Fodor's

BIG ISLAND
OF HAWAII

4th Edition

Fodor's Travel Publications   New York, Toronto, London, Sydney, Auckland
www.fodors.com

Portions of this book appear in *Fodor's Hawaii*.

FODOR'S BIG ISLAND OF HAWAII
Writers: Karen Anderson, Kristina Anderson, Cynthia Sweeney

Editor: Jess Moss
Editorial Contributor: Mark Sullivan

Production Editor: Carolyn Roth
Maps & Illustrations: Henry Colomb and Mark Stroud, Moon Street Cartography; David Lindroth, Inc., *cartographers;* Rebecca Baer, *map editor;* William Wu, *information graphics*
Design: Fabrizio La Rocca, *creative director;* Tina Malaney, Chie Ushio, Jessica Walsh, *designers;* Melanie Marin, *associate director of photography;* Jennifer Romains, *photo research*
Cover Photo: (Lava overflowing caldera of Puu Oo, Hawaii Volcanoes National Park) Frans Lanting/Corbis
Production Manager: Angela L. McLean

COPYRIGHT

4th Edition

ISBN 978-0-307-92920-4

ISSN 1934–5542

SPECIAL SALES

This book is available at special discounts for bulk purchases for sales promotions or premiums. Special editions, including personalized covers, excerpts of existing books, and corporate imprints, can be created in large quantities for special needs. For more information, write to Special Markets/Premium Sales, 1745 Broadway, MD 3-1, New York, NY 10019, or e-mail specialmarkets@randomhouse.com.

AN IMPORTANT TIP & AN INVITATION

Although all prices, opening times, and other details in this book are based on information supplied to us at press time, changes occur all the time in the travel world, and Fodor's cannot accept responsibility for facts that become outdated or for inadvertent errors or omissions. So **always confirm information when it matters,** especially if you're making a detour to visit a specific place. Your experiences—positive and negative—matter to us. If we have missed or misstated something, **please write to us.** Share your opinion instantly through our online feedback center at fodors.com/contact-us.

PRINTED IN COLOMBIA

10 9 8 7 6 5 4 3 2 1

CONTENTS

ABOUT THIS BOOK

Our Ratings

At Fodor's, we spend considerable time choosing the best places in a destination so you don't have to. By default, anything we recommend in this book is worth visiting. But some sights, properties, and experiences are so great that we've recognized them with additional accolades. Orange **Fodor's Choice** stars indicate our top recommendations; black stars highlight places we deem **Highly Recommended;** and **Best Bets** call attention to top properties in various categories. Disagree with any of our choices? Care to nominate a new place? Visit our feedback center at www.fodors.com/feedback.

Hotels

Hotels have private bath, phone, TV, and air-conditioning, and do not offer meals unless we specify that in the review. We always list facilities but not whether you'll be charged an extra fee to use them.

> For expanded hotel reviews, visit **Fodors.com**

Restaurants

Unless we state otherwise, restaurants are open for lunch and dinner daily. We mention dress only when there's a specific requirement and reservations only when they're essential or not accepted—it's always best to book ahead.

Credit Cards

We assume that restaurants and hotels accept credit cards. If not, we'll note it in the review.

Budget Well

Hotel and restaurant price categories from **$** to **$$$$** are defined in the opening pages of the respective chapters. For attractions, we always give standard adult admission fees; reductions are usually available for children, students, and senior citizens.

Listings
★ Fodor's Choice
★ Highly recommended
⊠ Physical address
✛ Directions or Map coordinates
🖅 Mailing address
☎ Telephone
🖷 Fax
⊕ On the Web

✎ E-mail
🎫 Admission fee
🕓 Open/closed times
Ⓜ Metro stations
▭ No credit cards

Hotels & Restaurants
🏠 Hotel
↘ Number of rooms
🛁 Facilities
🍽 Meal plans
✕ Restaurant
🖋 Reservations
🏛 Dress code
⤵ Smoking

Outdoors
🏌 Golf
⛺ Camping

Other
☕ Family-friendly
⇨ See also
⊠ Branch address
☞ Take note

Experience Big Island

1

WHAT'S WHERE

1 Kailua-Kona. A seaside town packed with tons of restaurants, shops, and a busy waterfront bustling with tourists along the main street, Alii Drive.

2 The Kona Coast. An area that stretches a bit north of Kailua-Kona and much farther south includes the gorgeous Kealakekua Bay. This is the place to come for world famous Kona Coffee to take farm tours and taste samples.

3 The Kohala Coast. The sparking coast is where all those long, white sand beaches are found, and the expensive resorts to go with them.

4 Waimea. Ranches sprawl across the cool, upland meadows of Waimea, known as paniolo (cowboy) country.

5 Mauna Kea. Climb (or drive) this 13,796-foot mountain for what's considered the world's best stargazing, with 13 telescopes perched on top.

6 The Hamakua Coast. Waterfalls, dramatic cliffs, ocean views, ancient hidden valleys, and rainforests and the stunning Waipio Valley are just a few of the treats that await you here.

7 Hilo. Known as the City of Rainbows for all its rain, Hilo is often skipped by tourists in favor of the sunny Kohala Coast. But for what many consider the "real" Hawaii, as well as incredible rainforests, waterfalls, and the best farmer's market on the island, Hilo can't be beat.

8 Puna. This section of the island was most recently covered by lava, and so it has brand-new jet-black beaches with volcanic hot springs.

9 Hawaii Volcanoes National Park and Vicinity. The land around the park is continually expanding, as the active Kilauea Volcano sends lava spilling into the ocean. The nearby town of Volcano provides a great base for exploring the park.

10 Kau and Ka Lae (South Point). Round the southernmost part of the island for two of Big Island's most famous beaches: Papakolea (Green Sand) Beach, and Punaluu (Black Sand) Beach.

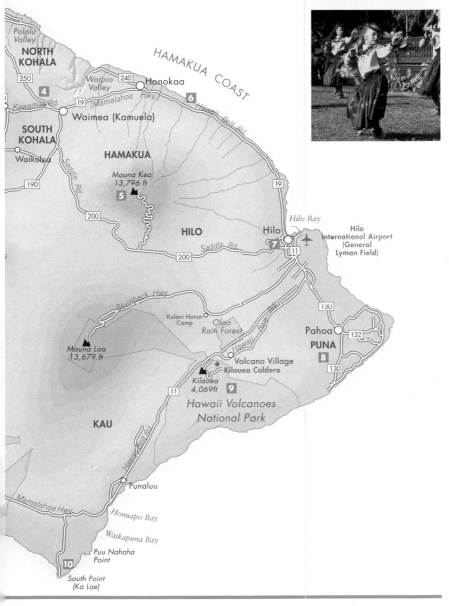

Pololu
Valley

**NORTH
KOHALA**

250

④

Kawaihae Rd.

HAMAKUA COAST

Waipio
Valley

240

Honokaa

19 (Mamalahoa Hwy.)

⑥

Hawaii Belt Rd.

**SOUTH
KOHALA**

Waimea (Kamuela)

Waikoloa

190

HAMAKUA

Saddle Rd.

Mauna Kea
13,796 ft

⑤

19

200

HILO

Saddle Rd.

Hilo

⑦

⑪

Hilo Bay

Hilo
International Airport
(General
Lyman Field)

200

Stainback Hwy.

Kulani Honor
Camp

Olaa
Rain Forest

Hawaii Belt Rd.

130

Pahoa

PUNA

⑧

132

Mauna Loa
13,679 ft

Volcano Village
Kilauea Caldera

130

⑪

Kilauea
4,069ft

⑨

*Hawaii Volcanoes
National Park*

KAU

Hawaii Belt Rd.

Punaluu

Mamalahoa Hwy

Honuapo Bay

Waikapuna Bay

Puu Nahaha
Point

⑩

South Point
(Ka Lae)

BIG ISLAND AND HAWAII TODAY

You could fit all the other Hawaiian Islands into the Big Island and still have a little room left over—hence the name. Locals refer to the island by side: the Kona side to the west and Hilo side to the east. Most of the resorts, condos, attractions, and restaurants are crammed into 30 mi of the sunny Kona side, while the rainy, windward Hilo side offers a much more local and "old Hawaii" experience.

Hawaiian culture and tradition here have experienced a renaissance over the last few decades. There's a real effort to revive traditions and to respect history as the Islands go through major changes. New developments often have a Hawaiian cultural expert on staff to ensure cultural sensitivity and to educate newcomers.

Nonetheless, development remains a huge issue for all Islanders—land prices are skyrocketing, putting many areas out of reach for the native population. Traffic is becoming a problem on roads that were not designed to accommodate all the new drivers, and the Islands' limited natural resources are being seriously tapped. The government, though sluggish to respond at first, is trying to make development in Hawaii as sustainable as possible.

Sustainability

Although sustainability is an effective buzzword and authentic direction for the Islands' dining establishments, 90% of Hawaii's food and energy is imported.

Most of the land was used for mono-cropping of pineapple or sugarcane, both of which have all but vanished. Sugarcane is now produced in only two plants on Kauai and Maui, while pineapple production has dropped precipitously. Dole, once the largest pineapple company in Hawaii, closed its plants in 1991, and

after 90 years, Del Monte stopped pineapple production in 2008. The next year, Maui Land and Pineapple Company also ceased its Maui Gold pineapple operation, although in early 2010 a group of executives took over one third of the land and created a new company. Low cost of labor and transportation from Latin American and Southeast Asian pineapple producers are factors contributing to the industry's demise in Hawaii. Although this proves daunting, it also sets the stage for great agricultural change to be explored.

Back-to-Basics Agriculture

Emulating how the Hawaiian ancestors lived and returning to their simple ways of growing and sharing a variety of foods has become a statewide initiative. Hawaii has the natural conditions and talent to produce far more diversity in agriculture than it currently does.

The seed of this movement thrives through various farmers' markets and partnerships between restaurants and local farmers. Localized efforts such as the Hawaii Farm Bureau Federation are collectively leading the organic and sustainable agricultural renaissance. From home-cooked meals to casual plate lunches to fine-dining cuisine, these sustainable trailblazers enrich the culinary tapestry of Hawaii and uplift the Islands' overall quality of life.

Tourism and the Economy

The over-$10 billion tourism industry represents a third of Hawaii's state income. Naturally, this dependency causes economic hardship as the financial meltdown of recent years affects tourists' ability to visit and spend.

One way the industry has changed has been to adopt more eco-conscious practices, as many Hawaiians feel that development

shouldn't happen without regard for impact to local communities and their natural environment.

Belief that an industry based on the Hawaiians' *aloha* should protect, promote, and empower local culture and provide more entrepreneurial opportunities for local people has become more important to tourism businesses. More companies are incorporating authentic Hawaiiana in their programs and aim not only to provide a commercially viable tour but also to ensure that the visitor leaves feeling connected to his or her host.

The concept of *kuleana*, a word for both privilege and responsibility, is upheld. Having the privilege to live in such a sublime place comes with the responsibility to protect it.

Sovereignty

Political issues of sovereignty continue to divide Native Hawaiians, who have formed myriad organizations, each operating with a separate agenda and lacking one collectively defined goal. Ranging from achieving complete independence to solidifying a nation within a nation, existing sovereignty models remain fractured and their future unresolved.

The introduction of the Native Hawaiian Government Reorganization Act of 2009 attempts to set up a legal framework in which Native Hawaiians can attain federal recognition and coexist as a self-governed entity. Also known as the Akaka Bill after Senator Daniel Akaka of Hawaii, this pending bill has been presented before Congress and is still awaiting a vote at the time of this writing.

Rise of Hawaiian Pride

After Hawaii became a state in 1959, a process of Americanization began. Traditions were duly silenced in the name of citizenship. Teaching Hawaiian language was banned from schools and children were distanced from their local customs.

But Hawaiians are resilient people, and with the rise of the civil rights movement they began to reflect on their own national identity, bringing an astonishing renaissance of the Hawaiian culture to fruition.

The people rediscovered language, hula, chanting, and even the traditional Polynesian arts of canoe building and wayfinding (navigation by the stars without use of instruments). This cultural resurrection is now firmly established in today's Hawaiian culture, with a palpable pride that exudes from Hawaiians young and old.

The election of President Barack Obama definitely increased Hawaiian pride and inspired a ubiquitous hope for a better future. The president's strong connection and commitment to Hawaiian values of diversity, spirituality, family, and conservation have restored confidence that Hawaii can inspire a more peaceful, tolerant, and environmentally conscious world.

BIG ISLAND PLANNER

When You Arrive

The Big Island's two main airports are almost directly across the island from each other. Kona International Airport on the west side is about a 10-minute drive from Kailua-Kona and 30 to 45 minutes from the Kohala Coast. On the east side, Hilo International Airport, 2 mi from downtown Hilo, is about 40 minutes from Volcanoes National Park. A 2½-hour drive connects Hilo and Kailua-Kona.

Visitor Information

Before you go, contact the Big Island Visitors Bureau to request a free official vacation planner. The Hawaii Island Chamber of Commerce also has links to dozens of museums, attractions, bed-and-breakfasts, and parks on its Web site. The Kona-Kohala Chamber of Commerce also has resources for the west side of the island.

Contacts Big Island Visitors Bureau ☎ 808/961–5797, 800/648–2441 ⊕ www. bigisland.org.

Hawaii Island Chamber of Commerce ☎ 808/935–7178 ⊕ www.hicc.biz.

Kona-Kohala Chamber of Commerce ☎ 808/329–1758 ⊕ www.kona-kohala.com.

Getting Here and Around

It's a good idea to rent a car with four-wheel drive, such as a Jeep, while visiting the Big Island. Some of the island's best sights (and most beautiful beaches) are at the end of rough or unpaved roads.

Most rental agencies require you sign an agreement that you won't drive to certain locations, such as over the Saddle Road or up to Mauna Kea and its observatories. Though a good portion of the road is smoothly paved, the Saddle Road is remote, winding, and bumpy in certain areas, unlighted and bereft of gas stations.

See Travel Smart Big Island for more information on renting a car and driving.

Island Driving Times

Due to the Big Island's size, it can take a long time to get from one region to another. And the island's increasing traffic is making driving times even longer, particularly between Kona and the Kohala Coast on weekday afternoons.

The state is widening portions of Highway 11 and Highway 19, which circle the island, and has opened a long-awaited bypass road between Keauhou and Kealakekua, both of which have alleviated congestion considerably. In general, you can expect the following average driving times.

Kailua-Kona to Kealakekua Bay	14 mi/30 min
Kailua-Kona to Kohala Coast	32 mi/50 min
Kailua-Kona to Waimea	40 mi/1 hr, 15 min
Kailua-Kona to Hamakua Coast	53 mi/1 hr, 40 min
Kailua-Kona to Hilo	75 mi/2 hrs
Kohala Coast to Waimea	16 mi/33 min
Kohala Coast to Hamakua Coast	29 mi/55 min
Hilo to Volcano	30 mi/45 min

Weather-Related Driving Tips

As a result of multiple microclimates and varying elevations, the Big Island experiences its share of extreme weather. During the same circle-the-island trip you may experience combinations of the following: intensely heavy tropical downpours; cold, windy conditions; searing heat; and even snow flurries. Be cautious on the mostly single-lane roads through rural areas, as these can be slick, winding, poorly lit, and prone to sudden flash floods. Pull over to the side of the road to wait out intense bursts of rain that may obscure vision and contribute to hazardous conditions. These are usually brief and might even end with a rainbow.

Dining and Lodging on the Big Island

Hawaii is a melting pot of cultures, and nowhere is this more apparent than in its cuisine. From luau and "plate lunches" to sushi and steak, there's no shortage of interesting flavors and presentations. The same "grow local, buy local" trend that is spreading through the rest of the country is also taking hold on the Big Island. This is a welcome shift from years past, in which all foods were imported, and it's a happy trend for visitors, who get to taste juicy, flavorful Waimea tomatoes, handmade Hamakua goat cheese, locally raised beef, or even island-grown wine. Whether you're looking for a quick snack or a multicourse meal, we cover the best eating experiences the island has to offer.

Consider spending part of your vacation at a resort and some of it at small inns or bed-and-breakfasts. The big resorts sit squarely on some of the best beaches on the Big Island, and they have a lot to offer—spas, golf, and great restaurants for starters. The B&Bs provide a more intimate experience in settings as diverse as an upcountry ranch, a rain-forest tree house, or a Victorian mansion perched on a dramatic sea cliff. Several romantic B&Bs nestle in the rain forest surrounding Hawaii Volcanoes National Park—very convenient (and romantic) after a nighttime lava hike.

WHAT IT COSTS

	$	$$	$$$	$$$$
Restaurants	under $17	$17–$26	$27–$35	over $35
Hotels	under $180	$180–$260	$261–$340	over $340

Restaurant prices are for a main course at dinner. Hotel prices are for two people in a standard double room in high season. Condo price categories reflect studio and one-bedroom rates.

Will I See Flowing Lava?

Without question, the best time to see lava is at night. However, you may not know until the day of your visit whether the lava flow will be in an accessible location. Your best bet is to call the visitor center at Hawaii Volcanoes National Park before you head out. No matter what's happening at the active lava flows, there's plenty to see and do inside the national park, where the Halemaumau Crater is located.

At times when lava is flowing inside the park, the hike out to the closest viewing might take a couple of hours. If it is expected to take longer than that, park rangers will usually advise against making the trek. Pay attention to all warning signs, and take safety advice from park rangers seriously. ■TIP→ Bring a flashlight, water, and sturdy shoes, and be prepared for some rough going over the lava fields at night.

When lava is flowing outside the park boundaries, hiking is strictly regulated because trails pass through private land. *For more information about visiting Hawaii Volcanoes National Park, see Chapter 2.*

BIG ISLAND OF HAWAII TOP ATTRACTIONS

The Lava Show
(A) Watch as fiery hot lava pours into the sea, creating huge steaming explosions; stare in awe at nighttime lava fireworks; and hike across the floor of a still-steaming crater at Hawaii Volcanoes National Park.

Green Sands Beach
(B) It's a bit off the beaten track, but this is one of the few places in the world to see green sand, which gets its unusual color from the mineral olivine. And it happens to be surrounded by turquoise waters and dramatic cliffs.

Exploring Waipio Valley
(C) Whichever way you choose to get there—on horseback, in a four-wheel drive, or on foot—you'll discover that the "Valley of the Kings" on the Hamakua Coast is full of sky-high waterfalls, lush green cliffs, and a mystical quality that can't quite be described or rivaled.

A Window on the Universe
(D) Teams of astronomers from all over the world come to Mauna Kea for the clearest skies and some of the best conditions anywhere. Head up the mountain in the late afternoon for the prettiest sunset on this island and the best stargazing on this planet.

Play at a Perfect Beach
(E) Whether you drive the paved roads to Hapuna, Kaunaoa (also known as Mauna Kea), Anaehoomalu Bay, or Kua Bay, or walk the rocky route to Makalawena, you'll find that the Big Island abounds with postcard-perfect beaches.

Stunning Waterfalls
(F) Watch rainbows forming in the mist, then take a refreshing dip in the cold, deep pools fed by the powerful waterfalls spilling over the dramatic cliffs of the Hamakua Coast.

Snooze with a Sea Turtle
(G) Hang out at Punaluu Black Sands Beach, fringed with coconut groves, where sea turtles surf the waves and nap on the black sands.

A Healing Lomilomi Massage
(H) The traditional Hawaiian *lomilomi* technique uses a combination of arms, elbows, hands, and breath to impart the overall sense of well-being associated with this ancient healing practice.

A Kona Coffee Farm Tour
(I) Spend an afternoon discovering why it is that Kona coffee commands those high prices. Visit a working estate and watch as "cherries" become beans, enjoy the smoky aromas of the roasting process, then indulge in the smoothest cup of coffee you'll ever taste. Did we mention that it's all free? Our favorite: Lions Gate Farms in the heart of Honaunau's coffee belt. The annual 10-day Kona Coffee Cultural Festival in November celebrates coffee with tours, cupping contests, tastings, and special events.

Whale the Day Away
(J) From November to late April, you can sit on any beach on the west side of the island and watch the breathtaking humpback whales. The sight of their backs, glistening as they move through the water, or the occasional perfect fluke cutting through the surface, is a matchless experience.

A Swim Through Coral Gardens
Diving or snorkeling in the crystal clear waters off the Kona Coast is like being let loose in your very own ocean-sized aquarium. Bright yellow, purple, and rose-colored coral creates surreal kingdoms ruled by octopi, turtles, rays, dolphins, and fish in every color of the rainbow.

GREAT ITINERARIES

Yes, the Big Island is big, and yes, there's a lot to see. If you're short on time, consider flying into one airport and out of the other. That will give you the opportunity to see both sides of the island without ever having to go backwards. Decide what sort of note you'd rather end on to determine your route—if you'd prefer to spend your last few days sleeping on the beach, go from east to west; if hiking through rain forests and showering in waterfalls sounds like a better way to wrap up the trip, move from west to east. If you're short on time, head straight for Hawaii Volcanoes National Park and briefly visit Hilo before traveling the Hamakua Coast route and making your new base in Kailua-Kona.

From exploring the shores of its green- and black-sand beaches to stargazing atop Mauna Kea, there's no shortage of ways to spend the day immersed in nature on the Big Island. Choose a couple or several of our favorite one-day itineraries to suit your interest and length of stay on the island.

Green Hawaii

Take full advantage of Hawaii's living classroom. Visit one of the island's botanical gardens or take a farm tour in the morning, then head to the Natural Energy Lab for a peek at how various enterprises raise shellfish, spirulina, and even seahorses. Wrap it up with an evening spent enjoying the delicious island-grown products at one of Waimea's top restaurants, such as local favorite Merriman's, or its nearby neighbor Daniel's.

Black and Green Sand

Check out some of the unusual beaches you'll find only on the Big Island. Start with a hike into Green Sands Beach near South Point and plan to spend some time sitting on the beach, dipping into the bay's turquoise waters, and marveling at the surreal beauty of this spot.

When you've had your fill, hop back in the car and head south about half an hour to Punaluu, the island's best-known black-sand beach and favorite nesting place of the endangered Hawaiian green sea turtle. Although the surf is often too rough to go swimming with the turtles, there are typically at least two or three napping on the beach at any given time of the day.

Sun and Stars

Spend the day lounging on a Kohala Coast beach (Hapuna, Kaunaoa—also known as Mauna Kea—or Kua Bay), but throw jackets and boots in the car because you'll be catching the sunset from Mauna Kea's summit. Bundle up and stick around after darkness falls for some of the world's best stargazing.

For the safest, most comfortable experience, book a summit tour or stop in at the Onizuka Center for International Astronomy, a visitor center located at about 9,000 feet, or join the free summit tour at 1 pm on Saturday or Sunday, and return to the center to use the telescopes for evening stargazing.

Hike Volcanoes

Devote a full day (at least) to exploring Hawaii Volcanoes National Park. Head out on the Kilauea Iki trail—a 4-mi loop at the summit—by late morning. Leave the park to grab lunch at nearby restaurants in Volcano Village just a few minutes away, or plan ahead and pack your own picnic lunch before you start your morning hike. Later you can take a stroll through the expansive Thurston Lava Tube and then hit the Jagger Museum, which offers great views of Halemaumau Crater's glow at night.

Majestic Waterfalls and Kings' Valleys

Take a day to enjoy the splendors of the Hamakua Coast—any gorge you see on the road is an indication of a waterfall waiting to be explored. For a sure bet, head to beautiful Waipio Valley. Book a horseback, hiking, or four-wheel-drive tour, or walk on in yourself (just keep in mind that it's an arduous hike back up—a 25% grade for a little over a mile).

Once in the valley, take your first right to get to the black-sand beach. Take a moment to sit here—the ancient Hawaiians believed this was where souls crossed over to the afterlife. Whether you believe it or not, there's something unmistakably special about this place.

Waterfalls abound in the valley, depending on the amount of recent rainfall. Your best bet is to follow the river from the beach to the back of the valley, where a waterfall and its lovely pool await.

Underwater Day

Explore the colorful reefs populated with tropical fish off the Big Island's coast for one day, and we defy you to stop thinking about the world beneath the waves when you're back on land. Our favorite spots include easily accessible Kahaluu Beach Park (off Alii Drive), Kealakekua Bay, and the Kapoho Tide Pools.

Early morning or late afternoon is the best time to see pods of Hawaiian spinner dolphins that rest in calm bays, but you're likely to encounter turtles any time of day, along with convict tangs, puffer fish, triggerfish, angelfish, spotted moray eels, trumpet fish, and hundreds of other brightly colored species.

Thermal Springs and Waterfalls

Due to its remote location, many visitors skip Puna. They don't know what they're missing. Venture into this isolated area for a morning, and you'll be rewarded with lava-tube hikes (Kilauea Caverns of Fire), volcanically heated pools (Ahalanui Park), and tide pools brimming with colorful coral, fish, and the occasional turtle (Kapoho Tide Pools).

Head to Hilo in the afternoon to visit Rainbow Falls, located right in town, or Akaka Falls, just outside town. Stroll Banyan Drive and Queen Liliuokalani Gardens before dining at one of Hilo's great restaurants.

Pololu and Paniolo Country

North Kohala is a world away from the resorts of the coast. Visit the quaint artists' community of Hawi, then head to the end of the road at Pololu Valley for amazing views.

A steep ½ mi hike leads to a fantastic black-sand beach surrounded by beautiful, sheer, green cliffs. Back on the road, head up Highway 250 to Waimea and the rolling hills and pastures of *paniolo* country. Indulge in a memorable meal at one of the town's fantastic restaurants.

Venture Off-Road

Book an ATV tour or take your four-wheel drive for a spin to check out some of the Big Island's isolated beaches. There are green beaches (in addition to *the* Green Sand Beach) waiting in the Kau region and ruggedly beautiful white beaches with perfect turquoise water along the Kohala Coast; deal with the tough, four-wheel-drive-only roads into these beaches and you're likely to be rewarded with a pristine tropical beach all to yourself.

THE HAWAIIAN ISLANDS

Oahu. The state's capital, Honolulu, is on Oahu; this is the center of Hawaii's economy and by far the most populated island in the chain—953,000 residents add up to 71% of the state's population. At 597 square miles Oahu is the third largest island in the chain; the majority of residents live in or around Honolulu, so the rest of the island still fits neatly into the tropical, untouched vision of Hawaii. Situated southeast of Kauai and northwest of Maui, Oahu is a central location for island hopping. Pearl Harbor, iconic Waikiki Beach, and surfing contests on the legendary North Shore are all here.

Maui. The second largest island in the chain, Maui is northwest of the Big Island and close enough to be visible from its beaches on a clear day. The island's 729 square miles are home to only 155,000 people but host more than 2 million tourists every year. With its restaurants and lively nightlife, Maui is the only island that competes with Oahu in terms of entertainment; its charm lies in the fact that although entertainment is available, Maui's towns still feel like island villages compared to the heaving modern city of Honolulu.

Hawaii (The Big Island). The Big Island has the second largest population of the Islands (almost 190,000) but feels sparsely settled due to its size. It's 4,038 square miles and growing—all the other Islands could fit onto the Big Island and there would still be room left over. The southernmost island in the chain (slightly southeast of Maui), the Big Island is home to Kilauea, the most active volcano on the planet. It percolates within Volcanoes National Park, which draws nearly 3 million visitors every year.

Kauai. The northernmost island in the chain (northwest of Oahu), Kauai is, at approximately 622 square miles, the fourth largest of all the Islands and the least populated of the larger Islands, with 64,000 residents. Known as the Garden Isle, this island is home to lush botanical gardens as well as the stunning Napali Coast and Waimea Canyon. The island is a favorite with honeymooners and others wanting to get away from it all—lush and peaceful, it's the perfect escape from the modern world.

Molokai. North of Lanai and Maui, and east of Oahu, Molokai is Hawaii's fifth-largest island, encompassing 260 square miles. On a clear night, the lights of Honolulu are visible from Molokai's western shore. Molokai is sparsely populated, with about 7,300 residents, the majority of whom are Native Hawaiians. Most of the island's 79,000 annual visitors travel from Maui or Oahu to spend the day exploring its beaches, cliffs, and former leper colony on Kalaupapa Peninsula.

Lanai. Lying just off Maui's western coast, Lanai looks nothing like its sister Islands, with pine trees and deserts in place of palm trees and beaches. Still, the tiny 140-square-mile island is home to about 3,200 residents and draws an average of 75,000 visitors each year to two resorts (one in the mountains and one at the shore), both operated by Four Seasons.

Hawaii's Geology

The Hawaiian Islands comprise more than just the islands inhabited and visited by humans. A total of 19 islands and atolls constitute the State of Hawaii, with a total landmass of 6,423.4 square miles.

The Islands are actually exposed peaks of a submersed mountain range called the Hawaiian Ridge-Emperor Seamounts

chain. The range was formed as the Pacific plate moves very slowly (around 32 miles every million years—or about as much as your fingernails grow in one year) over a hot spot in the Earth's mantle. Because the plate moves northwestwardly, the Islands in the northwest portion of the archipelago (chain) are older, which is also why they're smaller—they have been eroding longer and have actually sunk back into the sea floor.

The Big Island is the youngest, and thus the largest, island in the chain. It is built from five different volcanoes, including Mauna Loa, which is the largest mountain on the planet (when measured from the bottom of the sea floor). Mauna Loa and Kilauea are the only Hawaiian volcanoes still erupting with any sort of frequency. Mauna Loa last erupted in 1984. Kilauea has been continuously erupting since 1983.

Mauna Kea (Big Island), Hualalai (Big Island), and Haleakala (Maui) are all in what's called the post-shield-building stage of volcanic development—eruptions decrease steadily for up to a million years before ceasing entirely. Kohala (Big Island), Lanai (Lanai), and Waianae (Oahu) are considered extinct volcanoes, in the erosional stage of development; Koolau (Oahu) and West Maui (Maui) volcanoes are extinct volcanoes in the rejuvenation stage—after lying dormant for hundreds of thousands of years, they began erupting again, but only once every several thousand years.

There is currently an active undersea volcano to the south and east of the Big Island called Kamaehu that has been erupting regularly. If it continues its current pattern, it should breach the ocean's surface in tens of thousands of years.

Hawaii's Flora and Fauna

More than 90% of native Hawaiian flora and fauna are endemic (they evolved into unique species here), like the koa tree and the yellow hibiscus. Long-dormant volcanic craters are perfect hiding places for rare native plants. The silversword, a rare cousin of the sunflower, grows on Hawaii's three tallest peaks: Haleakala, Mauna Kea, and Mauna Loa, and nowhere else on Earth. Ohia trees—thought to be the favorite of Pele, the volcano goddess—bury their roots in fields of once-molten lava, and one variety sprouts ruby pom-pom-like lehua blossoms. The deep yellow petals of ilima (once reserved for royalty) are tiny discs, which make the most elegant lei.

But most of the plants you see while walking around, however, aren't Hawaiian at all and came from Tahitian, Samoan, or European visitors. Plumeria is ubiquitous; alien orchids run rampant on the Big Island; bright orange relatives of the ilima light up the mountains of Oahu. Though these flowers are not native, they give the Hawaiian lei their color and fragrance.

Hawaii's state bird, the nene goose, is making a comeback from its former endangered status. It roams freely in parts of Maui, Kauai, and the Big Island. Rare Hawaiian monk seals breed in the northwestern Islands. With only 1,500 left in the wild, you probably won't catch many lounging on the beaches, though they have been spotted on the shores of Kauai in recent years. Spinner dolphins and sea turtles can be found off the coast of all the Islands; and every year from November to April, the humpback whales migrate past Hawaii in droves.

WHEN TO GO

Long days of sunshine and fairly mild year-round temperatures make Hawaii an all-season destination. Most resort areas are at sea level, with average afternoon temperatures of 75°F–80°F during the coldest months of December and January; during the hottest months of August and September the temperature often reaches 90°F. Higher "upcountry" elevations typically have cooler and often misty conditions. Only at mountain summits do temperatures reach freezing.

Moist trade winds drop their precipitation on the north and east sides of the Islands, while the south and west sides remain warmer and drier. Rainfall can be higher in summer months, while winter brings higher surf and windier conditions.

Most travelers head to the Islands in winter, specifically from mid-November to mid-April. This high season means that fewer travel bargains are available; room rates average 10%–15% higher during this season than the rest of the year.

You can see humpback whales clearly off the western coast of the island from November to May. The Ironman triathlon takes place every October in Kailua-Kona. Shortly after the Ironman, the first 10 days of November are devoted to the Kona Coffee Cultural Festival. Each day brings numerous caffeinated events including cooking, picking, and barista competitions, and, of course, the coveted cupping competition, which measures the taste and quality of each estate coffee. Connoisseurs from all over the world flock to Kona for the festival, nearly every local coffee farmer participates, and the whole west side of the island goes crazy for coffee.

Hawaii Holidays

If you happen to be in the Islands on March 26 or June 11, you'll notice light traffic and busy beaches full of families—these are state holidays not celebrated anywhere else. March 26 recognizes the birthday of Prince Jonah Kuhio Kalanianaole, a member of the royal line who served as a delegate to Congress and spearheaded the effort to set aside homelands for Hawaiian people. June 11 honors the first island-unifying monarch, Kamehameha I; locals drape his statues with lei and stage elaborate parades.

May 1 isn't an official holiday, but May Day marks an important time when school kids and civic groups celebrate Hawaiian culture and the quintessential island gift, the flower lei.

Statehood Day is celebrated on the third Friday in August (admission to the Union was August 21, 1959).

Most Japanese and Chinese holidays are widely observed. On Chinese New Year, homes and businesses display bright-red good-luck mottoes, lions dance in the streets, and everybody eats *gau* (steamed pudding) and *jai* (vegetarian stew).

Climate

The following are average maximum and minimum temperatures for the Big Island; the temperatures throughout the Hawaiian Islands are similar.

HAWAIIAN HISTORY

Hawaiian history is long and complex; a brief survey can put into context the ongoing renaissance of native arts and culture.

The Polynesians

Long before both Christopher Columbus and the Vikings, Polynesian seafarers set out to explore the vast stretches of the open ocean in double-hulled canoes. From western Polynesia, they traveled back and forth between Samoa, Fiji, Tahiti, the Marquesas, and the Society Isles, settling on the outer reaches of the Pacific, Hawaii, and Easter Island, as early as AD 300. The golden era of Polynesian voyaging peaked around AD 1200, after which the distant Hawaiian Islands were left to develop their own unique cultural practices and subsistence in relative isolation.

The Islands' symbiotic society was deeply intertwined with religion, mythology, science, and artistry. Ruled by an *alii*, or chief, each settlement was nestled in an *ahupuaa*, a pie-shaped land division from the uplands where the alii lived, through the valleys and down to the shores where the commoners resided. Everyone contributed, whether it was by building canoes, catching fish, making tools, or farming land.

A United Kingdom

When the British explorer Captain James Cook arrived in 1778, he was revered as a god upon his arrival and later killed over a stolen boat. With guns and ammunition purchased from Cook, the Big Island chief, Kamehameha the Great, gained a significant advantage over the other alii. He united Hawaii into one kingdom in 1810, bringing an end to the frequent interisland battles that dominated Hawaiian life.

Tragically, the new kingdom was beset with troubles. Native religion was abandoned, and *kapu* (laws and regulations) were eventually abolished. The European explorers brought foreign diseases with them, and within a few short decades the Native Hawaiian population was decimated.

New laws regarding land ownership and religious practices eroded the underpinnings of pre-contact Hawaii. Each successor to the Hawaiian throne sacrificed more control over the Island kingdom. As Westerners permeated Hawaiian culture, Hawaii became more riddled with layers of racial issues, injustice, and social unrest.

Modern Hawaii

Finally in 1893, the last Hawaiian monarch, Queen Liliuokalani, was overthrown by a group of Americans and European businessmen and government officials, aided by an armed militia. This led to the creation of the Republic of Hawaii, and it became a U.S. territory for the next 60 years. The loss of Hawaiian sovereignty and the conditions of annexation have haunted the Hawaiian people since the monarchy was deposed.

Pearl Harbor was attacked in 1941, which engaged the United States immediately into World War II. Tourism, from its beginnings in the early 1900s, flourished after the war and naturally inspired rapid real estate development in Waikiki. In 1959, Hawaii officially became the 50th state. Statehood paved the way for Hawaiians to participate in the American democratic process, which was not universally embraced by all Hawaiians. With the rise of the civil rights movement in the 1960s, Hawaiians began to reclaim their own identity, from language to hula.

HAWAIIAN PEOPLE AND THEIR CULTURE

By October 2010, Hawaii's population was more than 1.3 million with the majority of residents living on Oahu. Nine percent are Hawaiian or other Pacific Islander, almost 40% are Asian American, 9% are Latino, and about 25% Caucasian. Nearly a fifth of the population list two or more races, making Hawaii the most diverse state in the United States.

Among individuals 18 and older, about 84% finished high school, half attained some college, and 26% completed a bachelor's degree or higher.

The Role of Tradition

The kingdom of Hawaii was ruled by a spiritual class system. Although the *alii,* or chief, was believed to be the direct descendent of a deity or god, high priests, known as *kahuna,* presided over every imaginable aspect of life and *kapu* (taboos) that strictly governed the commoners.

Each part of nature and ritual was connected to a deity—Kane was the highest of all deities, symbolizing sunlight and creation; Ku was the god of war; Lono represented fertility, rainfall, music, and peace; Kanaloa was the god of the underworld or darker spirits. Probably the most well known by outsiders is Pele, the goddess of fire.

The kapu not only provided social order, they also swayed the people to act with reverence for the environment. Any abuse was met with extreme punishment, often death, as it put the land and people's *mana,* or spiritual power, in peril.

Ancient deities play a huge role in Hawaiian life today—not just in daily rituals, but in the Hawaiians' reverence for their land. Gods and goddesses tend to be associated with particular parts of the land, and most of them are connected with many places, thanks to the body of stories built up around each.

One of the most important ways the ancient Hawaiians showed respect for their gods and goddesses was through the hula. Various forms of the hula were performed as prayers to the gods and as praise to the chiefs. Performances were taken very seriously, as a mistake was thought to invalidate the prayer, or even to offend the god or chief in question. Hula is still performed both as entertainment and as prayer; it is not uncommon for a hula performance to be included in an official government ceremony.

Who Are the Hawaiians Today?

To define the Hawaiians in a page, let alone a paragraph, is nearly impossible. Those considered to be indigenous Hawaiians are descendants of the ancient Polynesians who crossed the vast ocean and settled Hawaii. According to the government, there are Native Hawaiians or native Hawaiians (note the change in capitalization), depending on a person's background.

Federal and state agencies apply different methods to determine Hawaiian lineage, from measuring blood percentage to mapping genealogy. This has caused turmoil within the community because it excludes many who claim Hawaiian heritage. It almost guarantees that, as races intermingle, even those considered Native Hawaiian now will eventually disappear on paper, displacing generations to come.

Modern Hawaiian Culture

Perfect weather aside, Hawaii might be the warmest place anyone can visit. The Hawaii experience begins and ends with *aloha,* a word that envelops love, affection, and mercy, and has become a salutation for hello and good-bye. Broken

down, *alo* means "presence" and *ha* means "breath"—the presence of breath. It's to live with love and respect for self and others with every breath. Past the manicured resorts and tour buses, aloha is a moral compass that binds all of Hawaii's people.

Hawaii is blessed with some of the most unspoiled natural wonders, and aloha extends to the land, or *aina*. Hawaiians are raised outdoors and have strong ties to nature. They realize as children that the ocean and land are the delicate source of all life. Even ancient gods were embodied by nature, and this reverence has been passed down to present generations who believe in *kuleana,* their privilege and responsibility.

Hawaii's diverse cultures unfold in a beautiful montage of customs and arts—from music, to dance, to food. Musical genres range from slack key to *Jawaiian* (Hawaiian reggae) to *hapa-haole* (Hawaiian music with English words). From George Kahumoku's Grammy-worthy laid-back strumming, to the late Iz Kamakawiwoole's "Somewhere over the Rainbow," to Jack Johnson's more mainstream tunes, contemporary Hawaiian music has definitely carved its ever-evolving niche.

The Merrie Monarch Festival is celebrating almost 50 years of worldwide hula competition and education. The fine-dining culinary scene, especially in Honolulu, has a rich tapestry of ethnic influences and talent. But the real gems are the humble hole-in-the-wall eateries that serve authentic cuisines of many ethnic origins in one plate, a deliciously mixed plate indeed.

And perhaps, the most striking quality in today's Hawaiian culture is the sense of family, or *ohana*. Sooner or later, almost everyone you meet becomes an uncle or auntie, and it is not uncommon for near strangers to be welcomed into a home as a member of the family.

Until the last century, the practice of *hanai,* in which a family essentially adopts a child, usually a grandchild, without formalities, was still prevalent. While still practiced to a somewhat lesser degree, the *hanai,* which means to feed or nourish, still resonates within most families and communities.

How to Act Like a Local

Adopting local customs is a firsthand introduction to the Islands' unique culture. So live in T-shirts and shorts. Wear cheap rubber flip-flops, but call them slippers. Wave people into your lane on the highway, and, when someone lets you in, give them a wave of thanks in return. Never, ever blow your horn, even when the pickup truck in front of you is stopped for a long session of "talk story" right in the middle of the road.

Holoholo means to go out for the fun of it—an aimless stroll, ride, or drive. "Wheah you goin', braddah?" "Oh, holoholo." It's local speak for Sunday drive, no plan, it's not the destination but the journey. Try setting out without an itinerary. Learn to *shaka*: pinky and thumb extended, middle fingers curled in, waggle sideways. Eat white rice with everything. When someone says, "Aloha!" answer, "Aloha no!" ("And a real big aloha back to you"). And, as the locals say, "No make big body" ("Try not to act like you own the place").

KIDS AND FAMILIES

With dozens of adventures, discoveries, and fun-filled beach days, Hawaii is a blast with kids. Even better, the things to do here don't only appeal to small fry. The entire family, parents included, will enjoy surfing, discovering a waterfall in the rain forest, and snorkeling with sea turtles. And there are plenty of organized activities for kids that will give parents time for a few romantic beach strolls.

Choosing a Place to Stay

Resorts: All the big resorts make kids' programs a priority, and it shows. When you are booking your room, ask about "kids eat free" deals and the number of kids' pools at the resort. Also check out the size of the groups in the children's programs, and find out whether the cost of the programs includes lunch, equipment, and activities.

The Hilton Waikoloa Village is every kid's fantasy vacation come true, with dozens of pool slides, one lagoon for snorkeling and one filled with dolphins, and even a choice between riding a monorail or taking a boat to your room. Not to be outdone, the Four Seasons Resort Hualalai has a great program that will keep your little ones happy and occupied all day.

Condos: Condo and vacation rentals are a fantastic value for families vacationing in Hawaii. You can cook your own food, which is cheaper than eating out and sometimes easier (especially if you have a finicky eater in your group), and you'll get twice the space of a hotel room for about a quarter of the price. If you decide to go the condo route, be sure to ask about the size of the complex's pool (some try to pawn off a tiny soaking tub as a pool) and whether barbecues are available. One of the best reasons to stay in your own place is to hold a sunset family barbecue by the pool or overlooking the ocean.

Condos in Kailua-Kona (on or near Alii Drive) are the best value on the Big Island. We like Casa de Emdeko for its oceanfront pool and on-site convenience store. On the Kohala Coast, the Vista Waikoloa complex provides extra-large condos and is walking distance to beautiful Anaehoomalu Bay. Affordable food is available at restaurants in Kona, if you are looking for a family night out or, even better, a date night.

Ocean Activities

On the Beach: Most people like being in the water, but toddlers and school-age kids tend to be especially enamored of it. The swimming pool at your condo or hotel is always an option, but don't be afraid to hit the beach with a little one in tow. There are lots of family-friendly beaches on the Big Island, complete with protected bays and pleasant white sand. As always, use your judgment, and heed all posted signs and lifeguard warnings.

Calm beaches to try include Kamakahonu Beach and Kahaluu Beach Park in Kailua-Kona; Spencer Beach Park, Kaunaoa (aka Mauna Kea Beach), and Hapuna Beach on the Kohala Coast; Ahalanui Beach Park in Puna; and Leleiwi Beach Park in Hilo.

On the Waves: Surf lessons are a great idea for the older kids. Beginner lessons are always on safe and easy waves and tend to last anywhere from two to four hours. Most surf schools also offer instruction in the latest craze, stand-up paddle boarding.

For school-age and older kids, book a four-hour surfing lesson with Ocean Eco Tours and either join the kids out on the break or say aloha to a little parents-only time.

The Underwater World: If your kids are ready to try snorkeling, Hawaii is a great place to introduce them to the underwater world. Even without the mask and snorkel, they'll be able to see colorful fish darting this way and that, and they may also spot turtles and dolphins at many of the island beaches.

The easily accessible Kahaluu Beach in Kailua-Kona is a great introductory snorkel spot because if it many facilities. Protected by a natural breakwater, these shallow reefs attract large numbers of sea creatures, including the endangered Hawaiian green sea turtle. These turtles feed on seaweed near shore and sometimes can be spotted basking on the rocks.

On the southern tip of the island, Punaluu provides opportunities to see the sea turtles up close. Though the water can be rough, the sea turtles nest here and there are nearly always one or two napping on the black-sand beach. At nighttime, head to the Sheraton Keauhou or Huggo's on the Rocks in Kailua-Kona to view manta rays; each spot shines a bright spotlight on the water to attract the rays. Anyone, but especially kids, could sit and watch them fly through the ocean in graceful circles for hours. No snorkel required!

Another great option is to book a snorkel cruise or opt to stay dry inside the Atlantis Submarine that operates out of Kailua-Kona. Kids love crawling down into a real-life submarine and viewing the ocean world through its little portholes.

Land Activities

In addition to beach experiences, Hawaii has easy waterfall hikes, botanical gardens, petting zoos, and hands-on museums that will keep your kids entertained and out of the sun for a day.

Hawaii Volcanoes National Park is a must for any family vacation. Even grumpy teenagers will acknowledge the coolness of lava tubes, steaming volcanic rocks, and a fiery nighttime lava show.

On the Hilo side, the Panaewa Rain Forest Zoo is small, but free, and lots of fun for the little ones, with a small petting zoo on Saturday. Your kids will even get to hold a Hawaiian hawk. Just a few miles north, on the Hamakua Coast, the Hawaii Tropical Botanical Garden makes a beautiful and fun stop for kids, filled with huge lily pads and noisy frogs.

School-age and older kids will get a kick out of the ATV tours in North Kohala, and horseback rides through Waipio Valley with Naalapa Stables.

After Dark

At nighttime, younger kids get a kick out of luau, and many of the shows incorporate young audience members, adding to the fun. Teens and adults alike are sure to enjoy the music and overall theatrical quality of The Sheraton Keauhou's "Haleo," the story of the Keauhou *ahupuaa* (land division).

Stargazing from Mauna Kea is another treat. The visitor center has telescopes set up for all visitors to use. If you'd rather leave the planning to someone else, book a tour with Hawaii Forest and Trail. Its guides are also unbelievably knowledgeable and great at sharing that knowledge in a narrative form that kids—and adults for that matter—enjoy.

TOP 10 HAWAIIAN FOODS TO TRY

Food in Hawaii is a reflection of the state's diverse cultural makeup and tropical location. Fresh seafood, organic fruits and vegetables, free-range beef, and locally grown products are the hallmarks of Hawaii regional cuisine. Its preparations are drawn from across the Pacific Rim, including Japan, the Philippines, Korea, and Thailand—and "local food" is a cuisine in its own right. Don't miss Hawaiian-grown coffee, either, whether it's smooth Kona from the Big Island or coffee grown on other islands.

Saimin

The ultimate hangover cure and the perfect comfort food during Hawaii's mild winters, *saimin* ranks at the top of the list of local favorites. In fact, it's one of the few dishes deemed truly local, having been highlighted in cookbooks since the 1930s. Saimin is an Asian-style noodle soup so ubiquitous, it's even on McDonald's menus statewide. In mom-and-pop shops, a large melamine bowl is filled with homemade *dashi*, or chicken broth, and wheat-flour noodles and then topped off with strips of omelet, green onions, bright pink fish cake and *char siu* (Chinese roast pork) or canned luncheon meat, such as SPAM. Add shoyu and chili pepper water, lift your chopsticks and slurp away.

SPAM

Speaking of SPAM, Hawaii's most prevalent grab-and-go snack is SPAM *musubi*. Often displayed next to cash registers at groceries and convenience stores, the glorified rice ball is rectangular, topped with a slice of fried SPAM and wrapped in *nori* (seaweed). Musubi is a bite-sized meal in itself. But just like sushi, the rice part hardens when refrigerated. So it's best to gobble it up, right after purchase.

Hormel Company's SPAM actually deserves its own recognition—way beyond as a mere musubi topping. About 5 million cans are sold per year in Hawaii and the Aloha State even hosts a festival in its honor. It's inexpensive protein and goes a long way when mixed with rice, scrambled eggs, noodles or, well, anything. The spiced luncheon meat gained popularity in World War II days, when fish was rationed. Gourmets and those with aversions to salt, high cholesterol, or high blood pressure may cringe at the thought of eating it, but SPAM in Hawaii is here to stay.

Manapua

Another savory snack is *manapua*, fist-sized dough balls fashioned after Chinese *bao* (a traditional Chinese bun) and stuffed with fillings such as *char siu* (Chinese barbeque) pork and then steamed. Many mom-and-pop stores sell them in commercial steamer display cases along with pork hash and other dim sum. Modern-day fillings include curry chicken.

Fresh Ahi or Tako Poke

There's nothing like fresh ahi or *tako* (octopus) *poke* to break the ice at a backyard party, except, of course, the cold beer handed to you from the cooler. The perfect pupu, poke (pronounced poh-kay) is basically raw seafood cut into bite-sized chunks and mixed with everything from green onions to roasted and ground kukui nuts. Other variations include mixing the fish with chopped round onion, sesame oil, seaweed, and chili pepper water. Shoyu is the constant. These days, grocery stores sell a rainbow of varieties such as kimchi crab and anything goes, from adding mayonnaise to tobiko caviar. Fish lovers who want to take it to the next level order sashimi, the best cuts of ahi sliced and dipped in a mixture of shoyu and wasabi.

Tropical Fruits

Tropical fruits such as apple banana and strawberry papaya are plucked from trees in Island neighborhoods and eaten for breakfast—plain or with a squeeze of fresh lime. Give them a try; the banana tastes like an apple and the papaya's rosy flesh explains its name. Locals also love to add their own creative touches to exotic fruits. Green mangoes are pickled with Chinese five spice, and Maui Gold pineapples are topped with li hing mui powder (heck, even margarita glasses are rimmed with it). Green papaya is tossed in a Vietnamese salad with fish paste and fresh prawns.

Plate Lunch

It would be remiss not to mention the plate lunch as one of the most beloved dishes in Hawaii. It generally includes two scoops of sticky white rice, a scoop of macaroni or macaroni-potato salad, heavy on the mayo, and perhaps kimchi or *koko* (salted cabbage). There are countless choices of main protein such as chicken *katsu* (fried cutlet), fried mahimahi and beef tomato. The king of all plate lunches is the Hawaiian plate. The main item is laulau or kalua pig and cabbage along with poi, *lomilomi* salmon, chicken long rice, and sticky white rice.

Bento Box

The bento box gained popularity back in the plantation days, when workers toiled in the sugarcane fields. No one brought sandwiches to work then. Instead it was a lunch box with the ever-present steamed white rice, pickled *ume* (plum) to preserve the rice, and main meats such as fried chicken or fish. Today, many stores sell prepackaged bentos or you may go to an *okazuya* (Japanese deli) with a hot buffet counter and create your own.

Malasadas

The Portuguese have contributed much to Hawaii cuisine in the form of sausage, soup, and sweetbread. But their most revered food is *malasadas*, hot, deep-fried doughnuts rolled in sugar. Malasadas are crowd-pleasers. Buy them by the dozen, hot from the fryer, placed in brown paper bags to absorb the grease. Or bite into gourmet malasadas at restaurants, filled with vanilla or chocolate cream.

Shave Ice

Much more than just a snow cone, shave ice is what locals crave after a blazing day at the beach or a hot-as-Hades game of soccer. If you're lucky, you'll find a neighborhood store that hand-shaves the ice, but it's rare. Either way, the counter person will ask you first if you'd like ice cream and/or adzuki beans scooped into the bottom of the cone or cup. Then they shape the ice to a giant mound and add colorful fruit syrups. First-timers should order the Rainbow, of course.

Crack Seed

There are dozens of varieties of crack seed in dwindling specialty shops and at the drug stores. Chinese call the preserved fruits and nuts *see mui* but somehow the Pidgin English version is what Hawaiians prefer. Those who like hard candy and salty foods will love li hing mangoes and rock salt plums, and those with an itchy throat will feel relief from the lemon strips. Peruse large glass jars of crack seed sold in bulk or smaller hanging bags—the latter make good gifts to give to friends back home.

BIG ISLAND'S BEST FARMERS' MARKETS

The Big Island is home to more farmers' markets than most cities, each offering a different range of goods, but all providing at the very least a good place to pick up fresh produce, jarred goods such as jams and salsa, as well as homemade local Hawaiian treats. Not surprisingly, locally grown mango, papaya, pineapple, passion fruit, coconut, and guava are available in abundance at great prices, but you can also find delicious avocados, organic peppers, fantastic goat cheese, and, of course, coffee. Local handmade gifts abound, too.

Hawaii's farmers are experimenting with dozens of varieties of exotic fruits such as dragon fruit, poha berries, bilimbi, and mamey sapoy. Due to state government restrictions, these fruits generally can't leave the island, so this is your only chance to sample them.

Markets located in Kailua-Kona and Hilo are listed under the corresponding sections in the Shops and Spas chapter; the following markets are scattered about the Big Island. You might happily stumble upon them as you explore the coasts.

On the West Side

Hawaiian Homesteaders Association Farmers Market. Check out the crafts sold here in the Kuhio Hale Building before you head to Waimea's more expensive stores. Produce, flowers, plants, and baked goods are also available. It's open 7 am to noon every Saturday.

Under the Banyans Farmers Market. Fresh produce, seasonal fruit, plants, and craft items are sold at this market way up north in the village of Hawi. It's open Saturday from 7:30 am until 1 pm.

South Kona Farmers Market. This popular market features coffee, baked goods, and local honey and jams. It's located above Choice Mart Shopping Center in Captain Cook. It runs on Sunday morning until noon.

Kau Farmers Market. On a trip to South Point, stock up on local produce and freshly baked pastries at this market held at the Naalehu Theater. It's open every Saturday, 8 am to noon.

On the East Side

Downtown Honokaa Farmers Market. This good old-fashioned farmers' market in the midst of a charming old plantation town is a good stop during a drive up the Hamakua Coast. It begins at 8 am on Saturday.

The following markets are all south of Hilo:

Keaau Village Farmers Market. Fresh, local, farm produce featuring sweet corn and flowers is on offer daily from 7 am to 5 pm. On Friday, vendors also sell handmade Hawaiian arts and crafts.

Makuu Farmers Market. There's food and produce here, but what differentiates it from the rest are the Hawaiian crafts, plants, jewelry, shells, books, and secondhand clothing. It's along the Keaau/Pahoa Highway, and is open Sunday 8 am to noon.

Pahoa Village Farmers Market. This great market, held in a large, covered, outdoor space, offers local produce, prepared foods, coffee, clothing, and live music 9 am to 3 pm every Sunday.

Volcano Village Farmers Market. A favorite on the east side of the island, this market sells local produce, fresh flowers, prepared foods, baked goods, and hosts an occasional clothing swap. Held in the Cooper Center, you'll find it 8:30 to 11 every Sunday morning.

HAWAII AND THE ENVIRONMENT

Sustainability. It's a word rolling off everyone's tongues these days. In a place known as the most remote island chain in the world (check your globe), Hawaii relies heavily on the outside world for food and material goods—estimates put the percentage of food arriving on container ships as high as 90. Like many places, though, efforts are afoot to change that. And you can help.

Shop Local Farms and Markets

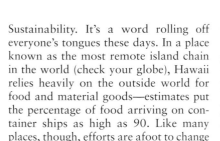

From Kauai to the Big Island, farmers' markets are cropping up, providing a place for growers to sell fresh fruits and vegetables. There is no reason to buy imported mangoes, papayas, avocados, and bananas at grocery stores, when the ones you'll find at farmers' markets are not only fresher and bigger but tastier, too. Some markets allow the sale of fresh-packaged foods—salsa, say, or smoothies—and the on-site preparation of food—like pork *laulau* (pork, beef and fish or chicken with taro, or luau, leaves wrapped and steamed in *ti* leaves) or roasted corn on the cob—so you can make your run to the market a dining experience.

Not only is the locavore movement vibrantly alive at farmers' markets, but Hawaii's top chefs are sourcing more of their produce—and fish, beef, chicken, and cheese—from local providers as well. You'll notice this movement on restaurant menus, featuring Kilauea greens or Hamakua tomatoes or locally caught mahimahi.

And while most people are familiar with Kona coffee farm tours on Big Island, if you're interested in the growing slow-food movement in Hawaii, you'll be heartened to know many farmers are opening up their operations for tours—as well as sumptuous meals.

Support Hawaii's Merchants

Food isn't the only sustainable effort in Hawaii. Buying local goods like art and jewelry, Hawaiian heritage products, crafts, music, and apparel is another way to "green up" the local economy. The County of Kauai helps make it easy with a program called **Kauai Made** (⊕ *www.kauaimade.net*), which showcases products made on Kauai, by Kauai people, using Kauai materials. The Maui Chamber of Commerce does something similar with **Made in Maui** (⊕ *www.madeinmaui.com*). Think of both as the Good Housekeeping Seal of Approval for locally made goods.

Then there are the crafty entrepreneurs who are diverting items from the trash heap by repurposing garbage. Take Oahu's **Muumuu Heaven** (⊕ *www.muumuuheaven.com*). They got their start by reincarnating vintage aloha apparel into hip new fashions. **Kini Beach** (⊕ *www.kinibeach.com*) collects discarded grass mats and plastic inflatables from Waikiki hotels and uses them to make pricey bags and totes.

Choose Green Tour Operators

Conscious decisions when it comes to Island activities go a long way to protecting Hawaii's natural world. The **Hawaii Ecotourism Association** (⊕ *www.hawaiiecotourism.org*) recognizes tour operators for, among other things, their environmental stewardship. The **Hawaii Tourism Authority** (⊕ *www.hawaiitourismauthority.org*) recognizes outfitters for their cultural sensitivity. Winners of these awards are good choices when it comes to guided tours and activities.

ONLY IN HAWAII

Traveling to Hawaii is as close as an American can get to visiting another country while staying within the United States. There's much to learn and understand about the state's indigenous culture, the hundred years of immigration that resulted in today's blended society, and the tradition of aloha that has welcomed millions of visitors over the years.

Aloha Shirt

To go to Hawaii without taking an aloha shirt home is almost sacrilege. The first aloha shirts from the 1920s and 1930s—called "silkies"—were classic canvases of art and tailored for the tourists. Popular culture caught on in the 1950s, and they became a fashion craze. With the 1960s' more subdued designs, Aloha Friday was born, and the shirt became appropriate clothing for work, play, and formal occasions. Because of its soaring popularity, cheaper and mass-produced versions became available.

Hawaiian Quilt

Although ancient Hawaiians were already known to produce fine *kapa* (bark) cloth, the actual art of quilting originated from the missionaries. Hawaiians have created designs to reflect their own aesthetic, and bold patterns evolved over time. They can be pricey because the quilts are intricately made by hand and can take years to finish. These masterpieces are considered precious heirlooms that reflect the history and beauty of Hawaii.

Popular Souvenirs

Souvenir shopping can be intimidating. There's a sea of Island-inspired and often kitschy merchandise, so we'd like to give you a breakdown of popular and fun gifts that you might encounter and consider bringing home. If authenticity is important to you, be sure to check labels and ask shopkeepers. Museum shops are good places for authentic, Hawaiian-made souvenirs.

Fabrics. Purchased by the yard or already made into everything from napkins to bedspreads, modern Hawaiian fabrics make wonderful keepsakes.

Home accessories. Deck out your kitchen or dining room in festive luau style with bottle openers, pineapple mugs, tiki glasses, shot glasses, slipper and surfboard magnets, and salt-and-pepper shakers.

Lei and shell necklaces. From silk or polyester flower lei to kukui or puka shell necklaces, lei have been traditionally used as a welcome offering to guests (although the artificial ones are more for fun, as real flowers are always preferable).

Lauhala products. *Lauhala* weaving is a traditional Hawaiian art. The leaves come from the hala, or pandanus, tree and are hand-woven to create lovely gift boxes, baskets, bags, and picture frames.

Spa products. Relive your spa treatment at home with Hawaiian bath and body products, many of them manufactured with ingredients found only on the Islands.

Vintage Hawaii. You can find vintage photos, reproductions of vintage postcards or paintings, heirloom jewelry, and vintage aloha wear in many specialty stores.

Luau

The luau's origin, which was a celebratory feast, can be traced back to the earliest Hawaiian civilizations. In the traditional luau, the taboo or *kapu* laws were very strict, requiring men and women to eat separately. However, in 1819 King Kamehameha II broke the great taboo and shared a feast with women and commoners ushering in the modern-era luau. Today, traditional luau usually

commemorate a child's first birthday, graduation, wedding, or other family occasion. They also are a Hawaiian experience that most visitors enjoy, and resorts and other companies have incorporated the fire-knife dance and other Polynesian dances into their elaborate presentations.

Nose flutes

The nose flute is an instrument used in ancient times to serenade a lover. For the Hawaiians, the nose is romantic, sacred, and pure. The Hawaiian word for kiss is *honi*. Similar to an Eskimo's kiss, the noses touch on each side sharing one's spiritual energy or breath. The Hawaiian term, *ohe hano ihu*, simply translated to "bamboo," with which the instrument is made; "breathe," because one has to gently breathe through it to make soothing music; and "nose," as it is made for the nose and not the mouth.

Slack-Key Guitar and the Paniolo

Kihoalu, or slack-key music, evolved in the early 1800s when King Kamehameha III brought in Mexican and Spanish vaqueros to manage the overpopulated cattle that had run wild on the Islands. The vaqueros brought their guitars and would play music around the campfire after work. When they left, supposedly leaving their guitars to their new friends, the Hawaiian *paniolo*, or cowboys, began to infuse what they learned from the vaqueros with their native music and chants, and so the art of slack-key music was born.

Today, the paniolo culture thrives where ranchers have settled.

Ukulele

The word *ukulele* literally translates to the "the jumping flea" and came to Hawaii in the 1880s by way of the Portuguese and Spanish. Once a fading art form, today it brings international kudos as a solo instrument, thanks to tireless musicians and teachers who have worked hard to keep it by our fingertips.

One such teacher is Roy Sakuma. Founder of four ukulele schools and a legend in his own right, Sakuma and his wife Kathy produced Oahu's first Ukulele Festival in 1971. Since then, they've brought the tradition to the Big Island, Kauai, and Maui. The free event annually draws thousands of artists and fans from all over the globe.

Hula

"Hula is the language of the heart, therefore the heartbeat of the Hawaiian people." —Kalakaua, the Merrie Monarch. Thousands—from tots to seniors—devote hours each week to hula classes. All these dancers need some place to show off their stuff. The result is a network of hula competitions (generally free or very inexpensive) and free performances in malls and other public spaces. Many resorts offer hula instruction.

TOP 5 OUTDOOR ADVENTURES

Getting out for active adventure is one of the top reasons people come to the Big Island.

There are endless options here for spending time outside, enjoying the land, the ocean, or the highest points of mountains and volcanoes. Here are a few of our favorites.

Bike Kulani Trails

Stands of 80-foot eucalyptus. Giant hapuu tree ferns. The sweet song of honeycreepers overhead. Add single-track of rock and root—no dirt here—and we're talking technical. Did we mention this is a rain forest? That explains the perennial slick coat of slime on every possible surface. Advanced cyclists only.

Snorkel at Kealakekua Bay

Yes, the snorkeling here is tops for the Big Island. Visibility reaches depths of 80 feet, and you'll spot colorful creatures swimming among jagged pinnacles and pristine coral habitats. But, to be real, the draw here are the Hawaiian spinner dolphins that come to rest in the bay during the daytime.

While it's enticing to swim with wild dolphins, getting too close can disrupt their sleep cycles. Observe from a distance and respect their space while still enjoying a fantastic experience communing with nature.

Search for Lava at Hawaii Volcanoes National Park

It's not too often that you can witness the creation of molten earth in action. That's just what happens at Hawaii Volcanoes National Park. The most dramatic examples occur where lava flows enter the sea. While Madame Pele rarely gives away her itinerary in advance, if you're lucky, a hike or boat ride may pay off with spectacu-

lar sights. Just before dawn and nighttime make for the best viewing opportunities.

Go Horseback Riding in Waipio Valley

The Valley of the Kings owes its relative isolation and off-the-grid status to the 2,000-foot-high cliffs book ending the valley. Really, the only way to explore this sacred place is on two legs—or four.

We're partial to the horseback rides that wend deep into the rain forest to a series of waterfalls and pools—the setting for a perfect romantic getaway.

Wade Through Waterfalls on the Hilo Side

The east side of Big Island—also called the Hilo side (as opposed to the western Kona side)—is essentially a rain forest, with an average rainfall of 130 inches a year. It's no wonder Hilo is called the "City of Rainbows"—and all that rain means tons of waterfalls. Some of our favorites include Peepee Falls (Boiling Pots) and Rainbow Falls, both easy to access from main roads.

BIG ISLAND'S TOP BEACHES

With over 265 mi of coastline, the Big Island—the largest and youngest island—offers the widest variety of beaches in Hawaii. Take your pick from black sand, soft white sand, crystalline green sand, award-winning beaches, and beaches off the beaten track.

Best Classic Beach

Mauna Kea (Kaunaoa) and nearby Hapuna Beach, Kohala Coast. Long, white stretches of pure soft sand and glistening, azure water are perfect for swimming, snorkeling, and sunbathing. These two beaches are consistently rated among the best in the world. Simply perfect.

Kekaha Kai State Park, Kona Coast. This beautiful beach in a postcardlike setting has outstandingly soft sand and great surf.

Best for Families

Spencer Beach Park, Kohala Coast. This protected sandy beach has consistently gentle surf so it's safe for swimming.

Anaehoomalu Beach, Kohala Coast. Even with half the beach wiped out in the 2011 tsunami, this is still a spectacular spot for swimming, snorkeling, stand-up paddling, and spotting turtles. The glass-bottom boat ride is cool too.

Onekahakaha Beach Park, Hilo. Parents can relax on the white-sand beach while kids explore the shallow, enclosed tide pools for exotic sea life.

Best for Interesting Sand

Punaluu Beach Park, Kau. It's busy for a reason. Between the turtles and the black sand it's tough not to camp out all day at this easily accessed beach.

Pololu Valley Beach, Kohala Coast. Jaw-droppingly scenic, this perfect crescent of black sand is backed by sheer green cliffs. The hike down to the beach is definitely worth the trip.

Papakolea Beach, Kau. Sure it's a 2-mi hike, but where else are you going to see a beach with green sand? The dry, barren landscape is surreal, and the beach sparkles with olivine crystals formed during volcanic eruptions.

Best Snorkeling

Kahaluu Beach Park, Kailua-Kona. Protective reefs keep the waters calm, and the abundant fish are not shy, as they are used to being fed by snorkelers.

Punaluu Beach Park, Kau. You're almost guaranteed to see sea turtles who nest in the black sand and swim in the waters just offshore.

Best Surfing

Hapuna State Park, Kohala Coast. Kawabunga, dude. When the surf's up, this beach is irresistible for anyone with a board. Careful of the shore break—it can be unforgiving.

Kua Bay, Kona Coast. Local surfers and body boarders love the challenge of the rough waves in winter. (If your surfer friend called in sick to work, this is where you'll find him.)

Honolii Beach Park, Hilo. Even if you don't surf, Hilo's main drag for surfers is a great place to hang out and watch.

Best Sunsets

We're going to say it one last time: westward-facing **Hapuna and Mauna Kea Beach** are not to be missed.

WEDDINGS AND HONEYMOONS

There's no question that Hawaii is one of the country's foremost honeymoon destinations. Romance is in the air here, and the white, sandy beaches, turquoise water, swaying palm trees, balmy tropical breezes, and perpetual sunshine put people in the mood for love. It's easy to understand why Hawaii is fast becoming a popular wedding destination as well, especially as the cost of airfare is often discounted, new resorts and hotels entice visitors, and as of January 2012, the state now recognizes and grants civil unions. A destination wedding is no longer exclusive to celebrities and the superrich. You can plan a traditional ceremony in a place of worship followed by a reception at an elegant resort, or you can go barefoot on the beach and celebrate at a luau. There are almost as many wedding planners in the Islands as real estate agents, which makes it oh-so-easy to wed in paradise, and then, once the knot is tied, stay and honeymoon as well.

The Big Day

Choosing the Perfect Place. When choosing a location, remember that you really have two choices to make: the ceremony location and where to have the reception, if you're having one. For the former, there are beaches, bluffs overlooking beaches, gardens, private residences, resort lawns, and, of course, places of worship. As for the reception, there are these same choices, as well as restaurants and even luau. If you decide to go outdoors, remember the seasons—yes, Hawaii has seasons. If you're planning a winter wedding outdoors, be sure you have a backup plan (such as a tent), in case it rains. Also, if you're planning an outdoor wedding at sunset—which is very popular—be sure you match the time of your ceremony to the time the sun sets at that time of year. If

you choose an indoor spot, be sure to ask for pictures of the location when you're planning. You don't want to plan a pink wedding, say, and wind up in a room that's predominantly red. Or maybe you do. The point is, it should be your choice.

Finding a Wedding Planner. If you're planning to invite more than a minister and your loved one to your wedding ceremony, seriously consider an on-island wedding planner who can help select a location, help design the floral scheme and recommend a florist as well as a photographer, help plan the menu and choose a restaurant, caterer, or resort, and suggest any Hawaiian traditions to incorporate into your ceremony. And more: Will you need tents, a cake, music? Maybe transportation and lodging? Many planners have relationships with vendors, providing packages—which mean savings.

If you're planning a resort wedding, most have on-site wedding coordinators; however, there are many independents around the Islands and even those who specialize in certain types of ceremonies—by locale, size, religious affiliation, and so on. A simple "Hawaii weddings" Google search will reveal dozens. What's important is that you feel comfortable with your coordinator. Ask for references—and call them. Share your budget. Get a proposal—in writing. Ask how long they've been in business, how much they charge, how often you'll meet with them, and how they select vendors. Request a detailed list of the exact services they'll provide. If your idea of your wedding doesn't match their services, try someone else. If you can afford it, you might want to meet the planner in person.

Getting Your License. The good news about marrying in Hawaii is that no waiting

period, no residency or citizenship requirements, and no blood tests or shots are required. However, both the bride and groom must appear together in person before a marriage-license agent to apply for a marriage license. You'll need proof of age—the legal age to marry is 18. (If you're 19 or older, a valid driver's license will suffice; if you're 18, a certified birth certificate is required.) Upon approval, a marriage license is immediately issued and costs $60, cash only. After the ceremony, your officiant will mail the marriage license to the state. Approximately four months later, you will receive a copy in the mail. (For $10 extra, you can expedite this process. Ask your marriage-license agent when you apply.) For more detailed information, visit ⊕ *www.ehawaii.gov.*

Also—this is important—the person performing your wedding must be licensed by the Hawaii Department of Health, even if he or she is a licensed minister. Be sure to ask.

Wedding Attire. In Hawaii, basically anything goes, from long, formal dresses with trains to white bikinis. Floral sundresses are fine, too. For the men, tuxedos are not the norm; a pair of solid-colored slacks with a nice aloha shirt is. In fact, tradition in Hawaii for the groom is a plain white aloha shirt (they do exist) with slacks or long shorts and a colored sash around the waist. If you're planning a wedding on the beach, barefoot is the way to go.

If you decide to marry in a formal dress and tuxedo, you're better off making your selections on the mainland and hand-carrying them aboard the plane. Yes, it can be a pain, but ask your wedding-gown retailer to provide a special carrying bag. After all, you don't want to chance losing your wedding dress in a wayward piece of luggage. And when it comes to fittings, again, that's something to take care of before you arrive in Hawaii.

Local Customs. The most obvious traditional Hawaiian wedding custom is the lei exchange in which the bride and groom take turns placing a lei around the neck of the other—with a kiss. Bridal lei are usually floral, whereas the groom's is typically made of *maile*, a green leafy garland that drapes around the neck and is open at the ends. Brides often also wear a *lei poo*—a circular floral headpiece. Other Hawaiian customs include the blowing of the conch shell, hula, chanting, and Hawaiian music.

The Honeymoon

Do you want champagne and strawberries delivered to your room each morning? A breathtaking swimming pool in which to float? A five-star restaurant in which to dine? Then a resort is the way to go. If, however, you prefer the comforts of a home, try a bed-and-breakfast. A small inn is also good if you're on a tight budget or don't plan to spend much time in your room. On the other hand, maybe you want your own private home in which to romp naked—or just laze around recovering from the wedding planning. Maybe you want your own kitchen so you can whip up a gourmet meal for your loved one. In that case, a private vacation-rental home is the answer. Or maybe a condominium resort. That's another beautiful thing about Hawaii: the lodging accommodations are almost as plentiful as the beaches, and there's one that will perfectly match your tastes and your budget.

CRUISING THE ISLANDS

Cruising has become extremely popular in Hawaii. For first-time visitors, it's an excellent way to get a taste of all the Islands; and if you fall in love with one or even two Islands, you know how to plan your next trip.

Cruising to Hawaii

Carnival Cruises. They call them "fun ships" for a reason—Carnival is all about keeping you busy and showing you a good time, both on board and on shore. Great for families, Carnival always plans plenty of kid-friendly activities, and their children's program rates high with the little critics. Carnival offers itineraries starting in Los Angeles, Ensenada, Vancouver, and Honolulu. Their ships stop on Maui (Kahului), the Big Island (Kailua-Kona and Hilo), Oahu, and Kauai. ☎ 888/227–6482 ⊕ www.carnival.com.

Holland America. The grande dame of cruise lines, Holland America has a reputation for service and elegance. Holland America's Hawaii cruises leave from and return to San Diego, California, with a brief stop at Ensenada. In Hawaii, the ship ties up at port in Maui (Lahaina), the Big Island (Hilo), Oahu, and Kauai (Nawiliwili). Holland America also offers longer itineraries (30-plus days) that include Hawaii, Tahiti, and the Marquesas and depart from or return to San Diego, Seattle, or Vancouver. ☎ 877/932–4259 ⊕ www.hollandamerica.com.

Princess Cruises. Princess strives to offer affordable luxury. Their prices start out a little higher, but you get more bells and whistles (affordable balcony rooms, nicer decor, more restaurants to choose from, personalized service). They're not fantastic for kids, but they do a great job of keeping teenagers occupied. *Golden Princess, Sapphire Princess,* and *Star Princess* sail from Los Angeles on a 14-day round-trip voyage with calls at Hilo on the Big Island, Honolulu, Kauai, and Lahaina on Maui, plus Ensenada, Mexico. There are also 15-day cruises out of San Francisco. In addition, the line offers longer cruises—up to 29 day—that include stops in Hawaii and the South Pacific. ☎ 800/774–6237 ⊕ www.princess.com.

Cruising within Hawaii

American Safari Cruises. Except for the summer months when its yachts cruise Alaska, American Safari Cruises offers round-trip, eight-day, seven-night interisland cruises departing from Lahaina, Maui. The *Safari Explorer* accommodates only 36 passengers; its smaller size allows it to dock at Moloka'i and Lana'i in addition to a stop on the island of Hawaii. The cruise is all-inclusive, with even shore excursions, water activities, and a massage included as part of the deal. ☎ 888/862–8881 ⊕ www.americansafaricruises.com.

Hawaii Nautical. Offering a completely different sort of experience, Hawaii Nautical provides private multiple-day interisland cruises on their catamarans, yachts, and sailboats. Prices are higher, but service is completely personal, right down to the itinerary. ☎ 808/234–7245 ⊕ www.hawaiinautical.com.

Norwegian Cruise Lines. Norwegian is the only major operator to offer interisland cruises in Hawaii. *Pride of America* sails year-round and offers seven day itineraries within the Islands stopping on Maui, Oahu, the Big Island (Hilo), and overnighting on Kauai. The ship has a vintage Americana theme and a big family focus with lots of connecting staterooms and suites. ☎ 800/327–7030 ⊕ www.ncl.com.

Exploring the Big Island

WORD OF MOUTH

"[Hawaii Volcanoes National Park] itself was magnificent and eerie even though the lack of fresh flowing lava was the major disappointment of our vacation. We spent one day driving first on Kilauea Crater Drive, then on the Chain of Craters road to the sea. On both drives, there are several half mile to mile long walks."

—cmstraf

Updated
by Cynthia
Sweeney

Nicknamed "The Big Island," Hawaii the island is a micro-cosm of Hawaii the state. From long white-sand beaches and crystal clear bays to rain forests, waterfalls, luau, exotic flowers, and birds, all things quintessentially Hawaiian are well represented here.

An assortment of happy surprises also distinguishes the Big Island from the rest of Hawaii—an active volcano (Kilauea) oozing red lava and cre-ating new earth every day, the clearest place in the world to view stars in the night sky (Mauna Kea), and some seriously good coffee from the famous Kona district and also from neighboring Kau.

GEOLOGY

Home to 11 climate zones, this is the land of fire (thanks to active Kilauea volcano) and ice (compliments of not-so-active Mauna Kea, topped with snow and expensive telescopes). At just under a million years old, Hawaii is the youngest of the Hawaiian Islands. The east rift zone on Kilauea has been spewing lava intermittently since January 3, 1983; an eruption began at Kilauea's summit caldera in March 2008 for the first time since 1982. Mauna Loa's explosions caused some changes back in 1984, and it could blow again any minute—or not for years. The third of the island's five volcanoes still considered active is Hualalai. It last erupted in 1801, and geologists say it will probably erupt again within 100 years. Mauna Kea is currently considered dormant, but may very well erupt again. Kohala, which last erupted some 120,000 years ago, is likely dead, but on volatile Hawaii Island, you can never be sure.

FLORA AND FAUNA

Sugar was the main agricultural and economic staple of all the Islands, but especially the Big Island. The drive along the Hamakua Coast, from Hilo or Waimea, illustrates recent agricultural developments on the island. Sugarcane stalks have been replaced by orchards of macadamia-nut trees, eucalyptus, and specialty crops from lettuce to strawberries. Macadamia nuts on the Big Island supply 90% of the state's yield, and coffee continues to be big business, dominating the mountains above Kealakekua Bay. Orchids keep farmers from Honoka to Pahoa afloat,

and small organic farms produce meat, fruits, vegetables, and even goat cheese for high-end resort restaurants.

HISTORY

Though no longer home to the capital, the state's history is nonetheless rooted in that of its namesake island, Hawaii. Kamehameha, the greatest king in Hawaiian history and the man credited with uniting the Islands, was born here, raised in Waipio Valley, and died peacefully in Kailua-Kona. The other man who most affected the history of Hawaii, Captain James Cook, spent the bulk of his time in the Hawaiian Islands here, docked in Kealakekua Bay (he landed first on Kauai, but had little contact with the natives there). Thus it was here that Western influence was first felt, and from here that it spread to the rest of the Islands.

KAILUA-KONA

Kailua-Kona is about 7 mi south of the Kona airport.

A fun and bustling seaside town, Kailua-Kona has the souvenir shops and open-air restaurants you'd expect in a major tourist hub, with the added bonus of a surprising number of historic sites. There are a few great restaurants here that are far more affordable than those at the resorts on the Kohala Coast and in Waimea.

Except for the rare deluge, the sun shines year-round. Mornings offer cooler weather, smaller crowds, and more birds singing in the banyan trees; you'll see tourists and locals out running on Alii Drive, the town's main drag, by about 5 am every day. Afternoons sometimes bring clouds and drizzly rain, but evenings are great for cool drinks, brilliant sunsets, gentle trade winds, and lazy hours spent gazing out over the ocean. Though there are better beaches north of the town on the Kohala Coast, Kailua-Kona is home to a few gems, including a fantastic snorkeling beach (Kahaluu) and a tranquil bay perfect for kids (Kamakahonu Beach, in front of the King Kamehameha Hotel).

Scattered among the shops, restaurants, and condo complexes of Alii Drive are the replica of the homestead where King Kamehameha I spent his last days (he died here in 1819), the last royal palace in the United States (Hulihee Palace), and a battleground dotted with the graves of ancient Hawaiians who fought for their land and lost. It was also here in Kailua-Kona that Kamehameha's successor, King Liholiho, broke and officially abolished the ancient *kapu* (roughly translated as "forbidden," it was the name for the strict code of conduct islanders were compelled to follow) system by publicly sitting and eating with women. The following year, on April 4, 1820, the first Christian missionaries came ashore here, changing the islands forever.

GETTING HERE AND AROUND

The town closest to the Kona International Airport (it's about 7 mi away), Kailua-Kona is a convenient home base from which to explore the island.

Half a day is plenty of time to explore Kailua-Kona, as most of the town's sights are located in or near the downtown area. Still, if you add in a beach trip (Kahaluu Beach has some of the best and easiest snorkeling on the island), it's easy to while away the bulk of a day here. Another option for making a day of it is to tack on a short trip down the Kona Coast to the charming artists' village of Holualoa or to the coffee farms in the mountains just above Kealakekua Bay.

The easiest place to park your car is at Courtyard King Kamehameha's Kona Beach Hotel ($15 per day). Some free parking is also available: When you enter Kailua via Palani Road (Hwy. 190), turn left onto Kuakini Highway, drive for a half block, and turn right into the small marked parking lot. Walk *makai* (toward the ocean) on Likana Lane a half block to Alii Drive, and you'll be in the heart of Kailua-Kona.

2

TOURS

Kona Historical Society. If you want to know more about the village's fascinating past, arrange for a 75-minute guided walking tour with the Kona Historical Society. ✉ *81-6551 Mamalahoa Hwy.* ☎ *808/323–3222* ⊕ *www.konahistorical. org.*

EXPLORING
TOP ATTRACTIONS

★ **Hulihee Palace.** A lovely rambling old stone home surrounded by jewel green grass and sweeping ocean views and fronted by an elaborate wrought-iron gate, Hulihee Palace is one of only three royal palaces in America (the other two are in Honolulu on Oahu). The two-story residence was built by Governor John Adams Kuakini in 1838, a year after he completed Mokuaikaua Church. During the 1880s it served as King David Kalakaua's summer palace. It's constructed of local materials, including lava, coral, koa wood, and *ohia* timber. The palace is operated by the Daughters of Hawaii, a nonprofit organization focused on maintaining the heritage of the Islands. ✉ *75-5718 Alii Dr.* ☎ *808/329–1877* ⊕ *www.daughtersofhawaii.org* 🔳 *$6 for adults, $4 for seniors, $1 for children under 18* ⏰ *Tues.–Sat. 10–3.*

Kailua Pier. Though most fishing boats use Honokohau Harbor, this pier dating from 1918 is still a hub of ocean activity. Outrigger canoe teams practice and boats shuttle cruise ship passengers to and from Kailua-Kona here, and tour boats depart from these docks most days. Along the seawall children and old-timers cast their lines daily, careful not to hook the pair of sea turtles nesting nearby. For youngsters, a bamboo pole and hook are easy to come by, and plenty of locals are willing to give pointers. Each October close to 1,500 international athletes swim 2.4 mi from the pier to begin the internationally famous Ironman World Championship triathlon competition. ✉ *Alii Dr., next to King Kamehameha's Kona Beach Hotel.*

QUICK BITES

Kope Lani Coffee. Grab a tasty croissant sandwich and locally made ice cream in tropical flavors, and knock back some of Kona's best coffee at Kope Lani Coffee, directly across from Hulihee Palace. ✉ *75-5719 Alii Dr.* ☎ *808/329–6152.*

Kona Inn Restaurant. If it's late afternoon, it's time to unwind with one of those umbrella drinks. For cocktails, head to the Kona Inn Restaurant, a local favorite. ✉ *75-5744 Alii Dr., #135* ☎ *808/329–4455.*

The Big Island of Hawaii

TO MAUI

THE KOHALA COAST AND WAIMEA

UPOLU PT.

NORTH KOHALA

Pololu Valley
Pololu Beach

Hawi
Kapaau
Mahukona

Kapaa Beach Park
Mahukona Beach Park
Lapakahi State Historical Park

250

Akoni Pule Hwy.

KOHALA MOUNTAINS

Kohala Mountain Rd.

Kohala Forest Reserve

Waiaka

Waimea (Kamuela)

270

Kawaihae

Kawaihae Rd.

Puukohola Heiau National Historic Site, Mailekini Heiau
Spencer Beach Park
Kaunooa Beach
Hapuna Beach State Park

Puako

19

SOUTH KOHALA

Waikoloa

Anaehoomalu

Anaehoomalu Bay

KOHALA COAST

Kiholo Bay

190

Puuanahulu

NORTH KONA

Mount Hualalai
8,271 ft

Huehue Ranch

Kalaoa

Kua Bay

Kekaha Kai State Park

Kona International Airport

19

Kaloko-Honokohau National Historical Park

Honokohau

KAILUA-KONA

Kailua Bay

White Sands Beach Park

Kahaluu

Holualoa

Kealakekua

11

Queen Kaahumanu Hwy.

Mamalahoa Hwy.

MAUNA KEA AND THE HAMAKUA COAST

HAMAKUA COAST

Honokaa

240

WAIPIO VALLEY OVERLOOK

Waipio Valley

19

Kukuihaele
Ookala

Kalopa State Rec. Area

19

Paauilo

Hwy. (Mamalahoa Hwy.)

Hawaii Belt Rd.

Laupahoehoe
Papaloa
Weloka
Ninole
Honohina
Hakalau

Kolekole Beach Park

Honomu

19

Wailea

Akaka Falls State Park

Hilo Forest Reserve

HAMAKUA

Mauna Kea
13,796 ft

Kawainui

Papaikou

Hilo Bay

Reeds Bay Beach Park
LELEIWI POINT
Onekahakaha Beach Park

Hilo International Airport (General Lyman Field)

HILO

NORTH HILO

Wainaku

SOUTH HILO

200

Saddle Rd.

Waikii

Saddle Rd.

200

Mauna Loa Observatory

Stainback Hwy.

Kulani Honor Camp

Olaa Rain Forest

Keaau

111

Kurtistown

Kukui

Mountain View

130

Kapoho Tide Pools

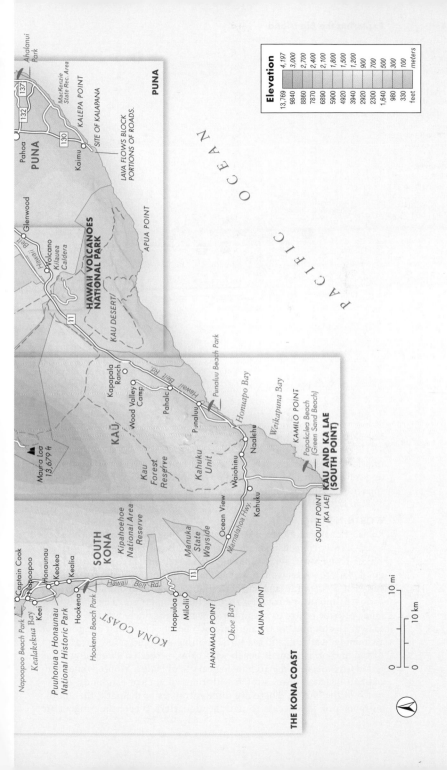

THE KONA COAST

PUNA

Ahalanui Park

MacKenzie State Rec. Area

137

132

130

Pahoa
PUNA

Glenwood

Volcano
Kilauea Caldera

Kaimu

KALEPA POINT

SITE OF KALAPANA

HAWAII VOLCANOES NATIONAL PARK

KAU DESERT

LAVA FLOWS BLOCK PORTIONS OF ROADS.

APUA POINT

Hawaii Belt

Mauna Loa
13,679 ft

KAU

Kau Forest Reserve

Kapapala Ranch

Wood Valley Camp

Pahala

Hawaii Belt Rd.

Punaluu

Punaluu Beach Park

Honuapo Bay

Kahuku Unit

Waiohinu

Naalehu

Weikapuna Bay

KAMILO POINT

Papakolea Beach
(Green Sand Beach)

KAU AND KA LAE (SOUTH POINT)

SOUTH POINT
(KA LAE)

SOUTH KONA

Kipahoehoe Natural Area Reserve

Manuka State Wayside

Ocean View

11

Kahuku

Mamalahoa Hwy.

Napoopoo Beach Park

Kealakekua Bay

Captain Cook

Napoopoo

Keei

Honaunau

Keokea

Kealia

Puuhonua o Honaunau National Historic Park

Hookena

Hawaii Belt Rd.

Hookena Beach Park

KONA COAST

Hoopuloa

Miloii

HANAMALO POINT

Okoe Bay

KAUNA POINT

PACIFIC OCEAN

Elevation

feet	meters
13,769	4,197
9840	3,000
8860	2,700
7870	2,400
6890	2,100
5900	1,800
4920	1,500
3940	1,200
2920	900
2300	700
1640	500
980	300
330	100
feet	meters

0   10 mi
0   10 km

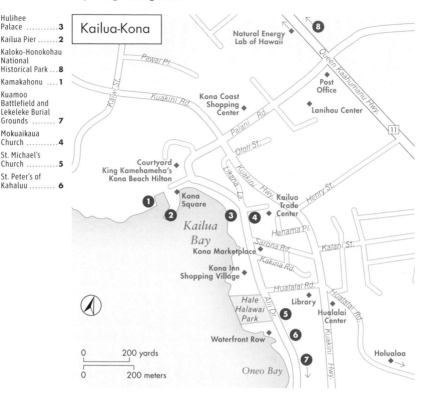

Kamakahonu. King Kamehameha I spent his last years, from 1812 to 1819, near what is now King Kamehameha's Kona Beach Hotel. Part of what was once a 4-acre homestead, complete with several houses and religious sites, has been swallowed by Kailua Pier, but a replica of the temple, **Ahuena Heiau,** keeps history alive. ✉ *75-5660 Palani Rd.* ☎ *808/329–2911.*

WORTH NOTING

Kaloko–Honokohau National Historical Park. The coastal trails at this sheltered 1,160-acre coastal park near Honokohau Harbor, just north of Kailua-Kona town, are popular among walkers and hikers. The park is a good place to see Hawaiian archaeological history and ruins intact; you can visit a *heiau* (an ancient Hawaiian place of worship), house platforms, fishponds, petroglyph rock etchings, and more. The park's wetlands provide refuge to a number of waterbirds, including the endemic Hawaiian stilt and coot. There are two beaches here that are good for swimming, walking, and sea turtle spotting—Aiopio, a few yards north of the harbor, is a small beach with calm, protected swimming areas (good for kids) near the archaeological site of Hale o Mono, while Honokohau Beach, a ¾-mi stretch with ruins of ancient fishponds, is also north of the harbor. There are three entrances to the park; the middle entrance provides access to park headquarters, where the rangers are

2

very helpful. ⊠ *Honokohau Harbor, 74-425 Kealakehe Pkwy., off Hwy. 19* ☎ *808/329–6881* ⊕ *www. nps.gov* ☉ *Park road gate 8–4.*

Kuamoo Battlefield and Lekeleke Burial Grounds. In 1819 an estimated 300 Hawaiians were killed on this vast, black-lava field, and you can still see their burial mounds there today

on the south end of Alii Dr. After the death of his father, King Kamehameha, Liholiho was crowned king; shortly thereafter he ate at a table with women, thereby breaking the ancient *kapu* (taboo) system. Chief Kekuaokalani, who held radically different views about religious traditions, unsuccessfully challenged King Liholiho in battle here. ⊠ *Alii Dr.*

Mokuaikaua Church. A thatch hut, erected on this site by missionaries in 1820, served as the first Christian church on the Islands. A more permanent structure was built in 1836 with black stone from an abandoned *heiau*. The stone was mortared with white coral and topped by an impressive steeple. Inside, behind a panel of gleaming koa wood, is a model of the brig *Thaddeus*. ⊠ *75-5713 Alii Dr.* ☎ *808/329–0655* ⊕ *mokuaikaua.org.*

St. Michael's Church. The site of Kona's first Catholic church, built in 1840, is marked by a small thatch structure to the left of the present church, which dates from 1850. In front of the church a coral grotto shrine holds 2,500 coral heads, harvested in 1940, when preservation was not yet an issue. ⊠ *75-5769 Alii Dr.* ☎ *808/326–7771.*

St. Peter's Church of Kahaluu. The definition of "quaint" with its crisp white and blue trim, this tiny old-fashioned steeple church sits on the rocks overlooking the ocean near Kahaluu Beach. It has appeared on many a Kailua-Kona postcard, and its charm and views bring hundreds of visitors every year. ⊠ *Alii Dr., just north of mile marker 5.*

THE KONA COAST

South of Kailua-Kona, Highway 11 hugs splendid coastlines, leaving busy streets behind. A detour along the winding narrow roads in the mountains above takes you straight to the heart of coffee country, where lush plantations and jaw-dropping views offer a taste of what Hawaii was like before the resorts took over. Tour one of the coffee farms to find out what the big deal is about Kona coffee, and enjoy a free sample while you're at it.

A half-hour drive on the highway from Kailua-Kona will lead you to beautiful Kealakekua Bay, where Captain James Cook arrived in 1778, changing the Islands forever. Hawaiian spinner dolphins frolic in the bay, now a marine preserve nestled alongside high green cliffs more reminiscent of popular images of Ireland than posters of Hawaii. Snorkeling is superb here, as it is a protected marine reserve, so you may want to bring your gear and spend an hour or so exploring the coral reefs. This is also a nice kayaking spot; the bay is normally extremely calm. ■TIP→ One of our favorite ways to spend a morning is to throw some snorkel gear in a kayak, paddle across the bay, go for a swim and a snorkel, and paddle back, dodging dolphins along the way.

North of Kona International Airport, along Highway 19, brightly colored bougainvillea stand out in relief against miles of black-lava fields stretching from the mountain to the sea. The dry, barren landscape may not be what you'd expect to find on a tropical island, but it's a good reminder of the island's volcanic past.

SOUTH KONA AND KEALAKEKUA BAY

Kealakekua Bay is 14 mi south of Kailua-Kona.

The winding road above Kealakekua Bay is home to a quaint little painted church, as well as several reasonably priced bed-and-breakfasts with great views. The communities surrounding the bay (Kainaliu and Captain Cook) are brimming with local and transplanted artists, making them great places to stop for a meal, some unique gifts, or an afternoon stroll.

After a morning of swimming and kayaking, head to one of the great cafés in nearby Kainaliu to refuel.

GETTING HERE AND AROUND

Between the coffee plantations, artsy towns, and Kealakekua Bay, South Kona has plenty of activities to keep you occupied for a day. Bring a swimsuit and snorkel gear, and hit Kealakekua Bay first thing in the morning. You'll have a better chance of a dolphin sighting, and you'll beat the large snorkel cruise groups. Follow the signs off Highway 11 to the bay, then park at Napoopoo Beach (not much of a beach, but it provides easy access into the water).

EXPLORING
COFFEE FARMS

Several coffee farms around the Kona coffee-belt area welcome visitors to watch all or part of the coffee process, from harvest to packaging. Some tours are self-guided and most are free, with the exception of the Kona Coffee Living History Farm.

Greenwell Farms. This 20-minute tour of a working Hawaiian farm is great for the entire family. Depending on the season, you will see various stages of coffee production, but you will always get to sample Greenwell Farms' Kona coffee at the end of your tour. ⊠ *81-6581 Mamalahoa Hwy., Kealakekua* ☎ *808/323–2295* ⊕ *www.greenwellfarms.com.*

Holualoa-Kona Coffee Company. There is a lot going on at this coffee farm and processing facility, from growing the beans to milling and drying. The processing plant next door to the farm lets you see how the beans are roasted and packaged as well. Holuakoa also processes beans for many other coffee farms in the area. The partially self-guided tours are weekdays only. ⊠ *77-6261 Old Mamalahoa Hwy., Hwy. 180, Holualoa* ☎ *808/322–9937, 800/334–0348* ⊕ *www.konalea.com.*

Hula Daddy. Learn the history of the farm and view different aspects of the coffee-making process here. You will get to pick and pulp your own

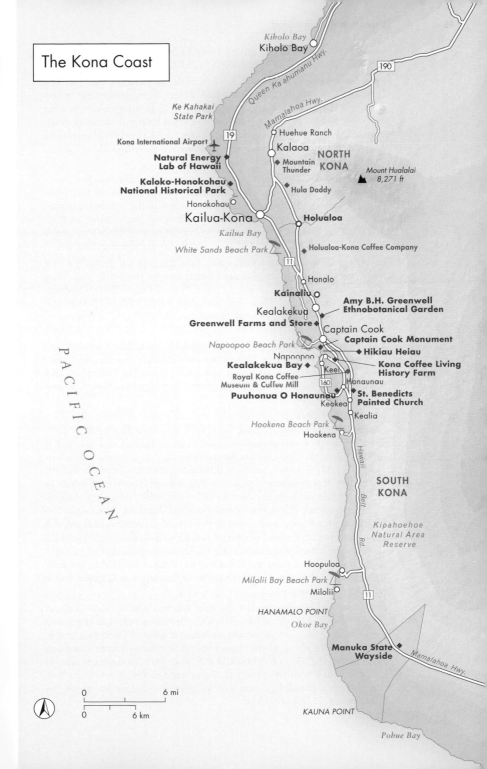

The Kona Coast

Kiholo Bay
Kiholo Bay

190

Queen Ka ahumanu Hwy.

Ke Kahakai State Park

Mamalahoa Hwy.

Kona International Airport ✈

19

Huehue Ranch

Kalaoa

NORTH KONA

Natural Energy Lab of Hawaii ◆

◆ Mountain Thunder

▲ *Mount Hualalai 8,271 ft*

Kaloko-Honokohau National Historical Park ◆

◆ Hula Daddy

Honokohau ○

Kailua-Kona

Holualoa

Kailua Bay

White Sands Beach Park

11

◆ **Holualoa-Kona Coffee Company**

Honalo ○

Kainaliu ○

Kealakekua ○

Amy B.H. Greenwell Ethnobotanical Garden

Greenwell Farms and Store ◆

Captain Cook

Captain Cook Monument

Napoopoo Beach Park

Napoopoo

◆ **Hikiau Heiau**

Kona Coffee Living History Farm

Keei

Kealakekua Bay ◆

Royal Kona Coffee Museum & Coffee Mill

160

Honaunau

Puuhonua O Honaunau

Keokea

St. Benedicts Painted Church

Kealia

Hookena Beach Park

Hookena ○

SOUTH KONA

Hawaii Belt Rd.

Kipahoehoe Natural Area Reserve

Hoopuloa

Milolii Bay Beach Park

Milolii ○

11

HANAMALO POINT

Okoe Bay

Manuka State Wayside ◆

Mamalahoa Hwy.

KAUNA POINT

Pohue Bay

PACIFIC OCEAN

0   6 mi
0   6 km

coffee bean. Hours are 10 am to 4 pm. ✉ *74-4944 Mamalahoa Hwy., Holualoa* ☎ *808/327–9744, 888/553–2339* ⊕ *www.huladaddy.com.*

Kona Coffee Living History Farm. Known as the D. Uchida Farm, this site is on the National Register of Historic Places. Completely restored by the Kona Historical Society, it includes a 1913 farmhouse surrounded by coffee trees, a Japanese bathhouse, *kuriba* (coffee-processing mill), and *hoshidana* (traditional drying platform). ✉ *82-6199 Mamalahoa Hwy., Kealakekua* ☎ *808/323–2006* ⊕ *www.konahistorical.org* 🖃 *$20* ☉ *Farm tours Mon.–Thurs. 10–2.*

Mountain Thunder. The largest organic coffee farm in Hawaii, this property in the rain forest above Kona teaches you about coffee from "bean to cup." The tour includes a tasting and access to the processing plant, where you can see everything from dry milling, sizing, coloring, sorting, and roasting. Hourly tours run daily from 10 to 4. ✉ *79-7469 Hawaii Belt Rd., Kainaliu* ☎ *888/414–5662* ⊕ *www.mountainthunder.com.*

Royal Kona Coffee Museum & Coffee Mill. Take this easy self-guided tour by following the descriptive plaques located around the coffee mill, then stop off at the small museum to see coffee-making relics and watch an informational film. Tours are weekdays only. ✉ *83-5427 Mamalahoa Hwy., next to tree house, Honaunau* ☎ *808/328–2511* ⊕ *www. hawaiicoffeeco.com.*

KONA'S COF-
FEE FESTIVAL **Kona Coffee Cultural Festival.** The fun annual Kona Coffee Cultural Festival runs for 10 days in November and includes parades and concerts, special tours, an art stroll and coffee tasting in Holualoa, and the Gevalia Kona Cupping Competition (a judged tasting). ⊕ *www. konacoffeefest.com.*

TOP ATTRACTIONS

★ **Captain Cook Monument.** No one knows for sure what happened on February 14, 1779, when English explorer Captain James Cook was killed on this spot. He had chosen Kealakekua Bay as a landing place in November 1778. Cook, arriving during the celebration of Makahiki, the harvest season, was welcomed at first. Some Hawaiians saw him as an incarnation of the god Lono. Cook's party sailed away in February 1779, but a freak storm forced his damaged ship back to Kealakekua Bay. Believing that no god could be thwarted by a mere rainstorm, the Hawaiians were not so welcoming this time, and various confrontations arose between them and Cook's sailors. The theft of a longboat brought Cook and an armed party ashore to reclaim it. One thing led to another: shots were fired, daggers and spears were thrown, and Captain Cook fell, mortally wounded.

A 27-foot-high obelisk marks the spot where Captain Cook died on the shore of Kealakekua Bay. The October 2006 earthquake caused the hillside above the monument to be come unstable, and as a result, there is no land access to the monument. You can see it from a vantage point across the bay at Kealakekua Bay State Park, or there are several licensed kayak tour operators that run trips to the monument. You can also get a one-day permit to land a noncommercial kayak by the mounument. ✉ *Captain Cook.*

Kealakekua Bay is one of the most beautiful spots on the Big Island.

Fodor's Choice **Kealakekua Bay.** This is one of the most beautiful spots on the island.
★ Dramatic cliffs surround crystal clear, turquoise water chock-full of stunning coral and tropical fish. The term "beach" is used a bit liberally for **Napoopoo Beach,** on the south side of the bay. There's no real beach to speak of, but there are easy ways to enter the water. This is a nice place to swim as it's well protected from weather or currents, so the water is almost always calm and clear. Excellent snorkel cruises can be booked through Fair Wind Cruises, the only company allowed to moor in Kealakekua Bay. ⊠ *Bottom of Napoopoo Rd.*

Holualoa. Hugging the hillside along the Kona Coast, the tiny village of Holualoa is just up winding Hualalai Road from Kailua-Kona. It's comprised almost entirely of galleries in which all types of artists, from woodworkers to jewelry makers and more traditional painters, work in their studios in back and sell the finished product up front. Formerly the exclusive domain of coffee plantations, it still has quite a few coffee farms offering free tours and cups of joe. ⊠ *Kailua-Kona.*

★ **Puuhonua O Honaunau** (*City of Refuge*). This 180-acre National Historic Park was once a safe haven for women in times of war as well as for *kapu* (taboo) breakers, criminals, and prisoners of war—anyone who could get inside the 1,000-foot-long wall, which was 10 feet high and 17 feet thick, could avoid punishment. **Hale-o-Keawe Heiau,** built in 1650 as the burial place of King Kamehameha I's ancestor Keawe, has been restored. If this place doesn't give you "chicken skin" (goose bumps), nothing will. ⊠ *Rte. 160, about 20 mi south of Kailua-Kona* 🕾 *808/328–2288* ⊕ *www.nps.gov/puho* 🖃 *$5 per vehicle* ☺ *Park daily 7 am–8 pm; visitor center daily 8 am–5:30 pm.*

CLOSE UP

Kona Coffee

From the cafés, stores, and restaurants selling Kona coffee, to the farm tours, to the annual Kona Coffee Cultural Festival, coffee is a major part of life on this side of the Big Island. More than 600 farms, most from just three to seven acres in size, grow the delicious—and luxurious, at generally more than $25 per pound—beans. Only coffee from the North and South Kona Districts can be called Kona.

Hawaii is the only U.S. producer of commercially grown coffee, and it has been growing in Kona since 1828, when Reverend Samuel Ruggles, an American missionary, brought a cutting over from the Oahu farm of Chief Boki, Oahu's governor. That coffee plant was a strain of Ethiopian coffee called coffee Arabica, and it is the same coffee still produced today, although a Guatemalan strain of Arabica introduced in the late 1800s is produced in far higher quantities.

In the early 1900s, the large Hawaiian coffee plantations subdivided their lots and began leasing parcels to local tenant farmers, a practice that continues today. Many tenant farmers were Japanese families. In the 1930s, local schools switched summer vacation to "coffee vacation" from August to November so that the kids could help with the coffee harvest, a practice that held until 1969.

Coffee is harvested as "cherries"—the beans are encased in a hard red shell. Kona beans are handpicked several times each season to guarantee the best product. The cherries are shelled and the beans roasted to a dark brown. Today most farms—owned and operated by Japanese-American families, west coast Mainland transplants, native Hawaiians, and descendants of Portuguese and Chinese immigrants—control production from harvest to cup.

WORTH NOTING

Amy B.H. Greenwell Ethnobotanical Garden. Easy to drive by on the twisting two-lane highway, this garden offers a wealth of Hawaiian ethnobotanical traditions. On 12 acres, 250 types of plants are grown that were typical in an early Hawaiian *ahupuaa,* the usually pie-shaped land divisions that ran from the mountains to the sea. The new visitor center, now on the south side of the garden, includes a gift shop. The garden is 12 mi south of Kailua-Kona, just past mile marker 110, across from the Manago Hotel. Call for information on guided tours. ⌧ *82-6160 Mamalahoa Hwy., Captain Cook* ☎ *808/323–3318* ⊕ *www. bishopmuseum.org/greenwell* ⌧ *$7* ☉ *Tues.–Sun. 9–4.*

Greenwell Store. Established in 1850, the homestead of Henry N. Greenwell served as cattle ranch, sheep station, store, post office, and family home all in one. Now, all that remains is the 1875 stone structure, which is listed on the National Register of Historic Places. It houses a fascinating museum that has exhibits on ranching and coffee farming. It's also headquarters for the **Kona Historical Society,** which organizes walking tours of Kailua-Kona. ⌧ *81-6551 Mamalahoa Hwy., Kealakekua* ☎ *808/323–3222* ⊕ *www.konahistorical.org* ⌧ *$7* ☉ *Mon.– Thurs. 10–2.*

DID YOU KNOW?

Kealakekua Bay is generally considered the best snorkeling spot on the Big Island, with stunning coral reefs—especially around the Captain Cook Monument—calm waters, and spinner dolphins.

Hikiau Heiau. This stone platform was once an impressive temple dedicated to the god Lono. When Captain Cook arrived in 1778, ceremonies in his honor were held here. ⊠ *Bottom of Napoopoo Rd.*

Kainaliu. Like many of the Big Island's old plantation towns, Kainaliu is experiencing a bit of a renaissance. In addition to a ribbon of funky old stores, a handful of new galleries and shops have sprung up in the last few years. Browse around Oshima's, established in 1926, and Kimura's, established in 1927, to find authentic Japanese goods beyond tourist trinkets, then pop into one of the local cafés for a tasty vegetarian snack. Cross the street to peek into the 1932 Aloha Theatre, where community-theater actors might be practicing a Broadway revue. ⊠ *Hwy. 11, mile markers 112–114, Kainaliu.*

St. Benedict's Painted Church. The walls, columns, and ceiling of this Roman Catholic church depict colorful biblical scenes through the paintbrush of Belgian-born priest Father Velghe. Mass is still held every weekend. The view of Kealakekua Bay from the entrance is amazing. ⊠ *Painted Church Rd., off Hwy. 160, Honaunau* ☎ *808/328–2227* ⊕ *www.thepaintedchurch.org.*

NORTH KONA

Most of the lava flows in North Kona are from the last eruptions of Mt. Hualalai, in 1800 and 1801. You will no doubt notice the miles of white-coral graffiti in the vast lava fields. This has been going on for decades, and locals still get a kick out of it, as do tourists. The first thing everyone asks is "where do the white rocks come from?" and the answer is this: they're bits of coral and they come from the ocean. If you want to write a message in the lava, you've got to use the coral that's already out there. This means that no one's message lasts for long, but that's all part of the fun. Some local couples even have a tradition of writing their names in the same spot on the lava fields every year on their anniversary.

GETTING HERE AND AROUND
Head north from Kona International Airport and follow Highway 19 along the coast. Take caution driving at night between the airport and where resorts begin on the Kohala Coast; it's extremely dark and there are few road signs and traffic lights.

EXPLORING
Natural Energy Lab of Hawaii. Driving south from the Kona International Airport towards Kailua-Kona, you'll spot a large mysterious group of buildings with an equally large and mysterious photovoltaic (solar) panel installation just inside its gate. Although it looks like some sort of top-secret military station, this is the site of the Natural Energy Lab of Hawaii, NELHA for short, where scientists, researchers, and entrepreneurs are developing and marketing everything from new uses for solar power to energy-efficient air-conditioning systems and environmentally friendly aquaculture techniques. Visitors are welcome at the lab, and there are 1½-hour tours for those interested in learning more about the experiments being conducted. ⊠ *73-4460 Queen Kaahumanu Hwy.,*

#101, Kailua-Kona ☎ 808/329–8073 ⊕ www.friendsofnelha.org ✉ $8 donation for tours ⊙ Tours Mon.–Thurs. at 10 am.

THE KOHALA COAST

The Kohala Coast is about 32 mi north of Kailua-Kona.

If you had only a weekend to spend on the Big Island, this is probably where you'd want to go. The Kohala Coast is a mix of the island's best beaches and swankiest hotels just minutes from ancient valleys and temples, waterfalls, and funky artist enclaves.

The resorts on the Kohala Coast lay claim to some of the island's finest restaurants and its only destination spas. But the real attraction here is the island's best beaches. On a clear day, you can see Maui and during the winter months, glistening humpback whales cleave the waters just offshore.

Rounding the northern tip of the island, the arid coast shifts rather suddenly to green villages and hillsides, leading to lush Pololu Valley in North Kohala, and the hot sunshine along the coast gives way to cooler temperatures.

As you drive north, you'll find the quaint sugar-plantations-turned-artsy-enclaves of Hawi and Kapaau, where new galleries are interspersed with charming reminders of old Hawaii—wooden boardwalks, quaint local stores, delicious neighborhood restaurants, friendly locals, and a delightfully slow pace. There's great shopping for everything from designer beachwear to authentic Hawaiian crafts.

GETTING HERE AND AROUND

Two days is sufficient time for experiencing each unique side of Kohala—one day for the resort perks: the beach, the spa, the golf, the restaurants; one day for hiking and admiring the waterfalls and valleys of North Kohala, coupled with a wander around Hawi and Kapaau.

Diving and snorkeling are great along this coast, so bring or rent equipment. If you're staying at one of the resorts, they will usually have any equipment you could possibly want. If you're feeling adventurous, get your hands on a four-wheel-drive vehicle and head to one of the unmarked beaches along the Kohala Coast—you may end up with a beach to yourself.

The best way to explore the valleys of North Kohala is with a hiking tour. Look for one that includes lunch and a dip in one of the area's waterfall pools. There are a number of casual lunch options in Hawi and Kapaau (sandwiches, sushi, seafood, local-style "plate lunch"), and a few good dinner spots.

ESSENTIALS

North Kohala Community Resource Center. Stop at this newly renovated plantation building for maps and information on North Kohala attractions. You can take a seat on the lanai and talk story with members of the local community. ✉ *55-3393 Akoni Pule Hwy., just past the "Welcome to Kohala" sign, North Kohala ☎ 808/889–5523 ⊕ www. northkohala.org ✉ Free ⊙ Weekdays 8:30–4:30, weekend hours vary.*

Continued on page 58

BIRTH OF THE ISLANDS

How did the volcanoes of the Hawaiian Islands evolve here, in the middle of the Pacific Ocean? The ancient Hawaiians believed that the volcano goddess Pele's hot temper was the key to the mystery; modern scientists contend that it's all about plate tectonics and one very hot spot.

Plate Tectonics & the Hawaiian Question: The theory of plate tectonics says that the Earth's surface is comprised of plates that float around slowly over the planet's molten interior. The vast majority of earthquakes and volcanic eruptions occur near plate boundaries—the San Francisco earthquakes in 1906 and 1989, for example, were the result of activity along the nearby San Andreas Fault, where the Pacific and North American plates meet. Hawaii, more than 1,988 miles from the nearest plate boundary, is a giant exception. For years scientists struggled to explain the island chain's existence—if not a fault line, what caused the earthquakes and volcanic eruptions that formed these islands?

What's a hotspot? In 1963, J. Tuzo Wilson, a Canadian geophysicist, argued that the Hawaiian volcanoes must have been created by small concentrated areas of extreme heat beneath the plates. Wilson hypothesized that there is a hotspot beneath the present-day position of the Big Island. Its heat produced a persistent source of magma by partly melting the Pacific Plate above it. The magma, lighter than the surrounding solid rock, rose through the mantle and crust to erupt onto the sea floor, forming an active seamount. Each flow caused the seamount to grow until it finally emerged above sea level as an island volcano. Plausible so far, but why then, is there not one giant Hawaiian island?

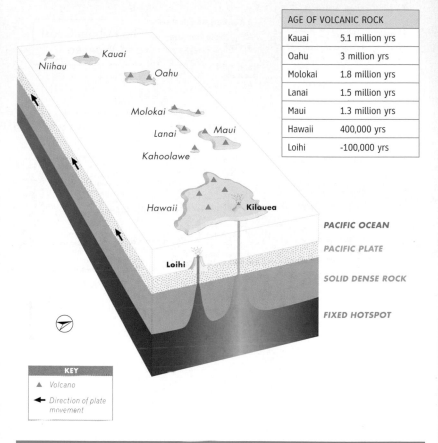

AGE OF VOLCANIC ROCK	
Kauai	5.1 million yrs
Oahu	3 million yrs
Molokai	1.8 million yrs
Lanai	1.5 million yrs
Maui	1.3 million yrs
Hawaii	400,000 yrs
Loihi	-100,000 yrs

PACIFIC OCEAN

PACIFIC PLATE

SOLID DENSE ROCK

FIXED HOTSPOT

KEY	
▲	Volcano
◄—	Direction of plate movement

Volcanoes on the Move: Wilson further suggested that the movement of the Pacific Plate itself eventually carries the island volcano beyond the hotspot. Cut off from its magma source, the island volcano becomes dormant. As the plate slowly moved, one island volcano would become extinct just as another would develop over the hotspot. After several million years, there is a long volcanic trail of islands and seamounts across the ocean floor. The oldest islands are those farthest from the hotspot. The exposed rocks of Kauai, for example, are about 5.1 million years old, but those on the Big Island are less than .5 million years old, with new volcanic rock still being formed.

An Island on the Way: Off the coast of the Big Island, the volcano known as Loihi is still submerged but erupting. Scientists long believed it to be a retired seamount volcano, but in the 1970s they discovered both old and new lava on its flanks, and in 1996 it erupted with a vengeance. It is believed that several thousand years from now, Loihi will be the newest addition to the Hawaiian Islands.

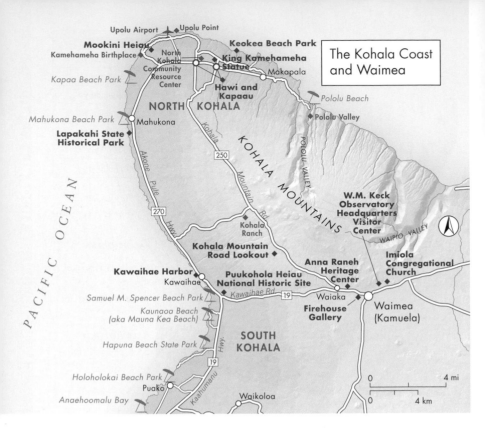

The Kohala Coast and Waimea

EXPLORING
TOP ATTRACTIONS

Hawi and Kapaau. Home to the birthplace of King Kamehameha, these neighboring towns thrived during the plantation days. There were hotels, saloons, and theaters—even a railroad. They took a hit when "Big Sugar" left the island, but both towns are blossoming once again today, thanks to strong local communities and an influx of artists keen on honoring the towns' past. Old historic buildings have been restored and now boast a wide variety of shops, galleries, and eateries.

Ackerman Gift Gallery. In Kapaau, browse through the extensive Hawaiian collection of the Ackerman Gift Gallery. ⊠ *54-3897 Akoni Pule Hwy., Hwy. 270, North Kohala* ☎ *808/889–5971* ⊕ *www.ackerman galleries.com.*

QUICK BITES

Kohala Coffee Mill & Tropical Dreams. If you're looking for something sweet—or savory—this cafe in downtown Hawi serves great local coffee, breakfast (bagels, espresso-machine steamed eggs) and lunch (hot dogs, vegan soup). Sit outside and watch the traffic go by as you enjoy locally made ice cream that is *ono* (translation: delicious). ⊠ *55-3412 Akoni Pule Hwy., Hawi* ☎ *808/889–5577.*

Keokea Beach Park. Not a beach per se, this shallow rocky inlet is a great place for a picnic. There's a pavilion and lookout area, but don't try to swim here—the water is very rough. Be careful on the hairpin curve going down. ⊠ *Hwy. 270, on the way to Pololu Valley near mile marker 27, North Kohala.*

WORD OF MOUTH

"I would suggest driving north on highway 19 then taking highway 270 from Kawaihae to Hawi—it's a lovely drive along the ocean and Hawi is a nice little town with shops and restaurants—either Bamboo or Sushi Rock for lunch."
—martym

★ **Kohala Mountain Road Lookout.** The road between North Kohala and Waimea is one of the most scenic drives in Hawaii, passing Parker Ranch, open pastures, and tree-lined mountains. There are a few places to pull over and take in the view; the lookout at mile marker 8 provides a splendid vista of the Kohala Coast and Kawaihae Harbor far below. On clear days, you can see well beyond the resorts, while other times an eerie, thick mist drifts over the view. ⊠ *Kohala Mountain Rd. (Hwy. 250), Kamuela.*

★ **Lapakahi State Historical Park.** A self-guided, 1-mi walking tour leads through the ruins of the once-prosperous fishing village Koaie, which dates as far back as the 15th century. Displays illustrate early Hawaiian fishing and farming techniques, salt gathering, games, and legends. Since the shoreline near the state park is an officially designated Marine Life Conservation District, and part of the site itself is considered sacred, swimming is discouraged. ⊠ *Hwy. 270, mile marker 14 between Kawaihae and Mahukona, North Kohala* ☎ *808/974–6200, 808/327–4958* ⊕ *www.hawaiistateparks.org* ⊡ *Free* ☉ *Daily 8–4.*

★ **Mookini Heiau.** This National Historic Landmark, an isolated *heiau* (an ancient place of worship), is so impressive in size it may give you what locals call "chicken skin" (goose bumps)—especially after you learn its history. The heiau's foundations date to about AD 480, but the high priest Paao from Tahiti expanded it several centuries later to offer sacrifices to please his gods. You can still see the lava slab where hundreds of people were sacrificed, which gives this place a truly haunted feel. The road is unpaved, and even with four-wheel-drive you could easily get stuck in the mud. Then it is a half-mile hike to the site. ⊠ *Turn off Hwy. 270 at sign for Upolu Airport, near Hawi, and hike or drive in a four-wheel-drive vehicle 1½ mi southwest North Kohala* ☎ *808/974–6200.*

★ **Puukohola Heiau National Historic Site.** In 1790 a prophet told King Kamehameha to build a *heiau* on top of Puukohola (Hill of the Whale) and dedicate it to the war god Kukailimoku by sacrificing his principal rival, Keoua Kuahuula. By doing so the king would achieve his goal of conquering the Hawaiian Islands. The prophecy came true in 1810. A short walk over arid landscape leads from the impressive, recently renovated visitor center to temples **Puukohola Heiau** and **Mailekini Heiau.** An even older temple, dedicated to the shark gods, lies submerged just offshore. Bring along your cellular phone to listen to a free audio tour while you visit the site. ⊠ *62-3601 Kawaihae Rd., Kawaihae* ☎ *808/882–7218* ⊕ *www.nps.gov/puhe/index.htm* ⊡ *Free* ☉ *Daily 7:45–5.*

WORTH NOTING

Kawaihae Harbor. This no-frills industrial harbor, where in 1793 the first cattle landed in Hawaii, is a hub of commercial and community activity. It's especially busy on weekends, when paddlers and local fishing boats float on the waves. Second in size only to Hilo Harbor on the east coast, the harbor is often home to the *Makalii,* one of three traditional Hawaiian sailing canoes. King Kamehameha and his men launched their canoes from here when they set out to conquer the neighboring islands. ■TIP→There are several restaurants with nice sunset views in Kawaihae should you be nearby at dinnertime. ✉ *Kawaihae Harbor Rd., off Hwy. 270, Kawaihae.*

King Kamehameha Statue. A statue of Kamehameha the Great, the legendary king who united the Hawaiian islands, stands watch over his descendants in North Kohala. The 8½-foot-tall figure bears the king's sacred feather *kihei, mahiole,* and *kaei* (cape, helmet, and sash). This is the original of the statue in front of the Judiciary Building on King Street in Honolulu. Cast in Florence in 1880, it was lost at sea when the German ship transporting it sank near the Falkland Islands. A replica was then commissioned and shipped to Honolulu. Two years after its disappearence, the original statue was found in a junkyard in the Falkland Islands; it was missing an arm, which has since been replaced. This statue was transported to the remote northern tip of the Big Island, Kamehameha's birthplace: it's in front of the old Kohala Courthouse in Kapaau, next to the highway on the way towards Pololu Valley.

Every year on King Kamehameha Day (June 11), Kohala residents honor their most famous son with a celebration that involves draping the statue in handmade floral lei and a parade. ✉ *54-3900 Kapaau Rd., Kapaau.*

QUICK BITES **Lighthouse Delicatessen.** In downtown Hawi's Kohala Trade Building, this eatery is reminiscent of a big-city delicatessen, but with a Kohala twist. Choose meats and cheeses from a tempting deli case to create your own sandwiches. There are also soups, salads, and vegetarian fare. The eggs Benedict on Sunday is a special treat. You can take out or eat in. ✉ *Kohala Trade Building, 55-3419 Akoni Pule Hwy., Hawi* ☎ *808/889–5757* ⊕ *www. lighthousedelihi.com* ⊗ *Mon.–Sat. 10–6, Sun. 9–4.*

WAIMEA

Waimea is 40 mi northeast of Kailua-Kona and 10 mi east of the Kohala Coast.

Thirty minutes over the mountain from Kohala, Waimea offers a completely different experience from the rest of the island. Rolling green hills, large open pastures, cool evening breezes and morning mists, abundant cattle, horses, and regular rodeos are just a few of the surprises you'll stumble upon here in *paniolo* (Hawaiian for "cowboy") country.

In addition to the horses and cattle, Waimea is also where some of the island's top Hawaii regional-cuisine chefs practice their art using

Mauna Kea's snowcapped summit towers ahead on a drive south from Waimea.

local ingredients, which makes it an ideal place to find yourself at dinnertime. In keeping with the recent Big Island restaurant trend toward locally farmed ingredients, a handful of Waimea farms and ranches supply most of the restaurants on the island, and many sell to the public as well. With its galleries, restaurants, beautiful countryside and paniolo culture, Waimea is well worth a stop if you're heading to Hilo or Mauna Kea. ■TIP➔ And the short highway, or mountain road, that connects Waimea to North Kohala (Hwy. 250) affords some of our favorite Big Island views.

GETTING HERE AND AROUND

You can see most of what Waimea has to offer in one day, but if you're heading up to Mauna Kea for stargazing (which you should), it could easily be stretched to two. If you stay in Waimea overnight (there are a few bed-and-breakfast options), spend the afternoon browsing through town or touring some of the area's ranches and historic sites, then indulge in a gourmet dinner—all before heading up Saddle Road for world-renowned stargazing atop Mauna Kea.

A word to the wise—there are no services or gas stations on Saddle Road, the only way to reach the summit of Mauna Kea. Fill up on gas and bring water, snacks, and warm clothes with you (there are plenty of gas stations, cafés, and shops in Waimea).

EXPLORING

★ **Anna Ranch Heritage Center.** Named after the "First Lady" of Hawaii ranching, Anna Lindsey Perry-Fiske, this ranch offers a rare opportunity to see a fully restored cattle ranch house on the Big Island. Wander the picturesque grounds and gardens on a self-guided walk, watch a master saddle maker and an ironsmith in action, and take a tour of the historic house, where Anna's elaborate *pau* (riding) costumes are on display. The knowledgeable staff will share anecdotes about Anna's amazing life. The ranch is on the National Register of Historic Places. On Wednesday afternoon a farmers' market is held here. ✉ *65-1480 Kawaihae Rd., Waimea* ☎ *808/885–4426* ⊕ *www.annaranch.org* 🎫 *Guided tours $10* ⊙ *Tues.–Sat. 10–4.*

WAIMEA OR KAMUELA?

Both, actually. Everyone knows it as Waimea, but the sign on the post office says Kamuela, which is Hawaiian for "Samuel," referring to Samuel Parker, the son of the founder of Parker Ranch. That designation is used to avoid confusion with communities named Waimea on the islands of Kauai and Oahu. But the official name of the town is Waimea.

Firehouse Gallery. Walk across the Parker Ranch Shopping Center parking lot to a historic 79-year-old fire station, now a gallery, to glimpse what the artists in Hamakua and Kohala are up to. The Waimea Arts Council sponsors free *kaha kii* (one-person shows). ✉ *67-1201 Mamalahoa Hwy.* ☎ *808/887–1052* ⊕ *www.waimeaartscouncil.org.* ⊙ *Wed.–Sat. 11–3.*

Imiola Congregational Church. Stop here to admire the dark koa interior and the unusual wooden calabashes hanging from the ceiling. Be careful not to walk in while a service is in progress, as the front entry of this church, which was established in 1832 and rebuilt in 1857, is behind the pulpit. ✉ *65-1084 Mamalahoa Hwy., on "Church Row"* ☎ *808/885–4987.*

W. M. Keck Observatory Headquarters Vistors Center. If you are keen on astronomy but don't have time to go all the way to the summit, visit Keck Observatory headquarters right in Waimea, with its educational exibits and informed staff. You can see models and images of the twin 10-meter Keck telescopes on Mauna Kea and learn about the latest discoveries. ✉ *65-1120 Kawaihae Rd., across from the hospital, Waimea* ☎ *808/885–7887* ⊙ *Tues.–Fri. 10–2.*

QUICK
BITES

Waimea Coffee Company. Stop by this shop for a steaming latté and a warm pastry. Sit out on their veranda, staring at the manicured lawns and ranch-style building and try to believe you're in Hawaii. ✉ *Parker Sq., 65-1279 Kawaihae Rd.* ☎ *808/885–8915.*

MAUNA KEA

Fodor's Choice ★ *Mauna Kea's summit is 18 mi southeast of Waimea and 34 mi northwest of Hilo.*

Mauna Kea ("white mountain") is the antithesis of the typical island experience. Freezing temperatures and arctic conditions are common at the summit, and snow can fall year-round. You can go even snowboarding up here. Seriously. But just because you can doesn't mean you'll want to. You should be in very good shape and a close-to-expert boarder or skier to get down the slopes near the summit and then up again in the thin air with no lifts. During the winter months, lack of snow is usually not a problem.

But winter sports are the least of the reasons that most people visit this starkly beautiful mountain. From its base below the ocean's surface to its summit, Mauna Kea is the tallest island mountain on the planet. It's also home to little Lake Waiau, one of the highest natural lakes in the world, though the word "pond" is closer to the truth.

Mauna Kea's summit—at 13,796 feet—is reputedly the best place in the world for viewing the night sky. For this reason, the summit is home to the largest and most productive astronomical observatory in the world. Research teams from 11 different countries operate 13 telescopes on Mauna Kea, several of which are record holders: the world's largest optical–infrared telescopes (the dual Keck telescopes), the world's largest dedicated infrared telescope (UKIRT), and the largest submillimeter telescope (the JCMT). A still-larger 30-meter telescope has just been cleared for construction, and is slated to open its record-breaking eye to the heavens in 2018.

Mauna Kea is tall, but there are higher mountains in the world, so what makes this spot so superb for astronomy? It has more to do with atmosphere than with elevation. A tropical-inversion-cloud layer below the summit keeps moisture from the ocean and other atmospheric pollutants down at lower elevations. As a result, the air around the Mauna Kea summit is extremely dry, which helps in the measurement of infrared and submillimeter radiation from stars, planets, and the like. There are also rarely clouds up here; the annual number of clear nights here blows every other place out of the water. And, because the mountain is far away from any interfering artificial lights (not a total coincidence—in addition to the fact that the nearest town is nearly 30 mi away, there's an official ordinance limiting light on the island), skies are dark for the astronomers' research. To quote the staff at the observatory, astronomers here are able to "observe the faintest galaxies that lie at the very edge of the observable universe."

Teams from various universities around the world have used the telescopes on Mauna Kea to make major astronomical discoveries, including new satellites around Jupiter and Saturn, new "Trojans" (asteroids that orbit, similar to moons) around Neptune, new moons and rings around Uranus, and new moons around Pluto. Their studies of galaxies are changing the way scientists think about time and the evolution of the universe.

What does all this mean for you? A visit to Mauna Kea is a chance to see more stars than you've likely ever seen before, and an opportunity to learn more about mind-boggling scientific discoveries in the very spot where these discoveries are being made. For you space geeks, a trip to Mauna Kea may just be the highlight of your trip.

If you're in Hilo, be sure to visit the Imiola Astronomy Center. It has presentations and planetarium films about the mountain and the science being conducted there, as well as exhibits describing the deep knowledge of the heavens possessed by the ancient Hawaiians.

GETTING HERE AND AROUND

The summit of Mauna Kea is only 34 mi from Hilo and 18 from Waimea, but the drive takes about an hour and a half from Hilo and an hour from Waimea thanks to the steep road. Between the ride there, sunset on the summit, and stargazing, we recommend allotting at least four hours for your Mauna Kea visit.

To reach the summit, you must drive on Saddle Road, which used to be a narrow, rough, winding highway, but has recently been rerouted and repaved, and is now a beautiful shortcut across the middle of the island (except for that stretch near Waimea). The road to the visitor center at Mauna Kea is fine, but the road from there to the summit is a bit more precarious because it's unpaved and very steep: although most cars can make it up slowly, four-wheel-drive vehicles are recommended. If you're worried about your rental making the drive, you can still head for the summit with one of a handful of tour operators who will take care of everything. If you plan to drive yourself, fill up on gas and bring water and snacks and warm clothes with you, as there is nowhere along the way to stock up.

The second thing, which is extremely important to remember, is the altitude. ■**TIP**➡ Take the change in altitude seriously—stop at the visitor center for at least half an hour, and don't overexert yourself, especially at the top. Scuba divers must wait at least 24 hours before attempting a trip to the summit to avoid getting the bends. The observatory recommends that children under 16, pregnant women, and those with heart, respiratory, or weight problems not go higher than the visitor center.

The last potential obstacle: it's cold, as in freezing. Military personnel stationed in Hawaii do their cold-weather training atop Mauna Kea. Most summit tours provide parkas, but it's difficult to find cold-weather clothing in Hawaii, so, if you plan to visit Mauna Kea, pack your favorite warm things from home.

ONIZUKA VISITOR CENTER

★ **Onizuka Center for International Astronomy Visitor Information Station.** At a 9,300-foot elevation, this is an excellent amateur observation site, with a handful of telescopes and a knowledgeable staff. It hosts nightly stargazing sessions from 6 to 10. This is also where you should stop for a while to acclimate to the altitude if you're heading for the summit. This is a pleasure to do as you drink hot chocolate and peruse the exhibits on ancient Hawaiian celestial navigation, the ancient history of the mountain as not only a quarry for the best basalt in the Hawaiian Islands, but also as one of its most revered spiritual retreats. Other exhibits cover modern astronomy and the unique natural history of the summit.

The gift shop is full of great books, posters, and other mementos. On weekends the Onizuka Center offers free escorted summit tours, heading up the mountain in a caravan. Participants must arrive at 1 pm, in your own all-wheel or four-wheel-drive vehicle. After watching a one-hour video, the caravan begins.

To get here from Hilo, which is about 34 mi away, take Highway 200 (Saddle Road), and turn right at mile marker 28 onto John A. Burns

Way, which is the only access road to the summit. ☎ *808/961–2180* ⊕ *www.ifa.hawaii.edu/info/vis* ☉ *Daily 9 am–9:30 pm.*

THE SUMMIT

Head to the summit before sunset so you're already there to witness the stunning sunset and emerging star show. Only the astronomers are allowed to use the telescopes and equipment up here, but the scenery is free for everybody. So, watch the sun sink into the horizon and then head down to the visitor center to warm up and stargaze some more. Or do your stargazing first and then head up here to get a different perspective—if you were blown away by the number of stars crowding the sky over the visitor center, this vantage point will really make you speechless. Just take it easy if you're driving back down in the dark— slow and cautious is the name of the game on this steep road.

If you haven't rented a four-wheel-drive vehicle, don't want to deal with driving to the summit, or don't want to wait in line to use the handful of telescopes at the visitor center, consider booking a tour. Operators provide transportation to and from the summit, and expert guides; some also provide parkas, gloves, telescopes, dinner, hot beverages, and snacks. Excursion fees range from $90 to $189.

GOING WITH A GUIDE

Arnott's Lodge & Hiking Adventures. Arnott's Mauna Kea summit tour focuses more on the experience of the mountain than astronomy. Each guest gets to use a pair of binoculars while the guide provides an informative lesson on major celestial objects and Polynesian navigational stars. The excursion departs from Hilo and costs $175 per person, including parkas and hot beverages. The outfitter also offers lava and waterfall tours. ✉ *Hilo* ☎ *808/969–7097* ⊕ *www.arnottslodge.com.*

Hawaii Forest & Trail. This outfitter leaves from Kona and also picks up guests at the Hilton Waikoloa Resort and at the Paniolo Greens Condominiums in Waikoloa Village. You'll stop for dinner along the way at a historic ranch. Hawaii Forest & Trail supplies parkas, gloves, and brings a telescope along. Cookies and hot chocolate make cold stargazing more pleasant. The price is $189 per person. ✉ *74-5035 Queen Kaahumanu Hwy., 3 mi. south of Kona airport, Kailua-Kona* ☎ *808/331–8505, 800/464–1993* ⊕ *www.hawaii-forest.com.*

Mauna Kea Summit Adventures. As the first company to specialize in tours to the mountain and the only company to offer only Mauna Kea tours, Mauna Kea Summit Adventures has a bit more cred than the rest of the pack. Expect cushy new van coaches for the tours, parkas and gloves provided, and dinner at the visitor center before heading up to view the sunset on the summit. A powerful telescope is also supplied. Find directions for pickup spots on the Web site; these include downtown Kona, the Hilton Waikoloa Resort, and the junction of Highway 190 and Saddle Road. The price is $200 per person, including tax. ✉ *Hilo* ☎ *808/322–2366* ⊕ *www.maunakea.com.*

CLOSE UP

Mauna Kea's Telescopes

There's a meeting of the minds on the mountaintop, with 13 telescopes operated by astronomers from around the world. Although the telescopes are owned and operated by various countries and organizations, any research team can book time on the equipment.

A U.S.–Japan team comprising astronomers from the University of Hawaii, University of Tokyo, Tohoku University, and Japan's Institute of Space and Astronautical Science made an important discovery of distant galaxies obscured by cosmic dust, using the JCMT telescope, which is jointly owned and operated by the United Kingdom, Canada, and the Netherlands. Similarly, a team of astronomers from the University of Hawaii used the Keck telescopes (owned and operated by Caltech and the University of California) to discover a distant galaxy that gives astronomers a glimpse of the Dark Ages, when galaxies and stars were first forming in the universe.

2

THE HAMAKUA COAST

The Hamakua Coast is about 25 mi east of Waimea.

The spectacular waterfalls, mysterious jungles, emerald fields, and stunning ocean vistas along Highway 19 northwest of Hilo are collectively referred to as the Hilo–Hamakua Heritage Coast. Brown signs featuring a sugarcane tassel reflect the area's history: thousands of acres of sugarcane are now idle, with no industry to support since "King Sugar" left the island in the early 1990s.

The 45-mi drive winds through little plantation towns, Papaikou, Laupahoehoe, and Paauilo among them. It's a great place to wander off the main road and see "real" Hawaii—untouched valleys, overgrown banyan trees, tiny coastal villages. ■TIP→ The "Heritage Drive," a 4-mi loop just off the main highway, is well worth the detour. Signs mark various sites of historical interest, as well as scenic views along the 40-mi stretch of coastline. Keep an eye out for them and try to stop at the sights mentioned—you won't be disappointed.

Once back on Highway 19, you'll pass the road to Honokaa, which leads to the end of the road bordering Waipio Valley, ancient home to Hawaiian royalty. The isolated valley floor has maintained the ways of old Hawaii, with taro patches, wild horses, and a handful of houses. The view from the lookout is breathtaking.

GETTING HERE AND AROUND

Any turn off along this coast could lead to an incredible view, so take your time and go exploring up and down the side roads. You'll find small communities still hanging on quite nicely, well after the demise of the big sugar plantations that first engendered them. You'll find homey cafés, gift shops, and galleries—and a way of life from a time gone by. If you're driving from Kailua-Kona, rather than driving around the northern tip of the island, cut across on the Mamalahoa Highway (190)

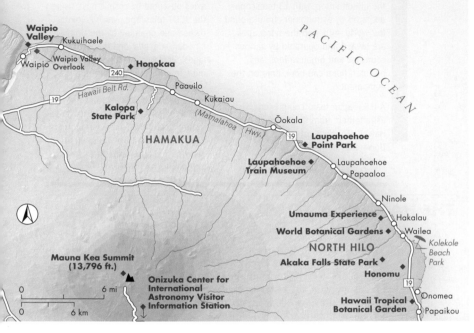

to Waimea, and then catch Highway 19 to the coast. It takes a little longer but is well worth it.

If you've stopped to explore the quiet little villages with wooden board-walks and dogs dozing in backyards, or if you've spent several hours in Waipio Valley, night will undoubtedly be falling by the time you've had your fill of the Hamakua Coast. Don't worry: the return to Hilo via Highway 19 only takes about an hour, or you can go in the other direction on the same road to stop for dinner in Waimea before heading back to the Kohala Coast resorts (another 25 to 45 minutes). Although you shouldn't have any trouble exploring the Hamakua Coast in a day, a handful of romantic bed-and-breakfasts are available along the coast if you want to spend more time.

TOURS

A guided tour is the best way to see Waipio Valley. You can walk down and up the steep narrow road yourself, but you won't see as much. Costs range from about $50 to $150, depending on the company and the transport mode.

Hawaiian Walkways. If you are serious about hiking, this is the company for you. Knowledgeable guides lead various personalized tours, from Waipio waterfall hikes to volcano discovery walks to a unique Saddle Road excursion. Tours range from 3½ to 7½ hours and from $119 for

DID YOU KNOW?

The dramatic Akaka Falls is only one of hundreds of waterfalls on the Hamakua Coast. Many falls tumble into pristine swimming holes, so bring your swimsuit when you explore this area.

the Waipio hike to $185 for the Saddle Road excursion. Hikes include a light lunch and hiking gear. It's best to call for reservations. ✉ *Honokaa* 🕾 *808/775–0372, 800/457–7759* ⊕ *www.hawaiianwalkways.com.*

Naalapa Stables. Friendly horses and friendly guides take guests on tours of the valley floor. The 2½-hour tours run Monday through Saturday (the valley rests on Sunday) with check-in times of 9 am and 12:30 pm. Cost is $88.50 per person. ✉ *Waipio Valley, Honokaa* 🕾 *808/775–0419* ⊕ *www.naalapastables.com.*

Waipio on Horseback. This is a great outfit offering guided horseback-riding trips on the valley floor for $85. It also offers ATV ranch tours for those 16 years and older, with awesome views of the valley and surrounding areas, for $100. ✉ *WOH Ranch, Hwy. 240, mile marker 7.5, northwest of Honokaa* 🕾 *808/775–7291, 877/775–7291* ⊕ *www. waipioonhorseback.com.*

Waipio Valley Shuttle. These informative 1½ to 2-hour four-wheel-drive tours explore the valley Monday through Saturday. The cost is $52. ✉ *48-5416 Government Main Rd., Honokaa* 🕾 *808/775–7121.*

Waipio Valley Wagon Tours. Mule-drawn wagon tours down through the valley run Monday through Saturday at 10:30, 12:30, and 2:30. The excursion lasts 1½ hours and costs $60. Reservations are highly recommended and can be made online. ✉ *Pickup 8 mi out of Honokaa, at the Last Chance Store, Honokaa* 🕾 *808/775–9518* ⊕ *www. waipiovalleywagontours.com.*

EXPLORING
TOP ATTRACTIONS

★ **Akaka Falls State Park.** A meandering 10-minute loop trail takes you to the best spots to see the two cascades, **Akaka** and **Kahuna.** The 400-foot Kahuna Falls is on the lower end of the trail. The majestic upper Akaka Falls drops more than 442 feet, tumbling far below into a pool drained by Kolekole Stream amid a profusion of fragrant white, yellow, and red torch ginger. ✉ *4 mi inland, off Hwy. 19, near Honomu* 🕾 *808/974–6200* 🖭 *$5 per vehicle (non-residents); $1 for walk-ins* ⊙ *Daily 7–7.*

★ **Hawaii Tropical Botanical Garden.** Eight miles north of Hilo, stunning coastline views appear around each curve of the 4-mi scenic jungle drive that accesses the privately owned nature preserve beside Onomea Bay. Paved pathways in the 17-acre botanical garden lead past ponds, waterfalls, and more than 2,000 species of plants and flowers, including palms, bromeliads, ginger, heliconia, orchids, and ornamentals. ✉ *27-717 Old Mamalahoa Hwy., Papaikou* 🕾 *808/964–5233* ⊕ *www. hawaiigarden.com* 🖭 *$15* ⊙ *Daily 9–4.*

ⓒ ★ **Kalopa State Park.** Past the old plantation town of Paauilo, at a cool elevation of 2,000 feet, lies this 100-acre state park. There's a lush forested area with picnic tables and restrooms, and an easy ¾-mi loop trail with additional paths in the adjacent forest reserve. Small signs identify some of the plants. ✉ *12 mi north of Laupahoehoe and 3 mi inland off Hwy. 19* 🕾 *808/775–8852* 🖭 *Free* ⊙ *Daily 7 am–8 pm.*

Fodor's Choice ★ **Waipio Valley.** Bounded by 2,000-foot cliffs, the "Valley of the Kings" was once a favorite retreat of Hawaiian royalty. Waterfalls drop 1,200 feet from the Kohala Mountains to the valley floor, and the sheer cliff faces make access difficult. Though completely off the grid today, Waipio was once a center of Hawaiian life; somewhere between 4,000 and 20,000 people made it their home between the 13th and 17th centuries. To preserve this pristine part of the island, commercial-transportation permits are limited—only five outfitters offer organized valley trips and they're not allowed to take visitors to the beach: environmental laws protect the swath of black sand. And on Sunday the valley rests. A road leads down from the **Waipio Valley Overlook**, but only four-wheel-drive vehicles should attempt the *very* steep road. There are no roads on the valley floor, and the going is often muddy. The walk down into the valley is less than a mile from the lookout point—just keep in mind the climb back up is strenuous. ⊠ *Follow Hwy. 240 8 mi northwest of Honokaa.*

WORTH NOTING

Honokaa. In 1881 Australian William Purvis planted the first macadamia-nut trees in Hawaii near what is now a very friendly, funky little town with a great antique shop, a few interesting galleries, and good cafés. But Honokaa's true heyday came when sugar was king in the early part of the 20th century. During World War II, this was the place for soldiers stationed around Waimea to cut loose. Today, it's still worth a look at its historic buildings, and a chat with its friendly residents. ⊠ *Hwy. 240, Honokaa.*

QUICK BITES

Tex Drive-In. A quick stop at Tex Drive-In will give you a chance to taste the snack that made it famous: *malasada*, a puffy, doughy Portuguese doughnut without a hole. These deep-fried beauties are best eaten hot. They also come in cream-filled versions, including vanilla, chocolate, and coconut. Or go for the Hawaiian burger with a fat juicy slice of sweet pineapple on top. ⊠ *45-690 Pakalana St., at Hwy. 19, Honokaa* ☎ *808/775–0598.*

Back to the 50's Highway Fountain. Midway along the coast, there's a great lunch spot in Laupahoehoe. Back to the 50's Highway Fountain serves just what you'd expect, good old-fashioned burgers, fries, onion rings, milk shakes, home-made pies plus lots of other entrées ranging from fish meatloaf to local specialties. The nicely restored old building is packed to the rafters with intriguing rock-and-roll and car culture memorabilia. Call for take-out. ⊠ *35-2074 Old Mamalahoa Hwy.* ☎ *808/962–0808* ⊙ *Closed Mon. and Tues.*

Honomu. Its sugar-plantation past is reflected in the wooden boardwalks and tin-roof buildings of this small community. It's fun to poke through old dusty shops such as Glass from the Past, where you'll find an assortment of old bottles. The Woodshop Gallery/Café showcases local artists. ⊠ *1 mi inland from Hwy. 19 en route to Akaka Falls State Park.*

Laupahoehoe Point Park. Come here to watch the surf pound the jagged black rocks at the base of the stunning point. This is not a safe place for swimming, however. Still vivid in the minds of longtime area residents is the 1946 tragedy in which 21 schoolchildren and three teachers were swept to sea by a tidal wave. ✉ *On northeast coastline, Hwy. 19, makai side, north of Laupahoehoe* ☎ *808/961–8311* 🎟 *Free* ⊙ *Daily 7 am–10 pm.*

Laupahoehoe Train Museum. Behind the stone-loading platform of the once-famous Hilo Railroad, constructed around the turn of the 20th century, the former manager's house is a poignant reminder of the era when sugar was the local cash crop. The railroad, used to transport sugar from the plantations to the port, was one of the most expensive built in its time. It was washed away by the 1946 tsunami. Today one of the vintage switch engines is on display at the museum, and on special occasions even runs a few yards on a short Y-track. ✉ *Hwy. 19, Laupahoehoe* ☎ *808/962–6300* ⊕ *www.thetrainmuseum.com* 🎟 *$6* ⊙ *Weekdays 9–4:30, weekends 10–2.*

Umauma Experience. This is the only place to see the famous triple-tier Umauma Falls. Like the World Botanical Gardens right next door, this park has a river walk, a zipline, and botanical gardens. This 200-acre park only opened two years ago, however, and the gardens here are not as lush and well-established as the gardens next door (though the competition is obvious). There is kayaking and a giant swing. ✉ *Hwy. 19, at mile marker 16, Honomu* ☎ *808/930–9477* 🎟 *$12* ⊙ *Daily 7:45–5.*

Ȼ **World Botanical Gardens.** Just off the highway, this garden park is on more than 300 acres of former sugarcane land. With wide views of the countryside and the ocean, this is the place to see the beautiful Kamaee waterfalls. You can also follow a walking trail with old-growth tropical gardens including orchids, palm trees, ginger, hibiscus, and heliconia; visit the 10-acre arboretum, which includes a maze made of orange shrubs; explore the river walk; ride the zipline; and take the only off-road Segway adventure on the island. The $13 admission (not including zipline and Segway) into the gardens is good for seven days, but if you skip the zipline, you can see it all in a few hours. ✉ *Hwy. 19, just past mile marker 16 from Hilo, Honomu* ☎ *808/963–5427* ⊕ *www.wbgi. com* 🎟 *$13* ⊙ *Daily 9–5:30.*

HILO

Hilo is 55 mi southeast of Waimea, 95 mi northeast of Kailua-Kona, and just north of the Hilo Airport.

When compared to Kailua-Kona, Hilo is often described as "the real Hawaii." With significantly fewer tourists than residents, more historic buildings, and a much stronger identity as a long-established community, life does seem more authentic on this side of the island. This quaint, traditional town stretches from the banks of the Wailuku River to Hilo Bay, where a few hotels line stately Banyan Drive. The characteristic old buildings that make up Hilo's downtown have been spruced up as part of a revitalization effort.

Nearby, the 30-acre Liliuokalani Gardens, a formal Japanese garden with arched bridges and waterways, was created in the early 1900s to honor the area's Japanese sugar-plantation laborers. It also became a safety zone after a devastating tidal wave swept away businesses and homes on May 22, 1960, killing 60 people.

With a population of almost 50,000 in the entire district, Hilo is the fourth-largest city in the state and home to the University of Hawaii at Hilo. Although it is the center of government and commerce for the island, Hilo is clearly a residential town. Mansions with yards of lush tropical foliage surround older wooden houses with rusty corrugated roofs. It's a friendly community, populated primarily by descendants of the contract laborers—Japanese, Chinese, Filipino, Puerto Rican, and Portuguese—brought in to work the sugarcane fields during the 1800s.

One of the main reasons visitors have tended to steer clear of the east side of the island is its weather. With an average rainfall of 130 inches per year, it's easy to see why Hilo's yards are so green, and its buildings so weatherworn. Outside of town, the Hilo District has rain forests and waterfalls, very unlike the hot and dry white-sand beaches of the Kohala Coast. But when the sun does shine—usually part of nearly every day—the town sparkles, and, during winter, the snow glistens on Mauna Kea, 25 mi in the distance. Best of all is when the mists fall and the sun shines at the same time, leaving behind the colorful arches that earn Hilo its nickname: the City of Rainbows.

GETTING HERE AND AROUND

Hilo is a great base for exploring the eastern and southern parts of the island—just be sure to bring an umbrella for sporadic showers. If you're just passing through town or making a day trip, make the first right turn into the town off Highway 19 (it comes up fast) and grab a parking spot in the lot on your left or on any of the surrounding streets. Downtown Hilo is best experienced on foot.

There are plenty of gas stations and restaurants in the area. Hilo is a good spot to load up on food and supplies—just south of downtown there are several large budget chains. If you're here on Wednesday or Saturday, be sure to stop by the expansive Hilo Farmers Market. The Merrie Monarch Hula Festival takes place in Hilo every year during the second week of April, and dancers and admirers flock to the city from all over the world. If you're planning a stay in Hilo during this time, be sure to book your room well in advance.

TOURS

Hilo Downtown Improvement Association. The Hilo Downtown Improvement Association provides an excellent and free self-guided walking tour to downtown Hilo. The tour includes historical information, a map, and directions to 18 historic sites. You can download it from their Web site or pick it up in person at their downtown Hilo office. ⊠ *329 Kamehameha Ave.* ☎ *808/935–8850* ⊕ *www.downtownhilo.com* ⊙ *Weekdays 8–4:30.*

EXPLORING

TOP ATTRACTIONS

Imiloa Astronomy Center. Part Hawaiian cultural center, part astronomy museum, the Imiloa Astronomy Center provides an educational and cultural complement to the research being conducted atop Mauna Kea. Although visitors are welcome at Mauna Kea, its primary function is

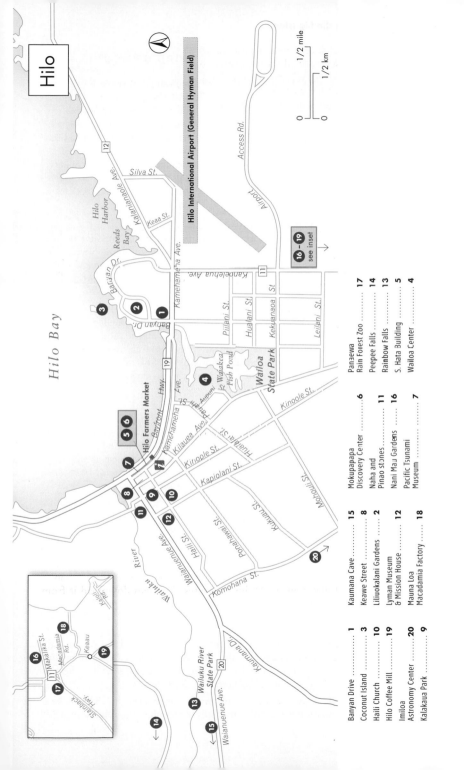

Hilo

Hilo Bay

Hilo Harbor

Reeds Bay

Hilo International Airport (General Hyman Field)

Silva St.

Keaa St.

Kalanianaole Ave.

Kamehameha Ave.

Kanoelehua Ave.

Access Rd.

Airport

Banyan Dr.

Waiakea Fish Pond

Wailoa State Park

Bayfront Hwy.

Hilo Farmers Market

Waianuenue Ave.

Wailuku River

Wailiki St.

Haili St.

Ponahawai St.

Kapiolani St.

Kinoole St.

Kilauea Ave.

Keawe St.

Kamehameha Ave.

Piilani St.

Huilani St.

Kekuanaoa St.

Leilani St.

Kinoole St.

Komohana St.

Kapiolani St.

Kaumana Dr.

Keaau

Wailuku River State Park

Stainback Hwy.

Makalika St.

Macadamia Rd.

Kolei Pl.

1/2 mile
1/2 km

16 – 19
see inset

Banyan Drive **1**
Coconut Island **3**
Haili Church **10**
Hilo Coffee Mill **19**
Imiloa
Astronomy Center **20**
Kalakaua Park **9**

Kaumana Cave **15**
Keawe Street **8**
Liliuokalani Gardens **2**
Lyman Museum
& Mission House **12**
Mauna Loa
Macadamia Factory **18**

Mokupapapa
Discovery Center **6**
Naha and
Pinao stones **11**
Nani Mau Gardens **16**
Pacific Tsunami
Museum **7**

Panaewa
Rain Forest Zoo **17**
Peepee Falls **14**
Rainbow Falls **13**
S. Hata Building **5**
Wailoa Center **4**

as a research center—not observatory, museum, or education center. Those roles have been taken on by Imiloa in a big way. With its interactive exhibits, full-dome planetarium shows, and regularly scheduled talks and events, the center is a must-see for anyone interested in the stars, the planets, or Hawaiian culture and history. The center, five minutes from downtown Hilo, also provides an important link between the scientific research being conducted at Mauna Kea and its history as a sacred mountain for the Hawaiian people. Admission includes one planetarium show. The lunch buffet at the adjoining Sky Garden Cafe is popular. ⊠ *600 Imiloa Pl., at the UH Hilo Science & Technology Park, off Nowelo and Komohana* ☎ *808/969–9700* ⊕ *www. imiloahawaii.org* ⊠ *$17.50* ☉ *Tues.–Sun. 9–5.*

WORD OF MOUTH

"You can see Waipio valley from the Honokaa side or the Hawi side. It will take you a while to drive all the way through Waimea and over to Hawi and back to Hilo. It would be a killer day. I would recommend Hawaii Botanical Gardens, then Akaka Falls, Honokaa Waipo lookout and then back to Hilo." —hiloliving

★ **Liliuokalani Gardens.** Designed to honor Hawaii's first Japanese immigrants, Liliuokalani's 30 acres of fish-filled ponds, stone lanterns, half-moon bridges, elegant pagodas, and ceremonial teahouse make it a favorite Sunday destination. The surrounding area used to be a busy residential neighborhood until a tsunami in 1960 swept the buildings away, taking the lives of 60 people in the process. ⊠ *Banyan Dr. at Lihiwai St.* ☎ *808/961–8311.*

Peepee Falls (*Boiling Pots*). Four separate streams fall into a series of circular pools, forming the Peepee Falls. The resulting turbulent action—best seen after a good rain—has earned this stretch of the Wailuku River the name Boiling Pots. ■**TIP→** There's no swimming allowed at Peepee Falls or anywhere in the Wailuku river, due to dangerous currents and undertows. ⊠ *3 mi northwest of Hilo, Waianuenue Ave, keep to right when road splits and look for a green sign for Boiling Pots.*

★ **Rainbow Falls.** After a hard rain, these falls thunder into the Wailuku River gorge, often creating magical rainbows in the mist. ⊠ *Take Waiānuenue Ave. west of town 1 mi; when the road forks, stay right and look for the Hawaiian warrior sign.*

WORTH NOTING

Banyan Drive. The more than 50 leafy banyan trees with aerial roots dangling from their limbs were planted some 60 to 70 years ago by visiting celebrities. You'll find such names as Amelia Earhart and Franklin Delano Roosevelt on plaques affixed to the trees. ⊠ *Begin at Hawai'i Naniloa Resort, 93 Banyan Dr.*

Coconut Island. This small island, just offshore from Liliuokalani Gardens, is accessible via a footbridge. It was considered a place of healing in ancient times. Today children play in the tide pools while fisherfolk try their luck. ⊠ *Liliuokalani Gardens, Banyan Dr.*

Haili Church. This church was originally constructed in 1859 by New England missionaries, but the church steeple was rebuilt in 1979

following a fire. The church is known for its choir, which sings hymns in Hawaiian during services. ✉ *211 Haili St.* ☎ *808/935–4847.*

Hilo Coffee Mill. With all the buzz about Kona coffee, it's easy to forget that coffee is produced throughout the rest of the island as well. The Hilo Coffee Mill is a pleasant reminder of that fact. In addition to farming their own coffee on-site, the Mill has partnered with several local small coffee farmers in East Hawaii in an effort to put the region on the world's coffee map. You can sample the efforts of the farmers, as well as tour the mill and watch the roasters in action. ✉ *17-995 Volcano Rd. (Hwy. 11), between mile markers 12 and 13, Mountain View* ☎ *808/968–1333* ⊕ *www.hilocoffeemill.com* ✉ *Free* ☉ *Mon.–Sat. 7–4.*

Kalakaua Park. King Kalakaua, who revived the hula, was the inspiration for Hilo's Merrie Monarch Festival. A bronze statue, erected in 1988, depicts the king with a taro leaf in his left hand to signify the Hawaiian peoples' bond with the land. The park also has a huge spreading banyan tree and small fishponds, but no picnic or recreation facilities. In a local tradition, families that have had recent funerals often leave leftover floral displays and funeral wreaths along the fishpond walkway as a way of honoring and celebrating their loved ones. ✉ *Kalakaua and Kinoole Sts.*

Kaumana Cave. Thanks to Hilo's abundant rainfall, this relatively new lava tube is lush with plant life. Concrete stairs lead down to the 2½-mi-long tube. Bring a flashlight and explore as far as you dare to go. There are restrooms and a covered picnic table at the cave, and parking across the street. ✉ *Waianuenue Ave., on the right just past mile marker 4 (veer left going towards Saddle Rd.)* ✉ *Free.*

Keawe Street. Buildings here have been restored to their original 1920s and '30s plantation styles. Although most shopping is along Kamehameha Avenue, the ambience on Keawe Street offers a nostalgic sampling of Hilo as it might have been 80 years ago.

Lyman Museum & Mission House. Built in 1839 for David and Sarah Lyman, Congregationalist missionaries, the Lyman House is the oldest frame building on the island. In the adjacent museum, dedicated in 1973, there's a realistic magma chamber and exhibits on the islands' formation. There's also an interesting section on Hawaiian flora and fauna. The gift shop sells Hawaiian books, cards, gifts, and music. It's best to call ahead for tour availability. ✉ *276 Haili St.* ☎ *808/935–5021* ⊕ *www.lymanmuseum.org* ✉ *$10* ☉ *Mon.–Sat. 10–4:30, Mission House tours 11–2.*

Mauna Loa Macadamia Factory. Acres of macadamia trees lead to a giant roasting facility and processing plant with viewing windows and self-guided tours. A videotape depicts the harvesting and preparation of the nuts, and there are free samples and plenty of gift boxes with mac nuts in every conceivable form of presentation to buy in the visitor center. Children can run off their energy on the nature trail. ✉ *Macadamia Rd., off Hwy. 11, 5 mi south of Hilo* ☎ *808/966–8618, 888/628–6256* ⊕ *www.maunaloa.com* ☉ *Daily 8:30–5.*

Mokupapapa Discovery Center. Visitors to this small but informative center will learn about the Papahanaumokuakea Marine National Monument,

The world's largest optical and infrared telescopes are located at the Keck Observatory on Mauna Kea's summit.

which encompasses about 140,000 square mi in the waters northwest of the main Hawaiian Islands, and is a UNESCO World Heritage site. Wall maps depict the northwestern Hawaiian Islands' extensive coral reefs and the more than 7,000 marine species that live there, one in four of which are found only in the Hawaiian archipelago. This center is run by devoted volunteers who are knowledgeable and give daily tours of the exhibits. Interactive programs and short films describe marine life and reef conditions. It's worth a stop just to get an up-close look at the center's huge stuffed albatross, with wings outstretched. ⊠ *S. Hata Bldg. fronting Hilo Bay, 308 Kamehameha Ave., Suite 109* ☎ *808/933–8195* ✉ *Free* ⊘ *Tues.–Sat. 9–4.*

Naha and Pinao stones. These two huge, oblong stones are legendary. The Pinao stone is purportedly an entrance pillar of an ancient temple built near the Wailuku River. King Kamehameha is said to have moved the 5,000-pound Naha stone when he was still in his teens. Legend decreed that he who did so would become king of all the islands. They're in front of the Hilo Public Library. ⊠ *300 Waianuenue Ave.*

Nani Mau Gardens. The name means "forever beautiful" in Hawaiian, and that's a good description of this 20-acre botanical garden filled with several varieties of fruit trees and hundreds of varieties of ginger, orchids, anthuriums, and other exotic plants. Guided tours by tram are available for groups. There is also a restaurant with a lunch buffet. ⊠ *421 Makalika St., off Hwy. 11* ☎ *808/959–3500* ⊕ *www. nanimaugardens.com* ✉ *$10* ⊘ *Daily 9:30–4.*

Ⓒ **Pacific Tsunami Museum.** A memorial to all those who lost their lives in tsunamis that have struck the Big Island, Hawaii and the world, this

CLOSE UP

A Walking Tour of Hilo

Put on some comfortable shoes, because Hilo is best explored on foot. All of the downtown destinations are within easy walking distance of each other. Start your excursion in front of the public library, on Waianuenue Avenue, four blocks from Kamehameha Avenue. Here, you'll find the massive **Naha and Pinao stones,** which legend says King Kamehameha I was able to move as a teenager, thus foretelling that someday he would be a powerful king. Cross the road to walk southeast along Kapiolani Street, and turn right on Haili Street to visit the historic **Lyman Museum & Mission House.** Back on Haili Street, follow this busy road toward the ocean; on your right you'll pass **Haili Church.**

Soon you'll reach **Keawe Street** with its plantation-style shop fronts. Stop at the Big Island Visitors Bureau on the right-hand corner for maps and brochures before taking a left. You'll bump into Kalakaua Street; for a quick respite turn left and rest on the benches in **Kalakaua Park.**

Continue *makai* (toward the ocean) on Kalakaua Street to visit the **Pacific Tsunami Museum** on the corner of Kalakaua and Kamehameha avenues. After heading three blocks east along the picturesque bay front, you'll come across the **S. Hata Building,** which has interesting shops and restaurants and the Mokupapapa: Discovery Center for Hawaii's Remote Coral Reefs Museum. Just next door, on either side of Mamo Street, is the **Hilo Farmers' Market.**

---

small but informative museum offers a poignant history of the devastating waves. In a 1931 C. W. Dickey–designed building—the former home of the First Hawaiian Bank—you'll find an interactive computer center, a science room, a theater, a replica of Old Hilo Town, a children's corner, and a knowledgeable, friendly staff. In the background, a striking quilt tells a silent story. ⊠ *130 Kamehameha Ave.* ☎ *808/935–0926* ⊕ *www.tsunami.org* ☜ *$8* ⊘ *Mon.–Sat. 9–4:15.*

ⓒ **Panaewa Rain Forest Zoo.** Advertised as "the only natural tropical rain forest zoo in the United States," this is the home of white Bengal tiger, Namaste. There is a variety of native Hawaiian species, such as the state bird, the *nene* (Hawaiian goose), as well as a small petting zoo every Saturday 1:30–2:30. Come in the afternoon and watch Namaste's feeding at 3:30 daily. ⊠ *Left on Mamaki off Hwy. 11, just past the "Kulani 19, Stainback Hwy" sign* ☎ *808/959–7224* ⊕ *www.hilozoo. com* ☜ *Free* ⊘ *Daily 9–4.*

S. Hata Building. Erected as a general store in 1912 by Sadanosuke Hata and his family, this historic structure now houses galleries, a restaurant, and the Mokupapapa Discovery Center. During World War II Hata family members were interned and the building was confiscated by the U.S. government. When the war was over, a daughter repurchased it for $100,000. A beautiful example of Renaissance-revival architecture, it won an award from the state for the authenticity of its restoration. ⊠ *308 Kamehameha Ave., at Mamo St.*

Banyan Drive's Trees

The history of the trees lining Hilo's Banyan Drive is one of the Big Island's most interesting and least known stories. Banyan Drive was named for these trees, which were planted by VIP visitors to Hilo. Altogether, some 50 or so banyans were planted between 1933 and 1972.

The majority are Chinese banyans, and each one is marked with a sign naming the VIP who planted it and the date on which it was planted. The first trees were planted on October 20, 1933, by a Hollywood group led by director Cecil B. DeMille, who was in Hilo making the film *Four Frightened People.* Soon after, on October 29, 1933, another banyan was planted by the one and only George Herman "Babe" Ruth, who was in town playing exhibition games.

President Franklin D. Roosevelt planted a tree on his visit to Hilo on July 25, 1934. And in 1935, famed aviator Amelia Earhart put a banyan in the ground just days before she became the first person to fly solo across the Pacific Ocean.

Trees continued to be planted along Banyan Drive until World War II. The tradition was then revived in 1952 when a young and aspiring U.S. senator, Richard Nixon of California, planted a banyan tree. Nixon's tree was later toppled by a storm and was replanted by his wife, Pat, during a Hilo visit in 1972. On a bright, sunny day, strolling down Banyan Drive is like going through a green, shady tunnel. The banyans form a regal protective canopy over Hilo's own "Walk of Fame."

Wailoa Center. This circular exhibition center, in Wailoa State Park, features shows by local artists that change monthly. Just in front of the center is a 12-foot-high bronze statue of King Kamehameha I, made in Italy in the late 1980s. Check out his gold Roman sandals. ⊠ *200 Piopio St., off Kamehameha Ave.* ☎ *808/933–0416* ⊘ *Mon., Tues., Thurs., and Fri. 8:30–4:30; Wed. noon–4:30.*

PUNA

Puna is about 6 mi south of Hilo.

The Puna District is wild in every sense of the word. The jagged black coastline is changing all the time; the trees are growing out of control, forming canopies over the few paved roads; the land is dirt cheap and there are no building codes; and the people—well, there's something about living in an area that could be destroyed by lava at any moment (as Kalapana was in 1990) that makes the laws of modern society seem silly. So it is that Puna has its well-deserved reputation as the "outlaw" region of the Big Island.

That said, it's a unique place that's well worth a detour, especially if you're in this part of the island anyway. There are volcanically heated springs, tide pools bursting with interesting sea life, and some mighty fine people-watching opportunities in Pahoa, a funky little town that the outlaws call home.

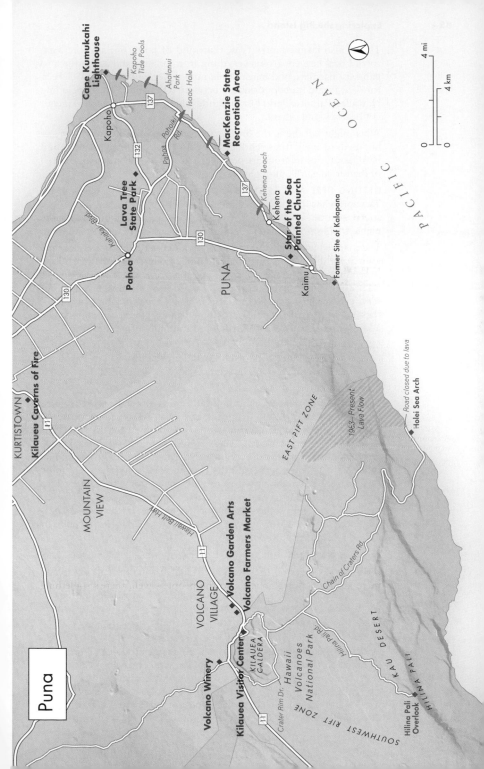

Puna

Cape Kumukahi Lighthouse ◆

Kapoho Tide Pools

Aholanui Park

Isaac Hale

Kapoho ◯

137

132

Pohoiki Rd.

Pahoa Rd.

MacKenzie State Recreation Area ◆

Lava Tree State Park ◆

Kahakai Blvd.

Pahoa ◆ ◯

Kehena Beach

Kehena ◯

137

130

Star of the Sea Painted Church ◆

130

PUNA

Kaimu ◆

Former Site of Kalapana ◆

KURTISTOWN

Kilauea Caverns of Fire ◆

11

MOUNTAIN VIEW

Hawaii Belt Hwy.

EAST RIFT ZONE

1963–Present Lava Flow

Road closed due to lava

Holei Sea Arch ◆

Volcano Garden Arts ◆

Volcano Farmers Market ◆

VOLCANO VILLAGE

11

Volcano Winery ◆

Kilauea Visitor Center ◆

KILAUEA CALDERA

Hawaii Volcanoes National Park

Chain of Craters Rd.

Crater Rim Dr.

11

Hilina Pali Rd.

KAU DESERT

HILINA PALI

SOUTHWEST RIFT ZONE

Hilina Pali Overlook ◆

PACIFIC OCEAN

0   4 mi

0   4 km

This is also farm country (yes, that kind of farm, but also the legal sort). Local farmers grow everything from orchids and anthuriums to papayas, bananas, and macadamia nuts. Several of the island's larger, rural, residential subdivisions are between Keaau and Pahoa, including Hawaiian Paradise Park, Orchidland Estates, Hawaiian Acres, Hawaiian Beaches, and others.

When night falls here, the air fills with the high-pitched symphony of hundreds of coqui frogs. Though they look cute on the signs and sound harmless, the coqui frogs are pests both to local crops and to locals tired of their loud, shrill, all-night song.

GETTING HERE AND AROUND
The sprawling Puna District includes part of the Volcano area and stretches northeast down to the coast. If you're staying in Hilo for the night, driving around wild lower Puna is a great way to spend a morning.

The roads connecting Pahoa to Kapoho and the Kalapana coast form a loop that's about 25 mi long; driving times are from two to three hours, depending on the number of stops you make and the length of time at each stop. There are restaurants, stores, and gas stations in Pahoa, but services elsewhere in the region are spotty. There are long stretches of the road that may be completely isolated at any given point; this can be a little scary at night but beautiful and tranquil during the day.

Compared to big-city living, it's pretty tame, but there is a bit of a "locals-only" vibe in parts of Puna, and a drug problem in Pahoa, so don't go wandering around at night.

EXPLORING
Cape Kumukahi Lighthouse. This lighthouse was miraculously unharmed during the 1960 volcano eruption here that destroyed the town of Kapoho. The lava flowed directly up to the lighthouse's base, but instead of pushing it over, actually flowed around it—an impressive sight now that the lava flows have hardened. Locals say that Pele, the volcano goddess, protected the Hawaiian fisherfolk by sparing the lighthouse. The building itself is a simple metal-frame structure with a light on top, similar to a tall electric-line transmission tower. To reach the lighthouse, keep going straight for 1½ mi when Highway 132 meets Highway 137 and turns into an unpaved road. ⊠ *Past intersection of Hwys. 132 and 137, Kapoho.*

Lava Tree State Park. Tree molds that rise like blackened smokestacks formed here in 1790 when a lava flow swept through the *ohia* forest. Some reach as high as 12 feet. The meandering trail provides close-up looks at some of Hawaii's tropical plants and trees. There are restrooms and a couple of picnic pavilions and tables. ■TIP→ Mosquitoes live here in abundance, so be sure to bring repellent. ⊠ *Hwy. 132, Pahoa* ☎ *808/974–6200* 🆓 *Free* ☉ *Daily 8–4:30.*

MacKenzie State Recreation Area. This is a coastal park located on rocky shoreline cliffs in a breezy, cool ironwood grove. There are picnic tables, restrooms, and a tent-camping area; bring your own drinking water. The park is significant for the restored section of the old "King's Highway" trail system, which circled the coast in the era before Hawaii was discovered by the Western world. In those days, regional chiefs used these trails to connect the coastal villages, allowing them to collect taxes and maintain control over the people. There are views of rugged coast, rocky beach, and coastal dry forest. ⊠ *Hwy. 137, Pahoa.*

Pahoa. Sort of like a town from the Wild West, this little town even has some wooden boardwalks and rickety buildings—not to mention a reputation as a wild and woolly place where pot growers make up a significant part of the community. Now things are more civilized in town, but there are still plenty of hippies and other colorful characters pursuing alternative lifestyles. The secondhand stores, tie-dye clothing boutiques, and art galleries in quaint old buildings are fun to wander through during the day. Pahoa's main street boasts a handful of island eateries, the best of which is **Luquin's Mexican Restaurant.** ⊠ *Turn southeast onto Hwy. 130 at Keaau, drive 11 mi to a right turn marked Pahoa, Pahoa.*

Star of the Sea Painted Church. This historic church, now a community center, was moved to its present location in 1990 just ahead of the advancing lava flow that destroyed the Kalapana area. The church, which dates from the 1930s, was built by a Belgian Catholic missionary priest, Father Everest Gielen, who also did the detailed paintings on the church's interior. Though similar in style, the Star of the Sea and St. Benedict's were actually painted by two different Belgian Catholic missionary priests. Star of the Sea also has several lovely stained-glass windows. ⊠ *Hwy. 130, 1 mi north of Kalapana, Kalapana.*

HAWAII VOLCANOES NATIONAL PARK AND VICINITY

Fodor'sChoice   *Hawaii Volcanoes National Park is about 22 mi southwest from the*
★   *start of the Puna district, and about 27 mi southwest of Hilo.*

Few visitors realize that in addition to "the volcano" (Kilauea)—that mountain oozing new layers of lava onto its flanks—there's also Volcano, the village. Conveniently located next to Hawaii Volcanoes National Park, Volcano village is a charming little hamlet in the woods that offers a dozen or so excellent inns and bed-and-breakfasts, a decent (although strangely expensive) Thai restaurant, some killer (although strangely expensive) pizza, and a handful of things to see and do that don't include the village's namesake.

For years, writers, artists, and meditative types have been coming to the volcano to seek inspiration, and many of them have settled in and around the village. Artist studios (open to the public by appointment) are scattered in the forest.

If you plan to visit the Halemaumau summit crater at night (which you absolutely should if it's glowing), or drive down Chain of Craters Road to the coast to try see lava steaming into the sea, spending a night in Volcano village is the ideal way to go about it.

Continued on page 90

HAWAII VOLCANOES NATIONAL PARK

Exploring the surface of the world's most active volcano—from the moonscape craters at the summit to the red-hot lava flows on the coast to the kipuka, pockets of vegetation miraculously left untouched—is the ultimate ecotour and one of Hawaii's must-dos.

The park sprawls over 520 square miles and encompasses Kilauea and Mauna Loa, two of the five volcanoes that formed the Big Island nearly half a million years ago. Kilauea, youngest and most rambunctious of the Hawaiian volcanoes, erupted at its summit from the 19th century through 1982. Since then, the top of the volcano had been more or less quiet, frequently shrouded in mist; an eruption in the Halemaumau Crater in 2008 ended this period of relative inactivity.

Kilauea's eastern side sprang to life on January 3, 1983, shooting molten lava four stories high. This eruption has been ongoing, and lava flows are generally steady and slow, appearing and disappearing from view. Over 500 acres have been added to Hawaii's eastern coast since the activity began, and scientists say this eruptive phase is not likely to end anytime soon.

If you're lucky, you'll be able to catch creation at its most elemental—when molten lava meets the ocean, cools, and solidifies into brand-new stretches of coastline. Even if lava-viewing conditions aren't ideal, you can hike 150 miles of trails and camp amid wide expanses of *aa* (rough) and *pahoehoe* (smooth) lava. There's nothing quite like it.

- P.O. Box 52, Hawaii Volcanoes National Park, HI 96718
- 808/985–6000
- www.nps.gov/havo
- $10 per vehicle; $5 for pedestrians and bicyclists. Ask about passes. Admission is good for seven consecutive days.
- The park is open daily, 24 hours. Kilauea Visitor Center: 7:45 am–5 pm. Thomas A. Jaggar Museum: 8:30–5. Volcano Art Center Gallery: 9–5.

(top) Kilauea Iki Trail
(left) Fuming rim of Puu Oo, source of the current eruption

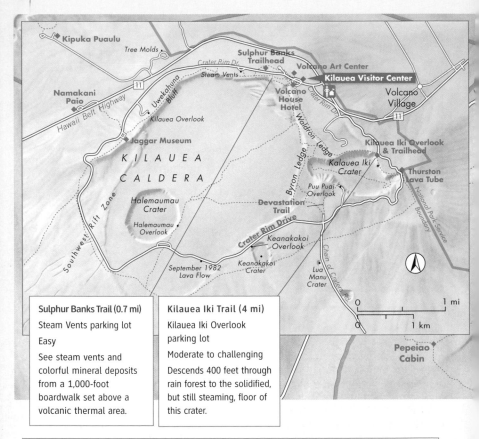

Sulphur Banks Trail (0.7 mi)

Steam Vents parking lot

Easy

See steam vents and colorful mineral deposits from a 1,000-foot boardwalk set above a volcanic thermal area.

Kilauea Iki Trail (4 mi)

Kilauea Iki Overlook parking lot

Moderate to challenging

Descends 400 feet through rain forest to the solidified, but still steaming, floor of this crater.

SEEING THE SUMMIT

The best way to explore the summit of Kilauea is to cruise along Crater Rim Drive to Kilauea Overlook. From Kilauea Overlook you can see all of Kilauea Caldera and Halemaumau Crater, an awesome depression in Kilauea Caldera measuring 3,000 feet across and nearly 300 feet deep. It's a huge and breathtaking view with pluming steam vents. At this writing, lava flows in the Southwest Rift Zone have closed parts of the 11-mile loop road indefinitely, including Halemaumau Overlook.

Near Kilauea Overlook is the Thomas A. Jaggar Museum, which offers simi-

lar views, plus geologic displays, video presentations of volcanic eruptions, and exhibits of seismographs once used by volcanologists at the adjacent Hawaiian Volcano Observatory (not open to the public).

Other Highlights along Crater Rim Drive include sulfur and steam vents, a walk-through lava tube, and deep fissures, fractures, and gullies along Kilauea's flanks. Kilauea Iki Crater, on the way down to Chain of Crater's Road, is smaller, but just as fascinating when seen from Puu Pai Overlook.

2

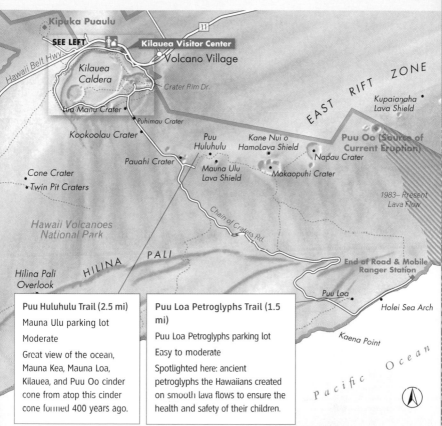

Kipuka Puaulu

SEE LEFT

Kilauea Visitor Center

Volcano Village

Hawaii Belt Hwy.

Kilauea
Caldera

Crater Rim Dr.

Loa Manu Crater

Puhimau Crater

EAST RIFT ZONE

Kupaianaha
Lava Shield

Kookoolau Crater

Puu
Huluhulu

Kane Nui o
HamoLava Shield

**Puu Oo (Source of
Current Eruption)**

Napau Crater

Pauahi Crater

Mauna Ulu
Lava Shield

Makaopuhi Crater

Cone Crater

Twin Pit Craters

Hawaii Volcanoes
National Park

Chain of Craters Rd.

1983– Present
Lava Flow

HILINA PALI

Hilina Pali
Overlook

**End of Road & Mobile
Ranger Station**

Puu Loa

Holei Sea Arch

Kaena Point

Pacific Ocean

Puu Huluhulu Trail (2.5 mi)

Mauna Ulu parking lot

Moderate

Great view of the ocean, Mauna Kea, Mauna Loa, Kilauea, and Puu Oo cinder cone from atop this cinder cone formed 400 years ago.

Puu Loa Petroglyphs Trail (1.5 mi)

Puu Loa Petroglyphs parking lot

Easy to moderate

Spotlighted here: ancient petroglyphs the Hawaiians created on smooth lava flows to ensure the health and safety of their children.

SEEING LAVA

Before you head out to find flowing lava, pinpoint the safe viewing spots at the Visitor Center. One of the best places usually is at the end of 18-mile Chain of Craters Road. Magnificent plumes of steam rise where the rivers of liquid fire meet the sea.

There are three guarantees about lava flows in HVNP. First: They constantly change. Second: Because of that, you can't predict when and where you'll be able to see them. Third: New land formed when lava meets the sea is highly unstable and can collapse at any time. Never go into areas that have been closed.

■ **TIP→** The view of brilliant red-orange lava flowing from Kilauea's east rift zone is most dramatic at night.

People watching lava flow at HVNP

PLANNING YOUR TRIP TO HVNP

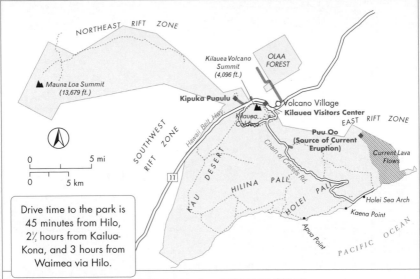

NORTHEAST RIFT ZONE

▲ Mauna Loa Summit
(13,679 ft.)

Kilauea Volcano Summit
(4,096 ft.)

OLAA FOREST

Kipuka Puaulu

○ Volcano Village
Kilauea Visitors Center

Kilauea Caldera

EAST RIFT ZONE

**Puu Oo
(Source of Current Eruption)**

Current Lava Flows

SOUTHWEST RIFT ZONE

Hawaii Belt Hwy.

Chain of Craters Rd.

KAU DESERT

HILINA PALI

HOLEI PALI

Holei Sea Arch

Kaena Point

Apua Point

11

PACIFIC OCEAN

0   5 mi
0   5 km

Drive time to the park is
45 minutes from Hilo,
2½ hours from Kailua-
Kona, and 3 hours from
Waimea via Hilo.

Lava entering the ocean

WHERE TO START

Begin your visit at the Visitor Center,
where you'll find maps, books, and
DVDs; information on trails, ranger-led
walks, and special events; and current
weather, road, and lava-viewing conditions. Free volcano-related film show-
ings, lectures, and other presentations
are regularly scheduled.

WEATHER

Weather conditions fluctuate daily,
sometimes hourly. It can be rainy and
chilly even during the summer; the
temperature usually is 14° cooler at
the 4,000-foot-high summit of Kilauea
than at sea level.

Expect hot, dry, and windy coastal conditions at the end of Chain of Craters
Road. Bring rain gear, and wear layered
clothing, sturdy shoes, sunglasses, a
hat, and sunscreen.

Photographer on lava table filming lava flow into ocean

FOOD

It's a good idea to bring your own favorite snacks and beverages; stock up on provisions in Volcano Village, 1½ miles away.

PARK PROGRAMS

Rangers lead daily walks at 10:30 and 1:30 into different areas; check with the Visitor Center for details as times and destinations depend on weather conditions.

Over 60 companies hold permits to lead hikes at HVNP. Good choices are Hawaii Forest & Trail (www.hawaii-forest.com), Hawaiian Walkways (www.hawaiianwalkways.com), and Native Guide Hawaii (www.nativeguide hawaii.com).

CAUTION

"Vog" (volcanic smog) can cause headaches; breathing difficulties; lethargy; irritations of the skin, eyes, nose, and throat; and other health problems. Pregnant women, young children, and people with asthma and heart conditions are most susceptible, and should avoid areas such as Halemaumau Crater where fumes are thick.

Wear long pants and boots or closed-toe shoes with good tread for hikes on lava. Stay on marked trails and step carefully. Lava is composed of 50% silica (glass) and can cause serious injury if you fall.

Carry at least 2 quarts of water on hikes. Temperatures near lava flows can rise above 100°F, and dehydration, heat exhaustion, and sunstroke are common consequences of extended exposure to intense sunlight and high temperatures.

Remember that these are active volcanoes, and eruptions can cause parts of the park to close at any time. Check the park's website or call ahead for last-minute updates before your visit.

Volcanologists inspecting a vent in the East Rift Zone

You may see flowing lava from Kilauea, the Big Island's youngest and most active volcano.

GETTING HERE AND AROUND

There are a handful of dining options, a couple of stores, and gas stations available in Volcano, so most of your needs should be covered. If you can't find what you're looking for, Hilo is about a 35-minute drive away, and the Keeau grocery store and fast-food joints are 25 minutes away.

Bring a fleece or a sweater if you plan to stay the night in Volcano; temperatures drop at night and mornings are usually cool and misty. One of the main reasons people choose to stay the night in Volcano is to see the dramatic glow at the summit vent and to drive to the coast to see the lava flow into the sea. ■TIP→ Make sure you have enough gas to get down to the flow and back up. The entrance to Volcanoes National Park is about one minute from Volcano village, but the drive down is a good 30 minutes. Remember that you'll be coming back around midnight, long after the rangers have gone home.

Speed limits in this area are low for a reason. Paved roads can become unpaved within a few feet; heed the speed limits so that you don't go flying onto a bumpy dirt road at 70 mph. There are also occasionally farm kids riding around on ATVs (and some of them might be going way faster than you're allowed to). It's best to be able to dodge them without ending up crashing into a lava rock.

EXPLORING

For information on Hawaii Volcanoes National Park, see the highlighted feature in this chapter.

Kilauea Caverns of Fire. Strap on a miner's hat and gloves and get ready to explore the underbelly of the world's largest active volcano. Tours through these fascinating caves and lava tubes underneath the volcano must be arranged in advance, but are well worth a little extra planning. Located off Highway 11 between Hilo and Volcanoes National Park, the caverns are comprised of four main tubes, each 500–700 years old and full of stalactites, stalagmites, and a variety of different-colored flowstone. The largest lava tube in the world is here—40 mi long, it has 80-foot ceilings and is 80 feet wide. Tours can range from safe and easy (safe enough for children five years old and up) to long and adventurous. ⊠ 16-1953 7th Rd., Hawaiian Acres, Off Hwy. 11, between Kurtistown and Mountain View ☏ 808/217–2363 ⊕ www.kilaueacavernsoffire.com ⊠ $29 for walking tour, $79 for adventure tour ⊙ By appointment only.

Volcano Farmers' Market. Local produce, flowers, and food products are on offer every Sunday morning at one of the better farmers' markets on the island. It's best to get there early, before 8 am, as vendors tend to sell out of the best stuff quickly. There's also a great bookstore (paperbacks 25¢, hardbacks 50¢, and magazines 10¢), and a thrift store with clothes and knickknacks. ■ TIP→ There are also more prepared-food vendors at the Volcano market than Hilo, with such temptations as fresh baked breads and pastries, vegetarian lunch items, and homemade Thai food. ⊠ Cooper Center, 19-4030 Wright Rd., Volcano ☏ 808/936–9705 ⊕ www.thecoopercenter.org ⊙ Sun. 6–10 am.

Volcano Garden Arts. Located on beautifully landscaped grounds with intriguing sculptures here and there, this charming complex includes an eclectic art gallery and excellent vegetarian café housed in redwood buildings built in 1908. A cute little one-bedroom "artist's cottage" is available for rent on the grounds as well. If you're lucky you'll get to meet the eccentric lord and master of this enclave, the one and only Ira Ono, known for his recycled "trash art," and his friendly hospitality. ⊠ 19-3438 Old Volcano Rd., Volcano ☏ 808/985–8979 ⊕ www.volcanogardenarts.com ⊠ Free ⊙ Tues.–Sat. 10–4.

Volcano Winery. Lava rock may not seem like ideal soil for the cultivation of grapes, but that hasn't stopped the Volcano Winery from producing some interesting wines. The Macadamia Nut Honey wine is a nutty, very sweet after-dinner drink; the new Infusion wine steeps Hawaiian-grown black tea—a new industry for the winery—with Macademia Nut wine for an alcohol-caffine kick. This is not Napa Valley, but these vintners take their wine seriously. If you're feeling adventurous, it's worth a stop. The tasting-room staff is friendly and knowledgeable; the gift store has a selection of local crafts and goods. Tours are available at 10 am or by appointment. It's located just past the entrance to Volcanoes National Park. ⊠ 35 Pii Mauna Dr., Volcano ☏ 808/967–7772 ⊕ www.volcanowinery.com ⊠ Free tasting ⊙ Daily 10–5:30.

KAU

Ka Lae (South Point) is 50 mi south of Kailua-Kona.

The most desolate region of the island, Kau, is home to spectacular sights. Mark Twain wrote some of his finest prose here, where macadamia-nut farms, remote green-sand beaches, and tiny communities offer rugged, largely undiscovered beauty. The 50-mi drive from Kailua-Kona to the turnoff for windswept Ka Lae (South Point), where the first Polynesians came ashore as early as AD 750, winds away from the ocean through a surreal moonscape of lava plains and patches of scrub forest. Coming from Volcano, as you near South Point, the barren lavascape gives way to lush vistas from the ocean to the hills.

At the end of the 12-mi two-lane road to Ka Lae, you can park and hike about an hour to Papakolea Beach (Green Sand Beach). Back on the highway, the coast passes verdant cattle pastures and sheer cliffs and the village of Naalehu on the way to the black-sand beach of Punaluu, a common nesting place of the Hawaiian green sea turtle.

GETTING HERE AND AROUND

Kau and Ka Lae are destinations usually combined with a quick trip to the volcano from Kona. This is probably cramming too much into one day, however. The volcano fills up at least a day (two is better), and the sights of this southern end of the island are worth more than a cursory glance.

Our recommendation? Make Green Sand Beach or Punaluu your destination for a beach day at some point during your stay, and stop to see some of the other sights on the way there or back. Bring sturdy shoes, water, and a sun hat if Green Sand Beach is your choice (reaching the beach requires a hike). And be careful in the surf here. Don't go in unless you're used to ocean waves. There are no lifeguards at this remote beach. It's decidedly calmer at Punaluu. Don't forget your snorkeling gear.

The drive from Kailua-Kona to Ka Lae is a long one (roughly 2½ hours); from Volcano it's approximately 45 minutes. It's a good idea to fill up on gas and pack a lunch before you leave, as there are few amenities along the way. Or you can eat or get picnic fixings in Naalehu. Weather tends to be warm, dry, and windy.

EXPLORING

★ **Ka Lae (South Point).** Windswept Ka Lae is the southernmost point of land in the United States. It's thought that the first Polynesians came ashore here. Check out the old canoe-mooring holes that are carved through the rocks, possibly by settlers from Tahiti as early as AD 750. Some artifacts, thought to have been left by early voyagers who never settled here, date to AD 300. Driving down to the point, you pass rows of giant electricity-producing windmills powered by the nearly constant winds sweeping across this coastal plain. Continue down the road (parts at the end are unpaved, but driveable), bear left when the road forks and park in the lot at the end; walk past the boat hoists toward the little lighthouse. South Point is just past the lighthouse at the southernmost cliff. ■ TIP➔ Don't leave anything of value in your car, and know that you don't have to pay for parking. It's a free, public park, so anyone trying to charge you is likely running some sort of scam. ⊠ *Turn right past mile marker 70 on Mamalahoa Hwy., then drive 12 mi down South Point Rd., Kau.*

Manuka State Wayside. This dry, upland forest spreads across several lava flows. A rugged trail follows a 2-mi loop past a pit crater and winds

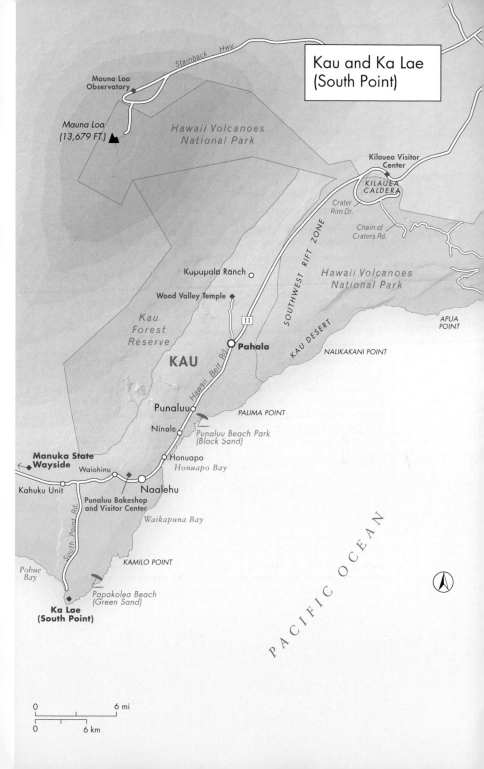

Kau and Ka Lae (South Point)

Stainback Hwy.

Mauna Loa Observatory

Mauna Loa (13,679 FT.)

Hawaii Volcanoes National Park

Kilauea Visitor Center

KILAUEA CALDERA

Crater Rim Dr.

Chain of Craters Rd.

Kupupala Ranch

Wood Valley Temple

SOUTHWEST RIFT ZONE

Hawaii Volcanoes National Park

APUA POINT

11

NALIKAKANI POINT

KAU DESERT

Pahala

Kau Forest Reserve

KAU

Hawaii Belt Rd.

Punaluu

PALIMA POINT

Ninole

Punaluu Beach Park (Black Sand)

Honuapo

Honuapo Bay

Manuka State Wayside

Waiohinu

Kahuku Unit

Naalehu

Punaluu Bakeshop and Visitor Center

Waikapuna Bay

South Point Rd.

Pohue Bay

KAMILO POINT

Papakolea Beach (Green Sand)

Ka Lae (South Point)

PACIFIC OCEAN

0 ___ 6 mi

0 ___ 6 km

around ancient trees such as *hau* and *kukui*. It's an okay spot to get out of the car and stretch your legs—you can wander through the well-maintained arboretum, snap a few photos of the eerie forest, and let the kids scramble around trees so large they can't get their arms around them. However, we don't recommend spending too much time here, especially if you're planning on driving all the way down to South Point. The pathways are not well maintained, but restrooms and picnic areas are available. ⊠ *Hwy. 11, north of mile marker 81* ☎ *808/974–6200* ⬚ *Free* ⊙ *Daily 7–7.*

QUICK BITES

Punaluu Bakeshop & Visitor Center. It's a bit of a tourist trap, but it's also a good spot to grab a snack before heading back out on the road, and the heavenly smell is worth the stop. Try some Portuguese sweet bread or a homemade ice-cream sandwich paired with some local Kau coffee (that's right, not Kona, but equally tasty). ⊠ *Hwy. 11, Naalehu* ☎ *808/929–7343* ⊕ *www.bakeshophawaii.com* ⊙ *Daily 9–5.*

OFF THE BEATEN PATH

Pahala. About 16 mi east of Naalehu, beyond Punaluu Beach Park, Highway 11 sidesteps this little town. You'll miss it if you blink. Pahala is a perfect example of a sugar-plantation town. Behind it, along a wide cane road, you enter Wood Valley, once a prosperous community, now just a road heavily scented by eucalyptus trees, coffee blossoms, and night-blooming jasmine.

Wood Valley Temple. In Pahala you'll find Wood Valley Temple, a serene and beautiful Tibetan Buddhist temple dedicated by the Dalai Lama during his 1980 visit. Today, you can visit the temple, meditate, attend a service, browse the gift shop, or book lodging in the temple's guesthouse for a complete Buddhist retreat. ⊠ *Pahala* ☎ *808/928–8539* ⊕ *www.nechung.org* ⊠ *Pahala.*

3

Beaches

WORD OF MOUTH

"Kahaluu Beach Park was our favorite snorkeling beach, and we came here often, even bringing a picnic lunch on one occasion. Even though it is also everybody else's favorite snorkeling site, the fish are surprisingly numerous and unafraid."

—billj

Updated
by Cynthia
Sweeney

Don't believe anyone who tells you that the Big Island lacks beaches. It's just one of the myths about Hawaii's largest island that has no basis in fact. It's not so much that the Big Island has fewer beaches than the other islands, just that there's more island, so getting to the beaches can be slightly less convenient.

That said, there are plenty of those perfect white-sand stretches you think of when you hear "Hawaii," and the added bonus of black- and green-sand beaches, thanks to the age of the island and its active volcanoes. New beaches appear and disappear regularly, created and destroyed by volcanic activity. In 1989 a black-sand beach, Kamoamoa, formed when molten lava shattered as it hit cold ocean waters; it was closed by new lava flows in 1992. It's part of the ongoing process of the volcano's creation-and-change dynamic.

The bulk of the island's beaches are on the northwest part of the island, along the Kohala Coast. Black-sand beaches and green-sand beaches are in the southern region, along the coast nearest the volcano. On the eastern side of the island, beaches tend to be of the rocky-coast–surging-surf variety, but there are still a few worth visiting, and this is where the Hawaiian shoreline is at its most picturesque.

KAILUA-KONA

There are a few good sandy beaches in the area near Kailua-Kona town. However, the coastline is generally rugged black lava rock, so don't expect long stretches of wide golden sand. The beaches near Kailua-Kona get lots of use by local residents, and visitors will enjoy them, too. Excellent opportunities for snorkeling, scuba diving, swimming, kayaking, and other water sports are easy to find.

The beaches here are listed from north to south.

○ **Old Kona Airport State Recreation Area.** This beach hugs the coast adjacent to the runway that served as Kona's airport until 1970. The old terminal building is now a public pavilion. The long shoreline is flat and spotted

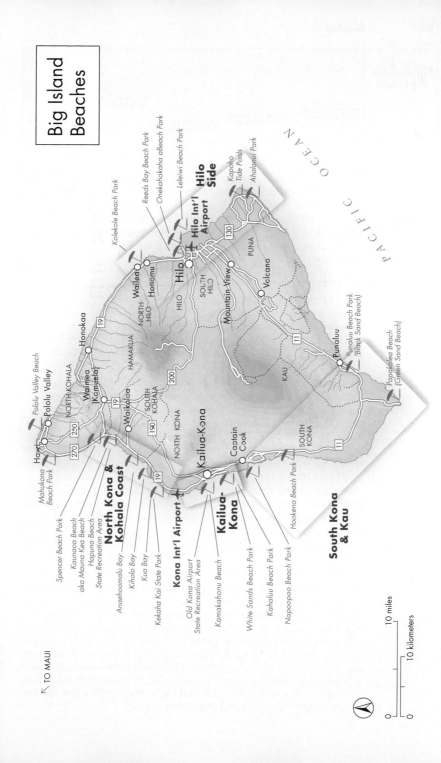

Big Island
Beaches

TO MAUI

PACIFIC OCEAN

Pololu Valley Beach
Pololu Valley
Hawi
NORTH KOHALA
270
250
Mahukona Beach Park
Spencer Beach Park
Kaunaoa Beach aka Mauna Kea Beach
Hapuna Beach State Recreation Area
19
Waimea (Kamuela)
Honokaa
19
HAMAKUA
Kolekole Beach Park
Honomu
Waikoloa
SOUTH KOHALA
190
19
200
NORTH HILO
Wailea
Reeds Bay Beach Park
Onekahakaha aBeach Park
Hilo
HILO
SOUTH HILO
Hilo Int'l Airport
Leleiwi Beach Park
Hilo Side
Anaehoomalu Bay
Kiholo Bay
Kua Bay
Kekaha Kai State Park
North Kona & Kohala Coast
Old Kona Airport State Recreation Area
Kona Int'l Airport
Kamakahonu Beach
Kailua-Kona
NORTH KONA
Mountain View
130
PUNA
Volcano
Kapoho Tide Pools
Ahalanui Park
White Sands Beach Park
Kahaluu Beach Park
Napoopoo Beach Park
Kailua-Kona
Captain Cook
SOUTH KONA
111
KAU
Punaluu
Punaluu Beach Park (Black Sand Beach)
Papakolea Beach (Green Sand Beach)
Hookena Beach Park
South Kona & Kau
11
N

10 miles
10 kilometers

BEACHES KEY

🚻	Restroom
🚿	Showers
🏄	Surfing
🤿	Snorkel/Scuba
👫	Good for kids
P	Parking

with rocks; calm waters make for good snorkeling. The sand is dotted with coral and generally clean. There is easy access to a few small coves of white sand with safe entry to the water and tide pools for children, while the shady areas are good for picnics or admiring the Kona "skyline," complete with a cruise ship or two. A well-cared-for walking and jogging trail on the other side of the runway is worth checking out for its landscape. Just north, an offshore surf break known as Old Airport is popular with local surfers. It's usually not crowded, but this area can be busy on weekends. **Amenities:** parking (no fee); showers; toilets. **Best for:** snorkeling; sunsets; walking. ⊠ *North end, Kuakini Hwy., where the road ends* ☎ *808/327–4958, 808/974–6200.*

🐢 **Kamakahonu Beach.** This is where King Kamehameha spent his final days—his Ahuena Heiau sits next to the sand. Fronting Courtyard's King Kamehameha's Kona Beach Hotel and next to Kailua Pier, this little crescent of white sand is the only beach in downtown Kailua-Kona. Protected by the harbor, the water here is almost always calm and the beach is clean making this a perfect spot for kids. For adults it's a great place for a swim, some stand-up paddleboarding, or just a lazy beach day, although it can get crowded in the afternoon. Though surrounded by an active pier, the water is surprisingly clear. Snorkeling can be good north of the beach, and snorkeling and kayaking equipment can be rented nearby. ■TIP➔ A little family of sea turtles likes to hang out next to the seawall, so keep an eye out. Park at the hotel for $15 a day. **Amenities:** food and drink; showers; toilets; water sports. **Best for:** snorkeling; swimming. ⊠ *75-5660 Palani Rd., at Alii Dr.*

White Sands Beach (*Magic Sands or Disappearing Sands Beach*). Towering coconut trees provide some shade and lend a touch of tropical beauty to this pretty little beach park (also called Laaloa), which may well be the Big Island's most intriguing stretch of sand. A migratory beach of sorts, it goes away in winter when waves wash away the small white-sand parcel (hence the name). In summer, the beach re-forms; you'll know you've found it when you see the body- and board surfers. Just south of Jameson's restaurant (closed at this writing), this is a popular summer hangout for young locals. **Amenities:** lifeguards; parking (no fee); toilets; shower. **Best for:** surfing. ⊠ *77-6470 Alii Dr., 4½ mi south of Kailua-Kona* ☎ *808/961–8311.*

The calm Kailua Bay is an excellent spot for kayaking, snorkeling, and swimming.

🐾 **Kahaluu Beach Park.** This salt-and-pepper beach is a combination of white and black sand mixed with lava and coral pebbles. It's one of the Big Island's most popular swimming and snorkeling sites, thanks to the fringing reef that helps keep the waters calm. But outside the reef there are very strong rip currents, so caution is advised. Some snorkelers hand-feed the unusually tame reef fish here, but we advise against it: the fish can become dependent and lose their natural survival instincts. ■**TIP→** Experienced surfers find good waves beyond the reef, and scuba divers like the shore dives—shallow ones inside the breakwater, deeper ones outside. This beach is very busy, and, consequently, littered. Snorkel equipment and boards are available for rent across the street. Hawaiian craft vendors set up on the beach but are inobtrusive. Kahaluu was a favorite of King Kalakaua, whose summer cottage is on the grounds of the neighboring Outrigger Keauhou Beach Resort. **Amenities:** food and drink; lifeguards; parking (no fee); shower; toilets; water sports. **Best for:** snorkeling; swimming. ✉ *78-6720 Alii Dr., 5½ mi south of Kailua-Kona, across from the Beach Villas, ½ mi north of the Keahou Resort* ☎ *808/961–8311.*

THE KONA COAST

The rugged beauty of this coastline harbors a couple of scenic beaches that take you off the beaten track. Napoopoo and Hookena offer great swimming, snorkeling, diving, and kayaking.

The beaches here are listed from north to south.

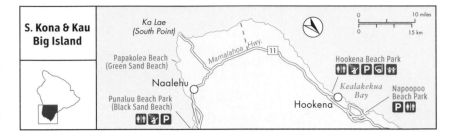

**S. Kona & Kau
Big Island**

Ka Lae
(South Point)

Papakolea Beach
(Green Sand Beach)

Naalehu

Punaluu Beach Park
(Black Sand Beach)

Mamalahoa Hwy.

11

0   10 miles
0   15 km

Hookena Beach Park

Kealakekua
Bay

Hookena

Napoopoo
Beach Park

NORTH KONA

Kua Bay. This lovely beach is on the northernmost portion of the stretch of coastline that comprises Kekaha Kai State Park. At one time you had to hike over a few miles of unmarked, rocky trail to get here, which kept many people out. Today, there's a separate entrance and a parking lot, making this bay much more accessible, and, as a result, more crowded. This is one of the most beautiful bays you'll ever see—the water is crystal clear, deep aquamarine, and peaceful in summer. The beach is a stretch of fine white sand and little shade. Rocky shores on either side keep the beach from getting too windy in the afternoon. △ The surf can get very rough in winter. **Amenities:** parking (no fee); showers; toilets. **Best for:** surfing; swimming. ⌧ *Hwy. 19, north of mile marker 88, directly across from the Veterans Cemetery, Kailua-Kona.*

Kekaha Kai State Park. It's slow going, down a 1½-mi, narrow, bumpy, gravel road off Highway 19 to this beach park, but it's worth it. Kehaha Kai State Park encompases three beaches (from north to south, Mahaiula, Makalawena, and Kua Bay, which has its own entrance). Mahaiula and Makalawena are beautiful, wide expanses of white-sand beach with dunes; there's a lot of space so you won't feel crowded. There are tidal pools for snorkeling and swimming, and you can hike along a historic 4½-mi trail to Kua Bay. If you're game, work your way to the top of Puu Kuili, a 342-foot-high cinder cone whose summit offers a fantastic view of the coastline. However, be prepared for the heat and bring lots of drinking water. The park is busy on the weekends. △ Watch out for rough surf and strong currents. **Amenities:** toilets. **Best for:** swimming; walking; sunsets. ⌧ *Hwy. 19, turnoff about 2 mi north of Keahole–Kona International Airport, Kailua-Kona* ☎ *808/327–4958, 808/974–6200* ⊕ *www.hawaiistateparks.org.*

SOUTH KONA

Napoopoo Beach Park. The shoreline is rocky with only a sliver of beach, but don't let that deter you—this is a popular park and a historically significant one. Captain James Cook first landed in Hawaii here in 1778 to refurbish his ships. When he returned a year later, he was killed in a skirmish with Hawaiians, now marked by a monument on the north end of Kealakekua Bay. The area is surrounded by high green cliffs, and when the water is calm the swimming, snorkeling, and diving is superb. You'll see a variety of marine life here, including colorful reef fish, corals, and, most likely, dolphins. This is also a great place to kayak. The trails behind the shore, leading to Hikiau Heiau, are rocky but walkable. △ Be aware of the off-limits area (in case of rockfalls) marked by orange buoys. **Amenities:** parking (no fee); toilets. **Best for:** snorkeling; swimming. ⊠ *Kealakekua Bay, Napoopoo Rd., off Hwy. 11, just south of mile marker 111, Kealakekua* ☎ *808/961–8311.*

Hookena Beach Park. The 2½-mi road down to this quiet, out-of-the-way beach is narrow and steep, but the views are awesome and you feel like you're venturing off the beaten path. The area is rich in cultural history, and remnants of the old steamship pier are still intact. This beach is frequented mostly by locals, so is usually only crowded on weekends. Backed by steep embankments, the dark sand is a clean, soft mix of lava and white sand. The bay is usually calm, with a small surf, good for swimming, snorkeling, kayaking, and diving. The ocean floor can be a little rocky, and caution is advised during high surf. Trails along the shoreline make for good exploring. South of Kealakekua Bay on Highway 11 you'll see a sign for Hookena Beach Park. **Amenities:** food and drink; parking (no fee); showers; toilets; water sports. **Best for:** snorkeling; sunset; swimming. ⊠ *Hwy. 11, 23 mi south of Kailua-Kona between mile markers 101 and 102* ☎ *808/961–8311.*

KOHALA COAST

Most of the Big Island's white sandy beaches are found on the Kohala Coast, which is also called the "Gold Coast," and is, understandably, home to the majority of the island's first-class resorts. Hawaii's beaches are public property and the resorts are required to provide public access to the beach, so don't be frightened off by a guard shack and a fancy sign. There is some limited public parking as well. The resort beaches aside, there are some real hidden gems on the Kohala Coast accessible only by boat, four-wheel drive, or a 15- to 20-minute hike. It's well worth the effort to get to at least one of these. ■ TIP→ The west side of the island tends to be calmer, but the surf still gets rough in winter.

The beaches here are listed in order from north (farthest from Kona) to south.

Pololu Valley Beach. On the North Kohala peninsula, this is one of the Big Island's most scenic black-sand beaches. After about 8 mi of lush, winding road past Hawi town, Highway 270 ends at the overlook of Pololu Valley. Snap a few photos of the stunning view, then take the 15-minute hike down (twice as long back up) to the beach. The trail is steep and rocky; it can also be muddy and slippery, so watch your step. The beach itself is a wide expanse of fine black sand surrounded by sheer green cliffs and backed by high dunes and pine trees. A gurgling stream leads from the beach to the back of the valley. △ This is not a particularly safe swimming beach even though locals do swim, body board, and surf here. Dangerous rip currents and usually rough surf pose a real hazard. And because this is a remote, isolated area far from emergency help, extreme caution is advised. **Amenities:** none. **Best for:** hiking. ⊠ *Hwy. 270, end of the road, Kapaau.*

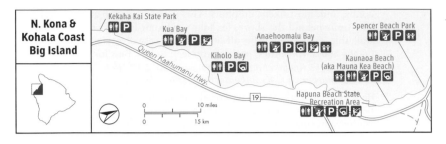

Mahukona Beach Park. Snorkelers and divers will find excitement in the clear waters of this beach park. Long ago, when sugar was the economic staple of Kohala, this harbor was busy with boats waiting for overseas shipments. Now it's a great swimming hole and an underwater museum of sorts. Remnants of shipping machinery, train wheels and parts, and what looks like an old boat are easily visible in the clear water. There's no actual beach here, but a ladder off the old dock makes getting in the water easy. It's best to venture out only on tranquil days, when the water is calm. A popular place for locals, Mahukona gets busy on weekends. A camping area on the south side of the park has picnic tables and an old covered pavillion. A trail also leads to nearby Lapakahi State Park, about a ½-mi hike. **Amenities:** showers; toilets. **Best for:** snorkeling; swimming. ⊠ *About 7 mi south of Hawi, Hwy. 270, between mile markers 14 and 15, watch for the sign, Kohala Coast* ☎ *808/961–8311.*

🌣 **Spencer Beach Park.** This white-sand beach is popular with local families because of its reef-protected waters. ■TIP➔ It's probably the safest beach in west Hawaii for young children. It's also safe for swimming year-round, which makes it an excellent spot for a lazy day at the beach. There is a little shade, plus a volleyball court and pavilion, and the soft sand is perfect for sand castles. It does tend to get crowded with families and campers on weekends, and the beach can be spotted with litter. Although you won't see a lot of fish if you're snorkeling here, in winter you can usually catch sight of a breaching whale or two. The beach park lies just below Puukohola Heiau National Historic Park, site of the historic temple built by King Kamehameha the Great in 1795. **Amenities:** lifeguards (weekends and holidays only); parking (no fee); showers; toilets. **Best for:** sunset; swimming. ⊠ *Hwy. 270, towards Kawaihae Harbor, just after the road forks from Hwy. 19, Kawaihae* ☎ *808/961–8311.*

🌣 **Kaunaoa Beach** (*Mauna Kea Beach*). Hands-down one of the most beau-
Fodor's Choice tiful beaches on the island, Kaunaoa is a long crescent of pure white
★ sand. The beach, which fronts the Mauna Kea Beach Hotel, slopes very gradually, and along the rocks it's a great place for snorkeling. This is a great spot to watch the sun set. When conditions permit, waves are good for body- and board surfing also. Currents can be strong and powerful in winter so be careful. ■TIP➔ Public parking is limited to 40 spaces, so arrive before 10 am or after 3 pm. If the lot is full, head to nearby Hapuna Beach, where there's a huge parking lot. Try this spot again another day—it's worth it! **Amenities:** lifeguards; parking (no fee); showers; toilets; water sports. **Best for:** sunset; swimming; walking. ⊠ *62-100*

Mauna Kea Beach Dr., entry through gate to Mauna Kea Beach Hotel, Kohala Coast.

(C) **Hapuna Beach State Recreation Area.** One of Hawaii's finest white-sand
Fodor'sChoice   beaches, Hapuna is a half-mi-long stretch of perfect white sand. The tur-
★   quoise water is calm in summer with just enough rolling waves to make
bodysurfing and body boarding fun. Watch for the undertow; in winter
the water can be rough. There is some excellent snorkeling around the
jagged rocks that border the beach on either side, but watch for strong
currents when the surf is high. Come here for awesome sunsets—it's
one of the best places on the island to see the "green flash" as the sun
dips below the horizon. The north end of the beach fronts the Hapuna
Beach Prince Hotel. You can rent water-sports equipment here, or stop
by the food concession and have lunch at the shaded picnic tables. There
is ample parking, although the lot can fill up by midday, and the beach
can be crowded on holidays. **Amenities:** food and drink; lifeguards;
parking (no fee); showers; toilets; water sports. **Best for:** sunset; swimming; surfing; walking. ⊠ *Hwy. 19, near mile marker 69, just south
of the Hapuna Beach Prince Hotel, Kohala Coast* ☎ *808/974–6200.*

(C) **Anaehoomalu Beach** (*A-Bay*). Also known as "A-bay," this expansive
★   stretch of white sand mixed with black lava grains fronts the Waikoloa
Beach Marriott and is a perfect spot for swimming, windsurfing, snorkeling, and diving. Although damaged by the 2011 tsunami (about 50%
of the beach is gone) it's still a vital and popular beach. The bay is well
protected, so even when surf is rough on the rest of the island, it's fairly
calm here. Snorkel gear, kayaks, and boogie boards are available for
rent at the north end, and the vendors are friendly and helpful. Snorkel
cruises and glass-bottom boat tours also depart from this bay. Behind
the beach are two ancient Hawaiian fishponds, **Kuualii** and **Kahapapa**,
that served the Hawaiian royalty in the old days. A walking trail follows
the coastline to the Hilton Waikoloa Village next door, passing by tide
pools, ponds, and a turtle sanctuary where you will often see sea turtles
sunbathing on the sand. Footwear is recommended for the trail. **Amenities:** food and drink; parking (no fee); showers; toilets; water sports.
Best for: snorkeling; swimming; walking. ⊠ *69-275 Waikoloa Beach
Dr., follow Waikoloa Beach Dr. to Kings' Shops, then turn left; parking
lot and beach just south of Waikoloa Beach Marriott, Kohala Coast.*

Kiholo Bay. The brilliant turquoise waters of this stunning bay are a
cooling invitation on a warm Kohala day, and a new gravel road to the
shoreline makes it an absolute must-see (it's still slow going, but in the
past you had to hike over lava for 20 minutes). The shore is rocky and
the water's a bit cold and hazy, but there are tons of green sea turtles
in residence year-round. The swimming and snorkeling are excellent
when the tide is calm. Thanks to the eruptions of Mauna Loa, what
was once the site of King Kamehameha's gigantic fishpond is now several freshwater ponds encircling this beautiful bay, with a picturesque
lava-rock island in the middle. If you follow the shoreline southwest
toward Kona, just past the big yellow house, you'll come to another
public beach which has naturally occurring freshwater pools inside a
lava tube. This area, called Queen's Bath, is as cool as it sounds. Recent
upgrades have been made for camping and unpaved parking. **Amenities:**

BEACH SAFETY

Hawaii's world-renowned, beautiful beaches can be extremely dangerous at times due to large waves and strong currents—so much so that the state rates wave hazards using three signs: a yellow square (caution), a red stop sign (high hazard), and a black diamond (extreme hazard). Signs are posted and updated three times daily or as conditions change.

Visiting beaches with lifeguards is strongly recommended, and you should only swim when there's a normal caution rating. Never swim alone or dive into unknown water or shallow breaking waves. If you're unable to swim out of a rip current, tread water and wave your arms in the air to signal for help.

Even in calm conditions, this is still the ocean and there are other dangerous things in the water to be aware of, including razor-sharp coral, jellyfish, eels, and sharks, to name a few.

Jellyfish cause the most ocean injuries, and signs are posted along beaches when they're present. Box jellyfish swarm to Hawaii's leeward shores 9–10 days after a full moon. Portuguese man-of-wars are usually found when winds blow from the ocean onto land. Reactions to a sting are usually mild (burning sensation, redness, welts); however, in some cases they can be severe (breathing difficulties). If you are stung by a jellyfish, pick off the tentacles, rinse the affected area with rubbing alcohol or urine (really) and apply ice. Seek first aid from a lifeguard if you experience severe reactions.

According to state sources, the chances of getting bitten by a shark in Hawaiian waters are very low; sharks attack swimmers or surfers three or four times per year. Of the 40 species of sharks found near Hawaii, tiger sharks are considered the most dangerous because of their size and indiscriminate feeding behavior (they eat just about anything at the water's surface). Tiger sharks are easily recognized by their blunt snouts and vertical bars on their sides.

To reduce your shark-attack risk, avoid swimming at dawn, dusk, and night, when some shark species may move inshore to feed. Steer clear of murky waters, harbor entrances, areas near stream mouths (especially after heavy rains), channels, or steep drop-offs.

The Web site ⊕ oceansafety.soest. hawaii.edu provides beach hazard maps for Oahu, Maui, Kauai and the Big Island, as well as weather and surf advisories, listings of closed beaches, and safety tips.

parking (no fee); toilets. **Best for:** snorkeling. ⊠ *Hwy. 19, unmarked gravel road between mile markers 82 and 83, just south of the lookout, Kohala Coast* ☎ *808/974–6200.*

THE HAMAKUA COAST

Although there are no actual beaches along the jagged cliffs of the Hamakua Coast, there are a few surf spots and swimming holes tucked into the lush landscape that are worth an afternoon stop.

The beaches here are listed from north to south.

Kua Bay is protected from wind by the rocky shores that surround it.

Kolekole Beach Park. This lush park is tucked away under a high bridge that crosses a gulch along Highway 19, about 13 mi north of Hilo, between Akaka and Umauma Falls. The beach is composed of large, smooth, waterworn lava rocks, where the Kolekole stream meets the ocean. Although the shoreline is rocky and the ocean is rough, the stream is usually calm and great for swimming. There's even a rope swing tied to a banyan tree on the opposite side. The park is popular with locals, especially on weekends when it can get rowdy. ■TIP→ Where the stream meets the ocean, the surf is rough and the currents strong. Only very experienced swimmers should venture here. **Amenities:** parking (no fee); showers; toilets. **Best for:** partiers. ⊠ *Hwy. 19, 13 mi north of Hilo, Honomu* ☏ *808/961–8311.*

HILO

Hilo isn't exactly known for its beautiful white beaches, but there are a few in the area that provide good swimming and snorkeling opportunities, and most are surrounded by lush rain forest.

The beaches here are listed from north to south.

Reeds Bay Beach Park. Safe swimming, proximity to downtown Hilo, and a freshwater-fed swimming hole, called the Ice Pond, that flows into the backwaters of Hilo Bay are the enticements of this cove. No, there really isn't ice in the swimming hole; it just feels that way on a hot sultry day. The large pond, between Hilo Seaside Hotel and Harrington's Restaurant, is a favorite of local kids who enjoy jumping into and frolicking in the chilly fresh- and saltwater mix. The water is usually calm but

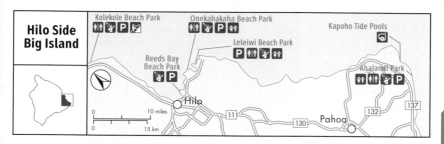

there is no real beach here. **Amenities:** parking (no fee); showers. **Best for:** swimming. ⊠ *Banyan Dr. and Kalanianaole Ave.* ☎ *808/961–8311.*

Onekahakaha Beach Park. Shallow, rock-wall-enclosed tide pools and an adjacent grassy picnic area make this park a favorite among Hilo families with small children. The protected pools are great places to look for Hawaiian marine life like sea urchins and anemones. There isn't much white sand, but access to the water is easy. The water is usually rough beyond the line of large boulders protecting the inner tide pools, so be careful if the surf is high. This beach gets crowded on weekends. **Amenities:** lifeguards (weekends and holidays only); parking (no fee); showers; toilets. **Best for:** swimming. ⊠ *Onekahakaha Rd. and Kalanianaole Ave., take Kanoelehua St. to Kalanianaole Ave. 3 mi east of Hilo, look for the sign* ☎ *808/961–8311.*

Leleiwi Beach Park and Richardson Ocean Center. You'll find plenty of sea life, from sea turtles to reef fish, at these beaches and protected inlets. Just east of Hilo, almost at the end of the road, these two adjacent parks make up one beautiful spot with a series of bays, inlets, lagoons, and pretty parks. This is one of the best snorkeling spots on this side of the island, as rocky outcrops provide shelter for schools of reef fish and you're almost sure to see turtles and dolphins. Local kids use the small black-sand pocket beach for body boarding. The shaded grassy areas are great for picnics. Be warned, this place is very crowded on the weekends. **Amenities:** lifeguards (weekends only); parking (no fee); showers; toilets. **Best for:** snorkeling; walking. ⊠ *Look for signs, almost at the end of the road, 2349 Kalanianaole Ave., 4 mi east of Hilo* ☎ *808/961–8311.*

PUNA

Puna's few beaches have some unique attributes—swaths of black sand, volcano-heated springs, and a coastline that is beyond dramatic (sheer walls of lava rock dropping into the bluest ocean you've ever seen).

The beaches here are listed from north to south.

Kapoho Tide Pools. Snorkelers will find tons of coral and the fish who feed off it in this large network of tide pools at the end of Kapoho-Kai Road. This is a great place for getting close-up looks at Hawaii's interesting marine life and reef fish. Some of the pools have been turned into private swimming pools in this residential area; those closest to the ocean are open to all. The pools are usually very calm, and some are volcanically heated and are divine. It's best to come during the week,

DID YOU KNOW?

You can swim with the turtles at the Big Island's Punaluu Beach Park, a black-sand beach and popular nesting and feeding spot for endangered Hawaiian green sea turtles. Resist touching the animals to avoid a hefty fine.

as the pools can get crowded on the weekend. Note: there is no real sandy beach here. Take the road to the end, then turn left and park. **Amenities:** none. **Best for:** snorkeling. ⌧ *Kapoho-Kai Rd., off Hwy. 13, about 9 mi southeast of Pahoa town, Puna.*

☞ **Ahalanui Park.** There's nothing like swimming in this natural, geothermally heated pool next to the ocean with palm trees swaying overhead. Popular with locals, this 3-acre beach park has a ½-acre pond of fresh spring water mixed with seawater that's heated by volcanic steam. There's no sand, but there is smooth rocky access to the ocean as well as the pool. ■TIP➔ The pool has had ongoing bacterial contamination problems that are typical of some ocean tidal pools in Hawaii. Those with skin-lesion problems, or chronic conditions like psoriasis, may want to avoid the water here. Others should have no problem. Check with the lifeguard on duty, and heed all posted signs. The parking lot fills up quickly. **Amenities:** lifeguards; parking (no fee); showers; toilets. **Best for:** swimming. ⌧ *Hwy. 137, 2½ mi south of Hwy. 132 junction, Puna* ☎ *808/961–8311* ☉ *Closed Wed.*

KAU

You shouldn't expect to find sparkling white-sand beaches on the rugged and rocky coasts of Kau, and you won't. What you will find is something a bit rarer and well worth the visit: black- and green-sand beaches. And there's the chance to see the endangered Hawaiian green sea turtles close up.

Beaches are listed from north to south.

★ **Papakolea Beach** (*Green Sand Beach*). Tired of the same old gold-, white-, or black-sand beach? Then how about a green-sand beach? You'll need good hiking shoes or sneakers to get to this olive-green crescent, one of the most unusual beaches on the island. It lies at the base of Puu o Mahana, at Mahana Bay, where a cinder cone formed during an early eruption of Mauna Loa. The greenish tint is caused by an accumulation of olivine crystals that form in volcanic eruptions. The dry, barren landscape is totally surreal. The surf is often rough, and swimming is hazardous due to strong currents, so caution is advised. Take the road off Highway 11 down to Ka Lae (South Point); at the end of the 12-mi "paved" road, take the road to the left and park at the end. ■TIP➔ Anyone trying to charge you for parking is running a scam. To reach the beach, follow the 2¼-mi coastal trail, which ends in a steep and dangerous descent down the cliff side on an unimproved trail. The hike takes at least an hour each way and it can get windy, so make sure to bring lots of drinking water. (Four-wheel-drive vehicles are no longer permitted on the trail). **Amenities:** none. **Best for:** solitude. ⌧ *Hwy. 11, 2½ mi northeast of South Point, Naalehu.*

★ **Punaluu Beach Park** (*Black Sand Beach*). This park is known for the endangered Hawaiian green sea turtles that nest here. Easily accessible, the beach is a long crescent of black sand backed by low dunes with some rocky outcroppings at the shoreline. You can see turtles feeding on the seaweed along the surf break or napping on the sand. If you

SUN SAFETY

Hawaii's weather—seemingly never-ending warm, sunny days with gentle trade winds—can be enjoyed year-round with good sun sense. Because of Hawaii's subtropical location, the length of daylight here changes little throughout the year. The sun is particularly strong, with a daily UV average of 14. Visitors should take the following steps to avoid sunburns and long-term cancer risks due to sun exposure.

■ Plan your beach, golf, hiking, and other outdoor activities for the early morning or late afternoon, avoiding the sun between 10 am and 4 pm when it's the strongest.

■ Apply a broad-spectrum sunscreen with a sun protection factor (SPF) of at least 30. Cover areas that are most prone to burning like your nose, shoulders, tops of feet, and ears. And don't forget to use sun protection products on your lips.

■ Apply sunscreen at least 30 minutes before you plan to be outdoors and reapply every two hours, even on cloudy days. Clouds scatter sunlight so you can still burn on an overcast day.

■ Wear light, protective clothing, such as a long-sleeved shirt and pants, broad-brimmed hat, and sunglasses.

■ Stay in the shade whenever possible—especially on the beach—by using an umbrella. Remember that sand and water can reflect up to 85% of the sun's damaging rays.

■ Children need extra protection from the sun. Apply sunscreen frequently and liberally on children over six months of age and minimize their time in the sun. Sunscreen is not recommended for children under six months.

swim with the turtles (they're used to people and will swim right next to you), resist the urge to touch or disturb them—they're protected by federal and state law and fines for touching them can be hefty. Don't venture too far from the shore; avoid going out past the boat ramp as very strong rip currents are active. ■ TIP→ It's quite rocky in the water, even close to shore—you might want to bring a pair of reef shoes if you plan to swim. Popular with locals and tour buses alike, this beach can be very busy, especially on weekends (the north parking lot is usually quieter). Shady palm trees provide an escape from the sun, and at the northern end of the beach, near the boat ramp, lie the ruins of Kaneeleele Heiau, an old Hawaiian temple. This area used to be a sugar port until the tidal wave of 1946 destroyed the buildings. Inland is a memorial to Henry Opukahaia. In 1809, when he was 17, Opukahaia swam out to a fur-trading ship in the harbor and asked to sign up as a cabin boy. When he reached New England, he entered the Foreign Mission School in Connecticut, but he died of typhoid fever in 1818. His dream of bringing Christianity to the Islands inspired the American Board of Missionaries to send the first Protestant missionaries to Hawaii in 1820. **Amenities:** parking (no fee); showers; toilets. **Best for:** snorkeling; walking. ⊠ *Hwy. 11, 27 mi south of Hawaii Volcanoes National Park between mile markers 55 and 56, Naalehu* ☎ *808/961–8311.*

Water Activities and Tours

WORD OF MOUTH

"LOVE Hapuna Beach. [It's] our favorite for boogie boarding. And if this 40something mom can do it, so can you and love it."

—oregonmom

Updated
by Cynthia
Sweeney

The ancient Hawaiians, who took much of their daily sustenance from the ocean, also enjoyed playing in the water. In fact, surfing was the sport of kings. Though it's easy to be lulled into whiling away the day baking in the sun on a white-, gold-, black-, or green-sand beach, getting into and onto the water will be a highlight of your trip.

All of the Hawaiian Islands are surrounded by the Pacific Ocean, making them some of the world's greatest natural playgrounds. But certain experiences are even better on the Big Island: nighttime scuba diving trips to see manta rays; deep-sea fishing in Kona's fabled waters, where dozens of Pacific blue marlin of 1,000 pounds or more have been caught; and kayaking among the dolphins in Kealakekua Bay, to name a few.

From any point on the Big Island, the ocean is never far away. With the variety of water sports that can be enjoyed—from body boarding and snorkeling to kayaking and surfing—there is something for everyone. For most activities, you can rent gear and go it alone or sign up for a group excursion with an experienced guide who can offer security as well as special insights into Hawaiian marine life and culture. Want to try surfing? You can take lessons as well.

The Kona and Kohala coasts of west Hawaii have the largest number of ocean sports outfitters and tour operators. They operate from the small-boat harbors and piers in Kailua-Kona, Keauhou, and at the Kohala Coast resorts. There are also several outfitters in the east Hawaii and Hilo areas.

As a general rule, the waves are gentler here than on the other Islands, but there are a few things to be aware of before heading to the shore. First, don't turn your back on the ocean. It's unlikely, but if conditions are right, a wave could come along and push you face-first into the sand or drag you out to sea. Conditions can change quickly, so keep your eyes open. Second, realize that ultimately you must keep yourself safe. We strongly encourage you to obey lifeguards and heed the advice of outfitters from whom you rent equipment. It could save your trip, or even your life.

DID YOU KNOW?

Kealakekua Bay, with its calm waters and spinner dolphins, is an excellent spot for kaya- king as well as snorkeling. Morning is the best time to see dolphins.

BODY BOARDING AND BODYSURFING

According to the movies, in the Old West there was always friction between cattle ranchers and sheep ranchers. Sometimes a similar situation exists between surfers and body boarders. That's why they generally keep to their own separate surfing areas. Often the body boarders, who lie on their stomachs on shorter boards, stay closer to shore and leave the outside breaks to the board surfers. Or the board surfers may stick to one side of the beach and the body boarders to the other. The truth is, body boarding (often called "boogie boarding," in homage to the first commercial manufacturer of this slick, little, flexible-foam board) is a blast. The only surfers who don't also sometimes carve waves on a body board are hard-core purists, and almost none of that type lives on this island.

■TIP→ Novice body boarders should catch shore-break waves only. Ask lifeguards or locals for the best spots. You'll need a pair of short fins to get out to the bigger waves offshore (not recommended for newbies). As for bodysurfing, just catch a wave and make like Superman going faster than a speeding bullet.

BEST SPOTS

Hapuna Beach State Recreation Area. When conditions are right, Hapuna Beach State Recreation Area, north of Kailua-Kona, is fabulous. The water is very calm in summer, with just enough rolling waves for bodysurfing or body boarding. But this beach isn't known as the "broken-neck capital" for nothing. Ask the lifeguards about conditions before heading into the water, and remember that if almost no one is in the water, there's a good reason for it. ⊠ *Hwy. 19, near mile marker 69, just south of the Mauna Kea Hotel, Kailua-Kona.*

White Sands, Magic Sands, or Disappearing Sands Beach Park. This is a great place for beginning and intermediate snorkelers, and in winter it's a good place to spot whales. Much of the sand at White Sands, Magic Sands, or Disappearing Sands Beach Park washes out to sea and forms a sandbar just offshore. This causes the waves to break in a way that's ideal for intermediate or advanced body boarding. There can be nasty rip currents at high tide. ■TIP→ If you're not using fins, wear reef shoes because of the rocks. ⊠ *Alii Dr., 4½ mi south of Kailua-Kona.*

Honolii Cove. North of Hilo, Honolii Cove is the best body boarding–surfing spot on the east side of the island. ⊠ *Off Hwy. 19, near mile marker 4, Hilo.*

EQUIPMENT

Equipment-rental shacks are located at many beaches and boat harbors, along the highway, and at most resorts. Body board rental rates are around $12–$15 per day and around $60 per week. Ask the vendor if he'll throw in a pair of fins—some will for no extra charge.

Orchid Land Surf Shop. This shop has a wide variety of water sports and surf equipment for sale or rent. They stock professional custom surfboards, body boards, and surf apparel, and do repairs. You can rent a body board here for $12 a day, or a surfboard for $20 a day. ⊠ *262 Kamehameha Ave., Hilo* ☎ *808/935–1533* ⊕ *www.orchidlandsurf.com.*

Body boarding is popular on the Big Island.

Pacific Vibrations. This family-owned surf shop has it all, from casual clothing to surf gear. This place stocks tons of equipment and is enthusiastic about GoPro digital cameras. You can rent a Morey or LMNOP body board for $5 a day, but you have to buy or bring your own fins. If you keep your board for more than five days, the rental rate drops to $3 a day. The shop rents surfboards, too. ⌧ *75-5702 Likana La., at Alii Dr., Kailua-Kona* ☎ *808/329–4140.*

DEEP-SEA FISHING

Along the Kona Coast you can find some of the world's most exciting "blue-water" fishing. Although July, August, and September are peak months, with the best fishing and a number of tournaments, charter fishing goes on year-round. You don't have to compete to experience the thrill of landing a Pacific blue marlin or other big-game fish. Some 60 charter boats, averaging 26 to 58 feet, are available for hire, most of them out of **Honokohau Harbor,** north of Kailua-Kona.

For an exclusive charter, prices generally range from $500 to $750 for a half-day trip (about four hours) and $800 to $1,300 for a full day at sea (about eight hours). For share charters, rates range from about $100 to $140 per person for a half day and $200 for a full day. If fuel prices increase, expect charter costs to rise. Most boats are licensed to take up to six passengers, in addition to the crew. Tackle, bait, and ice are furnished, but you'll usually have to bring your own lunch. You won't be able to keep your catch, although if you ask, many captains will send you home with a few fillets.

THE BIG ISLAND'S TOP WATER ACTIVITIES

Tour company/Outfitter	Length	AM/PM	Departure Point	Adult/Kid Price	Kids' Ages	Snack vs. Meal	Alcoholic Beverages Included	Boat Type	Capacity	Worth Noting
Scuba Diving										
Jack's Diving Locker	2-tank boat dive	AM	Honokohau Harbor	$125	10 and up	Snack	No	Large dive boat	24	Best for novice and intermediate divers
Kohala Divers	1-, 2-, or 3-tank boat dive	Both	Kawaihae Harbor	$129	All ages	None	No	Medium foot dive boat	15	Dive sites in the oldest part of the island
Ocean Eco Tours & Harbor Dive Ctr.	2-tank boat dive	Both	Kawaihae Harbor	$129	All ages	Snack	No	Small foot dive boat	6	Caters to small groups
Torpedo Tours	1-, 2- or 3-tank boat dive	Both	Honokohau Harbor	$110	10 and up	Meal	No	Medium dive boat	14	Underwater scooters available
Snorkeling										
Body Glove Cruises	3–4.5 hours	Both	Kailua-Kona	$78/ $58	All ages	Meals	No	Large catamaran	149	Kids under 5 are free
Captain Zodiac	4–5 hours	Both	Honokohau Harbor	$94/ $102	4 and up	Snack	No	Pontoon	16	Small size allows access to sea caves and unique sites
Fair Winds	4.5 hours	Both	Keauhou Harbor	$129/ $109	All ages	Meal	Yes	Large catamaran	100	Slide into the water; great for kids
Kona Boys	5.5 hours	Both	Kona Boys shop, just south of mile marker 113 on Hwy 11	$159	10 and up	Meal	No	Kayaks	2 per kayak	Great combo of kayaking and snorkeling

Snorkeling cont'd.

Torpedo Tours	3 hours	Both	Honokohau Harbor	$79	10 and up	Snack	No	Medium dive boat	14	Motorized torpedoes are easy to maneuver

Whale-Watching

Blue Sea Cruises	3 hours	PM	Kailua-Kona Pier	$79	All ages	Snack	No	Large catamaran	70–149	Glass bottom boat
Captain Dan McSweeney's	3 hours	Both	Honokohau Harbor	$79.50/$69.50	All ages	Snack	No	Large catamaran	42	Specializes in whale-watching and educational cruises
Captain Zodiac	3 hours	Both	Kailua-Kona	$65	All ages	Snack	No	Pontoon	16	Specialized rafts get you up close

Manta Ray Tours

Blue Sea Cruises	3 hours	PM	Kailua-Kona Pier	$65	All ages	Snack	Yes	Large catamaran	149	Watch from a glass bottom boat
Fair Wind Cruises: Hula Kai	3 hours	PM	Keahou Harbor	$99	18 and up	Snack	Yes	Large catamaran	42	Adults-only cruise
Jack's Diving Locker	3 hours	PM	Honokohau Harbor	$145	10 and up	Snack	No	Large dive boat	16	Late afternoon and night dives
Ocean Eco Tours & Harbor Dive Ctr.	3 hours	PM	Honokohau Harbor	$129	All ages	Snack	No	Small dive boat	6	Caters to small groups

Hawaiian International Billfish Tournament. These prize big-game fish have been sought after by deep-sea fishermen from all over the world who come to dip a line in Kona's fabled waters, most notably during the Hawaiian International Billfish Tournament. Held each August since 1959, this granddaddy of big-game-fishing tourneys has attracted teams from around the globe. Tournament records note that the largest marlin caught during the tourney was a 1,166-pound Pacific blue marlin taken on a 50-pound test line in 1993. That's a lot of sashimi! ☎ *808/836–3422* ⊕ *www. hibtfishing.com.*

> ### KONA'S "GRANDER ALLEY"
>
> Kona has the reputation of producing large marlin, mostly the Pacific blue variety. According to records, 63 marlin weighing 1,000 pounds or more have been caught off the Kona Coast, which has come to be known as "Grander Alley," a reference to the number of big fish that inhabit its waters. The largest "grander" ever, caught in 1984, weighed in at 1,649 pounds.

Honokohau Harbor's Fuel Dock. Big fish are weighed in at Honokohau Harbor's Fuel Dock. Show up around 11:30 am and watch the weigh-in of the day's catch from the morning charters, or around 3:30 pm for the afternoon charters. Weigh-ins are not a sure thing, but are fun when the big ones come in. If you're lucky, you'll get to see a "grander," a fish weighing in at 1,000-plus pounds. A surprising number of these are caught just outside Kona Harbor. ■TIP➔ On Kona's Waterfront Row, look for the "Grander's Wall" of anglers with their prizes. ✉ *Honokohau Harbor, Kealakekua Pkwy., Kailua-Kona.*

BOATS AND CHARTERS

Before you sign up with anyone, think about the kind of trip you want. Looking for a romantic cruise? A rockin' good time with your buddies? Serious fishing in one of the "secret spots"? A family-friendly excursion? Be sure to describe your expectations so your booking agent can match you with a captain and a boat that suits your style.

Captain Teddy Hoogs Big Game Fishing. Full-, half-, and quarter-day charters are available on the 46-foot *Bwana*. Built in 2008, the boat has all the latest electronics, top-of-the-line equipment, and air-conditioned cabins. Overnight fishing is also a possibility. Captain Teddy comes from a fishing family; father Peter, formerly of Pamela Big Game Fishing, is semiretired but still operates the Kona Charter Skippers Association. Rates start at $750. ✉ *Honokohau Harbor, just south of Kona airport, 74-381 Kealakehe Pkwy., Kailua-Kona* ☎ *808/936–5168* ⊕ *www.teddyhoogs.com.*

Charter Locker. This company can provide information on various charter-boat fishing trips and make all the arrangements—it can even book you on the luxurious *Blue Hawaii*, which has air-conditioned staterooms for overnight trips. ✉ *Honokohau Harbor, just south of the Kona airport, 74-381 Kealakehe Pkwy., Kailua-Kona* ☎ *808/326–2553* ⊕ *www.charterlocker.com.*

Charter Services Hawaii. Run for over 20 years by Ed and Audrey Barry, this booking service represents several Kona fishing boats and can assist with all the details in arranging a charter. ☎ *808/334–1881, 800/567– 2650* ⊕ *www.konazone.com.*

Honokohau Harbor Charter Desk. With about 60 boats on the books, this place can take care of almost anyone. You can make arrangements through your hotel activity desk, but we suggest you go down to the desk at the harbor and look things over for yourself. ✉ *74-381 Keal- akehe Pkwy., Kailua-Kona* ☎ *808/329–5735, 888/566–2487* ⊕ *www. charterdesk.com.*

Humdinger Sportfishing. This game fisher guide has more than three decades of fishing experience in Kona waters. The experienced crew are marlin specialists. The 37-foot *Humdinger* has the latest in electronics and top-line rods and reels. Half-day exclusive charters begin at $600, full-day exclusives at $950. ✉ *Honokohau Harbor, Slip B-4, Kailua- Kona* ☎ *808/936–3034, 800/926–2374* ⊕ *www.humdinger-online.com.*

Illusions Sportfishing. Captain Steve Sahines is one of Kona's top fishing tourney producers with several years of experience. The 39-foot *Illu- sions* is fully equipped with galley, restrooms, an air-conditioned cabin for guest comfort, plus the latest in fishing equipment. Half-day exclu- sive charters begin at $500, full-day exclusives at $800. ✉ *Honokohau Harbor, just south of Kona airport, 74-381 Kealakehe Pkwy., Kailua- Kona* ☎ *808/960–7371* ⊕ *www.illusionssportfishing.com.*

Kona Charter Skippers Association. In business since 1956, this company can help arrange half-day and full-day exclusive or share charters on several boats. The *Pamela* is the featured boat. ✉ *74-857 Iwalani Pl., Kailua-Kona* ☎ *808/936-4970* ⊕ *www.konabiggamefishing.com.*

KAYAKING

The leeward west coast areas of the Big Island are protected for the most part from the northeast trade winds, making for ideal near-shore kayaking conditions. There are miles and miles of uncrowded Kona and Kohala coastline to explore, presenting close-up views of stark, raw, lava-rock shores and cliffs, lava-tube sea caves, pristine secluded coves, and deserted beaches.

Ocean kayakers can get close to shore—where the commercial snorkel and dive cruise boats can't reach. This opens up all sorts of possibili- ties for adventure, such as near-shore snorkeling among the expansive coral reefs and lava rock formations that teem with colorful tropical fish, Hawaiian green sea turtles, and more. You can pull ashore at a quiet cove for a picnic and a plunge into turquoise waters. With a good coastal map and some advice from the kayak vendor, you can explore inland, where you might find ancient battlegrounds, burial sites, bath- ing ponds for Hawaiian royalty, or old villages.

Kayaking experiences can be enjoyed via a guided tour or on a self- guided paddling excursion. Either way, the kayak outfitter can brief you on recommended routes, manageable currents, and how you can help preserve and protect Hawaii's ocean resources and coral reef system.

KAYAK SAFETY

■ Whether you're a beginner or experienced kayaker, choose appropriate water and weather conditions for your kayak excursion.

■ Ask the outfitter about local conditions and hazards, such as tides and currents.

■ Beginners should practice getting into and out of the kayak and capsizing in shallow water.

■ Before departing, secure the kayak's hatches to prevent water intake.

■ Use a line to attach the paddle to the kayak to avoid losing it.

■ Always use a life vest or jacket and slather on plenty of sunblock.

■ Wear a helmet if kayaking in and around rough water and rocks.

■ Carry appropriate amounts of water and food.

■ Don't kayak alone. Create a float plan; tell someone where you're going and when you will return.

BEST SPOTS

Hilo Bay. Hilo Bay is a favorite kayak spot, and the best place to put in is at **Reeds Bay Beach Park.** Most afternoons you can share the bay with local paddling clubs. Stay inside the breakwater unless the ocean is calm (or you're feeling unusually adventurous). Conditions range from extremely calm to quite choppy. ⊠ *Banyan Way and Banyan Dr., 1 mi from downtown Hilo.*

Kailua Bay and Kamakahonu Beach. The small, sandy beach that fronts the King Kamehameha Kona Beach Hotel is a perfect place to launch your kayak. Because the bay is protected by the harbor, the water here is especially calm and teeming with ocean life. It's easy to get to and great for all skill levels. ⊠ *Alii Dr., next to Kailua Pier, Kailua-Kona.*

★ **Kealakekua Bay.** The excellent snorkeling and the likelihood of seeing dolphins makes Kealakekua Bay one of the most popular kayak spots on the Big Island. The bay is usually calm, and the kayaking is not difficult—except during high surf. If you're there in the morning, you may very well see spinner dolphins. Depending on your strength and the water conditions, you'll cross the bay in 30 to 60 minutes. You can snorkel from your kayak to the ancient canoe landing about 50 yards to the left of the **Captain Cook Monument,** but you need a special permit to land your canoe. Hawaii State Parks (⊕ *www.hawaiistateparks.org/ announcements*) has information about obtaining a permit. The coral around the monument makes for fabulous snorkeling. ⊠ *Bottom of Napoopoo Rd., Kailua-Kona.*

Oneo Bay. Oneo Bay is usually quite a placid place to kayak. It's easy to get to and great for all skill levels. If you can't find parking along the road, there's a lot across the street near the farmers' market. ⊠ *Alii Dr., Kailua-Kona.*

EQUIPMENT, LESSONS, AND TOURS

There are several rental outfitters on Highway 11 between mile markers 110 and 113. There's also one unofficial stand at the shore, at the house on the corner just across from the parking lot. After you've loaded your kayak onto the roof of your car, follow the 2-mi road down the rather steep hill to the parking lot below. ■TIP➔ There are usually local guys available to set up your kayak and get you into the water; tips of $5 to $10 are encouraged, expected, and appreciated.

Aloha Kayak Co. This Honalo outfitter offers guided tours out of Keauhou Bay—a four-hour morning tour ($89 per person) and a 2½-hour afternoon version ($69 per person). Both include snacks and beverages. There's also an hour-long evening tour ($99 per person). Daily kayak rental rates are $35 for a single, $60 for a double, and $85 for a triple. ✉ *79-7248 Mamalahoa Hwy., Honalo* ☎ *808/322–2868, 877/322–1444* ⊕ *www.alohakayak.com.*

Kohala Ditch Adventures. Formerly Flumin' Da Ditch, this 2½-hour guided kayak cruise through an old irrigation ditch reveals a dramatic part of Kohala history. The tour begins with an off-road excursion high in the Kohala mountains, followed by a short hike to the ditch, where you'll paddle along with the guides through 2½ mi of rain forest, tunnels, and water flumes. The valleys beyond provide water for the Kohala Ditch, which once brought water to the area's sugar plantations. The tour costs $129 per person. ✉ *Akoni-Pule Hwy., 1 mi past King Kamehameha Statue, Kapaau* ☎ *808/889–6000, 888/288–7288* ⊕ *www.kohaladitchadventures.com* ⊙ *Tours Mon.–Sat. at 8:30 and 1.*

Kona Boys. On the highway above Kealakekua Bay, this full-service outfitter handles kayaks, body boards, surf boards, stand-up paddleboards, and snorkeling gear. Single seat kayaks are $47 daily, while doubles are $67. If you want to learn surfing and stand-up paddling, the prices are $75 per person for group instruction or $150 for private lessons. The Kona Boys also lead two different half-day guided kayaking and snorkeling trips ($159 per person, including lunch, snacks, and beverages). One skirts the Kona coastline, and the other explores Kamakahonu Cove and Pawai Bay. There's also a sunset kayak and snorkel tour for $125 per person. Overnight camping trips are available. The Kona Boys also run a beach shack next to Kailua Pier, behind the King Kamehameha Kona Beach Hotel. ■TIP➔ This location offers the same rental equipment as well as Hawaiian outrigger canoe rides and charters, a uniquely Hawaiian experience. ✉ *79-7539 Mamalahoa Hwy., Kealakekua* ☎ *808/328–1234* ⊕ *www.konaboys.com* ✉ *75–5660 Palani Rd., Kailua-Kona.*

Ocean Safari's Kayak Adventures. On the guided 3½-hour morning sea-cave tour that begins in Keauhou Bay, you can visit lava-tube sea caves along the coast, then swim ashore for a snack. The kayaks will already be on the beach, so you won't have to hassle with transporting them. The cost is $64 per person. A two-hour dolphin-spotting tour leaves at 7 am on Tuesday. It's $35 per person. Kayak daily rental rates are $25 for singles and $40 for doubles. ✉ *End of Kamehameha III Rd., Kailua-Kona* ☎ *808/326–4699* ⊕ *www.oceansafariskayaks.com.*

Pineapple Park. Pineapple Park is actually a hostel with locations in Hilo, Kona, and Mountain View, but it's also one of the only outfitters for kayak rentals in Hilo. Kayaks are $38 for a single and $58 for a double, and the rental price includes oars, life jackets, bags to keep all your gear

4

dry, and harnesses to strap your kayak to your car. ■**TIP→** There's a 10% discount if you book ahead. ✉ *860 Piilani St., Hilo* ☎ *808/323–2224, 877/800–3800* ⊕ *pineapple-park.com.*

PARASAILING

Parasailing, gliding on the winds with a parachute while being pulled behind a powerboat, is a relaxing and thrilling experience. If you can handle heights, you'll revel in the experience of being suspended in air while soaring above Kailua Bay. The water is so clear you can almost see the ocean floor. And no swimming is required; takeoffs and landings are from the back of the boat.

EQUIPMENT AND LESSONS

UFO Parasail. This parasailing outfitter runs across Kailua Bay and along the Kona Coast, hoisting you up to 1,200 feet in the air. There's an optional "free fall" that stops short of the water, adding the rush of a parachute descent. A powerboat and winch provide dry takeoffs and landings, and guests can "fly" alone or in tandem. Although the flight is short, the boat ride takes about one hour. Flying up to 600 feet for seven minutes is $65, while the "out of this world" 1,200-foot flight lasts 10 minutes and costs $85. If you just want to enjoy the boat ride, the cost is $35. ✉ *75-5669 Alii Dr., Kailua-Kona* ☎ *888/359–4836, 808/325–5836* ⊕ *www.ufoparasailing.net.*

SAILING

For old salts and novice sailors alike, there's nothing like a cruise on the Kona or Kohala coasts of the Big Island. Calm waters, serene shores, and the superb scenery of Mauna Kea, Mauna Loa, and Hualalai, the Big Island's primary volcanic peaks, make for a great sailing adventure. You can drop a line over the side and try your luck at catching dinner, or grab some snorkel gear and explore when the boat drops anchor in one of the quiet coves and bays. A cruise may well be the most relaxing and adventurous part of a Big Island visit.

BOATS AND CHARTERS

Maile Charters. Private sailing charters for two to six passengers are available on the *Maile,* a 50-foot GulfStar sloop. You choose the itinerary, whether it's watching for dolphins and whales, snorkeling around coral reefs, or enjoying appetizers as the sun sinks below the horizon. Prices start at $997 for a sunset sail. You can also book day-long jaunts or overnight trips. Snorkeling equipment is provided, and food can be catered. ✉ *Kawaihae Harbor, Hwy. 270, Kawaihae* ☎ *808/960–9744* ⊕ *www.adventuresailing.com.*

SCUBA DIVING

The Big Island's underwater world is the setting for a dramatic diving experience. With generally calm waters, vibrant coral reefs and rock formations, and plunging underwater drop-offs, the Kona and Kohala coasts provide some great scuba diving. There are also some good dive locations in east Hawaii, not far from the Hilo area. Divers will find much to occupy their time, including marine reserves teeming with unique Hawaiian reef fish, Hawaiian green sea turtles, an occasional and rare Hawaiian monk seal, and even some playful Hawaiian spinner dolphins. On special night dives to see manta rays, divers descend with bright underwater lights that attract plankton, which in turn attract these otherworldly creatures. The best spots to dive are listed in order from north to south; all are on the west coast.

BEST SPOTS

Garden Eel Cove. A great spot to see manta rays is Garden Eel Cove. At this site you're likely to spot hundreds of tiny garden eels darting out from their sandy homes, as well as manta rays somersaulting overhead as they feast on a plankton supper. There's a steep drop-off and lots of marine life. ⊠ *Near Kona International Airport, Rte. 19, Kailua-Kona.*

Manta Village. One of Kona's best night-dive spots is Manta Village. Booking with a night-dive operator is required for the short boat ride to the area. If you're a diving or snorkeling fanatic, it's well worth it for the experience of seeing the manta rays. ⊠ *Off Sheraton Keauhou Bay Resort & Spa, 78-128 Ehukai St., Kailua-Kona.*

Pawai Bay Marine Reserve. The water is usually very clear at Pawai Bay Marine Reserve. This bay near Kailua-Kona has numerous underwater sea caves, arches, and rock formations, plus lots of marine life. It can be busy with snorkel boats, but is an easy dive spot. ⊠ *Kuakini Hwy., north of Old Kona Airport Beach Park, Kailua-Kona.*

Puako. Just south of Hapuna Beach State Recreation Area is Puako, which offers easy entry to some fine reef diving. Deep chasms, sea caves, and rock arches abound with varied marine life. ⊠ *Puako Rd., off Hwy. 19, Kohala Coast.*

EQUIPMENT, LESSONS, AND TOURS

There are quite a few good dive shops on the Kona Coast. Most are happy to take on all customers, but a few focus on specific types of trips. Trip prices vary, depending on whether you're already certified and whether you're diving from a boat or from shore. Instruction with PADI, SDI, or TDI certification in three to five days costs $600 to $850. Most instructors rent out dive equipment and snorkel gear, as well as underwater cameras. A few organize otherworldly manta ray dives at night or whale-watching cruises in season.

Jack's Diving Locker. The best place for novice and intermediate divers, Jack's Diving Locker has trained and certified tens of thousands of divers since opening in 1981. A massive operation, it has classrooms and a dive pool for beginning instruction. The company has four boats that can accommodate 10 to 24 divers. Heading to more than 80 established dive sites along the Kona coast, Jack's has plenty to offer, whether you want to see turtles, manta rays, garden eels, or schools of barracuda. It does a good job looking out for customers and protecting the coral reef. Daytime rates are $55 for snorkelers, $125 for divers. Night dives to see manta rays are $95 for snorkelers, $145 for divers. Snorkel charters, for a minimum of four passengers, cost $125 per person. ■ TIP➔ Kona's

HAWAII'S MANTA RAYS

Manta rays, one of Hawaii's most fascinating marine-life species, can be seen on some nighttime diving excursions along the Kona and Kohala coasts. They are generally completely harmless to divers, though of course no wild animal is totally predictable. If you don't want to get wet, head to the beach fronting the Mauna Kea Beach Hotel on the Kohala Coast, or the Sheraton Keauhou in Kailua-Kona, where each evening, visitors gather under the lights to watch manta rays feed in the shallows.

■ The manta ray (*Manta birostris*), called the devil fish by some, is known as *hahalua* by Hawaiians.

■ Its winglike fins, reaching up to 20 feet wide, allow the ray to glide through the water like a bird gliding through air.

■ The manta ray uses the two large flap-like lobes extending from its eyes to funnel food to its mouth. It eats microscopic plankton, small fish, and tiny crustaceans.

■ The manta ray, closely related to the shark, can weigh more than 3,000 pounds.

■ Its skeleton is made of cartilage, not bone.

■ A female ray gives birth to one or two young at a time; pups can be 45 inches long and weigh 20 pounds at birth.

best deal for scuba newbies is the introductory dive from Kailua Pier. It costs $80, including pool instruction. ⊠ *75-5813 Alii Dr., Kailua-Kona* ☎ *808/329–7585* ⊕ *www.jacksdivinglocker.com.*

Kohala Divers. The Kohala Coast's lava caves, vibrant coral reefs, and interesting smaller critters make it a great diving destination. Kohala Divers is a full-service PADI dive shop that has been certifying divers since 1984. A one-day intro dive course that will have you in the ocean the same day costs $204 per person. Full certification over four days is $595. The company also rents quality equipment and takes divers to the best diving spots. A two-tank dive is $129, plus $30 for your gear. Night dives are $139. Seasonal whale-watch tours are $75. ⊠ *Kawaihae Shopping Center, Hwy. 270, Kamuela* ☎ *808/882–7774* ⊕ *www. kohaladivers.com.*

Nautilus Dive Center. Across from Hilo Bay, Nautilus Dive Center is the oldest and most experienced dive shop on the island. It offers a broad range of services for both beginners and experienced divers. Owner Bill De Rooy has been diving around the Big Island for 30 years, and can provide you with underwater maps and show you the best dive spots in Hilo. He also provides PADI instruction and likes to repair gear. Dive-equipment rentals start at $35 per day. ⊠ *382 Kamehameha Ave., Hilo* ☎ *808/935–6939* ⊕ *www.nautilusdivehilo.com.*

★ **Ocean Eco Tours and Harbor Dive Center.** This eco-friendly outfit is eager to share a wealth of knowledge to beginners and advanced divers. It's close to a number of good reefs and other prime underwater locations. Divers and and snorkelers head out on one of two 30-foot craft. Excursions start at $129 for a four-hour daytime dive or for a nighttime dive

The Kona Coast's relatively calm waters and colorful coral reefs are excellent for scuba diving.

to spot manta rays. The PADI open-water certification classes can be completed in three to four days for $650. Seasonal whale-watch tours are $95. ⊠ *Honokohau Harbor, 74-425 Kealakehe Pkwy., Kailua-Kona* ☎ *808/324–7873* ⊕ *www.oceanecotours.com.*

★ **Torpedo Tours.** Mike and Nikki Milligan specialize in small groups, which means you'll spend more time diving and less time hanging out on the boat waiting to dive. Morning excursions featuring two-tank dives run $110 ($79 for smorkeling). Boat snorkelers and divers can try out the namesake torpedo scooters for $30. The scooters allow you to cover more ground with less kicking. ⊠ *Honokohau Harbor, 74-425 Keal-akehe Pkwy., Kailua-Kona* ☎ *808/938–0405* ⊕ *www.torpedotours.com.*

SNORKELING

A favorite pastime on the Big Island, snorkeling is perhaps one of the easiest and most enjoyable water activities for visitors. By floating on the surface, looking through your mask, and breathing through your snorkel, you can see lava rock formations, sea arches, sea caves, and coral reefs teeming with colorful tropical fish. While the Kona and Kohala coasts have more beaches, bays, and quiet coves to snorkel, the east side around Hilo and at Kapoho are also great places to get in the water.

If you don't bring your own equipment, you can easily rent all the gear needed from a beach activities vendor, who will happily provide directions to the best sites for snorkeling in the area. For access to deeper water and assistance from an experienced crew, you can opt for a snorkel cruise. Excursions generally range from two to five hours; be sure you know what equipment and food is included.

BEST SPOTS

Kahaluu Beach Park. Since ancient times, the waters around Kahaluu Beach Park have been a traditional net-fishing area (the water is shallower here than at Kealakekua). The swimming is good, and the snorkeling is even better. You'll see angelfish, parrot fish, needlefish, puffer fish, and a lot more. ■TIP→ Stay inside the breakwater and don't stray too far, as dangerous and unpredictable currents swirl outside the bay. ⊠ *Alii Dr., Kailua-Kona.*

Kapoho Tide Pools. Kapoho Tide Pools has the best snorkeling on the Hilo side. Fingers of lava from the 1960 flow that destroyed the town of Kapoho jut into the sea to form a network of tide pools. Conditions near the shore are excellent for beginners and challenging enough farther out for experienced snorkelers. ⊠ *End of Kapoho-Kai Rd., off Hwy. 137, Hilo.*

Fodor's Choice
★
Kealakekua Bay. Kealakekua Bay is, hands-down, the best snorkel spot on the island, with fabulous coral reefs around the Captain Cook monument and generally calm waters. And with any luck, you'll probably get to swim with dolphins. Overland access is difficult, so opt for one of several guided snorkel cruises or kayak across the bay to get to the monument. ■TIP→ Be on the lookout for kayakers who might not notice you swimming beneath them, and stay on the ocean side of the buoys near the cliffs. ⊠ *Bottom of Napoopoo Rd., Kailua-Kona.*

Puuhonua O Honaunau (*City of Refuge*). There is no swimming inside the actual park, but just north is a boat launch where the snorkeling is almost as good as at Kealakekua Bay, and it's much easier to reach. It's also a popular scuba diving spot. ⊠ *Hwy. 160, 20 mi south of Kailua-Kona* ⊕ *www.nps.gov/puho.*

White Sands, Magic Sands, or Disappearing Sands Beach Park. White Sands, Magic Sands, or Disappearing Sands Beach Park is a great place for beginning and intermediate snorkelers. In winter it's also a good place to see whales. ⊠ *Alii Dr., Kailua-Kona.*

EQUIPMENT, LESSONS, AND TOURS

ℭ
★
Body Glove Cruises. This operator is a good choice for families, particularly if at least one member is a certified diver and the rest want to snorkel. Kids love the waterslide and the high-dive platform, and parents appreciate the reasonable prices. The 51-foot catamaran sets off from Kailua-Kona pier daily for morning and afternoon dive and snorkel cruises that include breakfast and lunch buffets. Snorkelers pay $78 per person. A three-hour dinner cruise to Kealakekua Bay is a great way to relax, watch the sunset, and learn about Kona's history. Including a buffet and live music, it's $98 per person. Seasonal

Continued on page 132

SNORKELING IN HAWAII

The waters surrounding the Hawaiian Islands are filled with life—from giant manta rays cruising off the Big Island's Kona Coast to humpback whales giving birth in Maui's Maalaea Bay. Dip your head beneath the surface to experience a spectacularly colorful world: pairs of milletseed butterflyfish dart back and forth, redlipped parrotfish snack on coral algae, and spotted eagle rays flap past like silent spaceships. Sea turtles bask at the surface while tiny wrasses give them the equivalent of a shave and a haircut. The water quality is typically outstanding; many sites afford 30-foot-plus visibility. On snorkel cruises, you can often stare from the boat rail right down to the bottom.

Certainly few destinations are as accommodating to every level of snorkeler as Hawaii. Beginners can tromp in from sandy beaches while more advanced divers descend to shipwrecks, reefs, craters, and sea arches just offshore. Because of Hawaii's extreme isolation, the island chain has fewer fish species than Fiji or the Caribbean—but many of the fish that are here exist nowhere else. The Hawaiian waters are home to the highest percentage of endemic fish in the world.

The key to enjoying the underwater world is slowing down. Look carefully. Listen. You might hear the strange crackling sound of shrimp tunneling through coral, or you may hear whales singing to one another during winter. A shy octopus may drift along the ocean's floor beneath you. If you're hooked, pick up a waterproof fishkey from Long's Drugs. You can brag later that you've looked the Hawaiian turkeyfish in the eye.

Picasso Triggerfish	Milletseed Butterflyfish*	Yellow Tang
Moorish Idol	Hawaiian Whitespotted Toby*	Saddleback Wrasse*
Redlip Parrotfish	Hawaiian Turkeyfish*	Zebra Moray Eel
Stocky Hawkfish	Green Sea Turtle (Honu)	Spotted Eagle Ray

*endemic to Hawaii

POLYNESIA'S FIRST CELESTIAL NAVIGATORS: HONU

Honu is the Hawaiian name for two native sea turtles, the hawksbill and the green sea turtle. Little is known about these dinosaur-age marine reptiles, though snorkelers regularly see them foraging for *limu* (seaweed) and the occasional jellyfish in Hawaiian waters. Most female honu nest in the uninhabited Northwestern Hawaiian Islands, but a few sociable ladies nest on Maui and Big Island beaches. Scientists suspect that they navigate the seas via magnetism—sensing the earth's poles. Amazingly, they will journey up to 800 miles to nest—it's believed that they return to their own birth sites. After about 60 days of incubation, nestlings emerge from the sand at night and find their way back to the sea by the light of the stars.

SNORKELING

Many of Hawaii's reefs are accessible from shore.

The basics: Sure, you can take a deep breath, hold your nose, squint your eyes, and stick your face in the water in an attempt to view submerged habitats . . . but why not protect your eyes, retain your ability to breathe, and keep your hands free to paddle about when exploring underwater? That's what snorkeling is all about.

Equipment needed: A mask, snorkel (the tube attached to the mask), and fins. In deeper waters (any depth over your head), life jackets are advised.

Steps to success: If you've never snorkeled before, it's natural to feel a bit awkward at first, so don't sweat it. Breathing through a mask and tube, and wearing a pair of fins take getting used to. Like any activity, you build confidence and comfort through practice.

If you're new to snorkeling, begin by submerging your face in shallow water or a swimming pool and breathing calmly through the snorkel while gazing through the mask.

Next you need to learn how to clear water out of your mask and snorkel, an essential skill since splashes can send water into tube openings and masks can leak. Some snorkels have built-in drainage valves, but if a tube clogs, you can force water up and out by exhaling through your mouth. Clearing a mask is similar: lift your head from water while pulling forward on mask to drain. Some masks have built-in purge valves, but those without can be cleared underwater by pressing the top to the forehead and blowing out your nose (charming, isn't it?), allowing air to bubble into the mask, pushing water out the bottom. If it sounds hard, it really isn't. Just try it a few times and you'll soon feel like a pro.

Now your goal is to get friendly with fins—you want them to be snug but not too tight—and learn how to propel yourself with them. Fins won't help you float, but they will give you a leg up, so to speak, on smoothly moving through the water or treading water (even when upright) with less effort.

Flutter stroking is the most efficient underwater kick, and the farther your foot bends forward the more leg power you'll be able to transfer to the water and the farther you'll travel with each stroke. Flutter kicking movements involve alternately separating the legs and then drawing them back together. When your legs separate, the leg surface encounters drag from the water, slowing you down. When your legs are drawn back together, they produce a force pushing you forward. If your kick creates more forward force than it causes drag, you'll move ahead.

Submerge your fins to avoid fatigue rather than having them flailing above the water when you kick, and keep your arms at your side to reduce drag. You are in the water—stretched out, face down, and snorkeling happily away—but that doesn't mean you can't hold your breath and go deeper in the water for a closer look at some fish or whatever catches your attention. Just remember that when you do this, your snorkel will be submerged, too, so you won't be breathing (you'll be holding your breath). You can dive head-first, but going feet-first is easier and less scary for most folks, taking less momentum. Before full immersion, take several long, deep breaths to clear carbon dioxide from your lungs.

If your legs tire, flip onto your back and tread water with inverted fin motions while resting. If your mask fogs, wash condensation from lens and clear water from mask.

TIPS FOR SAFE SNORKELING

■ Snorkel with a buddy and stay together.

■ Plan your entry and exit points prior to getting in the water.

■ Swim into the current on entering and then ride the current back to your exit point.

■ Carry your flippers into the water and then put them on, as it's difficult to walk in them.

■ Make sure your mask fits properly and is not too loose.

■ Pop your head above the water periodically to ensure you aren't drifting too far out, or too close to rocks.

■ Think of the water as someone else's home—don't take anything that doesn't belong to you, or leave any trash behind.

■ Don't touch any sea creatures; they may sting.

■ Wear a T-shirt over your swimsuit to help protect you from being fried by the sun.

■ When in doubt, don't go without a snorkeling professional; try a guided tour.

Green sea turtle (Honu)

whale-watch cruises are $78. ⊠ *75-5629 Kuakini Hwy., Kailua-Kona* ☎ *808/326–7122, 800/551–8911* ⊕ *www.bodyglovehawaii.com.*

Captain Zodiac Raft Expedition. A four-hour trip on an inflatable raft takes you along the Kona Coast to explore gaping lava-tube caves, search for dolphins and turtles, and snorkel around Kealakekua Bay. The captain often throws in some Hawaiian folklore and Kona history, too. The morning trip departs at 8:15 am, the afternoon trip at 1 pm. The fee for the trips starts $94 per person. A seasonal three-hour whale-watching cruise is $65. ⊠ *Honokohau Harbor, Hwy. 19, Kailua-Kona* ☎ *808/329–3199* ⊕ *www.captainzodiac.com.*

Ⓒ **Fair Wind Cruises.** In business since 1971, Fair Wind offers morning
★ and afternoon snorkel trips. The company's custom-built 60-foot catamaran has two 15-foot waterslides, freshwater showers, and a staircase descending directly into the water for easy access. Snorkel gear is included (ask about prescription masks). These trips are great for families with small kids—there's lots of pint-size flotation equipment. Morning cruises are $129 per person; afternoon cruises are less, at $109 per person (but you're less likely to see dolphins).

The company also operates the adults-only *Hula Kai* snorkel cruise, a 55-foot luxury hydrofoil catamaran with theater-style seats for panoramic views. A five-hour morning snorkel cruise that includes a gourmet breakfast buffet and barbecue lunch is $165 for snorkelers, $196 for divers. ⊠ *Keauhou Bay, 78-7130 Kaleiopapa St., Kailua-Kona* ☎ *808/322–2788, 800/677–9461* ⊕ *www.fair-wind.com.*

SNUBA

Snuba—a cross between scuba and snorkeling—is a great choice for non-scuba divers who want to go a step beyond snorkeling. You and an instructor dive off a raft attached to a 25-foot hose and regulator; you can dive as deep as 20 feet or so. This is a good way to explore reefs a bit deeper than you can get to by snorkeling. If you need a break, the raft is ready to support you.

LESSONS

Ⓒ **Snuba Big Island.** Rendezvous with your instructor at the beach rental area near the swimming pool at King Kamehameha's Kona Beach Hotel in Kailua-Kona. A 30-minute class and a one-hour dive from the beach is $89 per person. Boat dives lasting three hours leave from Honakahou Harbor start at $145 per person. Kids aged four to seven can come along on the Snuba Doo program, which keeps them snorkeling safely on the surface. ⊠ *King Kamehameha's Kona Beach Hotel, 75-5660 Palani Rd., Kailua-Kona* ☎ *808/324–1650* ⊕ *www.snubabigisland.com.*

STAND-UP PADDLING

Stand-up paddling (or SUP for short), a sport with roots in the Hawaiian Islands, has grown popular worldwide over the past few years. It's available for all skill levels and ages, and even novice stand-up paddleboarders can get up, stay up, and have a great time paddling around a protected bay or exploring the gorgeous coastline. All you need is a large body of water, a board, and a paddle. The workout will test your core strength as well as your balance, but truly offers a unique vantage point from which to enjoy the beauty of the island and the ocean.

BEST SPOTS

Anaehoomalu Beach (A-Bay). This is a well-protected bay, so even when surf is rough on the rest of the island, it's fairly calm here. Boards are available for rent at the north end and the safe area for stand-up paddling is marked off by buoys. ✉ *Off Waikoloa Beach Dr., south of Waikoloa Beach Marriott.*

Kailua Bay and Kamakahonu Beach. The small, sandy beach that fronts the King Kamehameha Kona Beach Hotel is protected by the harbor; the water here is especially calm and teeming with ocean life. If you're more daring, you can easily paddle out of the bay and along the coast for some great scenic views. ✉ *Alii Dr., next to Kailua Pier, Kailua-Kona.*

Kealakekua Bay. The most protected deepwater bay in the islands, conditions at Kealakekua Bay are typically calm. You might see spinner dolphins (in the morning) or even the occasional whale in season. There aren't any shacks for rentals right at the bay, so you'll have to load up your board and transport it there yourself. ✉ *Bottom of Napoopoo Rd., Kailua-Kona.*

EQUIPMENT AND LESSONS

Kona Boys. If you rent from the main location above Kealakekua Bay, your rental comes with the necessary gear to transport your board to the water on your car; or visit the beach-shack location and carry your board straight from the shack to the water. Board rentals at this outfitter are $25 per hour or $65 per day. Kona Boys also offers group lessons for $75 per person, private lessons for $125 per person. ✉ *79-7539 Mamalahoa Hwy., Kealakekua* ☎ *808/328–1234, 808/329–2345* ⊕ *www.konaboys.com* ✉ *75–5660 Palani Rd., Kailua-Kona.*

Ocean Sports. At the Waikoloa Beach Marriott, this outfitter rents equipment, offers lessons, and has the perfect location for easy access to A-Bay. Stand-up paddleboard rentals are $30 per hour. Ocean Sports also has rental shacks at the Hilton Waikoloa Village, the Mauna Kea Beach Hotel, and the Waikoloa Queen's Marketplace. ✉ *Waikoloa Beach Marriott, 69-275 Waikoloa Beach Dr., Waikoloa* ☎ *808/886–6666* ⊕ *www.hawaiioceansports.com.*

SUBMARINE TOURS

☞ **Atlantis Adventures.** Want to stay dry while exploring the undersea world? Climb aboard the 48-foot *Atlantis VII* submarine anchored off Kailua Pier, across from King Kamehameha's Kona Beach Hotel in Kailua-Kona. A large glass dome in the bow and 13 viewing ports on the sides allow clear views of the aquatic world more than 100 feet down. This is a great trip for kids and nonswimmers. Each one-hour voyage costs $109 for adults. The company also operates on Oahu and Maui. ✉ *Kailua Pier, Alii Dr., Kailua-Kona* ☎ *808/326–7939, 800/548–6262* ⊕ *www.atlantisadventures.com.*

FodorsChoice
★

4

Passengers aboard the *Atlantis VII* submarine can visit the aquatic world without getting wet.

SURFING

The Big Island does not have the variety of great surfing spots found on Oahu or Maui, but it does have decent waves and a thriving surf culture. Local kids and avid surfers frequent a number of places up and down the Kona and Kohala coasts of west Hawaii. Expect high surf in winter and much calmer activity during summer. The surf scene is much more active on the Kona side.

BEST SPOTS

Pine Trees. Among the best places to catch the waves is Pine Trees. Keep in mind that this is a very popular local surf spot on an island where there aren't all that many surf spots, so be very respectful. ✉ *Off Hwy. 11, about 2 miles south of Kona Airport, Kailua-Kona.*

Kahaluu Beach Park. Slightly north of Kahaluu Beach Park, intermediate surfers brave the rocks to get out to a popular break just past the beach's calm lagoons and snorkelers. ✉ *Alii Dr., next to Sheraton Keauhou Beach Hotel, Kailua-Kona.*

Old Kona Airport State Recreation Area. The Old Kona Airport State Recreation Area is a good place for catching wave action. A couple of the island's outfitters conduct surf lessons here, as the break is far away from potentially dangerous rocks and reefs. ✉ *Kuakini Rd., Kailua-Kona.*

Honolii Cove. North of Hilo, Honolii Cove is the best surfing spot on the eastern side of the island. ✉ *Off Hwy. 19, near mile marker 4, Hilo.*

Humpback whales are visible off the coast of the Big Island between December and April.

EQUIPMENT, LESSONS, AND TOURS

Hawaii Lifeguard Surf Instructors. This certified school with experienced instructors helps novices become wave riders and offers tours that take more experienced riders to Kona's top surf spots. There's a one-hour introductory lesson ($75 for groups, $98 for individuals), but the two-hour lesson ($98 for groups, $175 for individuals) is recommended to get you ready to surf. ⊠ *75-5909 Alii Dr., Kailua-Kona* ☎ *808/324–0442, 808/936–7873* ⊕ *www.surflessonshawaii.com.*

Ocean Eco Tours Surf School. Kona's oldest surf school emphasizes the basics and specializes in beginners. All lessons are taught by certified instructors, and the school guarantees that you will surf. Lessons start at $95 per person. If you're hooked, sign up for a three-day package for $270. ⊠ *Honokohau Harbor, 74-425 Kealakehe Pkwy., Kailua-Kona* ☎ *808/324–7873* ⊕ *www.oceanecotours.com.*

Orchid Land Surf Shop. The shop has a wide variety of water sports and surf equipment for sale or rent. It stocks custom surfboards, body boards, and surf apparel. The staff also handles repairs. ⊠ *262 Kamehameha Ave., Hilo* ☎ *808/935–1533* ⊕ *www.orchidlandsurf.com.*

WHALE-WATCHING

Each winter, some two-thirds of the North Pacific humpback whale population (about 4,000–5,000 animals) migrate over 3,500 mi from the icy Alaska waters to the warm Hawaiian ocean to give birth to and nurse their calves. Recent reports indicate that the whale population is on the upswing—a few years ago one even ventured into the mouth of

Hilo Harbor, which marine biologists say is quite rare. Humpbacks are spotted here from early December through the end of April, but other species, like sperm, pilot, and beaked whales, can be seen year-round. Most ocean tour companies offer whale outings during the season, but two owner-operators *(listed below)* do it full-time. They are much more familiar with whale behavior and you're more likely to have a quality whale-watching experience. ■**TIP➔** If you take the morning cruise, you're likely to see dolphins as well. *In addition to the outfitters listed below see Snorkeling for additional outfitters that offer whale-watching cruises.*

TOURS

Blue Sea Cruises. The 46-foot *Makai* and the 70-foot *Spirit of Kona* cruise along the Kona Coast catching sight of dolphins, whales, and manta rays. Both boats have snack bars and restrooms, and the double-decker *Spirit of Kona* also has a glass bottom. Seasonal humpback whale watches are $79, dolphin cruises are $84, and night manta ray cruises are $69. Cruises last about three hours. ⊠ *Kailua-Kona Pier, 75-5660 Palani Rd., Kailua-Kona* ◻ *Box 2429, Kailua-Kona 96745* ☎ *808/331–8875* ⊕ *www.blueseacruisesinc.com.*

Captain Dan McSweeney's Year-Round Whale Watching Adventures. This is probably the most experienced small operation on the island. Captain Dan McSweeney offers three-hour trips on his double-decker, 40-foot cruise boat. In addition to humpbacks in the winter, he'll show you dolphins and some of the six other whale species that live off the Kona Coast throughout the year. Three-hour tours cost $89.50. McSweeney guarantees you'll see a whale or he'll take you out again free. ⊠ *Honokohau Harbor, 74-381 Kealakehe Pkwy., Kailua-Kona* ☎ *808/322–0028, 888/942–5376* ⊕ *www.ilovewhales.com.*

Golf, Hiking, and Outdoor Activities

WORD OF MOUTH

"We returned to the park at night to see a spectacular array of stars, the first time either of us had seen the Southern Cross as well as the red glow of [the volcano] caldera against the black night sky."

—cmstraf

Updated
by Kristina
Anderson

With the Big Island's predictably mild year-round climate, it's no wonder you'll find an emphasis on outdoor activities. After all, this is the home of the annual Ironman World Championship triathlon. Whether you're an avid hiker or a beginning bicyclist, a casual golfer or a tennis buff, you'll find plenty of land-based activities to lure you away from the sun and surf.

You can explore by bike, helicopter, ATV, or on horseback, or you can put on your hiking boots and use your own horsepower. No matter how you get around, you'll be treated to breathtaking backdrops along the Big Island's 266-mi coastline and within its 4,028 square mi (and still growing!). Aerial tours take in the latest eruption activity and lava flows, as well as the island's gorgeous tropical valleys, gulches, and coastal areas. Trips into the backcountry wilderness explore the rain forest, private ranch lands, coffee farms, and old sugar-plantation villages that offer a glimpse of Hawaii's earlier days.

Golfers will find acclaimed championship golf courses at the Kohala coast resorts—Mauna Kea Resort, Hapuna Beach Prince Hotel, Mauna Lani Resort, Waikoloa Resort, and Four Seasons at Hualalai, among others. And during the winter, if snow conditions allow, you can go skiing on top of Mauna Kea (elevation: 13,796 feet). It's a skiing experience unlike any other.

AERIAL TOURS

There's nothing quite like the aerial view of a waterfall crashing down a couple of thousand feet into cascading pools, or watching lava flow to the ocean, where clouds of steam billow into the air. You can get this bird's-eye view from a helicopter or a small plane. Most operators are reputable and fly with strict adherence to FAA safety rules. How to get the best experience for your money? ■TIP→ Before you choose

a company, be a savvy traveler and ask the right questions. What kind of aircraft do they fly? What is their safety record?

Blue Hawaiian Helicopters. The Eco-Star helicopters here live up to their reputation, with a smooth, comfortable ride and a great view from every seat. Pilots are knowledgeable about the island and offer accurate information about the sights, but are not excessively chatty. Flights into the Waimanu Valley, passing 2,500-foot cliffs and dramatic waterfalls, will take your breath away. Prices are between $396 and $495 per person (depending on the type of helicopter) for the two-hour Big Island Spectacular, which also includes the Kilauea Volcano area. ☒ *Waikoloa Heliport, Hwy. 19, Waikoloa* ☎ *808/961–5600* ⊕ *www.bluehawaiian.com.*

Iolani Air. These two- to six-passenger Gippsland and Cessna aircraft depart from both the Hilo and Kona airports, following the coastline all the way around for a view of the entire Big Island. You'll get a good view from every seat of fascinating geographic and historical points of interest. Four air tours are available, from a 60-minute tour of volcanoes and waterfalls at $175 per person to a 2½-hour full-circle tour starting at $289 per person. Highlights include the Waipio Valley and the Kona Coast. ☎ *808/329–0018, 800/538–7590* ⊕ *www.iolaniair.com.*

Fodor's Choice ★ **Paradise Helicopters.** This company offers a few great options no one else does. On landing tours, departing from Kona Airport, you can either touch down for a hike along the Hamakua Coast or for lunch in Hilo. In the six-passenger Bell 407, you can open small side windows for a little more air or to take photos without reflections on the glass. These aircraft can easily maneuver in the valleys, ensuring great views. In the four-passenger MD 500 helicopters, you can experience a very cool "doors off" adventure. Departing from the Hilo Airport, these flights allow you to feel the heat from the volcanoes. Flights start at $200 for a 50-minute flight to $495 for a three-hour landing tour. Pilots, many of whom come from Coast Guard backgrounds, are knowledgeable and personable. Free shuttles are available to and from the aiports. ☎ *808/969–7392, 866/876–7422* ⊕ *www.paradisecopters.com.*

ATV TOURS

A different way to experience the Big Island's rugged coastline and wild ranch lands is through an off-road adventure—a real backcountry experience. At higher elevations, the weather can be nippy and rainy, but views can be awesome. Protective gear is provided. Generally, you have to be 16 or older to ride your own ATV, though some outfitters allow children seven and older to be passengers.

ATV Outfitters Hawaii. These trips take in the scenic beauty of the rugged North Kohala Coast, traveling along coastal cliffs and into the forest in search of waterfalls. ATV Outfitters also offers double-seater ATVs for parents traveling with children or adults who don't feel comfortable operating their own vehicle. ☒ *Old Sakamoto Store, Hwy. 270, Kapaau* ☎ *808/889–6000, 888/288–7288* ⊕ *www.atvoutfittershawaii.com.*

Waipio Ride the Rim. This is one of the best ways to experience the extraordinary beauty at the top of the lush Waipio Valley. Fun and knowledgeable guides lead you to a gorgeous swimming pond, a lava-tube grotto, and a place to stand under a refreshing waterfall. You'll travel up to a series of lookouts where you can gaze all the way down to the black-sand beach. Bring a bathing suit and be prepared to get wet and muddy. The semi-challenging terrain offers the ideal ATV experience. Prices start at $159 per person. ⊠ *Waipio Valley Artworks Bldg., 48-5416 Kukuihaele Rd., Kukuihaele* ☎ *808/775–1450, 877/775–1450* ⊕ *www.RideTheRim.com.*

BIKING

The Big Island's biking trails and road routes range from easy to moderate coastal rides to rugged backcountry wilderness treks that will challenge the most serious cyclists. You can soak up the island's storied scenic vistas and varied geography—from tropical rain forest to rolling ranch country, from high country mountain meadows to dry lava deserts. It's dry, windy, and hot on Kona's and Kohala's coastal trails and cool, wet, and muddy in the upcountry Waimea and Volcano areas, as well as in lower Puna. There are long distances between towns and few services available in the Kau, Puna, South Kona and Kohala Coast areas, so plan accordingly for weather, water, food, and lodging before setting out.

Hawaii Cycling Club. The nonprofit Hawaii Cycling Club has tons of information on biking the Big Island. ☎ *74-5583 Luhia St., Kailua-Kona 96740* ⊕ *www.hawaiicyclingclub.com.*

BEST SPOTS

Fodor's Choice ★ **Kulani Trails.** Kulani Trails has been called the best ride in the state—if you really want to get gnarly. To reach the trailhead from the intersection of Highway 11 and Highway 19, take Highway 19 south about 4 mi, then turn right onto Stainback Highway and continue on 2½ mi, then turn right at the Waiakea Arboretum. Park near the gate. This technically demanding ride, which passes majestic eucalyptus trees, is for advanced cyclists.

Old Puna Trail. The Old Puna Trail is a 10½-mi ride through the subtropical jungle in Puna, one of the island's most isolated areas. You'll start out on a cinder road, which becomes a four-wheel-drive trail. If it's rained recently, you'll have to deal with some puddles—the first few of which you'll gingerly avoid until you give in and go barreling through the rest of them for the sheer fun of it. This is a great ride for all abilities and takes about 90 minutes. To get to the trailhead from Highway 130, take Kaloli Road to Beach Road.

EQUIPMENT AND TOURS

If you want to strike out on your own, there are several rental shops in Kailua-Kona and a couple in Waimea and Hilo. Many resorts rent bicycles that can be used around the properties. Most outfitters listed can provide a bicycle rack for your car. All offer reduced rates for rentals longer than one day.

Bike Works. This outfitter caters to cyclists of all skill levels with its rentals of deluxe road bikes, full-suspension mountain bikes, and

5

high-end triathlete bikes. Rentals start at $40 a day. ✉ *Hale Hana Centre, 74-5583 Luhia St., Kailua-Kona* ☎ *808/326–2453* ⊕ *www. bikeworkskona.com.*

Cycle Station. This shop has a variety of bikes for rent, from hybrids to racing models. Rental runs from $20 to $75 per day, and can be delivered to your hotel. ✉ *73-4976 Kamanu St., Kailua-Kona* ☎ *808/327–0087* ⊕ *www.cyclestationhawaii.com.*

Mid Pacific Wheels. This downtown shop carries a full line of bikes and related accessories. It also rents mountain bikes for exploring the Hilo area. Rentals start at $30 per day. The staff can provide information on the best places to go and what to see, do, and experience on a self-guided tour. ✉ *1133C Manono St., Hilo* ☎ *808/935–6211* ⊕ *www. midpacificwheelsllc.com.*

Volcano Bike Tours. Volcano Bike Tours takes you on a three- or five-hour bike ride through the rain forests and past the craters of Hawaii Volcanoes National Park. After a mostly downhill ride through the park, the five-hour tour ends at the Volcano Winery for a tasting at one of the country's most unique wineries. The three-hour tour costs $99, and the five-hour tour costs $129. There's also a spectacular seven-hour sunset tour that takes you to the active lava flow. ✉ *2352 Kalanianaole St., Hilo* ☎ *808/934–9199, 888/934–9199* ⊕ *www.bikevolcano.com.*

CAVING

The Kanohina Lava Tube system is about 1,000 years old and was used by the ancient Hawaiians for water collection and for shelter. More than 30 mi of these braided lava tubes have been mapped so far in the Kau District of the Big Island, near South Point. About 45 mi south of Kailua-Kona, these lava tubes are a great experience for cavers of all age levels and abilities.

Fodor'sChoice   **Kula Kai Caverns.** Embark on a fantastic adventure with expert cav-
★   ers (not "spelunkers") at Kula Kai Caverns, located near South Point. Braided lava tubes attract scientists from around the world, who come to study and map them (more than 30 mi have been mapped so far). Tours start at $15 and range from strolls along walkways in the lighted sections to down-and-dirty adventures lasting two to four hours. Tours are tailored to your group's interest and abilities, and all gear is provided. Knowledgeable guides provide great information about the caves. Advance reservations are required. ✉ *Kula Kai Estates, Lauhala at Kona Kai* ☎ *808/929–9725* ⊕ *kulakaicaverns.com.*

GOLF

For golfers, the Big Island is a big deal—starting with the Mauna Kea Golf Course, which opened in 1964 and remains one of the state's top courses. Black lava and deep blue sea are the predominant themes on the island. In the roughly 40 mi from the Kona Country Club out to the Mauna Kea Resort, nine courses are carved into sunny seaside lava plains, with four more in the hills above. Indeed, most of the Big Island's

TIPS FOR THE GREEN

Golf is golf, and Hawaii is part of the United States, but island golf nevertheless has its own quirks. Here are a few tips to make your golf experience in the Islands more pleasant.

■ Wear sunscreen, even in December. We recommend a minimum SPF of 30 and that you reapply on the 10th tee.

■ Stay hydrated. Spending four-plus hours in the sun and heat means you'll perspire away considerable fluids and energy.

■ All resort courses and many daily fee courses provide rental clubs. In many cases, they're the latest lines from Titleist, Ping, Callaway, and the like. This is true for both men and women, as well as left-handers, which means you don't have to schlep clubs across the Pacific.

■ Pro shops at most courses are stocked with balls, tees, and other accoutrements, so even if you bring your own bag, it needn't weigh a ton.

■ Come spikeless—very few Hawaii courses permit metal spikes.

■ Resort courses, in particular, offer more than the usual three sets of tees, sometimes four or five. So bite off as much or little challenge as you like. Tee it up from the tips and you'll end up playing a few 600-yard par-5s and see a few 250-yard forced carries.

■ In theory, you can play golf in Hawaii 365 days a year. But there's a reason the Hawaiian Islands are so green. Better to bring an umbrella and light jacket and not use them than to not bring them and get soaked.

■ Unless you play a muni or certain daily-fee courses, plan on taking a cart. Carts are mandatory at most courses and are included in the green fees.

best courses are concentrated along the Kona Coast, statistically the sunniest spot in Hawaii. Vertically speaking, although the majority of courses are seaside or at least near sea level, three are located above 2,000 feet, another one at 4,200 feet. This is significant because in Hawaii temperatures drop 3°F for every 1,000 feet of elevation gained.

Green Fees: Green fees listed here are the highest course rates per round on weekdays for U.S. residents. Courses with varying weekend rates are noted in the individual listings. (Some courses charge non–U.S. residents higher prices.) ■TIP→ Discounts are often available for resort guests and for those who book tee times on the Web, as well as for those willing to play in the afternoon instead of the morning. Twilight fees are also usually offered; call individual courses for information.

★ **Big Island Country Club.** Set 2,000 feet above sea level on the slopes of Mauna Kea, the Big Island Country Club is rather out of the way but well worth the drive. In 1997, Pete and Perry Dye created a gem that plays through upland woodlands—more than 2,500 trees line the fairways. On the par-5 15th, a giant tree in the middle of the fairway must be avoided with the second shot. Five lakes and a meandering natural mountain stream mean water comes into play on nine holes. The most dramatic is on the par-3 17th, where Dye creates a knockoff of his infamous 17th at the TPC at Sawgrass. ✉ *71-1420 Mamalahoa Hwy., Kailua-Kona* ☎ *808/325–5044* ⊕ *www.bigislandcountryclub.com* ⚑. *18 holes. 7075 yds. Par 72. Green fee: $70* ☞ *Facilities: Driving range, putting green, rental clubs, golf carts, pro shop, lessons.*

Hamakua Country Club. While the typical, modern 18-hole golf course requires at least 250 acres, this 9-hole, par-33 public Hamakua course fits into just 19. Compact is the word, and with several holes criss-crossing, this is BYO Hard Hat. Holes run up and down a fairly steep slope (a product of the island's plantation era) overlooking the ocean. There is no clubhouse or other amenities, and the 9th green is square, but for 15 bucks, whaddaya expect? ✉ *Hwy. 19, 41 mi north of Hilo, Honokaa* ☎ *808/775–7244* ⚑. *9 holes. 2520 yds. Par 33. Green Fee: $15* ☞ *Facilities: Putting green, golf carts, pull carts.*

Hapuna Golf Course. Hapuna's challenging play and environmental sensitivity make it one of the island's most unique courses. Designed by Arnold Palmer and Ed Seay, the course is nestled into the natural contours of the land from the shoreline to about 700 feet above sea level. There are spectacular views of mountains and sea (Maui is often visible in the distance). Holes wind through kiawe scrub, beds of jagged lava, and tall fountain grasses. Hole 12 is favored for its beautiful views and challenging play. ✉ *62-100 Kanunaoa Dr., Kamuela* ☎ *808/880–3000* ⊕ *www.princeresortshawaii.com/hapuna-golf* ⚑. *18 holes. 6875 yds. Par 72. Green fee: $125* ☞ *Facilities: Driving range, putting green, chipping green, golf carts, rental clubs, rental shoes, locker rooms, pro shop, lessons, restaurant.*

Hilo Municipal Golf Course. Hilo Muni is proof that you don't need a single sand bunker to create a challenging course. Trees and several meandering creeks are the danger here. The course, which offers views of Hilo Bay from most holes, has produced many of the island's top players over the years. Taking a divot reminds you that you're playing on a dormant volcano—the soil is dark black crushed lava. ✉ *340 Haihai St., Hilo* ☎ *808/959–7711* ⚑. *18 holes. 6325 yds. Par 71. Green Fee: $29 weekdays, $34 weekends* ☞ *Facilities: Driving range, putting green, golf carts, pull carts, rental clubs, pro shop, lessons, restaurant, bar.*

★ **Hualalai Resort.** Named for the volcanic peak that is the target off the first tee, the Nicklaus Course at Hualalai is semiprivate, open only to guests of the adjacent Four Seasons Resort Hualalai. From the forward and resort tees, this is perhaps Jack Nicklaus's most friendly course in Hawaii, but the back tees play a full mile longer. The par-3 17th plays across convoluted lava to a seaside green, and the view from the tee is so lovely, you may be tempted to just relax on the koa bench and enjoy the scenery. ✉ *100 Kaupulehu Dr., Kohala Coast* ☎ *808/325–8480* ⊕ *www. fourseasons.com/hualalai* ⚑. *18 holes. 7117 yds. Par 72. Green fee: $250 for all-day access* ☞ *Facilities: Driving range, putting green, pull carts, golf carts, rental clubs, lessons, pro shop, restaurant, bar.*

★ **Kona Country Club.** This venerable country club offers two very different tests with the aptly named Ocean and Alii Mountain courses. The Ocean Course (William F. Bell, 1967) is a bit like playing through a coconut plantation, with a few remarkable lava features—such as

Most of the Big Island's top golf courses are located on the sunny Kona Coast.

the "blowhole" in front of the par-4 13th, where seawater propelled through a lava tube erupts like a geyser. The Alii Mountain Course (front nine, William F. Bell, 1983; back nine, Robin Nelson and Rodney Wright, 1992) plays a couple of strokes tougher than the Ocean and is the most delightful split personality you may ever encounter. Both nines share breathtaking views of Keauhou Bay, and elevation change is a factor in most shots. The most dramatic view on the front nine is from the tee of the par-3 5th hole, one of the best golf vistas on the island. The back nine is links style, with less elevation change—except for the par-3 14th, which drops 100 feet from tee to green, over a lake. The routing, the sight lines and framing of greens, and the risk-reward factors on each hole make this one of the single best nines in Hawaii. ✉ *78-7000 Alii Dr., Kailua-Kona* ☎ *808/322–2595* ⊕ *www.konagolf. com* ⚑ *Ocean Course: 18 holes. 6613 yds. Par 72. Green fee: $165. Mountain Course: 18 holes. 6509 yds. Par 72. Green fee: $150* ☞ *Facilities: Driving range, putting green, golf carts, rental clubs, lessons, restaurant, bar.*

Makalei Country Club. Set on the slopes of Hualalai, at an elevation of 2,900 feet, Makalei is one of the rare Hawaii courses with bent-grass putting greens, which means they're quick and without the grain associated with Bermuda greens. Former PGA Tour official Dick Nugent (1992) designed holes that play through thick forest and open to provide wide ocean views. Elevation change is a factor on many holes, especially the par-3 15th, with the tee 80 feet above the green. In addition to fixed natural obstacles, the course is home to a number of wild peacocks and turkeys, which can make for an entertaining game. After noon, green fees dip drastically. ✉ *72-3890 Hawaii Belt Rd., Kailua-Kona* ☎ *808/325–6625* ⊕ *www.makalei.com* ⚑ *18 holes. 7091 yds. Par 72. Green fee: $85* ☞ *Facilities: Driving range, putting green, golf carts, rental clubs, pro shop, lessons, restaurant.*

★ **Mauna Kea Golf Course.** Originally opened in 1964, this golf course is one of the most revered in the state. It recently underwent a tee-to-green renovation by Rees Jones, son of the original architect, Robert Trent Jones Sr. New hybrid grasses were planted, the number of bunkers increased, and the overall yardage was expanded. The par-3 3rd hole is one of the most famous holes in the world (and one of the most photographed); you play from a cliff-side tee across a bay to a cliff-side green. Getting across the ocean is just half the battle because the third green is surrounded by seven bunkers, each one large and undulated. The course is definitely a shot-maker's paradise and follows Jones' "easy bogey/tough par" philosophy. Green fees drop after 11 am. ✉ *62-100 Kaunaoe Dr., Kamuela* ☎ *808/882–5400* ⊕ *www. maunakeagolf.com* ⚑ *18 holes 7250 yds. Par 72. Green fee: $250* ☞ *Facilities: Driving range, putting green, chipping green, golf carts, rental clubs, locker rooms, pro shop, lessons, shoe shine service, restaurant.*

Fodor's Choice
★ **Mauna Lani Resort.** Black lava flows, lush green turf, white sand, and the Pacific's multihues of blue define the 36 holes at Mauna Lani. The South Course includes the par-3 15th across a turquoise bay, one of the most photographed holes in Hawaii. But it shares "signature hole" honors with the 7th. A long par 3, it plays downhill over convoluted patches of black lava, with the Pacific immediately to the left and a dune to the right. The North Course plays a couple of shots tougher. Its most distinctive hole is the 17th, a par 3 with the green set in a lava pit 50 feet deep. The shot from an elevated tee must carry a pillar of lava that rises from the pit and partially blocks your view of the green. ✉ *68-1310 Mauna Lani Dr., Kohala Coast* ☎ *808/885–6655* ⊕ *www. maunalani.com* ⚑ *North Course: 18 holes. 6057 yds. Par 72. Green fee: $215. South Course: 18 holes. 6025 yds. Par 72. Green fee: $215* ☞ *Facilities: Driving range, putting green, golf carts, rental clubs, pro shop, lessons, restaurant, bar.*

Volcano Golf & Country Club. Just outside Volcanoes National Park—and barely a stone's throw from Halemaumau Crater—Volcano is by far Hawaii's highest course. At 4,200-feet elevation, shots tend to fly a bit farther than at sea level, even in the often cool, misty air. Because of the elevation and climate, Volcano is one of the few Hawaii courses with bent-grass putting greens. The course is mostly flat and holes play through stands of Norfolk pines, flowering *lehua* trees, and multitrunk *hau* trees. The uphill par-4 15th doglegs through a tangle of *hau*. ✉ *Pii Mauna Dr., off Hwy. 11, Volcanoes National Park* ☎ *808/967–7331* ⊕ *www.volcanogolfshop.com* ⚑ *18 holes. 6106 yds. Par 72. Green fee:*

$55 ☞ *Facilities: Driving range, putting green, golf carts, rental clubs, restaurant, bar.*

Fodor's Choice ★ **Waikoloa Beach Resort.** Robert Trent Jones Jr. built the Beach Course at Waikoloa (1981) on an old flow of crinkly *aa* lava, which he used to create holes that are as artful as they are challenging. The par-5 12th hole is one of Hawaii's most picturesque and plays through a chute of black lava to a seaside green. At the King's Course at Waikoloa (1990), Tom Weiskopf and Jay Morrish built a very links-esque track. It turns out lava's natural humps and declivities remarkably replicate the contours of seaside Scotland. But there are a few island twists—such as seven lakes. This is "option golf" as Weiskopf and Morrish provide different risk-reward tactics on each hole. Beach and King's have separate clubhouses. ✉ *600 Waikoloa Beach Dr., Waikoloa* ☎ *808/886–7888* ⊕ *www.waikoloagolf.com* ⚑ *Beach Course: 18 holes. 6566 yds. Par 70. Green fee: $135 for guests, $165 for nonguests. Kings' Course: 18 holes. 7074 yds. Par 72. Green fee: $135 for guests, $165 for nonguests.* ☞ *Facilities: Driving range, putting green, golf carts, rental clubs, lessons, restaurant, bar.*

Waikoloa Village Golf Course. Robert Trent Jones Jr., the same designer who created some of the most expensive courses on the Kohala Coast, designed this little gem, which is 20 minutes from the coast, in 1973. At a 450-foot elevation, it offers ideal playing conditions year-round. Holes run across rolling hills with sweeping mountain and ocean views. ✉ *68-1792 Melia St., Waikoloa* ☎ *808/883–9621* ⊕ *www.waikoloa.org* ⚑ *18 holes. 6230 yds. Par 72. Green fee: $83.50* ☞ *Facilities: Driving range, putting green, golf carts, rental clubs, lessons, restaurant, bar.*

WORD OF MOUTH

"You can see 'a' volcano on most of the islands; but 'the' volcano, the live one that erupts hot lava, is on the Big Island of Hawaii. You can hike out over the new lava fields, walk through the Thurston lava tube, tour Hawaii Volcanoes National Park and visitor center and visit the art studios and galleries in Volcano town." —Icuy

HIKING

Meteorologists classify the world's weather into 13 climates. Eleven are here on the Big Island, and you can experience them all by foot on the many trails that lace the island. The ancient Hawaiians cut trails across the lava plains, through the rain forests, and up along the mountain heights. Many of these paths are still in use today. Part of the King's Trail at Anaehoomalu winds through a field of lava rocks covered with prehistoric carvings called petroglyphs. Many other trails, historic and modern, crisscross the huge Hawaii Volcanoes National Park and other parts of the island. Plus, the serenity of remote beaches, such as Papakolea Beach (Green Sand Beach), is accessible only to hikers.

Department of Land and Natural Resources, State Parks Division. For information on all the Big Island's state parks, contact the Department of Land and Natural Resources, State Parks Division. ✉ *75 Aupuni St., Hilo* ☎ *808/587–0300* ⊕ *www.hawaiistateparks.org.*

BEST SPOTS

Fodor's Choice **Hawaii Volcanoes National Park.** Hawaii Volcanoes National Park is per-
★ haps the Big Island's premier area for hikers. The 150 mi of trails provide close-up views of fern and rainforest environments, cinder cones,
steam vents, lava fields, rugged coastline and current lava flow activity.
Day hikes range from easy to moderately difficult, and from one or
two hours to a full day. For a bigger challenge, consider an overnight
or multiday backcountry hike with a stay in a park cabin (available by
a remote coast, in a lush forest, or atop frigid Mauna Loa). To do so,
you must first obtain a free permit at the Kilauea Visitor Center. There
are also daily guided hikes led by knowledgeable and friendly park
rangers. ✉ *Hwy. 11, 30 mi south of Hilo* ☎ *808/985–6000* ⊕ *www.
nps.gov/havo/index.htm.*

Kekaha Kai (Kona Coast) State Park. A pair of 1½-mi-long unpaved roads
lead to the Mahaiula Beach and Kua Bay, on opposite sides of the park.
Connecting the two is the 4½-mi Ala Kahakai historic coastal trail. At
Mahaiula, you'll find picnic tables. Midway between the two white
sand beaches you can hike to the summit of Puu Kuili, a 342-foot-high
cinder cone with an excellent view of the coastline. It's dry and hot with
no drinking water, so be sure to pack sunblock and water. ✉ *Trailhead:
Hwy. 19, about 2 mi north of Keahole–Kona International Airport.*

Kealakekua Bay and Captain Cook Monument Trail. This trail is one of
South Kona's more popular moderately difficult hikes. About 100 yards
from the turnoff, the steep, loose gravel and dirt trail descends several
hundred feet across old lava flows. There are some steep switchbacks.
Shade along the upper section gives way to sun where the trail opens to
lava fields. Nearer to the bay, the trail passes through ancient Hawaiian
village ruins and by the Captain Cook Monument, a tall white obelisk
on the spot where the famed navigator was killed in 1779 in a dispute
with native Hawaiians. The bay, a protected Marine Life Conservation
District, is popular with divers and snorkelers. The 2½-mi hike is about
a three-hour round trip. The hike back up is steep and tiring, so allow
plenty of time. Park along the road. Bring sunscreen, a hat, water, and
food. ✉ *Trailhead on Napoopoo Rd., just off Hwy. 11, Captain Cook*
⊕ *hawaii.gov/dlnr/dar/coral/mlcd_kealakekua.html.*

Muliwai Trail. On the western side of mystical Waipio Valley, the Muliwai Trail leads to the back of the valley, then switchbacks up through
a series of gulches, and finally emerges at Waimanu Valley. Only very
experienced hikers should attempt the entire 18-mi trail. Completing
the trail can take two to three days of backpacking and camping, which
requires camping permits from the Division of Forestry and Wildlife
in Hilo. ✉ *Trailhead is at the end of Hwy. 240* ☎ *808/974–4221* ⊕ *ha-
waiitrails.ehawaii.gov.*

Onomea Bay Trail. Onomea Bay Trail is a short but beautiful trail packed
with stunning views of the cliffs, bays, and gulches of the Hamakua
coast on the east side of the island. The trail is just under a mile and
fairly easy, with access down to the shore if you want to dip your feet
in, although we don't recommend trying to swim in the rough waters.
Unless you pay the $15 entry fee to the nearby Botanical Garden,

Continued on page 152

HAWAII'S PLANTS 101

Hawaii is a bounty of rainbow-colored flowers and plants. The evening air is scented with their fragrance. Just look at the front yard of almost any home, travel any road, or visit any local park and you'll see a spectacular array of colored blossoms and leaves. What most visitors don't know is that many of the plants they are seeing are not native to Hawaii; rather, they were introduced during the last two centuries as ornamental plants, or for timber, shade, or fruit.

Hawaii boasts nearly every climate on the planet, excluding the two most extreme: arctic tundra and arid desert. The Islands have wine-growing regions, cactus-speckled ranchlands, icy mountaintops, and the rainiest forests on earth.

Plants introduced from around the world thrive here. The lush lowland valleys along the windward coasts are predominantly populated by non-native trees including yellow- and red-fruited **guava**, silvery-leafed **kukui**, and orange-flowered **tulip trees.**

The colorful **plumeria flower**, very fragrant and commonly used in lei making, and

the giant multicolored **hibiscus flower** are both used by many women as hair adornments, and are two of the most common plants found around homes and hotels. The umbrella-like **monkeypod tree** from Central America provides shade in many of Hawaii's parks including Kapiolani Park in Honolulu. Hawaii's largest tree, found in Lahaina, Maui, is a giant **banyan tree.** Its canopy and massive support roots cover about two-thirds of an acre. The native **ohia tree**, with its brilliant red brush-like flowers, and the **hapuu**, a giant tree fern, are common in Hawaii's forests and are also used ornamentally in gardens.

Bougainvillea	Guava	Monkeypod
Banyan	Ohia Lehua*	Tulip Tree
Plumeria	Pandanus	Hibiscus
Anthurium	Kukui	Hapuu

*endemic to Hawaii

DID YOU KNOW?

More than 2,200 plant species are found in the Hawaiian Islands, but only about 1,000 are native. Of these, 320 are so rare, they are endangered. Hawaii's endemic plants evolved from ancestral seeds arriving in the Islands over thousands of years as baggage with birds, floating on ocean currents, or drifting on winds from continents thousands of miles away. Once here, these plants evolved in isolation, creating many new species known nowhere else in the world.

Hawaii Volcanoes National Park's 150 mi of trails offer easy to moderately difficult hikes.

entering its gates (even by accident) will send one of the guards running after you to nicely but firmly point you back to the trail. ⊠ *Trailhead on Old Hawaiian Belt Rd., just before Botanical Garden* ⊕ *hawaiitrails. ehawaii.gov.*

TOURS

To get to some of the best trails and places, it's worth going with a skilled guide. Costs range from $95 to $165, and some hikes include picnic meals or refreshments, and gear, such as binoculars, ponchos, and walking sticks. The outfitters mentioned here also offer customized adventure tours.

Hawaii Forest & Trail. This locally owned and operated company has a reputation for great nature tours and eco-adventures of all kinds. The company has access to thousands of acres of restricted or private lands and employs certified guides who are experts in their fields. Try the Hakalau Forest National Wildlife Refuge Birdwatching Adventure, Kilauea Volcano Adventure, Kohala Waterfall Adventure, or the fun Kona Coffee & Craters Adventure. One of the most popular tours takes you to the top of Hawaii's tallest volcano for a sunset you'll never forget— as well as dinner and stargazing. ⊠ *74-5035B Queen Kaahahumanu Hwy., Kailua-Kona* ☎ *808/331–8505, 800/464–1993* ⊕ *www.hawaii-forest.com.*

Hawaiian Walkways. With the aid of knowledgeable guides, this company conducts several tours in unique spots—a Kona Cloud Forest botanical walk, a hike on Saddle Road between Mauna Kea and Mauna Loa, waterfall hikes and jaunts through Hawaii Volcanoes National Park—

as well as custom-designed trips. ⊠ *45-3625 Mamane St., Honokaa* ☎ *808/775–0372, 800/457–7759* ⊕ *www.hawaiianwalkways.com.*

Kapoho Kine Adventures. This outfitter offers several interesting tours of Hawaii Volcanoes National Park and surrounding areas, including a 14-hour tour that allows you to explore the region by day and see the lava at night. There is also a shorter day tour and a separate evening tour complete with a Hawaiian-style barbecue dinner. Prices range from $89 to $179 per person. ⊠ *25 Waianuinui Ave., Hilo* ☎ *808/964–1000, 866/965–9552* ⊕ *kapohokine.com.*

HORSEBACK RIDING

With its *paniolo* (cowboy) heritage and the ranches it spawned, the Big Island is a great place for equestrians. Riders can gallop through green pastures, or saunter through Waipio Valley for a taste of old Hawaii.

TOURS

Cowboys of Hawaii. Take a horseback ride at historic Parker Ranch, one of the largest privately held cattle ranches in the country and the spot where *paniolo* (Hawaiian cowboys) rode for the first time. Along the way, you might see some of the more than 5,000 head of Hereford cattle as they are driven down from the slopes of Mauna Kea. Morning and afternoon rides start at $79 per person. ⊠ *Parker Ranch, 67-133 Pukalani Rd., Waimea* ☎ *808/885–5006* ⊕ *www.cowboysofhawaii.com.*

King's Trail Rides. Take a four-hour excursion down an old Hawaiian trail to a small, uncrowded stretch of sand near Kealakekua Bay for snorkeling and lunch. A mask and snorkel is provided. The price is $135 per person. ⊠ *Hwy. 11, mile marker 111, Kealakekua* ☎ *808/323–2388* ⊕ *www.konacowboy.com.*

Naalapa Stables. This company is a good bet, especially for novice riders. The horses are well trained, and the stable is well run. You'll explore Waipio Valley, cross freshwater streams, and see waterfalls. Naalapa also offers open-range rides on the historic Kahua Ranch in North Kohala. ⊠ *Off Hwy. 240, Kukuihaele* ☎ *808/775–0419* ⊕ *www.naalapastables.com.*

Waipio Ridge Stables. Two different rides around the rim of Waipio Valley are offered—a 2½-hour trek for $85 and a 5-hour hidden-waterfall adventure (with swimming) for $165. Lunch is included. Riders meet at Waipio Valley Artworks. ⊠ *48-5416 Kukuihaele Rd., off Hwy. 240, Honokaa* ☎ *808/775–1007, 877/757–1414* ⊕ *www.waipioridgestables.com.*

HIKING BIG ISLAND TRAILS

■ Trails on the eastern or windward sides of the islands are often wet and muddy, making them slippery and unstable, so wear good hiking shoes or boots.

■ Bring plenty of water, rain protection, a hat, sunblock and a cell phone, but be aware that service is spotty in sections of the island.

■ Don't eat any unknown fruits or plants.

■ Darkness comes suddenly here, so carry a flashlight if there's a chance you'll be out after sunset.

Waipio on Horseback. Take a relaxing trek through this famous valley, where you'll visit a taro farm and enjoy the lush surroundings. Tours depart twice daily Monday through Saturday. The price is $78 per person. ⊠ *Last Chance Store, Off Hwy. 240, Kukuihaele* ☎ *808/775–7291, 877/775–7291* ⊕ *www.waipioonhorseback.com.*

JOGGING

Ironman 70.3 Hawaii. The Ironman 70.3 Hawaii Triathlon in early June begins with swimming at Hapuna Beach, then moves to biking for 56 miles on Queen Kaahumanu Highway, and finishes with a 13-mile run through paradise. ☎ *808/329–0063* ⊕ *www.ironman703hawaii.com.*

Ironman World Championship. Run annually since 1978, the Ironman World Championship is the granddaddy of all triathlons. For about two weeks in early October, Kailua-Kona takes on the vibe of an Olympic Village as 2,000 top athletes from across the globe roam the town, carbo-loading, training, and acclimating before competing in the world's premiere swim-bike-run endurance event. The competition starts at Kailua Pier with a 2.4-mi open-water swim, immediately followed by a 112-mi bicycle ride, then a 26.2-mi marathon. ☎ *808/329–0063* ⊕ *www.ironmanworldchampionship.com.*

SKIING

Where else but Hawaii can you surf, snorkel, and snow ski on the same day? In winter, the 13,796-foot Mauna Kea (Hawaiian for "white mountain") usually has snow at higher elevations—and along with that, skiing. No lifts, no manicured slopes, no faux-alpine lodges, no après-ski nightlife, but the chance to ski some of the most remote (and let's face it, unlikely) runs on the planet. Some people have even been known to use body boards as sleds, but we don't recommend it. As long as you're up there, fill your cooler with the white stuff for a snowball fight on the beach with local kids.

Ski Guides Hawaii. Christopher Langan of Mauna Kea Ski Corporation is the only licensed outfitter providing transportation, guide services, and ski equipment on Mauna Kea. Snow can fall from Thanksgiving to June, but the most likely months are February and March. The runs are fairly short, and hidden lava rocks and other dangers abound. Langan charges $450 per person for a daylong experience that includes lunch, equipment, guide service, transportation from Waimea, and a four-wheel-drive shuttle back up the mountain after each ski run. Ski or snowboard rentals are $50 per day. ⬦ *Box 1954, Kamuela 96743* ☎ *808/885–4188* ⊕ *www.skihawaii.com.*

TENNIS

Many of the island's resorts allow nonguests to play for a fee. They also rent rackets, balls, and shoes. On the Kohala Coast, try the Fairmont Orchid Hawaii, the Hilton Waikoloa Village, and Waikoloa Beach

DID YOU KNOW?

The Waipio Valley is a popular place to go horseback riding. Waipio means "curved water"; the valley is named for the Waipio River, which flows through it.

Marriott. In Kailua-Kona there's the Ohana Keauhou Beach Resort, King Kamehameha's Kona Beach Hotel, and the Royal Kona Resort.

County of Hawaii Department of Parks and Recreation. Contact the County of Hawaii Department of Parks and Recreation for information on all public courts. ⊠ *25 Aupuni St., Hilo* ☎ *808/961–8311* ⊕ *www.hawaii-county.com/directory/dir_parks.htm.*

Kailua Playground. In Kailua-Kona, you can play for free at the Kailua Playground. ⊠ *75-5794 Kuakini Hwy., Kailua-Kona.*

ZIPLINE TOURS

One of the few ways you can really see the untouched beauty of the Big Island is by flying over its lush forests, dense tree canopies, and glorious rushing waterfalls on a zipline course. You strap into a harness, get clipped to a cable and then zip, zip, zip your way through paradise. Most guide companies start you out easy on a slower, shorter line and by the end you graduate to faster, longer zips. It's an exhilarating adventure for all ages and has even been known to help some put aside their fear of heights (at least for a few minutes) to participate in the thrill ride. Check company credentials and specifics before you book to make sure your safety is their number one concern.

Big Island Eco Adventures II. This company knows ziplines—it built the first one on the Big Island. The three-hour tour takes you on eight ziplines and a 200-foot suspension bridge. You'll experience exhilarating crisscrossing thrills over the mountains and gulches of historic North Kohala, including the enormous Waianae Gulch. Along the way you get awesome views of the ocean, and, on clear days, all the way to Maui. If you are short on time, you can do the "quickie" Wiki Wiki Zip. ⊠ *55-514 Hawi Rd., Hawi* ☎ *808/889–5111* ⊕ *thebigislandzipline.com.*

Kohala Zipline. This company features nine zips, five suspension bridges, and a thrilling, above-the-canopy adventure in the forest. Designed for all ability levels, the Kohala Zipline offers plenty of safety equipment, including a dual line allowing for easy braking. You'll be hundreds of feet above the ground and feel like a pro by the time you reach the last line. Two certified guides accompany groups of no more than eight. The price includes transportation from your hotel in a six-wheel-drive, military-style vehicle. This course is especially fun for older kids. ⊠ *54-3676 Akoni Pule Hwy., Kapaau* ☎ *808/331–3620, 800/464–1993* ⊕ *www.kohalazipline.com.*

Shops and Spas

WORD OF MOUTH

"Just returned from our first visit to the Big Island. We enjoyed the town of Hawi and its art galleries and shops; good ice cream and coffee!"

—Uma

Updated
by Karen
Anderson

Residents like to complain that there isn't a lot of great shopping on the Big Island, but unless you're searching for winter coats or high-tech toys, you can find plenty to deplete your pocketbook.

Dozens of shops in Kailua-Kona offer a range of souvenirs from far-flung corners of the globe and plenty of local coffee and foodstuffs to take home to everyone you left behind. Housewares and artworks made from local materials (lava rock, coconut, koa, and milo wood) fill the shelves of small boutiques and galleries throughout the island. Upscale shops in the resorts along the Kohala Coast carry high-end clothing and accessories, as do a few boutiques scattered around the island. Galleries and gift shops, many showcasing the work of local artists, fill historic buildings in Waimea, Kainaliu, Holualoa, and Hawi. Hotel shops generally offer the most attractive and original resort wear but, as with everything else at resorts, the prices run higher than elsewhere on the island.

High prices are entirely too common at the island's resort spas, but a handful of truly unique experiences are worth every penny. Beyond the resorts, the Big Island is also home to independent massage therapists and day spas that offer similar treatments for lower prices, albeit usually in a slightly less luxurious atmosphere. In addition to the obvious relaxation benefits of any spa trip, the Big Island's spas have done a fantastic job incorporating local traditions and ingredients into their menus. Massage artists work with coconut or *kukui* (candlenut) oil, while hot-stone massages are conducted with lava stones, and ancient healing techniques such as *lomilomi*—a massage technique with firm, constant movement—are a staple at every island spa.

SHOPS

In general, stores on the Big Island open at 9 or 10 am and close by 6 pm. Hilo's Prince Kuhio Plaza stays open until 8 pm on weekdays and 9 pm on Friday and Saturday. In Historic Kona Village, most shopping plazas geared to tourists remain open until 9 pm. Grocery stores such as KTA Superstore are open until 11 pm.

KAILUA-KONA

SHOPPING CENTERS

Coconut Grove Marketplace. This meandering labyrinth of buildings includes cafés, restaurants, boutiques, a frozen-yogurt shop, and several art galleries. At night, locals gather to watch the outdoor sand volleyball games held in the courtyard or to grab a couple of beers at one of several sports bars. Jack's Diving Locker offers gear and scuba lessons. ✉ *75-5795–75-5825 Alii Dr.*

Crossroads Shopping Center. This in-town shopping center includes a Safeway with an excellent deli section for on-the-go snacks, as well a Wal-Mart, where visitors can find affordable Hawaiian souvenirs including discounted Kona coffee and macadamia nuts. ✉ *75-1000 Henry St.* ☎ *808/329–4822.*

Kaloko Light Industrial Park. This large retail complex includes Costco—the best place to stock up on food if you're staying in a condo for a week or more. For lunch, stop at Ceviche Dave's and enjoy some fresh fish. ✉ *Off Hwy. 19 and Hina Lani St., near Keahole-Kona International Airport.*

Keauhou Shopping Center. About 5 mi south of Kailua Village, this shopping center includes KTA Superstore, Longs Drugs, Kona Stories bookstore, and a multiplex movie theater. Kenichi Pacific, a great sushi restaurant, and Peaberry & Galette, a café that serves excellent crepes, are favorite eateries that have been joined by Bianelli's Pizza and Sam Choy's Kai Lanai. You can also grab a quick bite at Los Habaneros or L&L Hawaiian Barbecue. ✉ *78-6831 Alii Dr.* ☎ *808/322–3000* ⊕ *www.keauhoushoppingcenter.com.*

King Kamehameha Shopping Mall. Around the corner from King Kamehameha's Kona Beach Hotel, this neighborhood mall includes the Bangkok House, which serves up Thai cuisine. There's also a hair salon and women's clothier. ✉ *75-5626 Kuakini Hwy.*

Kona Commons. This new center features big-box retailers like Sports Authority (for snorkel and swim gear), as well as an array of fast-food standbys like Dairy Queen, Subway, Taco Del Mar, and Panda Express. The best-kept secret is Ultimate Burger, featuring locally produced beef and delicious homemade fries. Take the kids to Genki Sushi, where fresh sushi is delivered to patrons via a conveyor belt. Relocated from its previous site in Kailua Village, Kona Wine Market offers the best selection of premium wines, liquors, and spirits in Kona, along with some gourmet and gift items. ✉ *75-5450 Makala Blvd., Kailua-Kona.*

Kona Inn Shopping Village. Originally a hotel, the Kona Inn was built in 1928 to woo a new wave of wealthy travelers. As newer condos and resorts opened along the Kona and Kohala coasts, it was transformed into a low-rise mall with dozens of clothing boutiques, art galleries, gift shops, and island-style eateries. Broad lawns with coconut trees on the ocean side provide a lovely setting for an afternoon picnic. The open-air Kona Inn restaurant is a local favorite for evening mai tais. ✉ *75-5744 Alii Dr.*

6

Kona Marketplace. On the *mauka* (mountain) side of Alii Drive, this tourist destination in the heart Kailua Village includes galleries, clothing shops, souvenirs, and a dive-y karaoke bar, Sam's Hideaway. The best-kept secret here is You Make the Roll sushi shop, offering shaded outdoor seating and affordable sushi to go. ⊠ *75-5744 Alii Dr.*

Makalapua Center. This shopping center attracts islanders for the great bargains at Kmart, plus island-influenced clothing, jewelry, and housewares at the upscale Macy's. There's also one of the island's largest movie theaters here. ⊠ *Kamakaeha Ave. at Hwy. 19.*

ARTS AND CRAFTS

★ **Antiques and Orchids.** Housed in a historic building, this shop lives up to its name by offering a comprehensive collection of antiques and Hawaiiana interspersed with orchids of assorted colors and varieties. If you're on your way to Volcano, stop to enjoy a cup of Kona coffee served in antique china cups at the store's quaint coffee shop. ⊠ *81-6224 Mamalahoa Hwy., Captain Cook* ☏ *808/323–9851.*

Fodor's Choice **Eclectic Craftsman.** This longtime favorite occupies a beautiful space at
★ the Kona Inn Shopping Village. Brimming with handmade Hawaiian collectibles, the boutique focuses on local art and crafts. The 60 Big Island artists represented here include woodworker Craig Nichols and renowned painter Avi Kiraty. Affordable gifts range from bookmarks to salad servers to wine-bottle toppers. You won't find these items anywhere else, and they're all made in Hawaii. ⊠ *Kona Inn Shopping Village, 75-5744 Alii Dr., Kailua-Kona* ☏ *808/334–0562.*

Fodor's Choice **Hula Lamps of Hawaii.** Located in Kailua-Kona, this one-of-a-kind shop
★ features the bronze creations of Charles Moore. Inspired by the vintage hula-girl lamps of the 1930s, Moore creates art pieces sought by visitors and residents alike. Mix and match with an array of hand-painted lamp shades. ⊠ *74-5599 Luhia St., Unit F-5, Kailua-Kona* ☏ *808/326–9583.*

Just Ukes. As the name suggests, this place is all about ukuleles—from music books to T-shirts to accessories like cases and bags. Located at Kona Inn Shopping Village, this independently owned shop carries a variety of ukuleles ranging from low-priced starter instruments to high-end models made of koa and mango. There are branches in Kainaliu and at the Shops at Mauna Lani. ⊠ *Kona Inn Shopping Village, 75-5744 Alii Dr., Kailua-Kona* ☏ *808/769–5101.*

BOOKSTORES

Kona Stories Bookstore. This is the destination for more than 10,000 titles. The shop also sells Hawaiiana, children's books and toys, and whimsical gifts. Special events, such as readings, are held weekly. ⊠ *Keauhou Shopping Center, 78-6831 Alii Dr., Kailua-Kona* ☏ *808/324–0350.*

CLOTHING AND SHOES

★ **Hilo Hattie.** The well-known clothier matches his-and-her aloha wear and carries a huge selection of casual clothes, local art, books, music, jewelry, and souvenirs. ■TIP→ Call for free transportation from nearby hotels. ⊠ *75-5597 Palani Rd.* ☏ *808/329–7200* ⊕ *www.hilohattie.com.*

Honolua Surf Company. Surfer chic, compliments of Roxy, Volcom, and the like, is on offer here for both men and women. This is a great place to look for a bikini or board shorts, or to pick up a cool, casual T-shirt or beautifully embroidered sweat jacket. A second location at the Waikoloa Beach Resort focuses on *wahine* (women's) apparel. ⊠ *Kona Inn Shopping Village, 75-5744 Alii Dr.* ☎ *808/329–1001* ⊕ *www. honoluasurf.com.*

Paradise Found. This reputable shop carries contemporary silk and rayon clothing for women. Located in the upcountry town of Kainaliu, there's also a branch at Keauhou Shopping Center. ⊠ *79-740 Mamalahoa Hwy., Kainaliu* ☎ *808/322–2111.*

FOOD AND WINE

Kailua Candy Company. This chocolate company has been satisfying sweet tooths for more than three decades with decadent desserts and sinful bites of chocolate heaven. Many truffles and candies incorporate local ingredients (passion-fruit truffles and chocolate-covered mango—yum). There are also a variety of cheesecakes and mousse cakes that will melt in your mouth. Of course, tasting is part of the fun. Through a glass wall you can watch the chocolate artists at work Monday to Saturday from 9 to 5. ⊠ *Kamanu St. and Kauholo St.* ☎ *808/329–2522* ⊕ *www. kailuacandy.com.*

Kona Coffee & Tea Company. Its location across from the Honokohau Harbor makes this family-owned coffee company's retail outlet a good bet for some easy gourmet gift shopping—or just a coffee or tea stop. Try different roasts or a selection of flavored coffees from the coffee bar, and shop for other Hawaiian-made treats, from honey and jams to chocolate-covered coffee beans. The shop is behind the Tesoro gas station. ⊠ *74-5035 Queen Kaahumanu Hwy., 4 mi south of the airport, Kailua-Kona* ☎ *808/329–6577* ⊕ *www.konacoffeeandtea.com.*

Kona Wine Market. Kona's only wine market carries both local and imported varietals, gourmet foods, and local products (coffee or macadamia nuts, for example). As a bonus, the shop will deliver wine or any other product to your hotel. ⊠ *Kona Commons, 74-5450 Makala Blvd.* ☎ *808/329–9400* ⊕ *www.konawinemarket.com.*

GALLERIES

Pacific Fine Art. One of the oldest and largest galleries in Kona, Pacific Fine Art represents 42 artists from across the globe. The gallery features everything from original oil and acrylic paintings to limited editions, sculptures, glass, and raku ceramic pieces. ⊠ *Kona Inn Shopping Village, 75-5744 Alii Dr.* ☎ *808/329–5009.*

MARKETS

Alii Gardens Marketplace. This cluster of about 50 vendor stalls has beautiful tropical flowers, produce, coffee, jewelry, clothing, and even ukuleles. It's open Wednesday to Sunday 9 to 5. ⊠ *75-6129 Alii Dr., 1½ mi south of Kona Inn Shopping Village.*

Keauhou Farmers' Market. This cheerful market is the place to go on Saturday morning, and for good reason: live music, plus local produce (much of it organic), goat cheese, honey, meat, flowers, coffee, and macadamia nuts. Be sure to try Earthly Delight's fresh-baked pastries. Sample Lotus Cafe's savory breakfast offerings and fresh-squeezed

6

sugarcane juice. ⊠ *Keauhou Shopping Center, 78-6831 Alii Dr.* ⊕ *www. keauhoufarmersmarket.com.*

Kona Inn Farmers Market. An awesome flower vendor creates custom arrangements while you wait at this touristy farmers' market. A glass artist offers nice works of fine art. Here you can find the best prices on fresh produce anywhere in Kona. The market is held in the parking lot at the corner of Hualalai Drive and Alii Drive, Wednesday to Sunday from 7 to 3. ⊠ *75-7544 Alii Dr.*

Kona International Market. Vendors come from other islands to sell fresh flowers, local produce, handmade crafts, and random collectibles at this open-air tourist destination. It's open daily 9 to 5. There's also a shaded food court. Be sure to check out Mike's Just Barbecuing for fantastic pulled pork and brisket, slow-cooked over kiawe wood for a savory flavor. ⊠ *Luhia St.* ⊕ *www.konainternationalmarket.com.*

THE KONA COAST

ARTS AND CRAFTS

★ **Kimura's Lauhala Shop.** Originally a general store built in 1914, this shop features handmade products crafted by local weavers. Among the offerings are hats, baskets, containers, and mats, many of which are woven by the proprietors. Owner Alfreida Kimura-Fujita was born in the house behind the shop, and her daughter Renee is also an accomplished weaver. ⊠ *77-996 Mamalahoa Hwy., Holualoa* ☎ *808/324–0053.*

GALLERIES

Cliff Johns Gallery. Woodworker Cliff Johns can often be found on the front porch of his cool gallery in the heart of Holualoa Village, chatting with fellow artists or working on a new piece. The gallery features an array of works by Big Island artists, and an inventory of wood scultures, paintings, furniture, and other crafts that's decidedly different from the standard fare. ⊠ *76-5936 Mamalahoa Hwy., Holualoa* ☎ *808/322–6611.*

Holualoa Gallery. In the quaint village of Holualoa, this is one of several excellent galleries that occupy the narrow street. The gallery carries stunning contemporary *raku* pottery, original paintings by local artists, and other collectibles, including owner Matt Lovein's famous Wish Keepers ceramic sculptures. ⊠ *76-5921 Mamalahoa Hwy., Holualoa* ☎ *808/322–8484* ⊕ *www.lovein.com.*

THE KOHALA COAST

SHOPPING CENTERS

Kawaihae Harbor Center. This oceanfront shopping plaza houses the exquisite Harbor Gallery, which represents more than 150 Big Island artists. Take a look inside before or after your meal at the acclaimed Cafe Pesto, Kohala Burger and Taco, or Kawaihae Kitchen Sushi and Take-Out. Also here are Mountain Gold Jewelers, the Kawaihae Deli, and Kohala Divers. ⊠ *Hwy. 270, Kawaihae.*

Kings' Shops at Waikoloa Beach Resort. Here you can find fine stores such as Under the Koa Tree, with its upscale gift items crafted by artisans, along with such high-end chains as Coach, Tiffany, L'Occitane, and Louis Vuitton. Gourmet offerings include Merriman's Market Cafe, Roy's Waikoloa Bar & Grill, and the Eddie Aikau Restaurant and Surf Museum. Oahu-based Martin and MacArthur joined the tenant roster in late 2011, featuring koa furniture and fine accessories. ✉ *Waikoloa Beach Resort, 250 Waikoloa Beach Dr., Waikoloa* ☎ *808/886–8811* ⊕ *www.waikoloabeachresort.com.*

The Shops at Mauna Lani. This best part about this complex is its roster of restaurants, including Tommy Bahama's Tropical Café, Ruth's Chris Steakhouse, and Monstera. The boutiques are a bit overpriced, but you can find tropical apparel at Jams World, high-end housewares at Oasis, and original art at Lahaina Galleries and the Third Dimension Gallery. Kids love the movie theater, with the first "4-D" screens in Hawaii. ✉ *68-1330 Mauna Lani Dr., Kohala Coast* ☎ *808/885–9501* ⊕ *www. shopsatmaunalani.com.*

Waikoloa Queens' Marketplace. The largest shopping complex on the Kohala Coast, Queens' Marketplace houses several clothing shops, a jewelry store, a gallery, several gift shops, a food court, and a few restaurants, including Sansei Seafood Restaurant & Sushi Bar and Romano's Macaroni Grill. Island Gourmet Markets is a 20,000-square-foot grocery store. The marketplace sits adjacent to a performing arts amphitheater. ✉ *Waikoloa Beach Resort, 201 Waikoloa Beach Dr., Waikoloa* ☎ *808/886–8822* ⊕ *www.waikoloabeachresort.com.*

ARTS AND CRAFTS

Elements Jewelry & Fine Crafts. John Flynn showcases his exquisite jewelry pieces from his shop in Hawi. Look for the delicate silver lei and gold waterfalls. The shop also carries carefully chosen gifts, including unusual ceramics, paintings, prints, and glass items. ✉ *55-3413 Akoni Pule Hwy., Hawi* ☎ *808/889–0760* ⊕ *www.elementsjewelryandcrafts. com.*

Hawaiian Quilt Collection. The Hawaiian quilt is a work of art that is prized and passed down through generations. At this store you find everything from hand-quilted purses and bags to wall hangings and blankets. You can even get a take-home kit and make your very own Hawaiian quilt, if you have the time. ✉ *Waikoloa Queens' Marketplace, 201 Waikoloa Beach Dr., Waikoloa* ☎ *808/886–0494* ⊕ *www. hawaiianquilts.com.*

Island Pearls. This boutique carries a wide selection of fine pearl jewelry, including Tahitian black pearls, South Sea white and golden pearls, and chocolate Tahitian pearls. Also look for fresh-water pearls in the shell. Prices are high but you're paying for quality and beauty. ✉ *Waikoloa Queens' Marketplace, 201 Waikoloa Beach Dr., Waikoloa* ☎ *808/886–4817* ⊕ *www.waikoloabeachresort.com.*

Local Lizard & Friends. With their buggy eyes and scaly skin, geckos strike many people as creepy—but not the owners of this store! Local Lizard & Friends rejoices in these pint-size tropical houseguests with a wide variety of gecko-themed clothing, toys, and accessories—the perfect gift for the kids back home. ⊠ *Waikoloa Queens' Market-place, 201 Waikoloa Beach Dr., Waikoloa* ☎ *808/886–8900* ⊕ *www. waikoloabeachresort.com.*

CLOTHING AND SHOES

As Hawi Turns. This North Kohala shop, housed in the historic 1932 Toyama Building, adds a sophisticated touch to resort wear with items made of hand-painted silk in tropical designs by local artists. There are vintage and secondhand treasures, jewelry, and handmade ukuleles by David Gomes. ⊠ *55-3412 Akoni Pule Hwy., Hawi* ☎ *808/889–5023.*

Blue Ginger. The Waikoloa branch of this 25-year fashion veteran offers really sweet matching aloha outfits for the entire family. ⊠ *Waikoloa Queens' Marketplace, 201 Waikoloa Beach Dr., Waikoloa* ☎ *808/886–0022* ⊕ *www.blueginger.com.*

Cinnamon Girl. Popular for its original print dresses, skirts, and tops for women and girls, this store's feminine, flirty outfits are all designed in Hawaii and offer a contemporary twist on traditional "aloha" wear. In addition to clothing, the boutique carries jewelry, hats, slippers, stuffed animals, and other trinkets and toys. ⊠ *Kings' Shops at Waikoloa Beach Resort, 250 Waikoloa Beach Dr., Waikoloa* ☎ *808/886–0241* ⊕ *www. cinnamongirl.com.*

Exclusive Designs. Everything from the traditional to the contemporary can be found here when it comes to Hawaiian-style apparel. The shop offers options for casual, resort, and evening, as well as swimwear for women. Aloha styles are available for infants, children, men, and women. ⊠ *Waikoloa Queens' Marketplace, 201 Waikoloa Beach Dr., Waikoloa* ☎ *808/886–0350* ⊕ *www.waikoloabeachresort.com.*

Persimmon. This darling little boutique that's stocked with trendy women's clothing from lines such as Three Dots, Trinity, Sky, Michael Stars, Hard Tail, and Zen Knits also carries fantastic purses imported from Indonesia, as well as locally made jewelry. Other gift items include funky stationery and cards, and island-themed bath and body products. ⊠ *Waikoloa Queens' Marketplace, 201 Waikoloa Beach Dr., Waikoloa* ☎ *808/886–0303* ⊕ *www.persimmonboutique.com.*

Reyn's. Reyn Spooner's clothing has been well known throughout Hawaii since 1959. The store offers aloha shirts for both men and boys, men's shorts, and some dresses for women and girls. The aloha shirts, by the way, are high quality—and high price. ⊠ *Waikoloa Queens' Marketplace, 201 Waikoloa Beach Dr., Waikoloa* ☎ *808/886–1162* ⊕ *www.reyns.com.*

GALLERIES

Ackerman Fine Art Gallery. This gallery is truly a family affair. Painter Gary Ackerman's daughter, Alyssa, and her husband, Ronnie, run the gallery that showcases several family members' art. Don't miss the fine and varied collection of gifts for sale in their side-by-side gallery, café, and gift shop near the King Kamehameha statue. ⊠ *54-3897 Akoni Pule Hwy., Kapaau* ☎ *808/889–5971* ⊕ *www.ackermangalleries.com.*

Harbor Gallery. This venerable gallery has been enticing visitors for more than 20 years with a vast collection of paintings and sculptures by

DID YOU KNOW?

A hot-stone massage with lava rocks and coconut oil is the perfect way to pamper yourself on the Big Island. The only thing that makes a massage better is enjoying it at an oceanfront spa.

more than 150 Big Island artists. There are also antique maps and prints, stone artifacts, wooden bowls, paddles, koa furniture, jewelry, and glasswork. ⊠ *Kawaihae Harbor Center, 61-3665 Akoni Pule Hwy., Kawaihae* ☎ *808/882–1510.*

Rankin Gallery. Watercolorist and oil painter Patrick Louis Rankin showcases his own work in his shop in a restored plantation store next to the bright-green Chinese community and social hall, on the way to Pololu Valley. The building sits right on the road at the curve, in the Palawa *ahupuaa* (land division) near Kapaau. ⊠ *53-4380 Akoni Pule Hwy., Kapaau* ☎ *808/889–6849* ⊕ *www.patricklouisrankin.net.*

WAIMEA

SHOPPING CENTERS

Parker Ranch Center. With a snazzy ranch-style motif, this shopping hub includes a supermarket, some great local eateries, a coffee shop, natural foods store, and some clothing boutiques. The Parker Ranch Store and Parker Ranch Visitor Center and Museum are also here, and the Kahilu Center next door hosts plays and musical entertainment most nights. Check out Village Burgers and the Liliokoi Cafe for delicious and affordable meals. ⊠ *67-1185 Mamalahoa Hwy.* ⊕ *www.parkerranchcenterads.com.*

Parker Square. Browse the boutiques here, where you may find books and beads at Sweet Wind, locally crafted gold jewelry at Kamuela Goldsmiths, or salads, sandwiches, and Kona coffee at Waimea Coffee Company. Although Gallery of Great Things is the center's star attraction, Waimea General Store is packed with cool Hawaiian collectibles, books, cookware, and designer toiletries. ⊠ *65-1279 Kawaihae Rd.*

GALLERIES

Gallery at Bamboo. Inside Bamboo, one of the island's favorite eateries, this gallery seduces visitors with elegant koa-wood furniture pieces. It also has a wealth of gift items such as boxes, jewelry, and even aloha shirts. ⊠ *Hwy. 270, Hawi* ☎ *808/889–1441* ⊕ *www.bamboorestaurant.info.*

Fodor'sChoice
★
Gallery of Great Things. At this Parker Square shop, you might lose yourself exploring the treasure trove of fine art and collectibles in every price range. For almost three decades, the gallery has represented hundreds of local artists and has provided a low-key, unhurried atmosphere for customers. The "things" include: hand-stitched quilts, ceramic sculptures, vintage kimonos, original paintings, koa-wood furniture, etched glassware, Niihau shell lei, and feather art by Beth McCormick. ⊠ *65-1279 Kawaihae Rd.* ☎ *808/885–7706.*

Harbor Gallery. Though it carries some of the usual ocean-scene schlock, the Harbor Gallery has one of the better and more unique selections of art on the island. Expect to find fine art, furniture, and decorative pieces made with koa and other native woods. ⊠ *Kawaihae Harbor Center, Hwy. 270, Kawaihae* ☎ *808/882–1510* ⊕ *www.harborgallery.biz.*

Wishard Gallery. A Big Island–born artist whose verdant landscapes and *paniolo* (cowboy)-themed paintings have become iconic throughout the Islands, Harry Wishard's gallery at Parker Ranch Center showcases

Continued on page 170

ALL ABOUT LEI

Lei brighten every occasion in Hawaii, from birthdays to bar mitzvahs to baptisms. Creative artisans weave nature's bounty—flowers, ferns, vines, and seeds—into gorgeous creations that convey an array of heartfelt messages: "Welcome," "Congratulations," "Good luck," "Farewell," "Thank you," "I love you." When it's difficult to find the right words, a lei expresses exactly the right sentiment.

WHERE TO BUY THE BEST LEI

Florists **Ilima Flowers** (75-5660 Kopiko St., Kailua-Kona 808/769-5005); **Island Orchard Florist** (75-6082 Alii Dr., Kailua-Kona, 808/326-2266); and **Kona Flower Shoppe** (73-4273 Hulikoa Dr., Kailua-Kona, 808/329-0505) carry lei. Lei stands at the Kona and Hilo airports sell a surprisingly nice assortment of lei at reasonable prices. KTA, Safeway, and Costco also sell lei, but they tend to stick to "basics" like plumeria, orchid or tuberose.

LEI ETIQUETTE

■ To wear a closed lei, drape it over your shoulders, half in front and half in back. Open lei are worn around the neck, with the ends draped over the front in equal lengths.

■ Pikake, ginger, and other sweet, delicate blossoms are "feminine" lei. Men opt for cigar, crown flower, and ti leaf, which are sturdier and don't emit as much fragrance.

■ Lei are always presented with a kiss, a custom that supposedly dates back to World War II when a hula dancer fancied an officer at a U.S.O. show. Taking a dare from members of her troupe, she took off her lei, placed it around his neck, and kissed him on the cheek.

■ You shouldn't wear a lei before you give it to someone else. Hawaiians believe the lei absorbs your *mana* (spirit); if you give your lei away, you'll be giving away part of your essence.

ORCHID

Growing wild on every continent except Antarctica, orchids—which range in color from yellow to green to purple—comprise the largest family of plants in the world. There are more than 20,000 species of orchids, but only three are native to Hawaii—and they are very rare. The pretty lavender vanda you see hanging by the dozens at local lei stands has probably been imported from Thailand.

MAILE

Maile, an endemic twining vine with a heady aroma, is sacred to Laka, goddess of the hula. In ancient times, dancers wore maile and decorated hula altars with it to honor Laka. Today, "open" maile lei usually are given to men. Instead of ribbon, interwoven lengths of maile are used at dedications of new businesses. The maile is untied, never snipped, for doing so would symbolically "cut" the company's success.

ILIMA

Designated by Hawaii's Territorial Legislature in 1923 as the official flower of the island of Oahu, the golden ilima is so delicate it lasts for just a day. Five to seven hundred blossoms are needed to make one garland. Queen Emma, wife of King Kamehameha IV, preferred ilima over all other lei, which may have led to the incorrect belief that they were reserved only for royalty.

PLUMERIA

This ubiquitous flower is named after Charles Plumier, the noted French botanist who discovered it in Central America in the late 1600s. Plumeria ranks among the most popular lei in Hawaii because it's fragrant, hardy, plentiful, inexpensive, and requires very little care. Although yellow is the most common color, you'll also find plumeria lei in shades of pink, red, orange, and "rainbow" blends.

PIKAKE

Favored for its fragile beauty and sweet scent, pikake was introduced from India. In lieu of pearls, many brides in Hawaii adorn themselves with long, multiple strands of white pikake. Princess Kaiulani enjoyed showing guests her beloved pikake and peacocks at Ainahau, her Waikiki home. Interestingly, pikake is the Hawaiian word for both the bird and the blossom.

KUKUI

The kukui (candlenut) is Hawaii's state tree. Early Hawaiians strung kukui nuts (which are quite oily) together and burned them for light; mixed burned nuts with oil to make an indelible dye; and mashed roasted nuts to consume as a laxative. Kukui nut lei may not have been made until after Western contact, when the Hawaiians saw black beads from Europe and wanted to imitate them.

his original oils, plus works by such local artists as Kathy Long, Tai Lake, and Lynn Capell. ✉ *67-1185 Mamalahoa Hwy., Waimea* ☎ *808/937–8772.*

FOOD AND WINE

Kamuela Liquor Store. From the outside it doesn't look like much, but this shop sells the best selection of spirits, wines, and gourmet foods on the island. Wine-and-cheese tastings take place Friday afternoons—the store offers an extensive selection of artisanal cheeses from around the world, including France, Italy, Spain, England, Switzerland, and Wales. Favorites like pâté and duck mousse round out the inventory, and everything is priced within reason. ✉ *64-1010 Mamalahoa Hwy., Waimea* ☎ *808/885–4674.*

THE HAMAKUA COAST

ARTS AND CRAFTS

Glass from the Past. The best place to shop for a quirky gift or just to poke around, Glass from the Past is a truly unique store chock-full of antiques, vintage clothing, a colorful assortment of old bottles, and ephemera. ✉ *28-1672 Old Mamalahoa Hwy., Honomu* ☎ *808/963–6449.*

GALLERIES

Waipio Valley Artworks. In this remote gallery you can find finely crafted wooden bowls, koa furniture, paintings, and jewelry—all made by local artists. There's also a great little café where you can pick up a sandwich or ice cream before descending into Waipio Valley. ✉ *Off Hwy. 240, Kukuihaele* ☎ *808/775–0958* ⊕ *www.waipiovalleyartworks.com.*

Woodshop Gallery. Run by local artists Peter and Jeanette McLaren, this Honomu gallery showcases their woodwork and photography collections along with beautiful ceramics, woodwork, photography, glass, and paintings from other Big Island artists. The McLarens also serve up plate lunches, shave ice, homemade ice cream, and espresso to hungry tourists in the adjoining café. Their shop next door, called Same-Same, But Different, features made-in-Hawaii clothing and small gifts. The historic building still has a soda fountain dating from 1935. ✉ *28-1692 Old Government Rd., Honomu* ☎ *808/963–6363* ⊕ *www. woodshopgallery.com.*

HILO

SHOPPING CENTERS

Hilo Shopping Center. This shopping plaza encloses 40 shops, including and Lanky's Pastries and Island Naturals Market and Deli. Restaurants include Happy Valley Seafood, Sunlight Cafe, and Restaurant Niwa. You'll also find everying from a day spa to a pharmacy to a trendy boutique. There's plenty of free parking. ✉ *345 Kekuanaoa St., at Kilauea Ave.*

Prince Kuhio Plaza. Hilo's most comprehensive mall, Prince Kuhio Plaza is an indoor shopping center where you'll find entertainment and dining options including KFC, Kuhio Grille, Hot Dog on a Stick, Cinnabon, and the Big Island's only IHOP. Grab a bite at Maui Tacos before heading to the multiplex, stadium-seating movie theater, or drop the kids off at the arcade (located near the food court) while you browse the stores. ✉ *111 E. Puainako St., at Hwy. 11* ☎ *808/959–3555* ⊕ *www. princekuhioplaza.com.*

ARTS AND CRAFTS

Dan DeLuz's Woods. Master bowl-turner Dan DeLuz creates works of art from 50 types of exotic wood grown on the Big Island. The shop features a variety of items—from picture frames to jewelry boxes—made from koa, monkeypod, mango, kiawe, and other fine local hardwoods. ✉ *17-4003 Ahu Ahu Pl., Kurtistown* ☎ *808/968–6607.*

Most Irresistible Shop. This place lives up to its name by stocking unique gifts from around the Pacific, be it pure Hawaiian ohia lehua honey, kau coffee, or tinkling wind chimes. ✉ *256 Kamehameha Ave.* ☎ *808/935–9644.*

BOOKSTORES

Basically Books. More than a bookstore, this bay-front shop stocks one of Hawaii's largest selections of maps, including topographical and relief maps. You'll find books about Hawaii, including great choices for children. It also has the largest selection of Hawaiian music in Hilo. ✉ *160 Kamehameha Ave.* ☎ *808/961–0144, 800/903–6277* ⊕ *www. basicallybooks.com.*

CLOTHING AND SHOES

Fodor's Choice
★ **Hilo Hattie.** The east-coast outlet of the well-known clothier is slightly smaller than its Kailua-Kona cousin, but offers plenty of the same his-and-her aloha wear, casual clothes, slippers, jewelry, and souvenirs. ✉ *Prince Kuhio Plaza, 111 E. Puainako St.* ☎ *808/961–3077* ⊕ *www. hilohattie.com.*

★ **Sig Zane Designs.** This acclaimed boutique sells distinctive island wearables with bold colors and motifs designed by the legendary Sig Zane, well-known for his artwork honoring native flora and fauna. All apparel is handcrafted in Hawaii and is found nowhere else. ✉ *122 Kamehameha Ave.* ☎ *808/935–7077* ⊕ *www.sigzane.com.*

FOOD

★ **Big Island Candies.** A local legend in the cookie- and chocolate-making business, Big Island Candies is a must-see if you have a sweet tooth. Enjoy a free cookie sample and a cup of Kona coffee as you watch sweets being made through a plate-glass window. Big Island Candies has a long list of interesting and tasty products, but it is best known for its chocolate-dipped shortbread cookies. ✉ *585 Hinano St.* ☎ *808/935–8890* ⊕ *www.bigislandcandies.com.*

Two Ladies Kitchen. This hole-in-the-wall confections shop has made a name for itself thanks to its pillowy *mochi* (Japanese rice pounded into a sticky paste and molded into shapes). The proprietors are best known for their huge ripe strawberries wrapped in a white mochi covering. These won't last as long as a box of chocolates—most mochi items are only good for two or three days. To guarantee you get your fill, call and place your order ahead of time. ✉ *274 Kilauea Ave.* ☎ *808/961–4766* ⏱ *Closed Sun.–Tues.*

6

HOME DECOR

Dragon Mama. Step into this popular downtown Hilo spot to find authentic Japanese fabrics, futons, and antiques, along with a limited but elegant selection of clothing, sleepwear, and slippers for women. Handmade comforters, pillows, and futon pads are made of natural fibers. ⊠ *266 Kamehameha Ave.* ☏ *808/934–9081* ⊕ *www.dragon mama.com.*

WORD OF MOUTH

"My husband an I recently traveled to Kona with our best friends and we had a terrific experience at Mamalahoa Hot Tubs! We booked massages for the four of us and we soaked in the hot tubs for ½ hour before our massages."
—christawallis

MARKETS

★ **Hilo Farmers Market.** The 200 vendors here sell a profusion of tropical flowers, locally grown produce, aromatic honey, tangy goat cheese, and fresh baked goods at extraordinary prices. This colorful, open-air market—the most popular on the island—opens for business Wednesday and Saturday from 6 am to 4 pm. A smaller market on the other days features 20 to 30 vendors. ⊠ *Kamehameha Ave. and Mamo St.* ☏ *808/933–1000* ⊕ *www.hilofarmersmarket.com.*

South Kona Green Market. A favorite in Captain Cook, this Sunday market offers great hot breakfast and lunch items, produce from local farms, and artists selling their goods. ⊠ *Kealakekua Ranch Center, 82-6066 Mamalahoa Hwy., Captain Cook.*

HAWAII VOLCANOES NATIONAL PARK AND VICINITY

ARTS AND CRAFTS

2400 Fahrenheit. Just off Highway 11 on the way to Volcano, this small gallery and studio has unique, handblown glass inspired by the eruption of Kilauea. See the artist in action by appointment. ⊠ *Between mile markers 23 and 24 on Hwy. 11, very end of Old Volcano Rd., Puna* ☏ *808/985–8667* ☉ *Thurs.–Mon. 10–4, or by appointment.*

Kilauea Kreations. A stop at this unique shop should be part of your itinerary when visiting Volcano Village. Beautiful hand-stitched Hawaiian quilts grace the walls, quilting kits and books abound, and the vast inventory of tropical fabrics is amazing. The friendly proprietors also offer plentiful fine art, photography, and cool souvenirs you won't find anywhere else. ⊠ *19-3972 Volcano Rd., Volcano* ☏ *808/967–8090* ⊕ *www.kilaueakreations.com.*

SPAS

The Big Island's spa directors have produced menus full of "only in Hawaii" treatments well worth a holiday splurge. Local specialties include *lomilomi* massages, hot-lava-stone massages, and scrubs and wraps that incorporate plenty of coconut, ginger, orchids, and macadamia nuts. Also expect to find Swedish and deep-tissue massages and, at some spas, Thai massage. And in romantic Hawaii, couples can be pampered side by side in a variety of offerings. ∎**TIP**➔ Lomilomi massage is a quintessential Hawaiian deep-tissue massage, and most practitioners are happy to adjust the pressure to your needs. Most of the full-service spas on the Big Island are located at the resorts. With the exception of the Four Seasons Spa at Hualalai, these spas are open to anyone. In fact, many of the hotels outsource management of their spas, and there is no difference in price for guests and nonguests, although guests have the bonus of receiving in-room services.

KAILUA-KONA

Hoola Spa at the Sheraton Keauhou Bay. The Sheraton Keauhou Bay occupies one of the prettier corners of the island. That said, it's too bad that the Hoola Spa doesn't fully take advantage of its location, although there are plenty of windows with pretty views of the bay, and several outdoor treatment balconies. The spa menu includes a variety of locally influenced treatments, and the warm lava-rock massage is a little slice of heaven. The packages are an excellent deal, combining several services for far less than you would pay à la carte. For couples, the spa offers an ocean-side massage on a balcony overlooking the water, followed by a dip in a whirlpool bath. ✉ *Sheraton Keauhou Bay, 78-128 Ehukai St., Kailua-Kona* ☎ *808/930–4848* ⊕ *www.sheratonkeauhou.com* ☞ *$120 50-min lomilomi massage; $225–$380 packages. Hair salon, hot tub, sauna, steam room. Services: Aromatherapy, body scrubs and wraps, facials, massages, waxing.*

Kalona Salon & Spa at Keauhou Beach Resort. This spa is a great place to get a massage or body treatment for much less than you'd pay at the big resorts. Though not quite as nice as the bigger facilities, it's simple and clean, near the ocean, and staffed with well-trained therapists. The spa offers facials using its own line of products made from island ingredients. ✉ *Keauhou Beach Resort, 78-6740 Alii Dr., Kailua-Kona* ☎ *808/322–3441,* ⊕ *www.outrigger.com* ☞ *$95 50-min lomilomi massage, $225 half-day packages. Services: Facials, massage, nail treatments, waxing.*

The Lotus Center. Tucked away on the first floor of the Royal Kona Resort, the Lotus Center provides a convenient option for massage treatments, facials, and waxing. There's also a chiropractor on the premises. Ocean-side massage is available on a private patio outside of the treatment rooms. Alternative offerings include Reiki and crystal-energy sessions, biofeedback, and astrology readings. ✉ *Royal Kona Resort, 75-5852 Alii Dr., Kailua-Kona* ☎ *334–0445* ⊕ *www.konaspa.com* ☞ *$100–$135 lomilomi massage, $120–$150 hot-stone massage.*

The Spa at Hualalai. The spa is for the exclusive use of Four Seasons Resort guests, and features 28 massage treatment areas. Tropical breezes waft through 14 outdoor massage *hales*, situated in beautiful garden settings. The therapists are top-notch, and a real effort is made to incorporate local traditions. Apothecary services allow you to customize your treatment with ingredients like honey, kukui nuts, and coconut. Massage options range from traditional *lomilomi* to Thai. ✉ *72-100 Kaupulehu Dr., Kailua-Kona* ⊡ *Box 1269, Kaupulehu/Kona*

96740 ☎ 808/325–8000 ⊕ www.fourseasons.com ⌖ $170 50-min massage, $170 body scrub, $170 facials. Hair salon, outdoor hot tubs, sauna, steam room. Gym with: Cardiovascular machines, free weights, weight-training equipment. Classes and programs: Personal training, Pilates, Spinning, tai chi, yoga.

THE KONA COAST

Fodor's Choice
★
Mamalahoa Hot Tubs and Massage. Tucked into a residential neighborhood above Kealekekua, this little gem is a welcome alternative to the large resort spas. Soaking tubs are made of the finest quality wood, and they are enclosed in their own thatched gazebo with portholes in the roof for your stargazing pleasure. Tastefully laid out and run, there's no "hot tub party" vibe here, just a pleasant soak followed by, if you like, an hour-long massage. Mamalahoa offers *lomilomi*, Swedish, deep-tissue, and a Hawaiian hot-stone massage performed with lava rocks collected from around the island. Indulge in some romance with a twilight soak from 7:30 to 9 pm at $40 per couple. In addition to its secret-hideaway ambience, Mamalahoa's prices are lower than any other spa on the island. Call ahead for appointments. ⊠ 81-1016 St. John's Rd., Kealakekua ☎ 808/323–2288 ⊕ www.mamalahoa-hottubs. com ⊗ Wed.–Sat. noon–9 pm ⌖ $30 60-min soak; $95 30-min soak plus 60-min lomilomi, Swedish, or deep-tissue massage, $150 30-min soak plus 90-min hot-stone massage.

THE KOHALA COAST

Hawaii Island Retreat Maluhia Spa. This peaceful and elegant sanctuary in North Kohala offers three artfully appointed indoor treatment rooms and two massage platforms outside that overlook the valley. The spa is first-rate, with handcrafted wooden lockers, rain-style showerheads, and a signature line of lotions and scrubs that's made locally. The owners also create their own scrubs and wraps from ingredients grown on the property. The Papaya Delight lives up to its name, and features roasted ground papaya seeds mixed with goat yogurt and geranium. The roster of massages includes *lomilomi*, Thai, and deep tissue. Try the Shirodhara treatment of warm oil slowly drizzled over your third eye. ⊠ 250 Maluhia Rd., Kapaau ☎ 808/889–6336 ⊕ www.hawaiiislandretreat. com ⊗ Hours vary; call in advance ⌖ $130 60-minute lomilomi massage; signature facial $150. Hot tub, infinity pool. Services: Facial, massage. Classes and programs: Yoga.

★ **Kohala Spa at the Hilton Waikoloa Village.** The orchids that you'll find all over the Big Island suffuse the signature treatments at the Kohala Spa. By the end of the relaxing Orchid Isle Wrap, you're completely immersed in the scent. The island's volcanic character is also expressed in several treatments, as well as in the design of the lava-rock soaking tubs. Locker rooms are outfitted with a wealth of beauty and bath products; the spa's retail facility offers a signature line of Coco-Mango lotions, body washes, and shampoos. Open-air cabanas provide a delightful spot for a massage overlooking the ocean. The fitness center is equipped with the latest generation of machines, and group classes are plentiful, with everything from water aerobics to yoga. ⊠ *Hilton Waikoloa Village, 69-425 Waikoloa Beach Dr.* ☎ *808/886–2828, 800/445–8667* ⊕ *www. kohalaspa.com* ⌁ *$145 50-min lomilomi massage, $489–$599 half-day packages. Hair salon, hot tubs, sauna, steam room. Gym with: Cardiovascular machines, free weights, weight-training equipment. Services: Aromatherapy, body scrubs and wraps, facials, massage. Classes and programs: Aquaerobics, personal training, Pilates, Spinning, yoga.*

Kona Oceanfront Massage and Spa. With awesome views of Kailua Bay, Oceanfront Massage and Spa offers a full roster of massage treatments, as well as wraps, facials, and waxing. This is a convenient place to get pampered before you hit the village shops. ⊠ *75-5744 Alii Dr., Kailua-Kona* ☎ *808/937–9707* ⊕ *www.oceanfrontmassage.com* ⊗ *Hours vary; call for appointment* ⌁ *1-hour massage $79; 1½- hour massage $115. Services: Facial, massage, waxing, wraps. Classes and programs: Yoga.*

★ **Mandara Spa at the Waikoloa Beach Marriott Resort.** Overlooking the hotel's main pool with a distant view of the ocean, Mandara offers a very complete, if not unique, spa menu, with more facial options than you'll find at the island's other spas. Mandara, which operates spas all over the world, uses Elemis and La Therapie products in spa and salon treatments. The spa menu contains the usual suspects—*lomilomi*, scrubs, and wraps—but it incorporates local ingredients (lime and ginger in the scrubs, warm coconut milk in the wraps), and the facility, which fuses contemporary and traditional Asian motifs, is beautiful. ⊠ *Waikoloa Beach Marriott Resort, 69-275 Waikoloa Beach Dr., Waikoloa* ☎ *808/886–8191* ⊕ *www.mandaraspa.com* ⌁ *$145 50-min lomilomi massage; $450–$500 half-day packages. Steam room. Gym with: Cardiovascular machines, free weights, weight-training equipment.*

6

Mauna Kea Spa by Mandara. Mandara Spas blends European, Balinese, and indigenous treatments to create the ultimate spa experience. Things are no different at this spa at the Mauna Kea Beach Hotel. Though the facility is on the smaller side, the excellent treatments are up to the company's exacting standards. Try the Elemis Tri-Enzyme Resurfacing Facial or, even better, the Mandara Four Hand Massage, where two therapists work out the kinks simultaneously. Hawaiian traditional *lomilomi* is also available. The hotel operates a separate hair salon that offers manicures and pedicures in addition to standard salon services. ⊠ *Mauna Kea Beach Hotel, 69-100 Mauna Kea Beach Dr., Kohala Coast* ☎ *808/882–5630* ⊕ *www.mandaraspa.com* ⌁ *$181 50-min lomilomi. Services: Body treatments, facials, massage, waxing. Gym with: Cardiovascular machines, weight-training equipment. Classes and programs: Yoga.*

Fodor's Choice
★ **Mauna Lani Spa.** If you're looking for a one-of-a-kind experience, this is your destination. Most treatments take place in outdoor *hales* (houses) surrounded by lava rock. Wonderful therapists offer a mix of the traditional standbys (*lomilomi* massage, moisturizing facials) and innovative treatments influenced by ancient traditions and incorporating local products. One exfoliating body treatment is self-administered in one of the outdoor saunas. Watsu therapy, which mimics the feeling of being in the womb, takes place in a 1,000-square-foot grotto between two

lava tubes. You feel totally weightless, thanks to some artfully applied weights and the buoyancy of the warm salt water. It's a great treatment for people with disabilities that keep them from enjoying a traditional massage. The aesthetic treatments on the menu incorporate high-end products from Epicuran and Emmience, so a facial will have a real and lasting therapeutic effect on your skin. The spa also offers a full regimen of fitness and yoga classes. ⊠ *Mauna Lani Resort, 68-1365 Pauoa Rd., Kohala Coast* ☎ *808/881–7922* ⊕ *www.maunalani.com* ☞ *$159 50-min lomilomi massage; $345–$799 packages. Hair salon, hot tub, sauna, steam room. Gym with: Cardiovascular machines, free weights, weight-training equipment. Services: Aquatic therapy, baths, body wraps, facials, massage, nail treatment, scrubs, waxing, tinting. Classes and programs: Body sculpting, kickboxing, personal training, Pilates, Spinning, weight training, yoga.*

Paul Brown Salon & Spa at the Hapuna Beach Prince Hotel. It's not unusual for locals to drive an hour each way to get their hair styled here. The salon is still the center of the operation, but today it's joined by a full-service spa—nicely designed to let in lots of light—that has an extensive menu of massages, facials, and body treatments. The most popular massage is the *lomilomi* (traditional Hawaiian massage), but don't overlook the spa's unique body treatments. Consider the seaweed wrap, the detoxifying volcanic clay treatment, or the salt-and-aloe exfoliation. This is the best place for waxing. You can use the gym at the Hapuna Golf Course's clubhouse, accessible via a free shuttle. ⊠ *62-100 Kaunaoa Dr., Kohala Coast* ☎ *808/880–3335* ⊕ *www.paulbrownhawaii.com* ☞ *$115 50-min lomilomi massage, $338–$410 half-day package; $575 full-day package. Hair salon, sauna, steam room. Services: Acupuncture, body wraps, facials, massage.*

Fodor'sChoice
★
Spa Without Walls at the Fairmont Orchid Hawaii. This ranks among the best massage facilities on the island, partially due to the superlative setting—private massage areas are situated amid the waterfalls, saltwater pools, and meandering gardens, as well as right on the beach. In fact, the Fairmont Orchid is of the few resorts to offer beachside massage. Splurge on the 110-minute Alii Experience featuring hot-coconut-oil treatments, *lomilomi*, and hot-stone massage. There are other great treatments, including caviar facials, fragrant herbal wraps, and coffee-and-vanilla scrubs. And where else can you relax to the sounds of cascading waterfalls while watching tropical yellow tang swim beneath you through windows in the floor? ⊠ *Fairmont Orchid Hawaii, 1 N. Kaniku Dr., Kohala Coast* ☎ *808/887–7540, 808/885–2000* ⊕ *www.fairmont.com/ orchid* ☞ *$159–$179 50-min lomilomi massage. Sauna, steam room. Services: Baths, body wraps, facials, massage, scrubs. Classes and programs: Aquaerobics, guided walks, meditation, personal training, yoga.*

HILO

Hoomana Therapies. Two excellent massage therapists operate out of this small but peaceful location across the street from Hilo Bay. Tina Louise Cook specializes in deep-tissue massage, structural integration, and Zen therapies. Mariposa Blanco specializes in deep-tissue and cranial-sacral

Spa Without Walls at the Fairmont Orchid Hawaii

Mamalohoa Hot Tubs and Massage

Mauna Lani Spa

work, rebalancing the nervous system. Both will leave you feeling completely blissful. ✉ *1266 Kamehameha Ave.* ☎ *808/969–7075 for Tina, 808/938–7903 for Mariposa* ✆ *$65–$75 60-min deep-tissue massage.*

HAWAII VOLCANOES NATIONAL PARK AND VICINITY

★ **Hale Hoola Spa in Volcano.** Those staying in Volcano or Hilo have quick and easy access to the body treatments, massages, and facials—and at far more reasonable prices than on the other side of the island. Hale Hoola's menu features a bounty of local ingredients and traditional Hawaiian treatments, including a handful of unique Hawaiian massages, such as *lomi hula*, which is *lomilomi* massage choreographed to hula music; *laau hamo*, which blends *lomilomi* with traditional Hawaiian and Asian healing herbs and plant extracts. *Popokapai* is a divine blend of hot-stone massage and *laau hamo* that incorporates *lomilomi* massage with warm compresses filled with healing herbs. Facials and body scrubs use the traditional ginger, coconut, and macadamia nuts, but also some surprises, including taro, vanilla, and volcanic clay. ✉ *Mauna Loa Estates, 11-3913 7th St., Volcano* ☎ *808/756–2421* ⊕ *www.halehoola.net* ✆ *$75 60-min lomilomi massage, $150 half-day packages, $170 for couples. Services: Aromatherapy, body scrubs and wraps, facials, hair removal, makeup, massages, waxing.*

Entertainment and Nightlife

WORD OF MOUTH

"Many of the big luau start you at the buffet where there are all kinds of non-Hawaiian foods like cold cuts, cheeses, etc. You have to skip all that and go the place where the more genuine stuff is."

—charnees

Updated
by Karen
Anderson

If you're the sort of person who doesn't come alive until after dark, you might be a little lonely on the Big Island. Blame it on the plantation heritage. People did their cane raising in the morning, thus no late-night fun.

Still, there are a few lively bars on the island, a handful of great local playhouses, half a dozen or so movie houses (including those that play foreign and independent films), and plenty of musical entertainment to keep you occupied.

Also, many resorts have bars and late-night activities and events as well, and keep pools and gyms open late so there's something to do after dinner.

And let's not forget the luau. These fantastic dance and musical performances are combined with some of the best local food on the island and are plenty of fun for the whole family.

ENTERTAINMENT

DINNER CRUISES AND SHOWS

 Evening on the Reef Glass Bottom Dinner Cruise. Blue Sea Cruises offers a classier alternative to the booze cruise, with a buffet dinner, tropical cocktails, live entertainment, hula show, and open dancing. The focus is on the sunset and the scenery, with the chance to see spinner dolphins and manta rays, as well as whales from November to May. You can also enjoy what's below the surface through the boat's glass bottom. ⊠ *Kailua Pier, Alii Dr., next to King Kamehameha's Kona Beach Hotel, Kailua-Kona* 🕾 *808/331–8875* ⊕ *www.blueseacruisesinc.com* 🍽 *$98* ⊙ *Mon., Wed., Fri., and Sat., departure times vary.*

LUAU AND POLYNESIAN REVUES
KAILUA-KONA
Courtyard King Kamehameha's Kona Beach Hotel. Witness a dramatic fire-knife performance at the Island Breeze Luau, an oceanfront event that features live music and a bounty of food that includes kalua pig cooked in an authentic underground *imu.* ⊠ *75-5660 Palani Rd., Kai-*

lua-Kona ☎ 808/326–4969, 808/329–8111 ⊕ *www.islandbreezeluau.com* ✉ *$67.85* ◷ *Tues., Thurs., and Sun. 5–8.*

Royal Kona Resort. This resort lights its torches for a spectacular show and an oceanfront buffet four times a week. It's also one of a handful of luaus on the island that features food cooked in a traditional underground *imu* (oven). A fire-knife dancer caps off the show. Prices are cheaper if you book ahead. ✉ *75-5852 Alii Dr., Kailua-Kona* ☎ *808/329–3111* ⊕ *www.royalkona.com* ✉ *$78* ◷ *Mon., Tues. Wed., and Fri. at 5.*

Sheraton Keauhou Bay Resort & Spa. On the graceful grounds of the Sheraton Keauhou Bay, this luau takes you on a journey of song and dance, highlighted by a dramatic fire-knife finale. Before the show, you can participate in workshops on topics ranging from coconut-frond weaving to poi ball techniques. The excellent buffet features a feast of local favorites like kalua pig, poi, and ahi poke. Generous refills on the mai tais don't hurt, either. ✉ *75-5852 Alii Dr., Kailua-Kona* ☎ *808/930–4900* ⊕ *www.sheratonkeauhou.com* ✉ *$83* ◷ *Mon. at 5.*

THE KOHALA COAST

Fairmont Orchid. The Fairmont's "Gathering of the Kings Polynesian Feast" offers the most bang for your buck. The show is slickly produced and well choreographed, incorporating both traditional and modern dance and an array of beautiful costumes. The meal offers the most variety of any island luau, with four buffet tables representing New Zealand, Hawaii, Tahiti, and Samoa. ✉ *1 N. Kaniku Dr., Kohala Coast* ☎ *808/885–2000* ⊕ *www.fairmont.com/orchid* ✉ *$103* ◷ *Sat. at 6.*

Fodor's Choice ★ **Hapuna Beach Prince Hotel's Let's Go Crabbing.** While the Mauna Kea Beach Hotel's clambake gets all the acclaim, Let's Go Crabbing at the Hapuna Beach Prince Hotel is tastier, and at a fraction of the price. Held every Friday night on the hotel's terrace, the all-you-can-eat buffet features everything from prime rib and roasted breast of turkey to Washington mussels, steamed Manila clams, excellent shrimp salads, and corn-and-crab bisque. Expect an array of crab offerings, including wok-fried Dungeness crab and chilled snow-crab claws. Homemade ice cream is the star attraction of the dessert bar, which features hot fudge and other toppings. ✉ *Hapuna Beach Prince Hotel, 62-100 Kaunaoa Dr., Kohala Coast* ☎ *808/880–1111* ⊕ *www.princeresortshawaii.com.*

Hilton Waikoloa Village. This venue seats 400 people outdoors at the Kamehameha Court, where it presents the "Legends of the Pacific" review. A buffet dinner provides samplings of Hawaiian food as well as fish, beef, and chicken dishes that appeal to all tastes. ✉ *425 Waikoloa Beach Dr., Waikoloa* ☎ *808/886–1234* ⊕ *www.hiltonwaikoloavillage.com* ✉ *$99, includes two cocktails* ◷ *Tues., Fri., and Sun. at 6.*

Mauna Kea Beach Hotel. On the oceanfront North Pointe Luau Grounds of the Mauna Kea Beach Hotel, you can sample the best of island cuisine while listening to the music and hula of the renowned Lim family. Held every Tuesday and Friday, it includes an amazing fire-knife dance, spirited chanting, and traditional hula. You can relax under the stars and enjoy a traditional feast of kalua pig roasted in an underground oven. ✉ *62-100 Mauna Kea Beach Dr., Kohala Coast* ☎ *808/882–5810,*

Hawaiian Music on the Big Island

It's easy to forget that Hawaii has its own music until you step off a plane onto the Islands—and then there's no escaping it. It's a unique blend of the strings and percussion favored by the early settlers and the chants and rituals of the ancient Hawaiians. Hawaiian music today includes Island-devised variations on acoustic guitar—slack key and steel guitar—along with the ukulele and vocals that have evolved from ritual chants to more melodic compositions.

This is one of the few folk music traditions in the United States that is fully embraced by the younger generation, with no prodding from their parents or grandparents. More than half the radio stations on the Big Island play solely Hawaiian music, and concerts performed by Island favorites like Makana are filled with fans of all ages.

The best way to get an introduction to the music is to attend one of the annual festivals: The free **Annual Hawaii Slack Key Guitar Festival** (July) features a handful of greats performing throughout the day at the Sheraton Keauhou Bay; the **Annual Ukulele and Slack Key Guitar Institute** (November) at the Kahilu Theatre in Waimea takes it one step further, providing both a variety of concerts and workshops for those interested in learning to play the instruments; and the **Annual Big Island Hawaiian Music Festival** (July) at the UH Hilo Performing Arts Center is a weekend full of slack key, steel guitar, and ukulele madness.

Or, you can catch live performances most nights at one of a handful of local bars and clubs, including Remixx Lounge, **Huggo's on the Rocks,** or the **Kona Brewing Co.** in Kailua-Kona, and **Cronie's Bar and Grill** in Hilo.

808/882–7222 ⊕ *www.maunakeabeachhotel.com* ⊠ *$96* ⊗ *Tues. and Fri. at 5:45.*

Mauna Kea Beach Hotel Clambake. The Mauna Kea Beach Hotel's weekly clambake features an extensive menu that includes oysters on the half shell, Manila clams, Dungeness crab legs, and Keahole lobster sashimi. There's even prime rib for meat lovers. Live Hawaiian music is often accompanied by a graceful hula dancer. ⊠ *62-100 Mauna Kea Beach Dr., Kohala Coast* ☎ *808/882–5810, 808/882–7222* ⊕ *www. maunakeabeachhotel.com* ⊠ *$86* ⊗ *Sat. at 6.*

Waikoloa Beach Marriott. At this celebration, the entertainment includes a Samoan fire knife presentation as well as songs and dances from various Pacific cultures. Traditional dishes are served alongside more familiar fare, and there's also an open bar. ⊠ *69-275 Waikoloa Beach Dr., Waikoloa* ☎ *808/886–6789* ⊕ *www.marriott.com* ⊠ *$88* ⊗ *Wed. and Sat. 5–8:30.*

FESTIVALS

There is a festival dedicated to just about everything on the Big Island. Some of them are small community affairs, but a handful of film, food, and music festivals provide quality entertainment for visitors and locals alike. The following is a list of our favorites:

Black and White Night. This lovely annual outdoor party takes place in downtown Hilo. The stores stay open late, the sidewalks are dotted with live jazz bands, and everyone dresses in black and white, some in shorts and tees and others in gowns and tuxes, to enter the "best dressed" contest. ⊠ *329 Kamehameha Ave., Hilo* ☎ *808/935–8850* ⊕ *www.downtownhilo.com* ⊙ *First Friday in Nov.*

Chinese New Year. Every February, Hilo throws a big free party complete with live music, food, and fireworks to commemorate this holiday. There's a smaller celebration along Alii Drive in Kona. ⊠ *329 Kamehameha Ave., Hilo* ☎ *808/935–8850* ⊕ *www.downtownhilo. com* ⊙ *Feb.*

King Kamehameha Day Celebration Parade. Every June, Kailua-Kona rolls out its annual King Kamehameha Day Celebration Parade, featuring the beautiful pau riders on horseback representing the colorful flora of the Hawaiian Islands. A party usually follows. ⊠ *Kailua-Kona* ☎ *808/322–9944* ⊙ *June.*

Kona Brewers Festival. At this great annual celebration, roughly 30 breweries and 25 restaurants offer samples of their craft beer and ale. There's also live music, fashion shows, and home-brewer contest. The event is usually held on the grounds of Courtyard King Kamehameha's Kona Beach Hotel. ☎ *808/331–3033* ⊕ *www.konabrewersfestival.com* ⊙ *Early Mar.*

Kona Coffee Cultural Festival. Held over 10 days, the oldest food festival in Hawaii includes a coffee recipe contest, coffee picking competition, and a colorful parade. A highlight is the Holualoa Village Coffee and Art Stroll, during which you can enjoy original art and sample different cups of java. ☎ *808/323–2006* ⊕ *www.konacoffeefest.com* ⊙ *Early Nov.*

★ **Merrie Monarch Festival.** The mother of all Big Island festivals, the Merrie Monarch celebrates all things hula and completely overtakes Hilo for one fantastic weekend a year. The largest event of its kind in the world honors the legacy of King David Kalakaua, the man responsible for reviving fading Hawaiian traditions like the hula. The festival is staged at the spacious Edith Kanakaole Tennis Stadium during the first week following Easter Sunday. Hula *halau* (schools) compete in *kahiko* (ancient) and *auana* (modern) dance styles. ■TIP➔ You need to reserve accommodations and tickets up to a year in advance. ⊠ *Edith Kanakaole Tennis Stadium, 350 Kalanikoa St., Hilo* ☎ *808/935–9168* ⊕ *www. merriemonarchfestival.org* ⊙ *Apr.*

Moku O Keawe International Festival. An annual event held on the big stage at Waikoloa Bowl, this hula extravaganza features *halau* (groups) from Hawaii and Japan competing under the stars. During the day, workshops and cultural fairs take place at the Waikoloa Beach Marriott Resort. ⊠ *Waikoloa Bowl, 69-150 Waikoloa Beach Dr., Hilo* ☎ ⊕ *www. mokuokeawe.org* ⊙ *Nov.*

Taste of the Hawaiian Range. Since 1995, this culinary event has given locals and visitors a taste of what the region's best chefs and ranches have to offer, from grass-fed beef, lamb, and mutton to succulent veal. ⊠ *Kailua-Kona* ☎ *808/981–5199* ⊕ *www.tasteofthehawaiianrange.com* ⊙ *Sept. or Oct.*

Continued on page 188

HULA: MORE THAN A FOLK DANCE

Hula has been called "the heartbeat of the Hawaiian people" and also "the world's best-known, most misunderstood dance." Both are true. Hula isn't just dance. It is storytelling.

Chanter Edith McKinzie calls it "an extension of a piece of poetry." In its adornments, implements, and customs, hula integrates every important Hawaiian cultural practice: poetry, history, genealogy, craft, plant cultivation, martial arts, religion, protocol. So when 19th century Christian missionaries sought to eradicate a practice they considered depraved, they threatened more than just a folk dance.

With public performance outlawed and private hula practice discouraged, hula went underground for a generation, to rural villages. The fragile verbal link by which culture was transmitted from teacher to student hung by a thread. Even increasing literacy did not help because hula's practitioners were a secretive and protected circle.

As if that weren't bad enough, vaudeville, Broadway, and Hollywood got hold of the hula, giving it the glitz treatment in an unbroken line from "Oh, How She Could Wicky Wacky Woo" to "Rock-A-Hula Baby." Hula became shorthand for paradise: fragrant flowers, lazy hours. Ironically, this development assured that hundreds of Hawaiians could make a living performing and teaching hula. Many danced *auana* (modern form) in performance; but taught *kahiko* (traditional), quietly, at home or in hula schools.

Today, 30 years after the cultural revival known as the Hawaiian Renaissance, language immersion programs have assured a new generation of proficient—and even eloquent—chanters, songwriters, and translators. Visitors can see more, and more authentic, traditional hula than at any other time in the last 200 years.

Like the culture of which it is the beating heart, hula has survived.

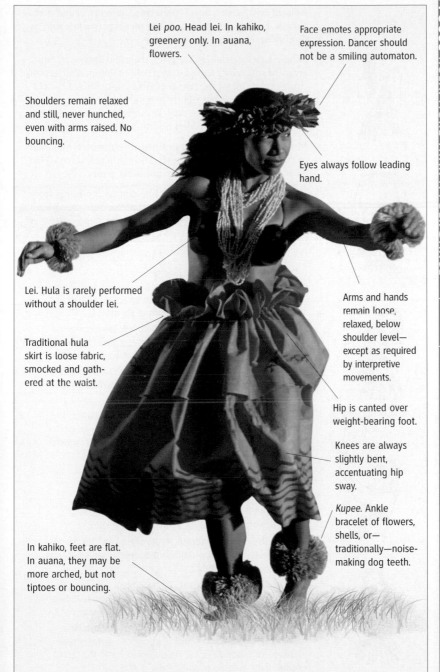

Lei *poo*. Head lei. In kahiko, greenery only. In auana, flowers.

Face emotes appropriate expression. Dancer should not be a smiling automaton.

Shoulders remain relaxed and still, never hunched, even with arms raised. No bouncing.

Eyes always follow leading hand.

Lei. Hula is rarely performed without a shoulder lei.

Arms and hands remain loose, relaxed, below shoulder level—except as required by interpretive movements.

Traditional hula skirt is loose fabric, smocked and gathered at the waist.

Hip is canted over weight-bearing foot.

Knees are always slightly bent, accentuating hip sway.

Kupee. Ankle bracelet of flowers, shells, or—traditionally—noise-making dog teeth.

In kahiko, feet are flat. In auana, they may be more arched, but not tiptoes or bouncing.

BASIC MOTIONS

Speak or Sing

Moon or Sun

Grass Shack or House

Mountains or Heights

Love or Caress

At backyard parties, hula is performed in bare feet and street clothes, but in performance, adornments play a key role, as do rhythm-keeping implements.

In hula *kahiko* (traditional style), the usual dress is multiple layers of stiff fabric (often with a pellom lining, which most closely resembles *kapa*, the paperlike bark cloth of the Hawaiians). These wrap tightly around the bosom but flare below the waist to form a skirt. In pre-contact times, dancers wore only kapa skirts. Men traditionally wear loincloths.

Monarchy-period hula is performed in voluminous muumuu or high-necked muslin blouses and gathered skirts. Men wear white or gingham shirts and black pants.

In hula *auana* (modern), dress for women can range from grass skirts and strapless tops to contemporary tea-length dresses. Men generally wear aloha shirts, but sometimes grass skirts over pants or even everyday gear.

SURPRISING HULA FACTS

■ Grass skirts are not traditional; workers from Kiribati (the Gilbert Islands) brought this custom to Hawaii.

■ In olden-day Hawaii, *mele* (songs) for hula were composed for every occasion—name songs for babies, dirges for funerals, welcome songs for visitors, celebrations of favorite pursuits.

■ Hula *mai* is a traditional hula form in praise of a noble's genitals; the power of the *alii* (royalty) to procreate gave *mana* (spiritual power) to the entire culture.

■ Hula students in old Hawaii adhered to high standards: scrupulous cleanliness, no sex, daily cleansing rituals, certain food prohibitions, and no contact with the dead. They were fined if they broke the rules.

WHERE TO WATCH

■ **Brown's Beach House** at the Fairmont Orchid. Hula dancers perform nightly on a moonlit grassy knoll.

■ **Kamahao "The Wondrous Myths of Hawaii."** The island's most talented dancers perform in this weekly luau production at the Sheraton Keauhou.

■ **Merrie Monarch Festival.** The king of all hula festivals, held annually the first Thursday after Easter Sunday in Hilo. Tickets are hard to get so book as early as possible.

■ **Volcano Center & Volcanoes National Park Na Mea Hawaii Hula Kahiko.** A series of free public performances takes place outdoors facing Halemaumau crater, the sacred home of the volcano goddess Pele.

FILM

FESTIVALS

Hawaii International Film Festival. With screenings at Hilo's Palace Theater and Kainaliu's Aloha Theatre, this festival has been blazing trails in the exhibition of Asian and Pacific feature films since 1981. It runs for about 10 days in late October. ⊕ *www.hiff.org.*

KAILUA-KONA

Keauhou 7 Cinemas. This is a splendid seven-theater complex, and there are several pre- or post-movie food options at the Keauhou Shopping Center. ⊠ *Keauhou Shopping Center, 78-6831 Alii Dr., Kailua-Kona* ☎ *808/324–7200.*

Makalapua Stadium Cinemas. The 10-screen theater in Kailua-Kona has stadium seating and digital surround sound. ⊠ *Makalapua Ave., next to Kmart, Kailua-Kona* ☎ *808/327–0444.*

HILO

Honokaa People's Theater. Screening art films during the week and more mainstream releases on weekends, the Honokaa People's Theater is the largest cinema on the Big Island, featuring a 50-foot screen, as well as a huge stage and a dance floor. Hula competitions, concerts, and other special events are held here. ⊠ *Mamane St., Hilo* ☎ *808/775–0000* ⊕ *www.honokaapeople.com.*

Kress Cinemas. Critically acclaimed films and the occasional art-house flick are shown on four screens in this pretty art-deco building. Since the movies are not-so-recently released, the price is right at $1 to $1.75 per person. You can even get a hot dog for $1.75 and free refills on large popcorns and sodas. ⊠ *174 Kamehameha Ave., Hilo* ☎ *808/961–0066.*

Palace Theatre. After decades of neglect, this theater dating from 1925 has been beautifully restored and showcases everything from old movies to musical productions to holiday concerts. ⊠ *38 Haili St., Hilo* ☎ *808/934–7010* ⊕ *www.hilopalace.com.*

Prince Kuhio Stadium Cinemas. First-run films are shown on the nine screens of the Prince Kuhio Stadium Cinemas. ⊠ *Prince Kuhio Plaza, 111 E. Puainako St., Hilo* ☎ *808/961–3456.*

THEATER

Aloha Angel Performing Arts Center. Local talent stages musicals and Broadway plays at this charming old plantation center near Kailua-Kona. ⊠ *Aloha Angel Theatre Café, 79-7384 Mamalahoa Hwy., Kainaliu* ☎ *808/322–2122.*

Aloha Theatre. Local groups stage musicals and plays at this charming old plantation theater near Kailua-Kona. ⊠ *79-7384 Mamalahoa Hwy., Kainaliu* ☎ *808/322–9924* ⊕ *www.alohatheatre.com.*

Kahilu Theater. For legitimate theater, the little town of Waimea is your best bet. The Kahilu Theater regularly hosts internationally acclaimed performers, interspersed with a variety of top-notch national and regional acts. In a recent season, Terence Blanchard, Ben Vereen, and the Martha Graham Company shared the calendar with modern dance performances and traditional Hawaiian dance shows. ⊠ *Parker Ranch*

Center, 67-1185 Mamalahoa Hwy., Waimea ☎ *808/885–6868* ⊕ *www. kahilutheatre.org.*

University of Hawaii at Hilo Performing Arts Center. This 600-seat venue hosts a full season of dance, drama, music, and other events. About 150 performances are held September to May. ✉ *200 W. Kawili St., Hilo* ☎ *808/974–7310* ⊕ *artscenter.uhh.hawaii.edu.*

★ **Volcano Art Center.** Hawaiian music and dance, as well as theater performances, are hosted by this local art center. Locals drive here from all over the island for the concerts. ✉ *19-4744 Old Volcano Rd., Volcano* ☎ *808/967–8222* ⊕ *www.volcanoartcenter.org.*

NIGHTLIFE

KAILUA-KONA

BARS

Humpy's Big Island Alehouse. If you're a beer drinker, you'll appreciate the numerous selections of fine craft brews on tap at this oceanfront restaurant on Alii Drive. Humpy's serves food as well, but when it comes to the menu, this spot is nothing to write home about. Happy-hour specials are available weekdays from 3 to 6 pm; the bar stays open until 2 am daily. ✉ *75-5815 Alii Dr., Kailua-Kona* ☎ *808/324–2337* ⊕ *www.humpys.com/kona.*

Kona Brewing Co. This place has been a local favorite practically since it opened. Good food, great locally brewed beer (go for the sampler and try them all), and an outdoor patio with live music on Sunday nights make sure it stays that way. ✉ *75-5629 Kuakini Hwy., Kailua-Kona* ☎ *808/334–2739* ⊕ *www.konabrewingco.com.*

Oceans Sports Bar & Grill. A popular gathering place, this sports bar in the back of the Coconut Grove Marketplace has a pool table and an outdoor patio, along with dozens of TVs screening the big game (whatever it happens to be that day). It really gets hopping on the weekends and for karaoke on Tuesday and Thursday. ✉ *Coconut Grove Marketplace, 75-5811 Alii Dr., Kailua-Kona* ☎ *808/327–9494.*

Okolemaluna Tiki Lounge. This addition to the Kailua-Kona cocktail scene is a cool, retro tiki bar where you can sip an exotic cocktail made with fresh, local, seasonal ingredients while munching on tasty tropical pupus. Happy hour, on weekdays from 3 pm to 6 pm, features $5 mai tais and $4 local draft beers. It's open Sunday to Thursday from 3 to 11 and Friday and Saturday 3 pm to midnight. ✉ *Alii Sunset Plaza, 75-5799 Alii Dr., by Lava Java, Kailua-Kona* ☎ *808/883–8454* ⊕ *www. okolemalunalounge.com.*

CLUBS

Huggo's on the Rocks. Jazz, country, and rock bands perform at this popular place, so call ahead to find out who's on the bill. Outside you might see people dancing in the sand to Hawaiian songs. The crowd is slightly older and better behaved than at Lulu's across the street.

7

✉ *75-5828 Kahakai Rd., at Alii Dr., Kailua-Kona* ☎ *808/329–1493* ⊕ *www.huggos.com.*

Lulu's. On weekends, a young crowd gyrates to hot dance music—hip-hop, R&B, and rock—spun by a professional DJ. The party lasts well into the evening. ✉ *Coconut Grove Marketplace, 75-5819 Alii Dr., Kailua-Kona* ☎ *808/331–2633.*

THE KOHALA COAST

BARS

Blue Dragon. If you're looking for live music and dancing, you can find it in Kawaihae at the Blue Dragon. Almost every night of the week you can hear live music, including jazz, R&B, and Motown grooves. ✉ *61-3616 Kawaihae Rd., Kawaihae* ☎ *808/882–7771.*

Luana Terrace. This wood-paneled lounge in the Fairmont Orchid has a large terrace and an impressive view. The bartenders are skilled, and service is impeccable. The crowd is subdued, so it's a nice place for an early evening cocktail or an after-dinner port. ✉ *Fairmont Orchid, 1 N. Kaniku Dr., Kohala Coast* ☎ *808/885–2000* ⊕ *www.fairmont.com/orchid.*

Malolo Lounge. A favorite after-work spot for employees from the surrounding hotels, this lounge in the Hilton Waikoloa Village offers decent music (usually jazz), friendly bartenders, and a pool table. ✉ *Hilton Waikoloa Village, 425 Waikoloa Beach Dr., Waikoloa* ☎ *808/886–1234* ⊕ *www.hiltonwaikoloavillage.com.*

HILO

BARS

Cronie's Bar & Grill. A sports bar and hamburger joint by day, Cronie's is a local favorite when the lights go down, when the bar gets packed. ✉ *11 Waianuenue Ave., Hilo* ☎ *808/935–5158.*

Mask-querade Bar. Hidden away in a little strip mall, this is one of the Big Island's most venerable gay bars. Drag shows, hot DJs, and Sunday barbecues are included in the roster of weekly events. ✉ *Kopiko Plaza, 75-5660 Kopiko St., behind Longs Drugs, Kailua-Kona* ☎ *808/329–8558* ⊕ *themask-queradebar.com.*

BEST SUNSET MAI TAIS

Huggo's on the Rocks (Kailua-Kona). Table dining in the sand, plus live music Friday and Saturday.

Kona Inn (Kailua-Kona). Wide, unobstructed view of the Kailua-Kona coastline.

Manta Ray Bar & Grill at the Sheraton Keauhou (Kailua-Kona). Fantastic sunset views from plush lounge chairs, followed by spotlighted glimpses of nearby manta rays.

Waioli Lounge in the Hilo Hawaiian Hotel (Hilo). A nice view of Coconut Island, live music Friday and Saturday nights.

Where to Eat

WORD OF MOUTH

"There are a number of restaurants along Alii Drive, south of King Kamehameha Hotel. Most are active, noisy, and crowded. They have dining on the second floor, looking out over Alii Drive to sunsets and the Kona harbor."

—BillJ

Updated
by Karen
Anderson

Between star chefs and myriad local farms, the Big Island restaurant scene has really heated up in the last 10 years. Food writers from national magazines are praising the chefs of the Big Island for their ability to turn the local bounty into inventive blends of the island's cultural heritage. The Big Island has become a destination for vacationing foodies who are drawn by the innovative offerings and reputations of some world-renowned chefs.

Hotels along the Kohala Coast have long invested in celebrated chefs who know how to make a meal memorable, from inventive entrées to spot-on wine pairings. But great food on the Big Island doesn't begin and end with the resorts. A handful of cutting-edge chefs have retired from the fast-paced hotel world and opened up their own small bistros closer to the farms in upcountry Waimea, or other places off the beaten track. And, as some historic towns transform into vibrant arts communities, unique and wonderful restaurants have cropped up in Hawi, Kainaliu, and Holualoa, and on the east side of the island in Hilo.

Though the larger, gourmet restaurants (especially those at the resorts) tend to be very pricey, there are still *ono grindz* (Hawaiian slang for tasty local food) to be found at budget prices throughout the island, from greasy plate lunch specials to reasonably priced organic fare at a number of cafés and health food markets. Less populated areas like Kau, the Hamakua Coast, and Puna offer limited choices for dinner, but there are usually at least one or two spots that have a decent plate lunch or surprisingly good food.

In addition to restaurants, festivals devoted to island products draw hundreds of attendees to learn about everything from breadfruit and mango to avocado, chocolate, and coffee. Island tourism bureaus have also made an effort to promote agritourism, and it has turned into a fruitful venture for farmers. Farm tours afford visitors the opportunity to meet with and learn from the local farmers and tour a variety of organic producers. Some tours conclude with a meal comprised of items sourced from the same farms. From goat farms churning creamy, savory goat cheese to Waimea farms planting row after row of bright tomatoes to high-tech aquaculture operations at NELHA (Natural Energy Lab Hawaii Authority), visitors can see exactly where their next meal will come from and taste the difference that local, fresh, and organic production can make.

BIG ISLAND DINING PLANNER

WITH KIDS
Little ones are welcome almost everywhere on the kid-friendly Big Island; the exceptions are a small handful of fine-dining restaurants that cater to adults. The majority of restaurants feature a kids' menu, and many have toys and gimmicks, from coloring kits to battery-operated spinning forks, to keep kids entertained.

SMOKING
Smoking is prohibited in all Hawaii restaurants and bars.

RESERVATIONS
Though it's rare to find a restaurant completely booked on the Big Island, a select few are sticklers about reservations. If you're bringing a large party or booking a special-occasion dinner, call ahead just in case, or check with your hotel concierge.

WHAT TO WEAR
There isn't a single place on the Big Island that requires formal attire. The general rule is anything goes, although there are a handful of restaurants (Pahuia at the Four Seasons, the CanoeHouse at the Mauna Lani, and Monettes at Mauna Kea) where you might feel out of place in your beach clothes. Resort wear, however, is acceptable at even the most upscale restaurants.

8

HOURS AND PRICES
Though it might seem at first glance like the Big Island's dining scene consists of either high-end restaurants or hole-in-the-wall dives, there is in fact a fairly large middle ground of quality restaurants that cater both to local and visiting families, with new places are cropping up all the time. Prices are generally higher than on the mainland due to the higher general cost of living here.

Tipping is similar here to elsewhere in the country: 15%–20% of the bill or $1 per drink at a bar. Bills for large parties generally include an 18% tip, as do bills at some resort restaurants, so be sure to check your bill before leaving extra.

WHAT IT COSTS				
	$	$$	$$$	$$$$
AT DINNER	under $17	$17–$26	$27–$35	over $35

Restaurant prices are for a main course at dinner, excluding 4.2% excise tax.

BEST BETS FOR BIG ISLAND DINING

Where can I find the best food the island has to offer? Fodor's writers and editors have selected their favorite restaurants by price, cuisine, and experience in the lists below. In the first column, the Fodor's Choice properties represent the "best of the best" across price categories. You can also search by area for excellent eats—just peruse our complete reviews on the following pages.

Fodor's Choice ★

Bamboo Restaurant, $$, p. 205

Beach Tree, $$$, p. 204

Brown's Beach House, $$$$, p. 205

CanoeHouse, $$$$, p. 206

Keei Café, $$, p. 203

Kona Brewing Co. Pub & Brewery, $, p. 198

Pahuia, $$$$, p. 204

By Price

$

Ceviche Dave's, p. 195

Island Lava Java, p. 197

Kalama's, p. 203

Kona Brewing Co. Pub & Brewery, p. 198

Lemongrass Bistro, p. 199

Lilikoi Café, p. 217

Pau, p. 217

Pho Saigon, p. 200

Sombat's Fresh Thai Cuisine, p. 221

$$

Bamboo Restaurant, p. 205

Jackie Rey's Ohana Grill, p. 197

Keei Café, p. 203

Kenichi Pacific, p. 198

Kiawe Kitchen, p. 222

Merriman's Market Café, p. 209

Sam Choy's Kai Lanai, p. 200

$$$

Beach Tree, p. 204

Kilauea Lodge, p. 222

$$$$

Brown's Beach House, p. 205

CanoeHouse, p. 206

KPC (Kamuela Provision Company), p. 209

Manta & Pavilion Wine Bar, p. 209

Pahuia, p. 204

Monettes, p. 209

By Cuisine

HAWAIIAN

Eddie Aikau Restaurant and Surf Museum, $$$, p. 207

Hilo Bay Café, $, p. 220

Manago Hotel, $, p. 203

Pahuia, $$$$, p. 204

Sam Choy's Kai Lanai, $$, p. 200

PLATE LUNCH

Blane's Drive-In, p. 218

Big Island Grill, p. 195

Café 100, p. 218

Kaaloa's Super Js Hawaiian Food, p. 203

Kalama's, p. 203

SUSHI

Kenichi Pacific, $$ p. 198

Monstera, $$, p. 210

Norio's Sushi Bar, $$$ p. 210

Sansei Seafood Restaurant & Sushi Bar, $$$, p. 211

Sushi Rock, $$, p. 211

Wasabi's, $, p. 201

By Experience

MOST KID-FRIENDLY

Bubba Gump Shrimp Company, $, p. 195

Lava Rock Café, $, p. 224

The Seaside Restaurant, $$, p. 221

MOST ROMANTIC

Beach Tree, $$$, p. 204

CanoeHouse, $$$$, p. 206

Manta & Pavilion Wine Bar, $$$$, p. 209

Huggo's, $$$, p. 196

Keei Café, $$, p. 203

Pahuia, $$$$, p. 204

BEST VIEW

Brown's Beach House, $$$$, p. 205

Bubba Gump Shrimp Company, $, p. 195

Don the Beachcomber, $$$, p. 196

Huggo's, $$$, p. 196

KPC (Kamuela Provision Company), $$$$, p. 209

The Coffee Shack, $, p. 201

KAILUA-KONA

$ ✕**Ba-Le.** Hidden away in a strip mall on Palani Road near KTA, Ba-Le
HAWAIIAN serves a decent plate lunch. It also offers Vietnamese-influenced food
such as pho, though there are more authentic options elsewhere. Ba-Le's
sandwiches are served on croissants or French baguettes, stuffed with
pickled daikon and carrots, cucumber, cilantro, homemade mayo, and
your choice of a variety of Asian-style meats. ✉ *Kona Coast Shopping
Center, 74-5588 Palani Rd., Kailua-Kona* ☎ *808/327–1212* ⊕ *www.
ba-le.com.*

$ ✕**Big Island Grill.** This typical, local Hawaiian restaurant looks like an
HAWAIIAN old coffee shop or a Denny's—it's dark and nondescript inside, with
☺ booths along the walls and basic tables with bingo-hall chairs in the
middle of the room. Local families love it for the huge portions of pork
chops, loco moco, and an assortment of fish specialties at very reasonable prices. "Biggie's" also serves a decent breakfast—the prices and
portions make this a good place to take large groups or families, if you
want to feel like a real *kamaaina* (local), that is. ✉ *75-5702 Kuakini
Hwy., Kailua-Kona* ☎ *808/326-1153* ☽ *Closed Sun.*

$ ✕**Bite Me Fish Market Bar & Grill.** This cool sit-down bar and grill overlooks
SEAFOOD the boat ramp of the Bite Me Fish Market in Honokohau Harbor. Sit at
the outdoor picnic tables and watch the day's catch get hoisted from the
boats; chances are it will end up on your plate that day. Sandwiches are
named after famous fishing lures in Kona (try the Kaya Bait Fish Reuben).
Fish tacos can be ordered à la carte for a couple of bucks. ✉ *Gentrys
Kona Marina at Honokohau Harbor, 74-425 Kealakehe Pkwy., No. 17,
Kailua-Kona* ☎ *808/327–3474* ⊕ *www.bitemefishmarket.com.*

$ ✕**Boston Basil's.** This tiny, traditional trattoria serves solid, family-style
ITALIAN Italian food and excellent pizzas at very good prices. The atmosphere
is similar to hundreds of Italian restaurants on the U.S. mainland—the
tablecloths are checkered, the candles are in Chianti bottles, there's
spaghetti on the menu, and it always feels a little hot and greasy inside.
But you can't beat the location in downtown Kailua-Kona, right across
the street from the ocean. ✉ *75-5707 Alii Dr., Kailua-Kona* ☎ *808/326–
7836* ⊕ *www.bostonbasils.com.*

$ ✕**Bubba Gump Shrimp Company.** Okay, it's a chain, and a chain that cen-
AMERICAN ters on an old Tom Hanks movie, no less. However, it has one of the nic-
☺ est oceanfront patios in Kailua-Kona, and the food's not bad, providing
you know what to order. Anything with popcorn shrimp in it is a good
bet, and the pear and berry salad (a combination of chicken, strawberries, pears, and glazed pecans) is the perfect size for lunch. ✉ *75-5776
Alii Dr., Kailua-Kona* ☎ *808/331–8442* ⊕ *www.bubbagump.com.*

$ ✕**Ceviche Dave's.** This cool little spot near Costco features beautiful
SEAFOOD tropical woodworking by Dave Weaver, who also serves up his own
ceviche concoctions, highlighted by the Taapuna, with fresh ono and
coconut milk. Order the sampler plate and you'll get to try four different ceviches, all served with chips and homemade bread baked daily
by Dave's wife, April. Dave likes to play guitar and tell stories about
surfing, Costa Rica, and music. Relax here after a day at the beach, and
enjoy the view of Pine Trees surf spot below. ✉ *73-4976 Kamanu St.,
Suite 100, near Costco, Kailua-Kona* ☎ *808/326-4737.*

8

$$$ ✕ **Don the Beachcomber at the Royal Kona Resort.** The "original home of the
HAWAIIAN mai tai," Don the Beachcomber includes a cool mai tai bar (bar service
is slow, so sit back and enjoy the view) and has recently become a popu-
lar local spot for lunch, thanks to fresh ono sandwiches and addictive
sweet-potato fries. Dinners are priced like those at the Kohala Coast
resort restaurants (high), but the location offers the absolute best view
in town of Kailua Bay. Try any of the nightly seafood specials or the
Huli Huli Chicken, but the Paniolo prime rib is the star attraction, slow
roasted for flavor and tenderness. Save room for the Molten Lava Cake.
✉ *Royal Kona Resort, 75-5852 Alii Dr., Kailua-Kona* ☎ *808/329–3111*
⊕ *www.royalkona.com/Dining.cfm.*

$$ ✕ **Fish Hopper.** The Hawaii location of the popular Monterey, Califor-
SEAFOOD nia, restaurant has an expansive menu, with inventive fresh-fish spe-
cials alongside the fish-and-chips and clam chowder that the original
restaurant is known for. The owners spent serious time and money
renovating the old and funky Ocean View Inn, and the restaurant itself
is lovely—lots of koa wood, Hawaiian art, and an open-air floor plan
that takes advantage of the Kailua Bay view. The food is decent, but
may not feel worth the price. The wine list is comprehensive, and there
are frequent bottle specials, so a money-saving option is to come for
wine and appetizers with a view. Ask your greeter for a card that will
get you a free appetizer or small discount off your meal. ✉ *75-5683
Alii Dr., Kailua-Kona* ☎ *808/326–2002* ⊕ *www.fishhopper.com/kona/.*

$ ✕ **Harbor House.** This open-air restaurant on the docks at Kona's busy
AMERICAN harbor is a fun place to grab a beer and a bite after a long day fishing,
surfing, or diving. The venue is nothing fancy but Harbor House is a
local favorite for fresh-fish sandwiches and a variety of fried fish-and-
chip combos. The icy schooners of Kona Brewing Company ale don't
hurt, either. ✉ *74-425 Kealakehe Pkwy., Suite 4, Honokohau Harbor,
Kailua-Kona* ☎ *808/326–4166* ⊕ *harborhouserestaurantkona.com.*

$$$ ✕ **Honu's on the Beach.** Featuring alfresco dining near the sand, Honu's
HAWAIIAN on the Beach is one of the few true beachfront restaurants in Kailua
Village. Part of Courtyard King Kamehameha's Kona Beach Hotel, the
newly transformed open-air venue offers prime views of Kailua Pier and
Kamakahonu Bay. Steak and seafood dominate the menu, highlighted
by the rib-eye, fresh catch, and the delicious seafood chowder made
with fish, clams, scallops, and shrimp. For lighter fare, there's an excel-
lent selection of entrée salads, including the grilled chicken and papaya
salad. A prime rib seafood buffet is available Friday and Saturday
nights. ✉ *Courtyard King Kamehameha's Kona Beach Hotel, 75-5660
Palani Road, Kailua-Kona* ☎ *808/331–6388* ⊕ *www.konabeachhotel.
com/dining.htm.*

$$$$ ✕ **Huggo's.** This is one of the few restaurants in town with prices and
HAWAIIAN atmosphere comparable to the splurge restaurants at the Kohala Coast
resorts. The dinner offerings sometimes fall short, considering the high
prices, but lunch is usually a good bet. Windows open out over the rocks
at the ocean's edge, and at night you can almost touch the marine life
swimming below. Relax with cocktails for two and feast on fresh local
seafood; the nightly chef's special is always changing. If you're on a

CLOSE UP

The Plate Lunch Tradition

To experience island history firsthand, take a seat at one of Hawaii's popular "plate lunch" eateries, and order a segmented Styrofoam plate piled with rice, macaroni salad, and maybe some "pig and poi," or lomilomi salmon. On the sugar plantations, native Hawaiians and immigrant workers from many different countries ate together in the fields, sharing food from their *kau kau* kits, the utilitarian version of the Japanese *bento* lunchbox. From this melting pot came the vibrant language of pidgin and its equivalent in food: the plate lunch.

At beach parks and events, you might see a few tiny kitchens-on-wheels, another excellent venue for sampling plate lunch. These portable restaurants are descendants of lunch wagons that began selling food to plantation workers in the 1930s. Try the deep-fried chicken *katsu* (rolled in Japanese panko flour and spices). The marinated beef teriyaki is another good choice, as is miso butterfish. The noodle soup, *saimin*, with its Japanese fish stock and Chinese red-tinted barbecue pork, is a distinctly local medley. Koreans have contributed spicy barbecue *kalbi* ribs, often served with chili-laden kimchi (pickled cabbage). Portuguese bean soup and tangy Filipino adobo stew are also favorites. The most popular Hawaiian contribution to the plate lunch is the *laulau*, a mix of meat or fish and young taro leaves, wrapped in more taro leaves and ti, and steamed.

---

budget, try Huggo's happy hour: pupus are half price from 5:30 to 6 pm and drink specials run from 4 to 6 pm daily.

Huggo's on the Rocks, next door, is a popular outdoor bar in the sand, and the burgers are pretty darn good, too. It's also Kailua-Kona's hot spot for drinks and live music on Friday nights. ⊠ *75-5828 Kahakai Rd., off Alii Dr., Kailua-Kona* ☎ *808/329–1493* ⊕ *www.huggos.com.*

$

AMERICAN ✕**Island Lava Java.** This place is always busy, especially on weekends. Order your food at the counter then sit outside at one of the wooden, umbrella-shaded tables where you can sip 100% Kona coffee and take in the ocean view. The variety-filled menu includes island-style pancakes for breakfast, fresh-fish tacos for lunch, and braised lamb shanks for dinner, plus towering, fresh bistro salads. There are also pizzas, sandwiches, and plenty of choices for both vegetarians and meat eaters. The giant cinnamon rolls are hugely popular. Portions are large and most of the menu is fresh, local, and organic. ⊠ *75-5799 Alii Dr., Kailua-Kona* ☎ *808/327–2161* ⊕ *www.islandlavajava.com.*

$$

MODERN HAWAIIAN ✕**Jackie Rey's Ohana Grill.** This brightly decorated, open-air restaurant is a favorite lunch destination and popular for dinner as well, thanks to the chef's chicken and angel hair pasta, nicely prepared local seafood dishes, and a few juicy meat standouts, including six-bone rack of lamb. Be sure to pair your meal with a selection from Jackie Rey's well-rounded wine list. At lunchtime, the fresh-fish sandwiches with wasabi mayo are excellent, and the fries are crisped to perfection. On the lighter side, inventive salads keep it healthy but flavorful. ⊠ *Pot-*

8

tery Terrace, 75-5995 Kuakini Hwy., Kailua-Kona 🕾 *808/327–0209* ⊕ *www.jackiereys.com* ⊘ *No lunch weekends.*

$$$
SOUTH PACIFIC

✕ **Kai at the Sheraton Keauhou Bay.** For a restaurant that faces Keauhou Bay, Kai doesn't fully take advantage of the view (there's no outdoor seating to speak of), but there are nice views through the large accordion windows depending on where you sit. Best bets include the poke, as well as the tender and flavorful filet mignon, and Kona coffee–crusted lamb. The risotto with truffle-oil infusion won't disappoint, and all seafood is freshly caught. On Sunday, the Pacific-to-Your Plate three-course menu is a standout. After dinner, head to the Manta Ray Bar and Grill to see manta rays swimming in the spotlights below the balcony. New hotel management plans to upgrade in 2012, so look for a new and improved venue in the near future. ✉ *78-128 Ehukai St., Kailua-Kona* 🕾 *808/930–4900* ⊕ *www.sheratonkeauhou.com.*

$
HAWAIIAN

✕ **Kanaka Kava.** A popular local hangout, and not just because the kava makes you mellow. Their *pupu* (appetizers) rock! Fresh poke, smoky, tender bowls of pulled kalua pork, and healthy organic greens are available in fairly large portions for less than you'll pay elsewhere. The restaurant also offers fresh-fish plates, vegetarian options, and even traditional Hawaiian *lau lau* (pork and butterfish wrapped in taro leaves and steamed). Seating is at a premium, but don't be afraid to share a table and make friends. ✉ *75-5803 Alii Dr., Space B6, in Coconut Grove Marketplace, Kailua-Kona* 🕾 *808/327–1660* ⊕ *www. kanakakava.com.*

$$
JAPANESE

✕ **Kenichi Pacific.** With its black-lacquer tables and lipstick-red banquettes, Kenichi provides one of the few upscale choices in town. Its location at Keauhou Shopping Center might feel like a secret, but visitors should seek it out. This is where residents go when they feel like splurging on top-notch sushi. It's a little on the pricey side, but you'll leave feeling satisfied. The signature rolls are inventive and tasty, especially the always-popular Dynamite Shrimp. If you're looking to save a buck or two, go early for happy hour (4:30 to 6:30 pm daily) when all sushi rolls are half price, or hang out in the cocktail bar where menu items average $6. ✉ *Keauhou Shopping Center, 78-6831 Alii Dr., D-125, Kailua-Kona* 🕾 *808/322–6400* ⊕ *www.kenichirestaurants. com* ⊘ *Closed Mon.*

$
AMERICAN
Fodor's Choice
★

✕ **Kona Brewing Co. Pub & Brewery.** This megapopular destination with a huge outdoor patio features an excellent and varied menu, including pulled-pork quesadillas, gourmet pizzas, and a killer spinach salad with Gorgonzola cheese, macadamia nuts, and strawberries. Your best bet for lunch or dinner is the veggie slice and salad for under $8—the garden salad is generous and the pizza is the best in town. Go for the beer-tasting menu—your choice of four of the eight available microbrews in miniature glasses that add up to about two regular-size mugs for the price of one. The Hefeweizen is excellent. If you're staying in town, purchase beer to go in a half-gallon jug ("growler") filled on-site from the brewery's own taps. The Growler Shack also sells beer by the keg. ✉ *75-5629 Kuakini Hwy., off Kaiwi St. at end of Pawai Pl., Kailua-Kona* 🕾 *808/329–2739* ⊕ *www.konabrewingco.com.*

$$ ✕**Kona Inn Restaurant.** This vintage
AMERICAN open-air restaurant offers a beautiful, oceanfront setting on Kailua Bay. It's a great place to have a mai tai and some appetizers while watching the sunset, or to enjoy a calamari or ono sandwich and a salad at lunch. Dinner is also available, but the entrées are less than stellar and for the prices there are better options once the sun disappears. ⊠ *75-5744 Alii Dr., Kailua-Kona* ☎ *808/329–4455* ⊕ *www.windandsearestaurants.com.*

$$$ ✕**La Bourgogne.** A genial husband-and-wife team owns this quiet, country-style bistro with dark-wood walls and private, romantic booths (no windows; it's located in a nondescript office building). The traditional French cuisine might not impress visitors from France, but the average guest can enjoy classics such as escargots, beef with a cabernet sauvignon sauce, rack of lamb with roasted garlic and rosemary, and the less traditional venison with a pomegranate glaze. Call well in advance for reservations. ⊠ *77-6400 Nalani St., Kailua-Kona* ☎ *808/329–6711* ⟐ *Reservations essential* ◎ *Closed Sun. and Mon. No lunch.*

$ ✕**Lemongrass Bistro.** This best-kept secret in Kailua-Kona occupies a
ASIAN small but tasteful venue across from the library near the Kona Inn Shopping Village. The Asian-fusion menu ranges from Thai and Vietnamese to Japanese, Laotian, and Filipino. Dishes are presented with a resort flair, yet most entrées average an afforable $14, with appetizers between $5 and $7. Best bets are the ono sashimi or the grilled marinated chicken salad with crispy wonton. Everything is made to order, plus it's one of the few restaurants in town open until 11 pm. ⊠ *75-5742 Kuakini Hwy., Suite 103, across the street from the library, Kailua-Kona* ☎ *808/331–2708* ⊕ *lemongrass-bistro.webs.com.*

$ ✕**Los Habaneros.** A surprising find in the corner of Keauhou Shopping
MEXICAN Center adjacent to the movie theater, Habaneros serves up fast Mexican food for low prices. Favorites are usually combos, which can be anything from enchilada plates to homemade sopes and chiles rellenos. The burritos are a solid pick, stuffed with meat, beans, cheese, and all the fixings. Wash it down with imported beer from Mexico. ⊠ *78-631 Alii Dr., Keauhou Shopping Center, Kailua-Kona* ☎ *808/324–4688* ◎ *Closed Sun.*

$ ✕**Pancho & Lefty's.** Across the street from the Kona Inn Shopping Village,
MEXICAN this Mexican restaurant is a good bet for nachos and margaritas on a lazy afternoon, or to watch the passersby below you on Alii Drive. The food is marginal, however, and some of the items on the menu are expensive. At 5 pm, the banyan tree across the street is filled with hundreds of chirping birds, a veritable happy hour in bird land. ⊠ *75-5719 Alii Dr., Kailua-Kona* ☎ *808/326–2171.*

$ ✕**Peaberry & Galette.** This little creperie is a welcome addition to the
FRENCH neighborhood. The menu includes Illy espresso, teas, excellent sweet and savory crepes, and rich desserts like lemon cheesecake and chocolate mousse that are made fresh daily. The small venue has a relaxed,

8

urban-café vibe, and is a nice place to hang for a bit if you're waiting for a movie at the theater next door, or just feel like taking a break from paradise to sip a decent espresso and flip through the latest W. ⊠ *Keauhou Shopping Center, 78-6831 Alii Dr., Kailua-Kona* ☎ *808/322–6020.*

$
VIETNAMESE

✕ **Pho Saigon.** Tucked away in the old Department of Motor Vehicles building near Big Island Grill, this new addition to Kona's dining scene also happens to be the Big Island's only authentic Vietnamese restaurant. All ingredients are the freshest of fresh, and the pho noodle soup (both chicken and beef) will satisfy aficionados. ⊠ *75-5722 Hanama Pl., Kailua-Kona* ☎ *808/326–2000* ☯ *Closed Sun.*

$
HAWAIIAN

✕ **Pine Tree Café.** Next to Matsuyama's market along Highway 11 on the way to the airport, the Pine Tree Café offers local classics such as *huli huli* (Hawaiian-style rotisserie) chicken and loco moco, alongside new inventions like crab curry bisque. The fresh-fish plate is decent, and all meals are served with fries or rice and macaroni salad. The prices are a bit higher than you might expect, but the portions are huge. It's a good place to stop for a last-minute bite before catching your flight back to the mainland. ⊠ *Kohanaiki Plaza, 73-4354 Mamalahoa Hwy. (Hwy. 11), Kailua-Kona* ☎ *808/327–1234.*

$
AMERICAN

✕ **Quinn's Almost by the Sea.** With the bar in the front and the dining patio in the back, Quinn's may seem like a bit of a dive at first glance, but this venerable restaurant serves up the best darn cheeseburger and fries in town. Appropriate for families, the restaurant stays busy for lunch and dinner, while the bar attracts a cast of colorful regulars. The menu has many tasty options, like fish-and-chips, meat loaf, or beef tenderloin tips. Quinn's stays open until 11 pm, later than almost any other restaurant in Kailua-Kona. If time gets away from you on a drive to the north beaches, Quinn's awaits your return with a cheap beer and a basket of fried calamari. Drinks are strong; there are no watered-down cocktails served here. Park across the street at the Courtyard King Kamehameha's Kona Beach Hotel and get free one-hour parking with validation. ⊠ *75-5655 Palani Rd., Kailua-Kona* ☎ *808/329–3822* ⊕ *quinnsalmostbythesea.com.*

$
JAPANESE

✕ **Restaurant Hayama.** Tucked into Kopiko Plaza, just below Long's, this local favorite for quality Japanese fare goes beyond sushi. Hayama serves traditional Japanese specialties like tempura, unagi, broiled fish, teriyaki, and *udon* noodles, all made from fresh local ingredients. Sushi is available as well, but only traditional *nigiri,* slices of raw fish layered with wasabi and rice, and sashimi. Lunch specials are a great deal, and dinner specials provide a three-course meal for two for $40. Despite its strip mall location, Hayama manages to pull off a Zen vibe that matches the quiet and attentive, albeit "island-time," service. ⊠ *75-5660 Kopiko St., Kailua-Kona* ☎ *808/331–8888* ☯ *Closed Sun.*

$$
HAWAIIAN

✕ **Sam Choy's Kai Lanai.** Perched on the bluff above Keauhou Shopping Center, the newly opened Sam Choy's Kai Lanai is already a Kona classic. Celebrity-chef Sam Choy has transformed an old Wendy's into a beautiful open-air restaurant complete with an awesome bar, The Short Bait, designed to look like a charter-fishing boat. Granite-topped tables offer sweeping ocean views from every seat in the house. Open for breakfast, lunch, and dinner, the venue presents reasonably priced entrées, highlighted by the macadamia-nut-crusted chicken, Oriental lamb chops, or Sam's trio of fish served with shiitake-mushroom cream sauce. The ahi salad (served in a deep-fried flour tortilla bowl) is a great deal for $14. *Keiki* (children's) menus accommodate families. Parking is at a premium, so you might have to park in the shopping center below. The restaurant can be noisy. ■ TIP➜ Arrive at 5 pm to nab the best patio seating. ✉ *Keauhou Shopping Center, 78-6831 Alii Dr., Suite 1000, Kailua-Kona* ☎ *808/333–3434* ⊕ *www.samchoy.com.*

$ ✕ **Tacos El Unico.** An array of authentic soft-taco choices (beef and
MEXICAN chicken, among others), burritos, quesadillas, and excellent homemade tamales. Order at the counter, take a seat outside at one of a dozen yellow tables with blue umbrellas, and enjoy all the good flavors served up in those red plastic baskets. ✉ *Kona Marketplace, 75-5729 Alii Dr., Kailua-Kona* ☎ *808/326–4033.*

$ ✕ **Thai Rin Restaurant.** The owner at this dependable joint adjacent to Lava
THAI Java is likely to take your order, cook it, and bring it to your table himself, but that doesn't mean the service is slow—just the opposite. Everything is cooked to order, and the menu is brimming with choices, including five curries, a green-papaya salad, and a popular platter that combines spring rolls, satay, beef salad, and *tom yum* (lemongrass soup). For a real treat, try the deep-fried fish. Piña colada fans will appreciate the excellent cocktails served here, and you can't beat the beautiful ocean view. Indoor and outdoor seating is available. ✉ *75-5799 Alii Dr., Kailua-Kona* ☎ *808/329–2929* ⊕ *www.aliisunsetplaza.com.*

$ ✕ **Ultimate Burger.** Located in the Sports Authority shopping complex
AMERICAN (Kona Commons), this excellent burger joint may look like a chain, but it's an independent, locally owned and operated eatery that serves 100% organic, grass-fed Big Island beef. Be sure to order a side of seasoned Big Daddy fries served with house-made aioli dipping sauce. ✉ *Kona Commons Shopping Center, 74-5450 Makala Blvd., Kailua-Kona* ☎ *808/329–2326.*

$ ✕ **Wasabi's.** A tiny place hidden in the back of the Coconut Plaza on
JAPANESE Alii Drive, Wasabi's features indoor and outdoor seating. Prices may seem steep, but the fish is of the highest quality, highlighted by a large selection of rolls and authentic Japanese offerings, along with a few unique inventions. And for those who will never be hip to the raw-fish thing, teriyaki, udon, and sukiyaki options abound. ✉ *75-5803 Alii Dr., Coconut Grove Marketplace, Kailua-Kona* ☎ *808/326–2352* ⊕ *www.wasabishawaii.com.*

THE KONA COAST

SOUTH KONA

$ ✕ **The Coffee Shack.** Visitors enjoy stopping here for lunch after a morn-
AMERICAN ing of snorkeling at Kealakekua Bay, and for good reason: the views of the Honaunau coast from this roadside restaurant in South Kona are stunning. Breads are all homemade, and you get to choose your favorite when ordering a generously sized sandwich brimming with Black Forest ham and the like. If you're in the mood for a Hawaiian

8

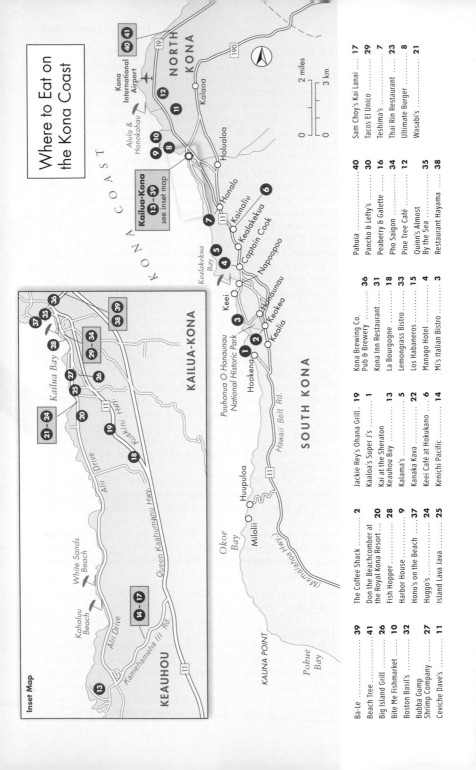

Where to Eat on the Kona Coast

NORTH KONA

Kona International Airport

Alula & Honokohau

Kalaoa

Holualoa

Kailua-Kona 13–39 see inset map

Honalo

Kainaliu

Kealakekua

Captain Cook

Napoopoo

Keei

Puuhonua O Honaunau National Historic Park

Honaunau

Keokea

Kealia

Hookena

Huupuloa

Miloli

SOUTH KONA

Kauna Point

Pohue Bay

Okoe Bay

Hawaii Belt Rd.

(Mamalahoa Hwy.)

KONA COAST

Kealakekua Bay

Kahaluu Beach

White Sands Beach

Inset Map

KEAUHOU

KAILUA-KONA

Kailua Bay

Alii Drive

Queen Kaahumanu Hwy.

Kamehameha III Rd.

Kuakini Hwy.

0   2 miles
0   3 km

smoothie, iced honey-mocha latte, or homemade luau bread, it's worth the detour, even though the parking lot can be tricky to maneuver. ✉ *83-5799 Mamalahoa Hwy., Captain Cook* ☎ *808/328–9555* ⊕ *www. coffeeshack.com* ☾ *No dinner.*

$ | ✕ **Kaaloa's Super Js Authentic Hawaiian Food.** It figures that the best *laulau*
HAWAIIAN | (meat wrapped in taro leaves and ti) in West Hawaii can be found at a roadside hole-in-the-wall rather than at an expensive resort luau. In fact, this humble family-run eatery was featured on the *Food Network*'s "The Best Thing I Ever Ate." Plate lunches to go include tender chicken or pork *laulau*, steamed for up to 10 hours. The kalua pig and cabbage is delicious, and the lomilomi salmon features vine-ripened tomatoes. Proprietors John and Janice Kaaloa also grind their own poi. ✉ *83-5409 Mamalahoa Hwy., between mile markers 106 and 107, Honaunau* ☎ *808/328–9566* ➟ *No credit cards.*

$ | ✕ **Kalama's.** The little yellow café near Kealakekua Bay is a great place
HAWAIIAN | to stop after a morning of kayaking or swimming with spinner dol-
☾ | phins. The Kauai-born proprietors serve up excellent Hawaiian offerings like the popular *laulau* burger made with cured pork, or complete entrées like grilled ahi or teriyaki short ribs. Be sure to try the mahimahi burger—it's might be the best mahimahi you'll ever eat. For the kids, Kalama's offers shave ice, musubi, hot deli sandwiches, hot dogs, and burgers grilled on the barbecue and served on a soft potato bun. Everything is cooked to order, so grab a table, change your watch to island time, relax, and enjoy the view. ✉ *82-5674 Kahau Pl., at Napoopoo Rd., Captain Cook* ☎ *808/328–2828.*

$$ | ✕ **Keei Café at Hokukano.** This beautiful restaurant, perched above the
ECLECTIC | highway just 15 minutes south of Kailua-Kona, serves delicious dinners
Fodor's Choice | with Brazilian, Asian, and European flavors highlighting fresh ingre-
★ | dients from local farmers. Favorites are the Brazilian seafood chowder or peanut-miso salad, followed by pasta primavera smothered with a basil-pesto sauce. There's an extensive wine list. Bob Miyashiro, the owner, is a Kona native, and his wife, Gina, is Brazilian. The husband-and-wife cooking team are also from Brazil, and have been with the restaurant since its humble beginnings at its previous location in Honaunau. Toast your friendly hosts with a refreshing mojito before dinner. ✉ *79-7511 Mamalahoa Hwy., ½ mi south of Kainaliu, Kealakekua* ☎ *808/322–9992* ⊕ *www.keeicafe.net* ☖ *Reservations essential* ➟ *No credit cards* ☾ *Closed Sun. and Mon.*

$ | ✕ **Manago Hotel.** About 20 minutes upcountry of Kailua-Kona, the his-
AMERICAN | toric Manago Hotel is a time-warp experience. A vintage neon sign identifies the hotel, while Formica tables and old photos add to the authentically retro flavor. The T-shirts (which are great souvenirs for friends at home) brag that the hotel's restaurant has the best pork chops in town, and it's not false advertising. The fresh fish is excellent as well, especially the ono and butterfish. Unless you request otherwise, the fish is sautéed with a tasty house butter-soy sauce concoction. Meals come with rice for the table and an assortment of side dishes that changes from time to time, but usually includes a macaroni, potato, and tuna salad, and a braised tofu and sautéed veggie dish. ✉ *82-6155 Mamala-*

8

hoa Hwy., Captain Cook ☎ *808/323–2642* ⊕ *www.managohotel.com* ⊘ *Closed Mon.*

$ ✕ **Mi's Italian Bistro.** A welcome addition to the South Kona dining scene, ITALIAN   Mi's is a classy, white-tablecloth establishment in a hole-in-the-wall location next to a liquor store on the mountain (*mauka*) side of Highway 11. The restaurant's husband-and-wife owners prepare homemade pastas and focaccia daily. Daily specials are always delicious and usually include a lasagna, focaccia, and risotto option. The homemade herb-cheese ravioli is rich and delicious, and even the salad options are a notch above, with ingredients such as candied macadamia nuts, roasted beets, and sautéed haricots verts. Homemade desserts are worth saving room for, particularly the banana-rum flambé. ⊠ *81-6372 Mamalahoa Hwy., Kealakekua* ☎ *808/323–3880* ⊕ *www.misitalianbistro.com.*

$ ✕ **Teshima's.** Locals show up at this small, historic restaurant 15 minutes JAPANESE   south of Kailua-Kona whenever they're in the mood for fresh sashimi, puffy shrimp tempura, or *hekka* (beef and vegetables cooked in an iron pot) at a reasonable price. Teshima's doesn't look like much, inside or out, but it's been a *kamaaina* (local) favorite since 1929 for a reason. You might want to try *teishoku* (tray) No. 3, featuring sashimi, tempura, sukiyaki beef, rice, miso soup, sunomono, and more. Or order the popular bento box lunch. The service is laid-back and friendly, and the restaurant has been family owned and operated by five generations of Teshimas. ⊠ *79-7251 Mamalahoa Hwy., Honalo* ☎ *808/322–9140* ⊟ *No credit cards.*

NORTH KONA

$$$ ✕ **Beach Tree at the Four Seasons Resort Hualalai.** This beautifully designed MODERN ITALIAN   venue provides a relaxed and elegant setting for alfresco dining near the ⟳   sand, with its boardwalk-style deck, outdoor seating under the trellis, **Fodor's Choice**   and enormous vaulted ceiling. Chef Nick Mastrascusa is a transplant ★   from the Four Seasons Hotel New York, bringing Italian and Spanish influences to his inventive menu. Outstanding entrées include the seafood paella for two and the grilled rib eye with shoestring fries. The tropical Peletini martini is a favorite, and at dinner, the premium wine list includes the Beach Tree's own signature reds and whites. There's also a great children's menu and activities to keep them busy, like a fun, rotating pasta fork, and an ice-cream-cone spinner. Live Hawaiian music is featured nightly. ⊠ *72-100 Kaupulehu Dr.* ⌷ *Box 1269, Kailua-Kona 96745* ☎ *808/325–8000* ⊕ *www.fourseasons.com/hualalai.*

$$$$ ✕ **Pahuia at the Four Seasons Resort Hualalai.** *Pahuia* means aquarium, so MODERN   it's fitting that a 9- by 4-foot aquarium in the entrance casts a dreamy HAWAIIAN   light through this exquisite restaurant. Presentation is paramount, and **Fodor's Choice**   the cuisine is first rate. Asian-influenced dishes stand out for their lay- ★   ers of flavor. Chef Jacob Anaya creates something spectacular with each plate. Opt for a tasting menu of up to seven small items or go for a full entrée—you'll be happy with whatever you choose. The chef changes the menu four times a year and focuses on showcasing local ingredients. You're likely to find unique preparations of your favorite dishes, such as baby abalone, white shrimp, Keahole lobster, Big Island moi, Hawaiian snapper, lamb, and prime beef. Breakfasts are superb; the lemon ricotta pancakes are so good they should be illegal. Reserve

Relax with a beachside meal at the Four Seasons Resort Hualalai

a table on the patio and you may be able to spot whales while dining. Pricey, but worth the splurge, at least once. ⊠ *Four Seasons Resort Hualalai, 100 Kaupulehu Dr., North Kona* ☎ *808/325–8000* ⊕ *www. fourseasons.com/hualalai* ⊙ *No lunch.*

THE KOHALA COAST

$$

ASIAN

Fodor'sChoice

★

✕ **Bamboo Restaurant.** It's out of the way, but the food at this spot in the heart of Hawi is good and the service and ambience have a Hawaiian–country flair. Creative entrées feature fresh island fish prepared several ways. The Thai-style fish, for example, combines lemongrass, Kaffir lime leaves, and coconut milk; it's best washed down with a passion-fruit margarita or passion-fruit iced tea. Bamboo accents, bold local artwork, and an old unfinished wooden floor make the restaurant cozy. Local musicians entertain on Friday or Saturday evenings. ⊠ *55-3415 Akoni Pule Hwy., Hwy. 270, Hawi* ☎ *808/889–5555* ⊕ *www. bamboorestaurant.info* ⊙ *Closed Mon. No dinner Sun.*

$$$$

MODERN

HAWAIIAN

Fodor'sChoice

★

✕ **Brown's Beach House at the Fairmont Orchid Hawaii.** Nestled alongside the resort's sandy bay, Brown's Beach House offers beautiful sunset dining and innovative cuisine by chef "TK" Keosavang. Attention to detail is evident in the sophisticated cuisine, like the delicious Manilla clams infused with subtle hints of tomato, onion, fennel, saffron, and white wine. Try the yummy tom yum soup with poached ono in coconut-lemongrass broth, or the tender braised short ribs with veggie risotto. The menu includes choices that accommodate diet-specific preferences such as macrobiotic, raw, vegan, gluten-free, and diabetic—amazingly,

The Fairmont Orchid Hawaii on the Kohala Coast is a great spot for sunset dining.

these offerings are as flavorful and inventive as everything on the main menu. ✉ *Fairmont Orchid Hawaii, 1 N. Kaniku Dr., Kohala Coast* ☎ *808/885–2000* ⊕ *www.fairmont.com/orchid* ☉ *No lunch.*

$$
ITALIAN

✕ **Café Pesto.** In the sleepy harbor town of Kawaihae, the original Café Pesto ranks as a hidden find for visitors. Gourmet pizzas are topped with eclectic goodies like pork and pineapple, chili-grilled shrimp, shiitake mushrooms, and cilantro crème fraîche. The menu is a bit pricey, and includes Asian-inspired pastas and risottos, plus fresh-fish entrées. Local brews and a full-service bar make this a good place to end the evening, and the lounge-y bar area with sofas and comfy chairs provides a nice place to grab a drink while you're waiting for a table. ✉ *61-3665 Akoni Pule Hwy., Kawaihae Harbor Center, Hwy. 270, Kawaihae* ☎ *808/882–1071* ⊕ *www.cafepesto.com.*

$$$$
ECLECTIC
Fodor'sChoice
★

✕ **CanoeHouse at the Mauna Lani Bay Hotel & Bungalows.** This landmark restaurant on the ocean showcases the inventive cuisine of executive chef Sandy Tuason, who previously served at the prestigious L'Atelier de Joël Robuchon restaurant in Manhattan. The progressive menu draws its influences from around the world while incorporating the flavors of the Islands. Dishes are artfully presented and feature delicious offerings like the Duo of Lamb, comprised of roasted loin and spiced lamb sausage; or the Keahole lobster salad with avocado-mango relish and crispy greens from Waimea. Don't miss the exquisite desserts, especially the homemade sorbets or the Waialua Chocolate Dome. The wine list is great, and the open-air beachfront setting makes the hefty price tag worth it on clear evenings. ✉ *Mauna Lani Bay Hotel & Bungalows, 68-1400 Mauna Lani Dr., Kohala Coast* ☎ *808/885–6622* ⊕ *www.maunalani.com.*

$$$
MODERN
HAWAIIAN
✕ **Coast Grille at Hapuna Beach Prince Hotel.** This open-air venue has high ceilings and a lanai that overlooks the pool and beach. American bistro-style dishes showcase the bounty of Big Island ingredients, including fresh Kona shrimp and lobster (raised at the Natural Energy Lab), seasonal fresh oysters, and specially prepared seafood. Every Friday is "Let's Go Crabbing" night, a splendid buffet with everything from steamed Manilla clams and soft-shell crab tempura to crab-and-corn bisque and a full salad bar. ⊠ *Hapuna Beach Prince Hotel, 62-100 Kaunaoa Dr., Kohala Coast* ☎ *808/880–3192* ⊕ *www.princeresortshawaii.com* ⊗ *No lunch.*

$$$
HAWAIIAN
✕ **Eddie Aikau Restaurant and Surf Museum.** The lastest addition to the upscale Kings' Shops in Waikoloa, this two-level venue commemorates the late, big-wave-surfing legend of "Eddie Would Go" fame. The restaurant is owned and operated by Eddie's family in partnership with a group of Hawaiian-born restaurateurs. Although the menu approaches resort prices, the restaurant is fun and casual, with cocktail bars upstairs and downstairs, plus lakeside seating. Don't miss the 16-oz. grilled Aikau rib eye or the Kalua spring rolls laden with special sauce. Chef Scott Lutey's take on contemporary Hawaiian cuisine includes an inventive Luau Plate with taro hash. Memorabilia including Eddie's red surf trunks are on display. ⊠ *Kings' Shops Waikoloa, 69-250 Waikoloa Beach Dr., Suite C1, Kohala Coast* ☎ *808/886–8433* ⊕ *www.eddieaikaurestaurant.com.*

$$$$
SEAFOOD
✕ **Hakone Buffet.** Open on Saturday evening only, Hakone restaurant offers an excellent steak-and-seafood buffet featuring assorted sushi, daily catch, shrimp and veggie tempura, and grilled teriyaki steak. There's also a limited à la carte menu. The restaurant doesn't offer ocean views, but the upscale setting features Asian decor, fountains, shoji screens, and linen tablecloths. Be sure to try the signature martini—a hibiscus sake made with Sprite and a little cranberry juice. Yum. ⊠ *Hapuna Beach Prince Hotel, 62-100 Kaunaoa Dr., Kohala Coast* ☎ *808/880–1111* ⊕ *www.princeresortshawaii.com* ⊗ *Closed Sun.–Fri. No lunch.*

8

$$$$
JAPANESE
✕ **Imari Japanese Restaurant at the Hilton Waikoloa Village.** This elegant restaurant, complete with waterfalls and a teahouse, serves sukiyaki and tempura aimed to please mainland tastes. Beyond the impressive display of Imari porcelain at the entrance, you can find teppanyaki (beef or shrimp cooked table-side), *washoku* (a traditional Japanese dining experience that allows you to enjoy new-wave and classical cuisine), and a sushi–sashimi bar. The restaurant can get loud. ⊠ *425 Waikoloa Beach Dr., Kohala Coast* ☎ *808/886–1234* ⊕ *www.hiltonwaikoloavillage.com* ⊗ *No lunch.*

$$
SEAFOOD
✕ **Kawaihae Seafood Bar.** Upstairs in a structure that dates from the 1850s, this seafood bar has been a hot spot since it opened in 2003, serving up a dynamite and well-priced bar menu with tasty *pupu* (appetizers), and an always expanding dinner menu that includes at least four fresh-fish specials daily. There's fare for landlubbers, too, including boneless braised short ribs, rib-eye steak, specialty pizza and lots of salad options. Don't miss their escargot, oysters Rockefeller, and ginger steamed clams. At lunch, the menu ranges from sandwiches and burgers to sashimi and poke. Breakfast is served only on weekends, and happy

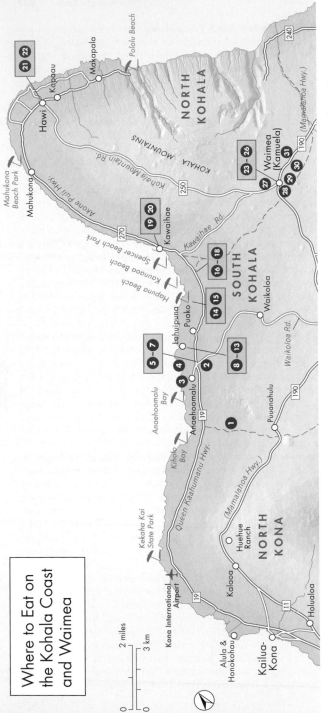

Where to Eat on the Kohala Coast and Waimea

0 — 2 miles
0 — 3 km

hour runs daily from 3 to 5:30 pm, and again from 10 pm until close (2 am). If you've got the late-night munchies, this is a great spot—they serve food until 11:30 pm. ✉ *61-3642 Kawaihae Harbor, Hwy. 270, Kawaihae* ☎ *808/880–9393* ⊕ *www.seafoodbargrill.com.*

$$$$
MODERN
HAWAIIAN
✕ **KPC (Kamuela Provision Company) at the Hilton Waikoloa Village.** The breezy lanai with a sweeping view of the Kohala Coast is the perfect accompaniment to the elegant yet down-to-earth Hawaii regional cuisine. The lanai offers the best seats in the house—get there by 5:30 if you want to score a seat for the sunset, because KPC offers a better view than any other restaurant on the Big Island. The specialty cocktails are some of the best on the island, as well; ask for the mango martini. Entrées are on the pricy side, but the ginger-steamed monchong (a deep-water Hawaiian fish) is a winner. If you're in the mood for appetizers, the Kona lobster and Hokkaido pumpkin bisque tastes as good as it sounds. The restaurant's number one seller is the Kona Coffee Mud Slide; don't miss it. The Baked Mauna Kea (KPC's take on a Baked Alaska) is equally decadent. ✉ *Hilton Waikoloa Village, 69-425 Waikoloa Beach Dr., Waikoloa* ☎ *808/886–1234* ⊕ *www.hiltonwaikoloavillage.com* ◷ *No lunch.*

$$$$
MODERN
HAWAIIAN
✕ **Manta & Pavilion Wine Bar at the Mauna Kea Beach Hotel.** Perched on the edge of a bluff overlooking the sparkling waters of Kaunaoa Beach, this is an amazing spot for a romantic meal at sunset, especially at one of the outside tables. The restaurant's Enomatic wine system allows guests to sample 48 different wines by the glass. Main dishes include macadamia nut–crusted lamb, Big Island butterfish, Kau coffee beef filet, butter-poached Keahole lobster, and a perfectly prepared seared ahi with Molokai sweet-potato puree and foie-gras spring roll. The crispy pork-belly appetizer with Kona baby abalone is not to be missed; try the squash soup topped with ohelo berry. This is also the spot for Sunday brunch, with an impressive spread that includes an omelet station, prime rib, smoked salmon, tempura, lobster bisque, and a build-your-own-sundae bar. ✉ *62-100 Mauna Kea Beach Dr., Kohala Coast* ☎ *808/882–5810* ⊕ *www.maunakeabeachhotel.com* ◷ *No lunch.*

$$
MEDITERRANEAN
✕ **Merriman's Market Café.** From Peter Merriman, one of Hawaii's star chefs, comes a more affordable alternative to his upscale Waimea and Maui restaurants. The Mediterranean-influenced menu includes a variety of pasta dishes, tasty appetizers, and salads teeming with fresh ingredients from nearby Waimea farms. Its outdoor patio beckons locals and visitors alike. It's open daily for lunch, followed by happy hour from 3 pm to 5:30 pm, then dinner until 8:45 pm. ✉ *Kings' Shops at Waikoloa Beach Resort, 250 Waikoloa Beach Dr., Waikoloa* ☎ *808/886–1700* ⊕ *merrimanshawaii.com/market_cafe.htm.*

$$$$
MODERN
AMERICAN
✕ **Monettes.** Chef Michael Minshull has arrived, and with him comes a refined and lightened menu to which he's adding new favorites. This superpricey restaurant at the Mauna Kea Beach Hotel unveils a beautiful koa-and-mahogany bar, plus a huge, glass-fronted wine cellar that houses an award-winning selection of more than 4,500 premium wines. Signature dishes range from Kobe beef to Colorado rack of lamb. Try the rich and buttery lobster bisque. Be sure to sample one of the delicious martinis served in a cone-shaped glass embedded in a bowl of

8

crushed ice. ⊠ *Mauna Kea Beach Hotel, 62-100 Mauna Kea Beach Dr., Kohala Coast* ☎ *808/443–2850* ⊕ *www.monetteshawaii.com.*

$$ ✕ **Monstera.** It may not be beachfront with a view of the sunset, but this
JAPANESE   addition to the Shops at Mauna Lani is worth a visit for its casual Japanese pub food with a touch of local inspiration. Chef Norio Yamamoto's tasty lunch and dinner menu includes his signature tuna tataki, crispy whole moi, *hamachi kama* (broiled Japanese yellowtail cheek) and seafood papaya (shrimp and scallops with veggies baked in a papaya). There are excellent sizzling plate items like short ribs and rib-eye steak, hot and cold noodle dishes, and, of course, the outstanding sushi. Most people make a meal out of sharing several small plate items so you can sample a bit of everything. Save room for the tempura banana drizzled with chocolate and caramel for dessert. It's best to make a reservation; you can also get some of the menu to go. ⊠ *The Shops at Mauna Lani, 68-1330 Mauna Lani Dr., Waikoloa* ☎ *808/887–2711* ⊕ *www. monterasushi.com.*

$$$ ✕ **Norio's Japanese Restaurant and Sushi Bar.** Located inside the Fairmont
JAPANESE   Orchid at the garden level, this restaurant appeals to both steak and seafood lovers. Chef Darren Ogasawara has completely revamped the former Norio's menu, highlighting everything from Australian A6 Wagyu rib eye (seasoned with five different kinds of Hawaiian sea salt) to the delicious hamachi-and-avocado sashimi served with ponzu-garlic sauce. Everything on the menu is made from scratch, including the sauces, plus the fish is as fresh as it gets. ⊠ *Fairmont Orchid Hawaii, 1 N. Kaniku Dr., Kohala Coast* ☎ *808/885–2000* ⊕ *www.fairmont.com/ orchid* ⊗ *Closed Tues. and Wed. No lunch.*

$$ ✕ **Number 3 at the Mauna Kea Beach Hotel.** Though it sits right on the edge
AMERICAN   of the hotel's golf course, this is not just a restaurant for golfers. A short walk from the main entrance to the hotel, the newly renovated, spacious dining room has seating both inside and out, and service is quick and correct. Number 3 serves up a great lunch menu with dishes such as ahi sashimi and beer-battered fresh-fish tacos. ⊠ *62-100 Mauna Kea Beach Dr., Kohala Coast* ☎ *808/882–5810* ⊕ *www.maunakeabeachhotel.com* ⊗ *No dinner.*

$$$ ✕ **Roy's Waikoloa Bar & Grill.** If you're looking for consistently decent
MODERN   food and you're staying nearby, Roy's fits the bill. The venue overlooks
HAWAIIAN   the lake at the Kings' Shops, which, granted, is not an oceanfront setting by any means. If you're simply in the mood for a light meal, you can easily fill up on the enormous selection of great appetizers, and the extensive wine-by-the-glass list offers good pairing options. The three-course meal is a good bet, or try the butterfish for a melt-in-your-mouth encounter. ⊠ *Kings' Shops at Waikoloa Village, 250 Waikoloa Beach Dr., Kohala Coast* ☎ *808/886–4321* ⊕ *www.roysrestaurant.com* ⊗ *No lunch.*

$$$$ ✕ **Ruth's Chris Steakhouse.** Located at the Shops at Mauna Lani, the
STEAKHOUSE Hawaii location of the popular Louisiana steakhouse chain serves the same sizzling steaks and heaping sides the restaurant is known for throughout the country. Ask about early evening "Prime Time" specials that include a salad, entrée, side, and dessert for a fraction of the price. They also have vegetarian options, but Ruth's Chris is a true steakhouse

in every way and as such is best suited to meat lovers. Steaks come sizzling; tasty, classic sides, which are à la carte, include creamed spinach, sautéed mushrooms, and potatoes au gratin. ⊠ *Shops at Mauna Lani, 68-1330 Mauna Lani Dr., Kohala Coast* ☎ *808/887–0800* ⊕ *www.ruthschris.com* ⊘ *No lunch.*

$$$ ✕**Sansei Seafood Restaurant & Sushi Bar.** This restaurant serves heavenly
JAPANESE   interpretations of sushi and contemporary Asian cuisine. More than a few dishes have won awards, including the shrimp dynamite in a creamy garlic masago aioli and unagi glaze, and the Dungeness crab ramen with Asian truffle broth. There are tried-and-true favorites that are mainstays, however, the menu is consistently updated to include new and exciting options such as the Hawaiian *moi* sashimi rolls and the Japanese yellowtail nori aioli poke. You can certainly make a meal out of the appetizers and sushi rolls, or try some of Sansei's great entrées from both land and sea. Go for an early dinner on Sunday and Monday when sushi and other food items are half off from 5 to 6 pm (limited seating; first come, first served). Or opt for a late-night meal on Friday and Saturday when sushi and appetizers are half off from 10 pm until 1:30 am (you just have to put up with the karaoke singers; 21 and older). ⊠ *201 Waikoloa Beach Dr., 801 Queens' MarketPlace, Waikoloa* ☎ *808/886–6286* ⊕ *www.dkrestaurants.com* ⊘ *No lunch.*

$$ ✕**Sushi Rock.** In the funky Without Boundaries shop in Hawi, Sushi
JAPANESE   Rock isn't big on ambience—its narrow dining room is brightly painted and casually decorated with various Hawaiian and Japanese knick-knacks—but hungry locals and visiting couples flock here for some of the island's best sushi. The restaurant prides itself on using fresh local ingredients like grass-fed beef tenderloin, goat cheese, macadamia nuts, and mango in their Island-inspired sushi rolls. They also serve up a variety of cooked seafood, chicken, noodle dishes, and salads for lunch and dinner. Everything is plated beautifully and served either at the sushi bar, at one of the handful of indoor tables in the restaurant's narrow dining room, or on the covered front patio. There's also a full bar. ⊠ *55-3435 Akoni Pule Hwy., Hawi* ☎ *808/889–5900* ⊕ *sushirockrestaurant.net* ⊘ *Closed Wed.*

$$$ ✕**Tommy Bahama Tropical Café.** This breezy, open-air restaurant, located
MODERN   upstairs at the Shops at Mauna Lani, offers an excellent roster of appe-
HAWAIIAN   tizers: don't miss the seared-scallop sliders or the coconut-crusted crab cakes. The chef here has freedom to cook up his own daily specials, and the macadamia-crusted *opakapaka* (Pacific red snapper) is a standout. Other entrées include maple-brined pork chops and crab-stuffed shrimp. Homemade breads and creamy butters set the stage for a nice meal, which most definitely should include one of Tommy's outstanding martinis, the tastiest and strongest anywhere on the island. Desserts are decadent and meant for sharing. ⊠ *Shops at Mauna Lani, 68-1330 Mauna Lani Dr., No. 102, Kohala Coast* ☎ *808/881–8686* ⊕ *www.tommybahama.com.*

$ ✕**Waikoloa Grill'n Bar.** Amid the sea of expensive resort restaurants on
HAWAIIAN   the Kohala Coast, this is an affordable alternative, a best-kept secret in the Waikoloa Beach Resort area. Its location on the 14th tee near the Marriott offers casual, fine dining with a menu that's a throwback

8

to Hawaii's retro steakhouses of the 1960s. Decor is simple, and so is the concept. Legendary restaurateur Dickie Furtado boasts many signature dishes, highlighted by the delicious calamari steak cooked with lemon butter and capers in a delicate panko crust. (Don't miss it; it's probably the best calamari you'll ever eat.) Generous-size steaks include the kiawe-grilled rib eye and the giant 14-oz. porterhouse. No watered-down cocktails here—the restaurant offers an excellent happy hour with free pupus, while the well-stocked salad bar features more than 30 items. ⊠ *Waikoloa Beach Resort, 69-1022 Keana Pl., Kohala Coast* ☎ *808/886–8797.*

> **WORD OF MOUTH**
>
> "I really enjoy Kona Brewing Co.… great beers and really good pizzas!" —beanweb24

WAIMEA

$$$
HAWAIIAN

✕ **Allen's Table.** Formerly executive chef at the acclaimed Merriman's restaurant in Waimea, Chef Allen Hess recently opened his own namesake restaurant at the former Huli Sue's down the highway. Foodies will appreciate his "slow food" take on regional cuisine inspired by Hawaii's plantation era. Don't miss the braised short ribs, the fried pork chop, the goat tacos, and the Kona lobster bouillabaisse. Chef Allen makes everything in-house, including sausages, patés, and dry-aged meats sourced from Big Island beef producers. As for seafood, his broiled local kampachi is the highlight of the fresh-catch offerings. ⊠ *64-957 Mamalahoa Hwy., Waimea* ☎ *808/885–6268* ⊕ *www. allenstable.com* ۞ *Closed Sun.*

$
MEXICAN

✕ **Big Island Brewhaus/Tako Taco.** Tako Taco has always been a favorite Waimea eatery, and owner Tom Kerns is a veteran brewer. He's now churning out some decent ales, lagers, and specialty beers from his on-site brewery. With a focus on fresh ingredients, Tako Taco whips up excellent tacos, burritos, Mexican salads, enchiladas, rellenos, and quesadillas fresh to order. You'll want refills on the habanero salsa, perhaps accompanied by a top-shelf margarita, either classic or *lilikoi* (passion fruit). And nothing beats a cold local brew to wash down that spicy enchilada. ⊠ *64-1066A Mamalahoa Hwy. (Hwy. 11), Waimea* ☎ *808/887–1717* ⊕ *www.bigislandbrewhaus.com.*

$$
MODERN
HAWAIIAN

✕ **Daniel's.** This fine-dining restaurant features the creations of respected local chef Daniel Thiebaut in a quaint yellow building that once housed the historic Chock In Store, which catered to the ranching community beginning in 1900. Collectibles abound, such as antique porcelain pieces. Under new ownership, but still retaining the services of chef Daniel, the revamped establishment has unveiled an all-organic, locally sourced, sustainable menu that includes everything from handmade pastas to eggplant napoleon with hamakua mushrooms to Cajun-style ahi niçoise, pan-seared scallops, and a variety of sautéed seafood options. The place to be in Waimea on a Sunday afternoon, Daniel's offers a popular Sunday brunch from 10 to 2, featuring live local music and

Continued on page 217

LUAU: A TASTE OF HAWAII

The best place to sample Hawaiian food is at a backyard luau. Aunts and uncles are cooking, the pig is from a cousin's farm, and the fish is from a brother's boat.

But even locals have to angle for invitations to those rare occasions. So your choice is most likely between a commercial luau and a Hawaiian restaurant.

Some commercial luau are less authentic; they offer little of the traditional diet and are more about umbrella drinks, spectacle, and fun.

For greater authenticity, folksy experiences, and rock-bottom prices, visit a Hawaiian restaurant (most are in anonymous storefronts in residential neighborhoods). Expect rough edges and some effort negotiating the menu.

In either case, much of what is known today as Hawaiian food would be as foreign to a 16th-century Hawaiian as risotto or chow mien. The pre-contact diet was simple and healthy—mainly raw and steamed seafood and vegetables. Early Hawaiians used earth ovens and heated stones to cook seafood, taro, sweet potatoes, and breadfruit and seasoned their food with sea salt and ground kukui nuts. Seaweed, fern shoots, sweet potato vines, coconut, banana, sugarcane, and select greens and roots rounded out the diet.

Successive waves of immigrants added their favorites to the ti leaf–lined table. So it is that foods as disparate as salt salmon and chicken long rice are now Hawaiian—even though there is no salmon in Hawaiian waters and long rice (cellophane noodles) is Chinese.

AT THE LUAU: KALUA PORK

The heart of any luau is the *imu*, the earth oven in which a whole pig is roasted. The preparation of an imu is an arduous affair for most families, who tackle it only once a year or so, for a baby's first birthday or at Thanksgiving, when many Islanders prefer to imu their turkeys. Commercial luau operations have it down to a science, however.

THE ART OF THE STONE

The key to a proper imu is the *pohaku*, the stones. Imu cook by means of long, slow, moist heat released by special stones that can withstand a hot fire without exploding. Many Hawaiian families treasure their imu stones, keeping them in a pile in the backyard and passing them on through generations.

PIT COOKING

The imu makers first dig a pit about the size of a refrigerator, then lay down *kiawe* (mesquite) wood and stones, and build a white-hot fire that is allowed to burn itself out. The ashes are raked away, and the hot stones covered with banana and ti leaves. Well-wrapped in ti or banana leaves and a net of chicken wire, the pig is lowered onto the leaf-covered stones. *Laulau* (leaf-wrapped bundles of meats, fish, and taro leaves) may also be placed inside. Leaves—ti, banana, even ginger—cover the pig followed by wet burlap sacks (to create steam). The whole is topped with a canvas tarp and left to steam for the better part of a day.

OPENING THE IMU

This is the moment everyone waits for: The imu is unwrapped like a giant present and the imu keepers gingerly wrestle out the steaming pig. When it's unwrapped, the meat falls moist and smoky-flavored from the bone, looking just like Southern-style pulled pork, but without the barbecue sauce.

WHICH LUAU?

Fairmont Orchid. Blends modern and traditional music with stories of the kings of Hawai'i, Tahiti, Samoa, and New Zealand. Foods from all four cultures are served.

Royal Kona Resort Popular show features the unveiling of the pig from the underground oven (imu), plus generous menu and cocktails.

King Kamehameha's Kona Beach Hotel. This Luau features pig cooked in an imu, and Samoan fireknife dancers.

MEA AI ONO.
GOOD THINGS TO EAT.

LAULAU
Steamed meats, fish, and taro leaf in ti-leaf bundles: fork-tender, a medley of flavors; the taro resembles spinach.

Laulau

LOMI LOMI SALMON
Salt salmon in a piquant salad or relish with onions, tomatoes.

POI
Poi, a paste made of pounded taro root, may be an acquired taste, but it's a must-try during your visit.

Consider: The Hawaiian Adam is descended from *kalo* (taro). Young taro plants are called "keiki"–children. Poi is the first food after mother's milk for many Islanders. Ai, the word for food, is synonymous with poi in many contexts.

Lomi Lomi Salmon

Not only that, we love it. "There is no meat that doesn't taste good with poi," the old Hawaiians said.

But you have to know how to eat it: with something rich or powerfully flavored. "It is salt that makes the poi go in," is another adage. When you're served poi, try it with a mouthful of smoky kalua pork or salty lomi lomi salmon. Its slightly sour blandness cleanses the palate. And if you don't like it, smile and say something polite. (And slide that bowl over to a local.)

Poi

8

E HELE MAI AI! COME AND EAT!

Hawaiian restaurants tend to be inconveniently located in well-worn storefronts with little or no parking, outfitted with battered tables and clattering Melmac dishes, but they personify aloha, invariably run by local families who welcome tourists who take the trouble to find them.

Combination plates are a standard feature: one or two entrées, a side such as chicken long rice, choice of poi or steamed rice and—if the place is really old-style—a tiny portion of coarse Hawaiian salt and some raw onions for relish.

Most serve some foods that aren't, strictly speaking, Hawaiian, but are beloved of ka-maaina, such as salt meat with watercress (preserved meat in a tasty broth), or *akubone* (skipjack tuna fried in a tangy vinegar sauce).

Our two favorites: **Kanaka-Kava and Kualoa's Super J's Authentic Hawaiian.**

MENU GUIDE

Much of the Hawaiian language encountered during a stay in the Islands will appear on restaurant menus and lists of luau fare. Here's a quick primer.

ahi: yellowfin tuna.

aku: skipjack, bonito tuna.

amaama: mullet; it's hard to get but tasty.

bento: a box lunch.

chicken luau: a stew made from chicken, taro leaves, and coconut milk.

haupia: a light, pudding-like sweet made from coconut.

imu: the underground oven in which pigs are roasted for luau.

kalua: to bake underground.

kau kau: food. The word comes from Chinese but is used in the Islands.

kimchee: Korean dish of pickled cabbage made with garlic and hot peppers.

Kona coffee: coffee grown in the Kona district of the Big Island.

laulau: literally, a bundle. Laulau are morsels of pork, chicken, butterfish, or other ingredients wrapped with young taro leaves and then bundled in ti leaves for steaming.

lilikoi: passion fruit, a tart, seedy yellow fruit that makes delicious desserts, juice, and jellies.

lomi lomi: to rub or massage; also a massage. Lomi lomi salmon is fish that has been rubbed with onions and herbs; commonly served with minced onions and tomatoes.

luau: a Hawaiian feast; also the leaf of the taro plant used in preparing such a feast.

luau leaves: cooked taro tops with a taste similar to spinach.

mahimahi: mild-flavored dolphinfish, not the marine mammal.

mai tai: potent rum drink with orange liqueurs and pineapple juice, from the Tahitian word for "good."

malasada: a Portuguese deep-fried doughnut without a hole, dipped in sugar.

manapua: steamed chinese buns filled with pork, chicken, or other fillings.

mano: shark.

niu: coconut.

onaga: pink or red snapper.

ono: a long, slender mackerel-like fish; also called wahoo.

ono: delicious; also hungry.

opihi: a tiny shellfish, or mollusk, found on rocks; also called limpets.

papio: a young ulua or jack fish.

poha: Cape gooseberry. Tasting a bit like honey, the poha berry is often used in jams and desserts.

poi: a paste made from pounded taro root, a staple of the Hawaiian diet.

poke: cubed raw tuna or other fish, tossed with seaweed and seasonings.

pupu: appetizers or small plates.

saimin: long thin noodles and vegetables in broth, often garnished with small pieces of fish cake, scrambled egg, luncheon meat, and green onion.

sashimi: raw fish thinly sliced and usually eaten with soy sauce.

ti leaves: a member of the agave family. The leaves are used to wrap food while cooking and removed before eating.

uku: deep-sea snapper.

ulua: a member of the jack family that also includes pompano and amberjack. Also called crevalle, jack fish, and jack crevalle.

slack-key players. ⊠ *65-1259 Kawaihae Rd., Waimea* ☎ *808/881–8282* ⊕ *www.danielthiebaut.com* ☾ *Closed Mon. No dinner Sun.*

$ ✕ **Huli Sue's BBQ and Grill.** Huli Sue's serves large portions of updated

MODERN Hawaiian classics in a casual little restaurant along the highway in

HAWAIIAN Waimea. The barbecue menu, which includes your choice of meat (classics like ribs, pork roast, brisket) with one of four sauces, is melt-in-your-mouth delicious. The menu includes many other options, including a baked potato stuffed with your choice of meat, cilantro sour cream, and Fontina cheese, a variety of curry dishes, and a handful of fantastic appetizers. ⊠ *64-957 Mamalahoa Hwy. (Hwy. 11), Waimea* ☎ *808/885–6268* ⊕ *www.hulisues.com.*

$ ✕ **Lilikoi Café.** This gem of a café is tucked away in the back of the Parker

EUROPEAN Ranch Shopping Center. Locals love that it's hard to find because they want to keep Lilikoi Café's delicious breakfast crepes, freshly made soups, and croissants Waimea's best-kept secret. Owner and chef John Lorda puts out an impressive display of salad choices daily, including chicken curry, beet, fava bean, chicken pesto, and Mediterranean pasta. The Israeli couscous with tomato, red onion, cranberry, and basil is a hit, as is the half avocado stuffed with tuna salad. There's also a nice selection of sandwiches and hot entrées. The food is fresh, many of the ingredients are organic, and everything is homemade. ⊠ *67-1185 Mamalahoa Hwy. (Hwy. 11), Waimea* ☎ *808/887–1400* ☾ *Closed Sun. No dinner.*

$$$$ ✕ **Merriman's.** By far one of the best restaurants in Waimea, this is the

MODERN signature restaurant of Peter Merriman, one of the pioneers of Hawai-

HAWAIIAN ian regional cuisine. Merriman's is the home of the original wok-charred ahi, usually served with buttery Wainaku corn. If you prefer meat, try the Kahua Ranch lamb, raised locally to the restaurant's specifications, or the prime bone-in New York steak, grilled to order. The extensive wine list is impressive and includes many selections poured by the glass. Be forewarned: Merriman's is pricey, so prepare to splurge. ⊠ *Opelo Plaza, 65-1227 Opelo Rd., Waimea* ☎ *808/885–6822* ⊕ *www.merrimanshawaii.com* ☙ *Reservations essential.*

$ ✕ **Pau.** The name here is the Hawaiian word for "done," which we're

ITALIAN guessing alludes to how eagerly you will gobble up their sensational pizzas. You order at the counter and find your own seat in the small but neat inside dining area. The big draw is the wide selection of appetizers, salads, sandwiches, pastas, and pizzas loaded with lots of local, fresh ingredients. Try the "Superfood" salad with quinoa, brown rice, edamame, grapes, and spiced nuts or the tangy vintner's salad with local organic greens, spiced pecans, apples, Gorgonzola, and Pau's champagne vinaigrette. All sauces and salad dressings are made in-house. When it comes to the pizzas, anything goes: order one of Pau's 16-inch signature pies or create your own. Lunch is a deal if you order the Slice of Italy: a quarter pizza cut into three slices plus a side salad for just $9. The restaurant is a little tricky to find, but it's right next to Merriman's in Waimea. ⊠ *65-1227 Opelo Rd., Waimea* ☎ *808/885–6325* ⊕ *www.paupizza.com* ☾ *Closed Sun.*

$$$ ✕ **The Red Water Cafe.** Chef David Abraham has transformed the for-

ECLECTIC mer Fujimamas into a place for Hawaiian café food with a twist. They

☾ specialize in "multicultural cuisine" like the "Thai Caesar salad" with

8

crispy calamari croutons that is big enough to share. There's a full sushi bar as well. Don't miss the "Fuji" roll with shrimp, ahi, crab, avocado, and cucumber that is tempura-battered and deep-fried. Wash it all down with the signature saketini. Lunch is a great bet here, too, with a build-your-own *saimin* option (broth with noodles), a huge Cobb salad, and a juicy 8-ounce burger with lots of fixings. This place is popular among locals and is a great spot for the whole family—the kids' menu was developed by Abraham's eight-year-old daughter. ⊠ 65-1299 Kawaihae Rd., Waimea ☎ 808/885–9299 ⊕ www.redwater-cafe. com ◷ Closed Sun.

$
AMERICAN
✕ **Village Burger.** Village Burger brings a whole new meaning to gourmet hamburgers. This little eatery in Parker Ranch Center serves up locally raised, grass-fed, hormone-free beef that is ground fresh, hand-shaped daily at their restaurant, and grilled to perfection right before your eyes. Top your burger (be it ahi, veal, Kahua Ranch wagyu beef, Hamakua mushroom, or Waipio Taro) with everything from local avocados, baby greens, and chipotle goat cheese to tomato marmalade. Even the ice cream for their milkshakes is made right in Waimea, and the delicious brioche buns that house these juicy burgers are baked fresh in nearby Hawi. At this place, you really can taste the difference. ⊠ *Parker Ranch Center, 67-1185 Mamalahoa Hwy. (Hwy. 11), Waimea* ☎ *808/885–7319* ⊕ *villageburgerwaimea.com.*

HILO

$
DINER
☾
✕ **Bears' Coffee.** A favorite Hilo breakfast spot, much loved for their fresh-fruit waffles and tasty morning coffee. Service can be a little slow, but where are you running off to anyway? For lunch they serve up huge deli sandwiches and decent entrée-size salads. In keeping with its name, the little diner is full of stuffed bears, ceramic bears, even bear wallpaper. ⊠ *106 Keawe St., Hilo* ☎ *808/935–0708* ⊟ *No credit cards.*

$
ITALIAN
✕ **Big Island Pizza.** Gourmet pizza is the star here, topped with things like shrimp and smoked salmon. They also serve sandwiches, wraps, pastas, and salads. There are only a handful of tables for eating in, but they do a brisk take-out business and also deliver to the eastern side of the island. There's another brand-new location above Costco in Kailua-Kona, where they specialize in European-style pizzas with artisan crusts. ⊠ *760 Kilauea Ave., Hilo* ☎ *808/934–8000* ⊕ *www.bigislandpizza.com.*

$
HAWAIIAN
✕ **Blane's Drive-In.** With a vast menu second only to Ken's House of Pancakes, Blane's serves up everything from standard hamburgers to chicken *katsu*. There's a mean plate lunch with tons of fresh fish for only $8. At one point it was a real drive-in, with car service. Now, customers park, order at the window, and then eat at one of the few picnic tables provided or take their food to go. ⊠ *217 Wainuenue Ave., Hilo* ☎ *808/969–9494.*

$
HAWAIIAN
✕ **Café 100.** Established in 1948, this family-owned restaurant is famous for its tasty loco moco, prepared in more than a three dozen ways, and its dirt-cheap breakfast and lunch specials. (You can stuff yourself for $3 if you order right.) The word "restaurant," or even "café," is used liberally here—you order at a window and eat on one of the outdoor

Big Island Farm Tours

As local ingredients continue to play a prominent role on Big Island menus, chefs and farmers are working together to support a burgeoning agritourism industry in Hawaii. Several local farms have cropped up over the past few years to make specialty items that cater to the island's gourmet restaurants. The **Hawaii Island Goat Dairy** (⊕ www.hawaiiislandgoatdairy. com) produces specialty cheese; lone beekeeper Richard Spiegel of **Volcano Island Honey Co.** (⊕ www. volcanoislandhoney.com) produces a rare and delicious white honey now available not only in local restaurants but on the shelves of high-end stores like Neiman Marcus; and the **Hamakua Heritage Farm** (⊕ www. fungaljungle.com) has turned harvested koa forests into a safe haven for gourmet mushrooms. While a handful of farms—like **Mountain Thunder** (⊕ mountainthunder. com), which produces 100% organic Kona coffee, and **Hawaiian Vanilla Company** (⊕ www.hawaiianvanilla. com), which is cultivating vanilla from orchids on the Hamakua Coast—are open to the public and offer free tours, others have opted instead to offer limited tours through group operators. The **Big Island Farm Bureau** (⊕ www.bigislandfarmbureau. org) has also tried to encourage local farming and agritourism through the creation of **Hawaii AgVentures** (⊕ www.hawaiiagventures.com), an organization that schedules farm visits (to either single or multiple farms) for interested parties.

benches provided—but you come here for the food and prices, not the ambience. ⊠ 969 *Kilauea Ave., Hilo* ☎ 808/935–8683 ☯ *Closed Sun.*

$$
ITALIAN
✕ **Café Pesto.** One of the better restaurants in Hilo, Café Pesto offers exotic pizzas (with fresh Hamakua mushrooms, artichokes, and rosemary Gorgonzola sauce, for example), Asian-inspired pastas and risottos, fresh seafood, delicious salads, and appetizers that you could make a meal of. Products from local farmers feature heavily on the menu here—everything from the Kulana free-range beef to the Kawamata Farms tomatoes to the Kapoho Farms lehua-blossom honey made on the island. Live local musicians provide entertainment at dinner Thursday through Sunday. ⊠ *308 Kamehameha Ave., Hilo* ☎ *808/969–6640* ⊕ *www.cafepesto.com.*

$
THAI
✕ **Full Moon Cafe.** This cozy restaurant in a newly renovated downtown Hilo building offers a small American menu of burgers, fish, and steak, but where the eatery truly stands out is in its fresh and tasty traditional Thai fare. The owners grow their own spices, herbs, and papayas organically on their Puna farm. The chefs here also sauté with olive oil to keep things heart-healthy. Try the hot and sour Tom Yum soup that is loaded with fresh veggies, pineapple curry, and the Thai basil eggplant. Wash it all down with a Thai iced tea or coffee as a musician strums relaxing Hawaiian music (weekends from 6 to 8:30). Also look for outdoor seating on the lanai and a new coffee shop next door that serves breakfast. ⊠ *51 Kalakaua St., Hilo* ☎ *808/961–0599* ⊕ *www.fullmooncafe.net.*

8

$ ✕ **Happy Valley Seafood Restaurant.** Don't let the name fool you. Though
CHINESE   Hilo's best Chinese restaurant does specialize in seafood (the salt-and-pepper prawns are fantastic), they also offer a wide range of other Cantonese treats, including a sizzling lamb platter, salt-and-pepper pork, Mongolian beef or chicken, and vegetarian specialties like garlic eggplant and crispy green beans. The food is good, portions are large, and the price is right, but don't come here expecting any ambience—this is a funky and cheap Chinese restaurant, with a few random pieces of artwork tacked up here and there. ✉ *1263 Kilauea Ave., Ste. 320, Hilo* ☎ *808/933–1083* ✆ *No lunch Sun.*

$ ✕ **Hilo Bay Café.** What this eatery lacks in setting—it's in a strip mall
AMERICAN   that contains Office Max and Wal-Mart—it makes up for with modern decor and fantastic food. It's a popular restaurant among locals for "special" occasions like birthdays and anniversaries due to the high quality of food, but truth be told, the prices are reasonable enough you can come just to celebrate a Tuesday. Highly recommended are the roasted eggplant Parmesan custard and the peppered local beef carpaccio with horseradish cream. The vegan offerings, like potpie, are good enough to seduce meat eaters. Daily specials always include a vegetarian, meat, and fish choice, and the menu changes twice a year to keep things fresh. The chef tries to use organic and local products wherever possible. ✉ *315 Makaala St., Hilo* ☎ *808/935–4939* ⊕ *www. hilobaycafe.com* ✆ *No dinner Sun.*

$ ✕ **Ken's House of Pancakes.** For years, this 24-hour diner on Banyan
AMERICAN   Drive between the airport and the hotels has been a gathering place for Hilo residents and visitors. Breakfast is the main attraction: Ken's serves more than 11 different types pancakes, plus all kinds of fruit waffles (banana, peach), and popular omelets, like "Da Bradda," teeming with a variety of meats. The menu features 180 other tasty local specialties (loco moco, tripe stew, oxtail soup) and American-diner-inspired items from which to choose. Sunday is all-you-can-eat spaghetti night, Tuesday is all-you-can-eat tacos, and Wednesday is prime rib night. ✉ *1730 Kamehameha Ave., Hilo* ☎ *808/935–8711* ⊕ *kenshouseofpancakes-hilohi.com.*

$ ✕ **Kuhio Grille.** There's no atmosphere to speak of, and water is served in
HAWAIIAN   unbreakable plastic, but if you're searching for local fare—that eclectic and undefinable fusion of ethnic cuisines—Kuhio Grille is a must. Sam Araki serves a 1-pound *laulau* (a steamed bundle of taro leaves and pork) that is worth the trip. Other *grindz* include loco moco, oxtail soup, plate lunch specialties, pork chops, steaks, saimin, stir-fry, and daily specials. This local diner opens at 6 am, and is at the edge of Hilo's largest mall above the parking lot near Longs. ✉ *Prince Kuhio Shopping Plaza, 111 E. Puainako St., at Hwy. 11, Hilo* ☎ *808/959–2336* ⊕ *www.kuhiogrill.com.*

$ ✕ **Ocean Sushi.** What this restaurant lacks in ambience it certainly makes
JAPANESE   up for in quality and price. We're talking about light and crispy tempura; tender, moist teriyaki chicken; and about 25 specialty sushi rolls that, on average, will cost you a mere $5 per roll. If you're a sushi lover, be sure to try the "hospital roll" with shrimp tempura, cream cheese, cucumber, and spicy ahi, or the "volcano roll," a California

roll topped with flying fish eggs, dried fish shavings, green onions, and spicy mayo. Don't let the low price tag fool you—the service is friendly and the food here is fresh, filling, and delicious. Open Monday through Saturday, 10 am to 2 pm, and 5 pm to 9 pm. ⊠ *250 Keawe St., Hilo* ☎ *808/961–6625* ⊙ *Closed Sun.*

$ ✕ **Pescatore.** With dim lights, stately high-back chairs, and dark-wood
ITALIAN paneling, Pescatore conjures up an Italian trattoria. The food is good,
☺ but not amazing, with plenty of Italian basics such as lasagna, chicken marsala, and chicken or veal parmigiana. Lunch and dinner are available daily; lunch consists of Italian-style sandwiches. Brunch is served on Sunday only and features omelettes and crepes. Families love the simple pastas made to please choosy children. ⊠ *235 Keawe St., at Haili St., Hilo* ☎ *808/969–9090.*

$ ✕ **Reuben's Mexican Restaurant.** It's not the best Mexican food you've ever
MEXICAN had, but if you're in Hilo and you're jonesing for some carne asada or chicken flautas, Reuben's has got you pretty well covered. You could make a meal out of their warm chips and salsa alone, and they're known for pouring a stiff margarita in all sorts of interesting flavors like *lilikoi* (passion fruit), guava, mango, coconut, and watermelon. This is a lively place to spend your afternoon or evening, and it's open all day for lunch and dinner. ⊠ *336 Kamehameha Ave., Hilo* ☎ *808/961–2552* ⊕ *www.reubensmexican.com.*

$ ✕ **Royal Siam.** A downtown Hilo fixture, this authentic Thai eatery keeps
THAI things simple in the ambience department. But you don't need a dramatic view when you can choose from a menu that includes five kinds of curries and plenty of stir-fried meals. The tangy stir-fried garlic shrimp with coconut milk and wild mushrooms is particularly good. Don't leave Hawaii without sampling some green papaya salad. ⊠ *70 Mamo St., Hilo* ☎ *808/961–6100* ⊕ *www.royalsiamthai.com.*

$$ ✕ **The Seaside Restaurant & Aqua Farm.** The Nakagawa family has been
SEAFOOD running this eatery since the early 1920s. The latest son to manage the
☺ restaurant has transformed both the menu and the decor, and that, paired with the setting (the restaurant sits on a 30-acre natural brackish water fishpond) makes this one of the most romantic and interesting places to eat in Hilo. You can't get fish fresher than this. Islanders travel great distances for the fried *aholehole* (young Hawaiian flagtail) that's raised on the aqua-farm. Other great dishes from the sea include furikake salmon, miso butterfish, and macadamia nut–crusted mahimahi. The Pacific Rim menu includes plenty of selections for landlubbers, too. Arrive before sunset and request a table by the window for a view of the egrets roosting around the fishponds. ⊠ *1790 Kalanianaole Ave., Hilo* ☎ *808/935–8825* ⊕ *www.seasiderestaurant.com* ⊙ *Closed Mon. No lunch.*

$ ✕ **Sombat's Fresh Thai Cuisine.** The name says it all. Fresh local ingredients
THAI highlight proprietor Sombat Parente's menu (many of the herbs come from her own garden) to create authentic and tasty Thai treats like

8

coconut curries, fresh basil rolls, eggplant stir-fry, and green papaya salad. You can have most dishes prepared with your choice of tofu, pork, beef, chicken, or fish. The weekday lunch plate special is a steal ($7–$9). And if you can't leave the island without it, Sombat's famous pad thai sauce is available to take home in jars. ⊠ *Waiakea Kai Plaza, 88 Kanoelehue Ave., Hilo* ☎ *808/969–9336* ⊕ *www.sombats.com* ⊘ *Closed Sun., no lunch Sat.*

$ ✕ **Verna's Drive-In.** Verna's is a favorite among locals who come for the
HAWAIIAN   moist homemade burgers and filling plate lunches. The price is right with a burger combo that includes fries and a drink for just $5. If you're hungry for more, try the traditional Hawaiian plate with *laulau*, beef stew, chicken long rice, *lomilomi* salmon; or the smoked meat plate (a local specialty) smothered in onions and served with rice and macaroni salad. Whatever you choose, you won't leave hungry. Late-night revelers take note: Verna's is one of the only joints in Hilo that's open 24 hours every day. ⊠ *1765 Kamehameha Ave., Hilo* ☎ *808/935–2776.*

PUNA

$ ✕ **Luquin's Mexican Restaurant.** Long an island favorite for tasty, albeit
MEXICAN   greasy, Mexican grub, Luquin's is still going strong in the funky town of Pahoa. Tacos are great here (go for crispy), especially when stuffed with grilled, seasoned local fish on occasion. Chips are warm and salty, the salsa's got some kick, and the beans are thick with lard and topped with melted cheese. Not something you'd eat before a long swim, but perfect after a long day of exploring. ⊠ *15-2942 Pahoa Village Rd., Pahoa* ☎ *808/965–9990* ⊕ *luquinsmexicanrestauranthawaii.com.*

HAWAII VOLCANOES NATIONAL PARK AND VICINITY

With Volcano House still closed at this writing, there are few options for food inside the park. Many park visitors stop in Volcano on their way in or out to refuel at one of the handful of eateries here.

VOLCANO

$$ ✕ **Kiawe Kitchen.** Everyone around here says the same thing: "Kiawe has
ITALIAN   awesome pizza, but it's a little expensive." And it's true—the wood-fired pizza at this warm and pretty Italian eatery, with red walls and wood floors, has a perfect thin crust and an authentic Italian taste, but you have to be prepared to spend around $15 on a typical pie. Food options are limited in this area, though. Go for it. ⊠ *19-4005 Old Volcano Rd., Volcano* ☎ *808/967–7711.*

$$$ ✕ **Kilauea Lodge.** Chef Albert Jeyte combines contemporary trends with
EUROPEAN   traditional cooking styles from the mainland, France, and his native Hamburg, Germany. The menu changes daily, and features such entrées as venison, duck à l'orange with an apricot-mustard glaze, and authentic *hasenpfeffer* (braised rabbit). The coconut-crusted Brie appetizer is huge, melty, and absolutely delicious, as are Jeyte's made-from-scratch

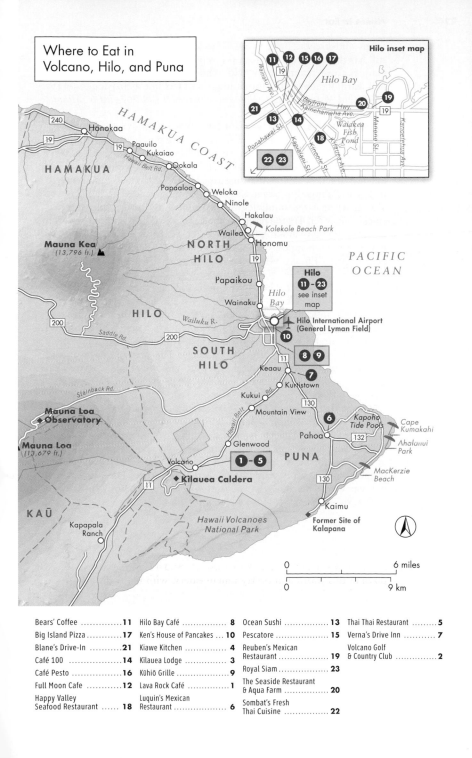

Where to Eat in Volcano, Hilo, and Puna

Hilo inset map

Hilo Bay

HAMAKUA COAST

240
Honokaa
19
Paauilo
Kukaiao
Ookala
Hawaii Belt Rd.

HAMAKUA

Papaaloa
Weloka
Ninole
Hakalau
Wailea
Kolekole Beach Park

Mauna Kea
(13,796 ft.)

NORTH HILO

Honomu
19

Papaikou

Hilo Bay
Wainaku

PACIFIC OCEAN

Hilo
11 – 23
see inset map

HILO

Wailuku R.

200

Saddle Rd.
200

Hilo International Airport
(General Lyman Field)
10

SOUTH HILO

11
Keaau
8 9
7
Kukui Rd.
Kurtistown
130
Kukui
Mountain View
6
Kapoho Tide Pools
Cape Kumakahi

Mauna Loa Observatory
Stainback Rd.

Hawaii Belt Rd.
Glenwood
Pahoa
132
Ahalanui Park

Mauna Loa
(13,679 ft.)
Volcano
1 – 5
PUNA
MacKerzie Beach

11
♦ **Kilauea Caldera**
130
Kaimu

KAŪ
Kapapala Ranch
Hawaii Volcanoes National Park
Former Site of Kalapana

0   6 miles
0   9 km

Bears' Coffee **11**	Hilo Bay Café **8**	Ocean Sushi **13**	Thai Thai Restaurant **5**
Big Island Pizza **17**	Ken's House of Pancakes ... **10**	Pescatore **15**	Verna's Drive Inn **7**
Blane's Drive-In **21**	Kiawe Kitchen **4**	Reuben's Mexican Restaurant **19**	Volcano Golf & Country Club **2**
Café 100 ....**14**	Kīlauea Lodge **3**		
Café Pesto **16**	Kūhiō Grille **9**	Royal Siam **23**	
Full Moon Cafe **12**	Lava Rock Café **1**	The Seaside Restaurant & Aqua Farm **20**	
Happy Valley Seafood Restaurant **18**	Luquin's Mexican Restaurant **6**	Sombat's Fresh Thai Cuisine **22**	

soups and breads. Built in 1937 as a YMCA camp, the restaurant still has the original "Friendship Fireplace" embedded with coins and plaques from around the world. The roaring fire, koa-wood tables, and warm lighting make the dining room feel like a cozy lodge. ⊠ *19-3948 Old Volcano Hwy., Volcano Village* ☎ *808/967–7366* ⊕ *www. kilauealodge.com.*

$ ✕ **Lava Rock Café.** This is an affordable place to grab a sandwich or a

DINER coffee and check your email (Wi-Fi is free with purchase of meal) before

☺ heading to HVNP. The homey, sit-down diner caters to families, serving up heaping plates of pancakes and French toast for breakfast. For lunch, burgers highlight the menu—everything from bacon-cheese to turkey to Paniolo burgers made with Hawaii grass-fed beef. There are also generous-sized sandwiches, loco moco, and soups, plus beef or chicken teriyaki. Try the haupia cake for dessert. Bottled beer is served here too. If you're looking for a place to take the kids, Lava Rock Café is the only real option in Volcano Village. ⊠ *19-3972 Old Volcano Hwy., behind Kilauea General Store, Volcano* ☎ *808/967–8526* ⊘ *No dinner Sun. and Mon.*

$ ✕ **Thai Thai Restaurant.** The food is authentic, and the prices are reason-

THAI able at this little Volcano Village find. A steaming hot plate of curry is the perfect antidote to a chilly day on the volcano. The chicken satay is excellent—the peanut dipping sauce the perfect match of sweet and spicy. Be careful when you order, as "medium" is more than spicy enough even for hard-core chili addicts. The service is warm and friendly and the dining room is pleasant, with white tablecloths, Thai art, and a couple of silk wall hangings. ⊠ *19-4084 Old Volcano Rd., Volcano* ☎ *808/967–7969* ⊘ *No lunch Wed.*

$ ✕ **Volcano Golf & Country Club.** This restaurant doesn't feel much like a

AMERICAN country club—it's simple and not at all fancy, with oak tables filled with local old-timers talking story and chowing down on greasy local favorites. Locals love this spot for its large portions and classic breakfasts: ordering the breakfast burger (with fried egg, cheese, and your choice of meat) and a cup of Kona coffee is the way to go. If it's lunchtime, you can't beat the burgers. ⊠ *Pii Mauna Dr., off Hwy. 11, Volcano* ☎ *808/967–8228* ⊘ *No dinner Fri. and Sun.*

Where to Stay

WORD OF MOUTH

"We had 10 days on the Big Island, and split it with 4 on the Hilo side and 6 on the Kona side. I was very glad we did both. It's really very long to do day trips, and there are lots of things to see and do on the west side. I would split the time."

—china_cat

Updated
by Karen
Anderson

Even among locals, there is an ongoing debate about which side of the Big Island is "better," so don't worry if you're having a tough time deciding where to stay. Our recommendation? Do both. Each side of the island offers a different range of accommodations, restaurants, and activities.

Consider staying at one of the upscale resorts along the Kohala Coast or in a condo in Kailua-Kona for half of your trip. Then, shift gears and check into a romantic bed-and-breakfast on the Hamakua Coast, South Kona, Hilo, or near the volcano. If you've got children in tow, opt for a vacation home or a stay at one of the island's many family-friendly hotels. On the west side, explore the island's most pristine beaches or try some of the fine-dining restaurants; on the east side, hike through rain forests, witness majestic waterfalls, or go for a plate lunch.

Some locals like to say that the east is "more Hawaiian," but we argue that King Kamehameha himself made Kailua-Kona his final home during his sunset years. Another reason to try a bit of both: your budget. You can justify splurging on a stay at a Kohala Coast resort for a few nights because you'll spend the rest of your time paying one-third that rate at a cozy cottage in Volcano or a condo on Alii Drive. And although food at the resorts is very expensive, you don't have to eat every meal there. Condos and vacation homes can be ideal for a family trip or for a group of friends looking to save money and live like *kamaainas* (local residents) for a week or two. Many of the homes also have private pools and hot tubs, lanai, ocean views, and more—you can go as budget or as high-end as you like.

If you choose a bed-and-breakfast, inn, or an out-of-the-way hotel, explain your expectations fully and ask plenty of questions before booking. Be clear about your travel and location needs. Some places require stays of two or three days. No matter where you stay, you'll want to rent a car. Some rental car companies do have restrictions about taking their vehicles to certain Big Island scenic spots, so make sure to ask about rules before you book.

BIG ISLAND LODGING PLANNER

PROPERTY TYPES

HOTELS AND RESORTS

The resorts—most clustered on the Kohala Coast—are expensive, there are no two ways about it. That said, many offer free nights with longer stays (fifth or seventh night free) and sometimes team with airlines or consolidators to offer package deals that may include a rental car, spa treatments, golf, and other activities. Some hotels allow children under 17 to stay for free. Ask about specials when you book, and check the Web sites as well—many resorts have Internet-only deals.

CONDOS AND VACATION RENTALS

Condos and vacation rental homes offer a range of options in every district of the island. With your own vacation pad, not only do you have more space to spread out, you can save a substantial amount of money by eating in.

See Condos and Vacation Rentals box for more information and rental agencies.

B&BS AND INNS

Bed-and-breakfasts and locally run inns offer a nice alternative to hotels or resorts in terms of privacy and location. Guests enjoy the perks of a hotel (breakfast and maid service), but without the extras that drive up rates.

Be sure to check industry association Web sites as well as property Web sites, and call to ask questions. There are still a few "B&Bs" that are really just dumpy rooms in someone's house, and you don't want to end up there. Members of the Big Island–based **Hawaii Island Bed & Breakfast Association** (⊕ *www.stayhawaii.com*) are listed with phone numbers and rates in a comprehensive online brochure. In order to join this network, bed-and-breakfasts must be evaluated and meet fairly stringent minimum requirements, including a yearly walk-through by association officers, to maintain their membership. Another bed-and-breakfast association includes **Hawaii's Best Bed & Breakfasts** (☎ *808/985–7488, 800/262–9912* ⊕ *www.bestbnb.com*).

9

RESERVATIONS

You'll almost always be able to find a room on the Big Island, but you might not get your first choice if you wait until the last minute. Make reservations six months to a year in advance if you're visiting during the peak seasons (summer, Christmas holiday, and spring break). During the week after Easter Sunday, for example, the Merrie Monarch Festival is in full swing, and most of Hilo's rooms are booked. Kailua-Kona is packed in mid-October during the Ford Ironman World Triathlon Championship. ■ TIP➔ September and February are great months to visit Hawaii; fares are lower, crowds are less, and accommodations prices are reduced.

PRICES

Keep in mind that many of the resorts charge "resort fees" for things like parking, Internet, daily newspaper service, beach gear, and activities. Most condos and vacation rental owners charge an additional cleaning fee. Always ask about hidden fees as well as specials and discounts when you book, and look online for great package deals.

WHAT IT COSTS				
	$	$$	$$$	$$$$
For Two People	under $180	$180–$260	$261–$340	over $340

Hotel prices are for two people in a standard double room in high season, excluding tax. Condo price categories reflect studio and one-bedroom rates.

For expanded hotel reviews, visit Fodors.com.

KAILUA-KONA

Kailua-Kona, a bustling historic village full of restaurants, shops, and entertainment options, boasts tons of lodging options. In addition to half a dozen hotels, oceanfront Alii Drive is brimming with condo complexes and vacation homes on both sides of the street. All the conveniences are here, and there are several grocery stores and big-box retailers nearby for those who choose to go the condo or vacation rental route and need to stock up on supplies. Kailua-Kona has a handful of beaches—White Sands, Kahaluu, and Kamakahonu (at the pier) among them. The downside to staying here is that you'll have to drive 30 to 45 minutes up the road to the Kohala Coast to visit Hawaii's signature, long, white-sand beaches. However, you'll also pay about half what you would at any of the major resorts, not to mention that Kailua-Kona offers a bit more local charm.

$$ **Aston Kona by the Sea.** Complete modern kitchens, tile lanai, and
RENTAL   washer-dryer units can be found in every suite of this comfortable oceanfront condo complex. **Pros:** oceanfront; swimming pool and Jacuzzi. **Cons:** no beach. ⊠ *75-6106 Alii Dr., Kailua-Kona* ☎ *808/327–2300, 877/997–6667* ⊕ *www.astonhotels.com* ➵ *73 units* ⚭ *In-room: a/c, kitchen. In-hotel: pool, spa* ♦ *No meals.*

$ **Casa de Emdeko.** A large and pretty complex on the *makai* (ocean-
RENTAL   front) side of Alii Drive, Casa de Emdeko offers a few more amenities than most condo complexes, including a florist, hair salon, and an on-site convenience store that makes sandwiches. **Pros:** oceanfront fresh- and saltwater pools; hidden from the street; very private. **Cons:** quality and prices depend on owner; not kid-friendly. ⊠ *75-6082 Alii Dr., Kailua-Kona* ☎ *808/329–2160* ⊕ *www.casadeemdeko.org* ➵ *106 units* ⚭ *In-room: a/c, kitchen. In-hotel: pool, beach* ♦ *No meals.*

$ **Courtyard King Kamehameha's Kona Beach Hotel.** A splendid renovation
HOTEL   has given new life to this previously aging landmark hotel in Kailua-Kona; new highlights include modern room decor that evokes a quintessential Hawaiian charm, plus a jazzed-up lobby that displays historical artifacts. **Pros:** central location; tastefully appointed rooms; historic ambience; aloha-friendly staff. **Cons:** most rooms have partial ocean views. ⊠ *75-5660 Palani Rd., Kailua-Kona* ☎ *808/329–2911* ⊕ *www.konabeachhotel.com* ➵ *457 rooms* ⚭ *In-room: a/c, safe, Internet, Wi-Fi. In-hotel: restaurant, pool, tennis court, spa, water sports* ♦ *No meals.*

BEST BETS FOR BIG ISLAND LODGING

Fodor's writers and editors have selected their favorite hotels, resorts, condos, vacation rentals, and bed-and-breakfasts by price and experience. Fodor's Choice properties represent the "best of the best" across price categories. You can also search by area for excellent places to stay—check out our complete reviews on the following pages.

Fodor's Choice ★

9

Where to Stay on the Kona Coast and Kau

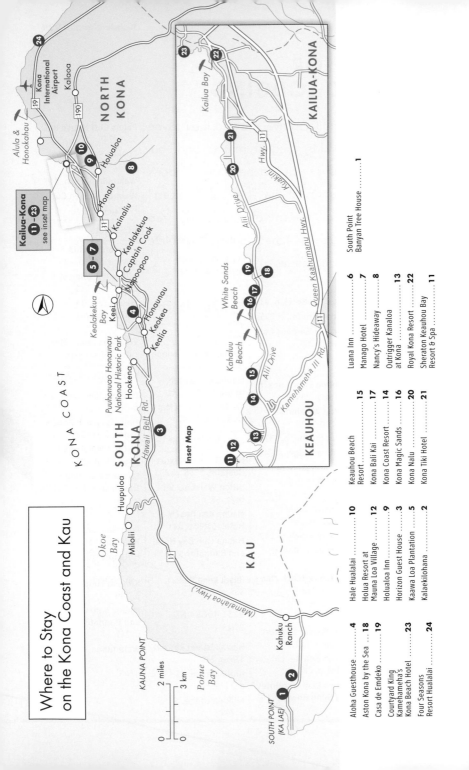

KONA COAST

Alula & Honokahau
KAUNA POINT
SOUTH POINT (KA LAE)
Pohue Bay
Kahuku Ranch
Mamalahoa Hwy.
KAU
Miloli'i
Okoe Bay
Huupuloa
Hawaii Belt Rd.
SOUTH KONA
Hookena
Puuhonuao Honaunau National Historic Park
Kealia
Keokea
Honaunau
Kealakekua Bay
Kei'i
Keauhou
Kealakekua
Captain Cook
Kainaliu
Honalo
Holualoa
Kalaoa
NORTH KONA
Kona International Airport
19
190
11

Kailua-Kona 11–23 see inset map

Inset Map

Kailua Bay
KAILUA-KONA
Kuakini Hwy.
Ali'i Drive
White Sands Beach
Kahaluu Beach
Ali'i Drive
Kamehameha III Rd.
Queen Kaahumanu Hwy.
KEAUHOU

0 2 miles
0 3 km

WHERE TO STAY ON THE BIG ISLAND

	Local Vibe	Pros	Cons
Kailua-Kona	Kailua-Kona is a bustling little village. Alii Drive is brimming with hotels and condo complexes.	Plenty to do, day and night; main drag of shops, historic landmarks, and seaside attractions within easy walking distance of most hotels; many grocery stores in the area.	More traffic than anywhere else on the island; limited number of beaches; traffic noise on Alii Drive.
South Kona and Kau	A great place to stay if you want to be near some of the best water attractions on the island; there are plenty of bed-and-breakfasts and vacation rentals at or near Kealakekua Bay.	Kealakekua Bay is one of the most popular destinations on the island for kayaking and snorkeling; several good dining options nearby; coffee-farm tours in Captain Cook and Kainaliu towns.	Vog from Kilauea often settles here; fewer sand beaches in the area; farther south, the Kau district is quite remote.
The Kohala Coast	The Kohala Coast is home to most of the Big Island's major resorts. Blue, sunny skies prevail here, along with the island's best beaches.	Beautiful beaches; high-end shopping and dining; lots of activities for adults and children.	Pricey; long driving distances to Volcano, Hilo, and Kailua-Kona.
Waimea	Though it seems a world away, Waimea is only about a 15- to 20-minute drive from the Kohala Coast.	Beautiful scenery, paniolo (cowboy) culture; home to some exceptional local restaurants.	Can be cool and rainy year-round; nearest beaches are a 20-minute drive away.
The Hamakua Coast	The Hamakua Coast is a nice spot for those seeking peace, tranquility, and an alternative to the tropical-beach-vacation experience.	Close to Waipio Valley; foodie and farm tours in the area; good spot for honeymooners.	Beaches are an hour's drive away; convenience shopping is nonexistent.
Hilo	Hilo is the wetter, more lush eastern side of the Big Island. It is also less touristy than the west side.	Proximity to waterfalls, rain-forest hikes, museums, and botanical gardens; good bed-and-breakfast options.	The best white-sand beaches are on the other side of the island; noise from coqui frogs can be distracting at night.
Puna	Puna doesn't attract nearly as many visitors as other regions on the island, so you'll find good deals on rentals and B&Bs here.	A few black-sand beaches; off the beaten path with lots of outdoor wilderness to explore; lava flows into the sea here.	Few dining and entertainment options; no resorts or resort amenities; noisy coqui frogs at night.
Hawaii Volcanoes National Park and Vicinity	If you are going to visit Hawaii Volcanoes National Park, stay the night at any number of enchanting bed-and-breakfast inns in the fern-shrouded Volcano Village.	Good location for watching lava at night bubbling inside Halemaumau Crater; great for hiking, nature tours, and bike riding; close to Hilo and Puna.	Not many dining options; not much nightlife; can be cold and wet.

9

$ ⊡ **Hale Hualalai.** Perfect for couples, Hale Hualalai offers two exception-
B&B/INN   ally large suites with exposed beams, whirlpool bathtubs, and private
lanai. **Pros:** gourmet breakfasts; new and tastefully decorated house;
whirlpool tubs; large living space. **Cons:** not kid-friendly; removed from
local beaches and restaurants. ✉ *74-4968 Mamalahoa Hwy., Holualoa*
☎ *808/326–2909* ⊕ *www.hale-hualalai.com* ⊷ *2 suites* ⌂ *In-room: no
a/c, Wi-Fi* ⦿ *Breakfast.*

$$ ⊡ **Holualoa Inn.** Six spacious rooms and suites are available in this beau-
B&B/INN   tiful cedar home on a 30-acre coffee-country estate, a few miles above
Fodor's Choice   Kailua Bay and steps away from the artists' town of Holualoa. **Pros:**
★   within walking distance of art galleries and cafés; well-appointed, with
wood floors, fine art, and lots of windows; panoramic views. **Cons:**
not kid-friendly. ✉ *76-5932 Mamalahoa Hwy., Box 222, Holualoa*
☎ *808/324–1121, 800/392–1812* ⊕ *www.holualoainn.com* ⊷ *6 rooms*
⌂ *In-room: no a/c, kitchen, no TV. In-hotel: pool* ⦿ *Breakfast.*

$ ⊡ **Holua Resort at Mauna Loa Village.** Tucked away by Keauhou Bay amid
RESORT   a 36-hole championship golf course and a plethora of coconut trees, this
well-maintained enclave of blue-roofed villas offers lots of amenities,
including an 11-court tennis center (with a center court, pro shop, and
lights), swimming pools, hot tubs, fitness center, manicured gardens,
waterfalls, covered parking, and a Tuesday-night cocktail party. **Pros:**
tennis center; upscale feeling. **Cons:** no beach. ✉ *78-7190 Kaleiopapa
St., Kailua-Kona* ☎ *808/324–1550* ⊕ *www.shellhospitality.com/Holua-
Resort-at-Mauna-Loa-Village* ⊷ *73 units* ⌂ *In-room: a/c, safe, kitchen,
Wi-Fi. In-hotel: golf course, pool, tennis court, gym* ⦿ *No meals.*

$ ⊡ **Keauhou Beach Resort.** This hotel preserves a unique part of Hawaiian
RESORT   history (the grounds include a *heiau* [temple], a sacred fishpond, and a
replica of the summer home of King David Kalakaua) and is adjacent
to Kahaluu, one of the best snorkeling beaches on the island. **Pros:**
large rooms; free full breakfast daily; historic Hawaiian ambience; great
tennis center. **Cons:** limited dining options. ✉ *78-6740 Alii Dr., Kailua-
Kona* ☎ *808/322–3441, 866/326–6803* ⊕ *www.keauhoubeachresort.
com* ⊷ *306 rooms, 3 suites* ⌂ *In-room: a/c, safe, Internet. In-hotel:
restaurant, bar, pool, tennis court, gym, beach, laundry facilities*
⦿ *Breakfast.*

$ ⊡ **Kona Bali Kai.** These slightly older condominium units, spread out
RENTAL   among three low-rises on the ocean side of Alii Drive, are situated at
Kona's most popular surfing spot, Banyans. **Pros:** close to town and
beaches; convenience mart and beach-gear rental nearby. **Cons:** moun-
tain-view rooms close to noisy street; oceanfront rooms don't have
a/c. ✉ *76-6246 Alii Dr., Kailua-Kona* ☎ *808/329–9381, 800/535–0085*
⊕ *www.castleresorts.com* ⊷ *67 units* ⌂ *In-room: no a/c, kitchen. In-
hotel: pool, laundry facilities* ⦿ *No meals.*

$ ⊡ **Kona Coast Resort.** Just below Keauhou Shopping Center, Kona Coast
RENTAL   Resort offers furnished condos on 21 acres with pleasant ocean views
and a host of on-site amenities including a swimming pool, beach vol-
leyball, cocktail bar, hot tub, tennis courts, hula classes, equipment
rental, and children's activites. **Pros:** nice location in Keauhou. **Cons:**
dated decor; not on the beach. ⌂ *78-6842 Alii Dr., Kailua-Kona 96740*
☎ *808/324–1721* ⊕ *www.shellhospitality.com* ⊷ *75 rooms* ⌂ *In-room:*

a/c, kitchen, Internet. In-hotel: bar, pool, tennis court, water sports, children's programs, laundry facilities, parking ¶| *No meals.*

$
RENTAL
☶ **Kona Magic Sands.** Cradled between a lovely grass park on one side and White Sands Beach on the other, this condo complex is great for swimmers, surfers, and sunbathers. **Pros:** next door to popular beach; affordable; oceanfront view from all units. **Cons:** studios only; some units are dated. ⊠ *77-6452 Alii Dr., Kailua-Kona* ☎ *808/329–9393, 800/622–5348* ⊕ *www.konahawaii.com/ms.htm* ↝ *37 units* ⚿ *In-room: a/c, kitchen. In-hotel: pool* ¶| *No meals.*

$$
RENTAL
☶ **Kona Nalu.** One of the smaller complexes on the ocean side of Alii Drive, Kona Nalu features large, beautifully furnished units with supersize lanai, and ocean views from all units. **Pros:** extra-large units; ocean views. **Cons:** not within walking distance to stores or restaurants; sandy cove doesn't provide easy ocean entry. ⊠ *76-6212 Alii Dr., Kailua-Kona* ☎ *808/329–6438* ⊕ *www.sunquest-hawaii.com* ↝ *15 units* ⚿ *In-room: a/c, kitchen, Wi-Fi. In-hotel: pool, beach, laundry facilities* ¶| *No meals.*

$
HOTEL
☶ **Kona Tiki Hotel.** The best thing about this three-story walk up budget hotel, about a mile south of downtown Kailua Village, is that all the units have lanai right next to the ocean. **Pros:** very low price; oceanfront lanai and pool; friendly staff; free parking. **Cons:** older hotel in need of update; no TV; doesn't accept credit cards, but will take Paypal. ⊠ *75-5968 Alii Dr., Kailua-Kona* ☎ *808/329–1425* ⊕ *www.konatikihotel.com* ↝ *15 rooms* ⚿ *In-room: no a/c, no TV, Wi-Fi. In-hotel: pool, parking* ⊟ *No credit cards* ¶| *Breakfast.*

$
B&B/INN
☶ **Nancy's Hideaway.** A few miles up the hill from Kailua-Kona, this charming cottage and studio offer modern comforts; each has its own entrance, a lanai, ocean views, and a wet bar. **Pros:** plenty of privacy; ocean views. **Cons:** slightly inconvenient location; not kid-friendly. ⊠ *73-1530 Uanani Pl., Kailua-Kona* ☎ *808/325–3132, 866/325–3132* ⊕ *www.nancyshideaway.com* ↝ *2 rooms* ⚿ *In-room: no a/c* ¶| *Breakfast.*

$$$
RENTAL
☶ **Outrigger Kanaloa at Kona.** The 16-acre grounds provide a peaceful and verdant background for this low-rise condominium complex bordering the Keauhou-Kona Country Club. **Pros:** across the street from acclaimed golf course and within walking distance of Keauhou Bay; three pools with hot tubs. **Cons:** no restaurant on property. ⊠ *78-261 Manukai St., Kailua-Kona* ☎ *808/322–9625, 808/322–2272, 800/688–7444* ⊕ *www.*

KONA CONDO COMFORTS

The Safeway at Crossroads Shopping Center (⊠ *75-1000 Henry St., Kailua-Kona* ☎ *808/329–2207*) offers an excellent inventory of groceries and produce, although prices can be steep.

You can rent DVDs at Blockbuster in the Kona Coast Shopping Center (⊠ *74-5588 Palani Rd., Kailua-Kona* ☎ *808/326–7694*).

For pizza, **Kona Brewing Co. Pub & Brewery** (⊠ *75-5629 Kuakini Hwy., just past Palani intersection on right, Kailua-Kona* ☎ *808/329–2739*) is the best bet, if you can pick it up. Otherwise, for delivery, try Domino's (☎ *808/329–9500*).

9

outrigger.com ⚓166 units ☝In-room: *a/c, safe, kitchen. In-hotel: pool, tennis court, laundry facilities* |◎|*No meals.*

$ 🏨 **Royal Kona Resort.** This is a great

RESORT option if you're on a budget—the location is central; the bar, lounge, pool, and restaurant are right on the water; and the rooms feature

contemporary Hawaiian decor with Polynesian accents. **Pros:** convenient location; waterfront pool; low prices. **Cons:** can be crowded; parking is tight. ✉ *75-5852 Alii Dr., Kailua-Kona* ☎ *808/329–3111, 800/222–5642* ⊕ *www.royalkona.com* ⚓*436 rooms, 8 suites* ☝*In-room: a/c, safe, Internet. In-hotel: restaurant, bar, pool, tennis court, gym, spa, laundry facilities* |◎|*No meals.*

$ 🏨 **Sheraton Keauhou Bay Resort & Spa.** What it might lack in architectural

RESORT ambience (it's a big concrete structure), the Sheraton makes up for with

☺ its beautifully manicured grounds, a historic sense of place, and stunning location on Keauhou Bay. **Pros:** cool pool; manta rays on view nightly; resort style at lower price. **Cons:** no beach; daily resort fee for Wi-Fi and parking; only one restaurant. ✉ *78-128 Ehukai St., Kailua-Kona* ☎ *808/930–4900* ⊕ *www.sheratonkeauhou.com* ⚓*510 rooms, 11 suites* ☝*In-room: a/c, safe, Internet, Wi-Fi. In-hotel: restaurant, bar, pool, tennis court, gym, spa, water sports* |◎|*No meals.*

THE KONA COAST

SOUTH KONA

There are no resorts in this area, but there are plenty of fantastic bed-and-breakfasts and vacation rental homes at Kealakekua Bay and in the hills above. The towns of Captain Cook and Kainaliu feature some excellent dining and shopping options, and there are several coffee farms open for tours as well. You can get to the volcano in about an hour and a half, and you're also close to several less well-known but wonderful beaches, including Hookena. Kailua-Kona is a 30-minute drive away from Captain Cook, while the great, sandy beaches of the Kohala Coast are an hour or more away.

$ 🏨 **Aloha Guesthouse.** In the hills above Honaunau, Aloha Guest-

B&B/INN house offers quiet elegance, complete privacy, and ocean views from every room. **Pros:** eco-conscious; full breakfast; views of the South Kona coastline. **Cons:** remote location up a bumpy 1-mile dirt road. ✉ *Old Tobacco Rd., off Hwy. 11 near mile marker 104, Honaunau* ☎ *808/328–8955* ⊕ *www.alohaguesthouse.com* ⚓*5 rooms* ☝*In-room: no a/c, Wi-Fi. In-hotel: business center* |◎|*Breakfast.*

$$ 🏨 **Horizon Guest House.** Surrounded by McCandless Ranch on 40 acres

B&B/INN in South Kona, Horizon Guest House may seem remote, but it's actually just a short drive from some of the best water attractions on the island, including Place of Refuge, Kealakekua Bay, and Hookena Beach.

Pros: private and quiet; heated pool with Jacuzzi; beautiful views. **Cons:** not on the beach; 40 minutes from Kailua-Kona. ✉ *Mamalahoa Hwy., between mile markers 101 and 100, Captain Cook* ☎ *808/328–2540* 🌐 *www.horizonguesthouse.com* *4 suites* *In-room: no a/c, Wi-Fi. In-hotel: pool, laundry facilities, parking* *Breakfast.*

$ B&B/INN **Kaawa Loa Plantation.** Proprietors Mike Martinage and Greg Nunn operate a grand bed-and-breakfast inn on a 5-acre coffee farm above Kealakekua Bay. **Pros:** nice views; excellent breakfast; Hawaiian steam room. **Cons:** not within walking distance of bay. ✉ *82-5990 Napoopoo Rd., Captain Cook* ☎ *808/323–2686* 🌐 *kaawaloaplantation.com* *4 rooms, 1 cottage* *In-room: no a/c, Wi-Fi. In-hotel: laundry facilities* *Breakfast.*

$ B&B/INN **Luana Inn.** The best part of this bed-and-breakfast near Kealakekua Bay is the fabulous gourmet breakfast prepared by proprietors Ken and Erin. **Pros:** excellent food; sterling hospitality. **Cons:** not on the bay or beach. ✉ *82-5856 Napoopoo Rd., Captain Cook* ☎ *808/328–2612* 🌐 *www.luanainn.com* *5 rooms* *In-room: a/c, kitchen, Wi-Fi. In-hotel: pool* *Breakfast.*

$ HOTEL **Manago Hotel.** This historic hotel is a good option if you want to escape the touristy thing but still be close to the water and attractions like Kealakekua Bay and Puuhonua O Honaunau National Historical Park. **Pros:** local color; rock-bottom prices; terrific on-site restaurant. **Cons:** not the best sound insulation between rooms. ✉ *81-6155 Mamalahoa Hwy., Box 145, Captain Cook* ☎ *808/323–2642* 🌐 *www.managohotel.com* *64 rooms, 42 with bath* *In-room: no a/c, no TV. In-hotel: restaurant* *No meals.*

NORTH KONA

$$$$ RESORT Fodor's Choice ★ **Four Seasons Resort Hualalai.** Beautiful views everywhere, polished wood floors, custom furnishings and linens in warm earth and cool white tones, and Hawaiian fine artwork make Four Seasons Resort Hualalai a peaceful retreat. **Pros:** beautiful location; excellent restaurants. **Cons:** not the best beach among the resorts. ✉ *72-100 Kaupulehu Dr., Box 1269, Kailua-Kona* ☎ *808/325–8000, 800/819–5053, 888/340–5662* 🌐 *www.fourseasons.com/hualalai* *243 rooms, 51 suites* *In-room: a/c, safe, Internet, Wi-Fi. In-hotel: restaurant, bar, golf course, pool, tennis court, gym, spa, beach, children's programs* *No meals.*

THE KOHALA COAST

The Kohala Coast is home to most all of the Big Island's megaresorts. (As of this writing, Kona Village Resort remains closed indefinitely due to tsunami damage in March 2011. It's expected to reopen after extensive renovations are completed.) Dotting the coastline, manicured lawns and golf courses, luxurious hotels, and white-sand beaches break up the long expanse of black lava rock along Queen Kaahumanu Highway. Many visitors to the Big Island check in here and rarely leave, except to try the restaurants, spas, or golf courses at neighboring resorts. If

CLOSE UP

Condos and Vacation Rentals

Renting a condo or vacation house gives you much more living space than the average hotel, plus the chance to meet more people (neighbors are usually friendly), lower nightly rates, and the option of cooking or barbecuing rather than eating out. When booking, remember that most properties are individually owned, with rates and amenities that differ substantially depending on the place. Some properties are handled by rental agents or agencies while many are handled directly through the owner. The following is a list of our favorite booking agencies for various lodging types throughout the island. Be sure to call and ask questions before booking.

Abbey Vacation Rentals (⊕ *www. waikoloarentals.com*) has luxury condos on the Kohala Coast.

Big Island Villas (⊕ *www. bigislandvillas.com*) lists a variety of condos attached to the Four Seasons Hualalai, Mauna Kea, and Mauna Lani resorts.

CJ Kimberly Realty (⊕ *www. cjkimberly.com*) offers fantastic deals on some oceanfront homes and condos.

Hawaiian Beach Rentals (⊕ *www. hawaiianbeachrentals.com*) and **Tropical Villa Vacations** (⊕ *www.tropicalvillavacations.com*) are excellent for high-end, ocean- or beach-front homes.

Hawaii Vacation Rentals (⊕ *www. vacationbigisland.com*) lists several properties on the beach in Puako, a sleepy beach settlement just up the road from the Kohala coast resorts.

Keauhou Property Management (⊕ *www.konacondo.net*) has condos along the Kona coast, just south of Kailua-Kona around Keauhou Bay.

Kolea Vacations (⊕ *www. koleavacations.com*) lists dozens of condos at the Kolea at Waikoloa complex as well as a stunning oceanfront home on Alii in Kailua-Kona.

Kona Coast Vacations (⊕ *www. konacoastvacations.com*) offers a large variety of condos on the west side of the island and wins high marks for good service.

Kona Hawaii Vacation Rentals (⊕ *www.konahawaii.com*) offers very affordable condos in Kailua-Kona.

Knutson and Associates (⊕ *www. konahawaiirentals.com*) handles rentals for a wide variety of Kailua-Kona condos and oceanfront vacation homes.

Property Network (☎ *808/329–7977* ⊕ *www.hawaii-kona.com*) lists and manages dozens of condo rentals in and around Kailua-Kona.

Rent Hawaii Home (⊕ *www. renthawaiihome.com*) offers several affordable cottage and beach-house rentals, ideal for those who are staying for awhile and want some room and privacy but don't want to spend half a year's salary on a beachfront palace.

South Kohala Management (⊕ *www. southkohala.com*) lists a wide variety of luxury Kohala Coast condos.

Vacation Rental By Owner (⊕ *www. vrbo.com*) has homes and condos for rent all over the island.

Four Seasons Resort Hualalai

Holualoa Inn

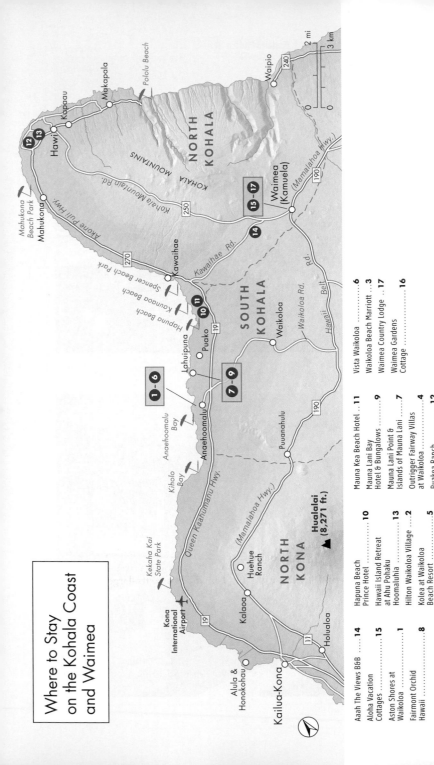

Where to Stay on the Kohala Coast and Waimea

Aaah The Views B&B **14**
Aloha Vacation
Cottages **15**
Aston Shores at
Waikoloa **1**
Fairmont Orchid
Hawaii **8**

Hapuna Beach
Prince Hotel **10**
Hawaii Island Retreat
at Ahu Pohaku
Hoomaluhia **13**
Hilton Waikoloa Village **2**
Kolea at Waikoloa
Beach Resort **5**

Mauna Kea Beach Hotel .. **11**
Mauna Lani Bay
Hotel & Bungalows **9**
Mauna Lani Point &
Islands of Mauna Lani ... **7**
Outrigger Fairway Villas
at Waikoloa **4**
Puakea Ranch **12**

Vista Waikoloa **6**
Waikoloa Beach Marriott ...**3**
Waimea Country Lodge .. **17**
Waimea Gardens
Cottage **16**

you're looking to be pampered (for a price) and lounge on the beach or by the pool all day with an umbrella drink in hand, this is where you need to be. That's not to say that staying at a resort makes it difficult to see the rest of the island. On the contrary, most of the hiking and adventure-tour companies on the island offer pickups at the Kohala Coast resorts, and many of the hotels have offers with various rental car agencies so you can be as active or lazy as you like.

> ## KOHALA CONDO COMFORTS
>
> If you require anything not provided by the management, both the **Kings' Shops** (✉ 250 *Waikoloa Beach Dr., Waikoloa* ☎ *808/886–8811*) and the **Queens' Marketplace** (✉ 201 *Waikoloa Beach Dr., Waikoloa* ☎ *808/886–8822*) in the Waikoloa Beach Resort are good places to go. There are a small grocery store, a liquor store, and several nice restaurants at the Kings' Shops. The newer Queens' Marketplace also has a food court, as well as a gourmet market where you can get pizza baked to order. It's not exactly cheap, but you're paying for the convenience of not having to drive into town.

$$ **Aston Shores at Waikoloa.** Villas with terra-cotta-tile roofs are
RENTAL set amid landscaped lagoons and waterfalls at the edge of the championship Waikoloa Village Golf Course. **Pros:** good prices for the area; great location; fully self-sufficient condos with maid service. **Cons:** daily fee for Internet access. ✉ *69-1035 Keana Pl., Waikoloa* ☎ *808/886–5001, 800/922–7866* ⊕ *www.astonhotels.com* ⬦ *69 units* ⬥ *In-room: a/c, kitchen, Internet. In-hotel: pool, tennis court, gym* ⑲ *No meals.*

$$$ **Fairmont Orchid Hawaii.** You can't go wrong booking a stay at the
RESORT Fairmont Orchid, a first-rate resort that overflows with tropical gar-
Fodor'sChoice dens, cascading waterfalls, beautiful wings with "open sesame" doors,
★ a meandering pool, and nicely appointed rooms with all the amenities. **Pros:** oceanfront location; great restaurants; excellent pool; aloha hospitality. **Cons:** top resort features come at a high price. ✉ *1 N. Kaniku Dr., Kohala Coast* ☎ *808/885–2000, 800/845–9905* ⊕ *www.fairmont. com/orchid* ⬦ *486 rooms, 54 suites* ⬥ *In-room: a/c, safe, Wi-Fi. In-hotel: restaurant, bar, golf course, pool, tennis court, gym, spa, beach, water sports, children's programs* ⑲ *No meals.*

$$ **Hapuna Beach Prince Hotel.** More reasonably priced than its neighbor
HOTEL resorts, Hapuna Beach Prince Hotel occupies the northern corner of
☺ the largest sand beach on the Big Island. **Pros:** extra-large rooms; all ocean-facing rooms; direct access to one of island's best beaches. **Cons:** fitness center located off-site at the golf course; daily fees for Wi-Fi and parking. ✉ *62-100 Kaunaoa Dr., Kohala Coast* ☎ *808/880–1111, 800/882–6060* ⊕ *www.princeresortshawaii.com* ⬦ *350 rooms, 61 suites* ⬥ *In-room: a/c, Internet. In-hotel: restaurant, bar, golf course, pool, tennis court, gym, spa, beach, children's programs* ⑲ *No meals.*

$$$ **Hawaii Island Retreat at Ahu Pohaku Hoomaluhia.** Here, sustainability
B&B/INN meets luxury without sacrificing comfort. **Pros:** stunning location; new and beautiful construction with no expense spared; eco-friendly. **Cons:** not within walking distance of restaurants; off the beaten path. ✉ *250*

9

The Fairmont Orchid Hawaii

Mauna Kea Beach Hotel

Maluhia Rd., follow signs off Hwy. 270 in Kapaau, North Kohala, Kapaau ☎ *808/889–6336* ⊕ *www. hawaiiislandretreat.com* ➥ *9 rooms* ♿ *In-room: no a/c, no TV. In-hotel: pool, spa* ⦿ *Breakfast.*

WORD OF MOUTH

"I admit that the Mauna Kea has the better beach. However, there is more to life than a beach. If you love to snorkel, like history and a natural setting, Mauna Lani is the place." —wbpiii

$$ ⌂ **Hilton Waikoloa Village.** Dolphins
RESORT swim in the lagoon; a pint-size
♺ daredevil zooms down the 175-
foot waterslide; a bride poses on
the grand staircase; a fire-bearing runner lights the torches along the seaside path at sunset—these are some of the scenes that may greet you at this 62-acre megaresort. **Pros:** family-friendly; lots of restaurant and activity options. **Cons:** gigantic, crowded; restaurants are pricey. ⊠ *69-425 Waikoloa Beach Dr., Waikoloa* ☎ *808/886–1234, 800/445–8667* ⊕ *www.hiltonwaikoloavillage.com* ➥ *1,240 rooms, 57 suites* ♿ *In-room: a/c, safe, Internet. In-hotel: restaurant, bar, golf course, pool, tennis court, gym, spa, water sports, children's programs, laundry facilities* ⦿ *No meals.*

$$$ ⌂ **Kolea at Waikoloa Beach Resort.** Kolea appeals to the high-end visitor
RENTAL typically associated with the Mauna Lani Resort. **Pros:** high design; close to beach and activities; some resort amenities. **Cons:** pricey; no on-property restaurants. ⊠ *Waikoloa Beach Resort, 69-1000 Kolea Kai Circle, Waikoloa* ☎ *808/987–4519* ⊕ *www.waikoloavacationrentals. com/kolea-rentals* ➥ *28 villas, 1 home* ♿ *In-room: a/c, kitchen. In-hotel: pool, gym* ⦿ *No meals.*

$$$$ ⌂ **Mauna Kea Beach Hotel.** The grande dame of Kohala Coast, the Mauna
HOTEL Kea Beach Hotel was designed by Laurance S. Rockefeller in the early
Fodor's Choice 1960s and opened in 1965. **Pros:** beautiful beach; extra-large contem-
★ porary rooms; excellent restaurants. **Cons:** small swimming pool; over-priced sundries shop. ⊠ *62-100 Mauna Kea Beach Dr., Kohala Coast* ☎ *808/882–7222, 800/882–6060* ⊕ *www.maunakeabeachhotel.com* ➥ *258 rooms, 10 suites* ♿ *In-room: a/c, safe, Internet. In-hotel: restaurant, bar, golf course, pool, tennis court, gym, beach, water sports, children's programs* ⦿ *No meals.*

$$$$ ⌂ **Mauna Lani Bay Hotel & Bungalows.** A Kohala Coast classic, popular
HOTEL with honeymooners and anniversary couples for decades, the elegant
Fodor's Choice Mauna Lani Bay Hotel & Bungalows is still one of the most beautiful
★ resorts on the island, highlighted by a breathtaking, open-air lobby with cathedral-like ceilings, Zen-like koi ponds, and illuminated sheets of cascading water. **Pros:** beautiful design; award-winning spa; no hidden fees; complimentary valet parking. **Cons:** no luau. ⊠ *68-1400 Mauna Lani Dr., Kohala Coast* ☎ *808/885–6622, 800/367–2323* ⊕ *www. maunalani.com* ➥ *324 rooms, 14 suites, 5 bungalows* ♿ *In-room: a/c, safe, Wi-Fi. In-hotel: restaurant, bar, golf course, pool, tennis court, gym, spa, beach, children's programs* ⦿ *No meals.*

$$$$ ⌂ **Mauna Lani Point and Islands of Mauna Lani.** Surrounded by the emer-
RENTAL ald greens of a world-class ocean-side golf course, spacious two-story suites at Islands of Mauna Lani offer a private, independent home away from home. **Pros:** privacy; soaking tubs; extra-large units. **Cons:** can get

9

very pricey; no access to nearby resort amenities. ✉ *68-1050 Mauna Lani Point Dr., Kohala Coast* ☎ *808/885–5022, 800/642–6284* ⊕ *www. classicresorts.com* ⟿ *61 units* ♿ *In-room: a/c, kitchen. In-hotel: pool* †⊘| *No meals.*

$$ ⊞ **Outrigger Fairway Villas at Waikoloa.** These large and comfy town
RENTAL houses and condominiums are located just off the fairway of the Waikoloa golf course and are just a short walk from Anaehoomalu Bay. **Pros:** good location for beach, shopping, dining, and golf; infinity pool; kid-friendly. **Cons:** no ocean views. ✉ *Waikoloa Beach Resort, 69-200 Pohakulana Pl., Waikoloa* ☎ *808/886–0036* ⊕ *www.outrigger. com* ⟿ *80 units* ♿ *In-room: a/c, kitchen, Wi-Fi. In-hotel: pool, gym, laundry facilities, business center* †⊘| *No meals.*

$$$ ⊞ **Puakea Ranch.** Four beautifully restored ranch houses and bungalows
RENTAL occupy this historic country estate in Hawi, where guests enjoy their
Fodor'sChoice own private swimming pools, horseback riding, round-the-clock con-
★ cierge availability, and plenty of fresh fruit to pick from the orchards.
Pros: horseback lessons and trail riding; charmingly decorated; beau-
tiful bathrooms; private swimming pools. **Cons:** not on the beach.
✉ *56-2864 Akoni Pule Hwy., Kohala Coast* ☎ *808/315–0805* ⊕ *www. puakearanch.com* ⟿ *4 private bungalows* ♿ *In-room: no a/c, kitchen, Wi-Fi. In-hotel: pool* †⊘| *No meals.*

$ ⊞ **Vista Waikoloa.** Older and more reasonably priced than most of the
RENTAL condo complexes along the Kohala Coast, the two-bedroom, two-
bath Vista condos offer ocean views and a great value for this part of
the island. **Pros:** centrally located; reasonably priced; very large units;
75-foot lap pool. **Cons:** hit or miss on decor because each unit is individually owned. ✉ *Waikoloa Beach Resort, 69-1010 Keana Pl., Waikoloa*
☎ *808/886–3594* ⊕ *www.waikoloavacationrentals/kolea.com* ⟿ *122 units* ♿ *In-room: a/c, kitchen. In-hotel: pool, gym, laundry facilities, business center* †⊘| *No meals.*

$$$ ⊞ **Waikoloa Beach Marriott.** The most affordable resort on the Kohala
RESORT Coast, the Waikoloa Beach Marriott covers 15 acres and encompasses
ancient fishponds, historic trails, and petroglyph fields. **Pros:** more low-
key than the Hilton Waikoloa; well-designed interiors. **Cons:** only one
restaurant. ✉ *69-275 Waikoloa Beach Dr., Waikoloa* ☎ *808/886–6789, 800/228–9290* ⊕ *www.marriott.com* ⟿ *523 rooms, 22 suites* ♿ *In-room: a/c. In-hotel: restaurant, bar, golf course, pool, tennis court, gym, spa, beach, laundry facilities* †⊘| *No meals.*

WAIMEA

Though it seems a world away, Waimea is only about a 15- to 20-minute drive from the Kohala Coast resorts, which means it takes less time to get to the island's best beaches from Waimea than it does from Kailua-Kona. Yet, few visitors think to book lodging in this pleasant upcountry village, where you can enjoy cool mornings and evenings after a day spent basking in the sun. To the delight of residents and visitors, a few retired resort chefs have opened up their own little projects in Waimea. Sightseeing is easy from here, too: Mauna Kea is a short drive away, and Hilo and Kailua-Kona can be reached in about an hour. Because

Mauna Lani Bay Hotel & Bungalows

Puakea Ranch   Waianuhea

Waimea doesn't attract as many visitors as the coast, you won't find as many condos and hotels, but there are some surprising bed-and-breakfast options in the area. Some also offer some of the island's best lodging deals, especially when you consider that their vantage point affords spectacular views of Mauna Kea, the ocean, and the beautiful, green hills of Waimea.

$
B&B/INN
⌐ Aaah The Views Bed and Breakfast. The name aptly sums up the experience at this tranquil, stream-side inn built specifically to be a bed-and-breakfast—and it's the only lodging in Waimea that includes breakfast. **Pros:** away from it all; friendly hosts; beautiful countryside views; free beach gear. **Cons:** no pool. ✉ *66-1773 Alaneo St., off Akulani, just past mile marker 60 on Hwy. 19, Waimea* ☎ *808/885–3455* ⊕ *www.aaahtheviews.com* ⌐ *3 suites* ᗽ *In-room: no a/c, kitchen, Wi-Fi* ⫙ *Breakfast.*

$
RENTAL
⌐ Aloha Vacation Cottages. Set on several acres in upper South Kohala, these two rental cottages are clean, comfortable, and well stocked with beach toys, towels and mats, snorkel gear, body boards, kayaks, fishing gear, laptop computers, books, cable TV, videos, you name it. **Pros:** each cottage equipped with gas grill; free Wi-Fi; 10-minute drive from great beaches. **Cons:** somewhat remote location; can't walk to restaurants or stores; no pool. ⌂ *Box 1395, Waimea 96743* ☎ *877/875–1722, 808/885–6535* ⊕ *www.alohacottages.net* ⌐ *2 units* ᗽ *In-room: no a/c, kitchen, Wi-Fi. In-hotel: parking* ⫙ *No meals.*

$
HOTEL
⌐ Waimea Country Lodge. In the heart of cowboy country, this modest ranch house–style lodge offers views of the green, rolling slopes of Mauna Kea. **Pros:** affordable; large rooms equipped with kitchenettes. **Cons:** rooms could use some updating; no pool. ✉ *65-1210 Lindsey Rd., Waimea* ☎ *808/885–4100, 800/367–5004* ⊕ *www.castleresorts.com* ⌐ *21 rooms* ᗽ *In-room: no a/c, kitchen, Internet. In-hotel: laundry facilities, parking* ⫙ *No meals.*

$
RENTAL
⌐ Waimea Gardens Cottage. Surprisingly luxe, yet cozy and quaint, three charming country cottages at this historic Hawaiian homestead are surrounded by flowering private gardens and a backyard stream. **Pros:** no detail left out; beautiful self-contained cottages; gardens; complete privacy. **Cons:** requires payment in full six weeks prior to arrival. ⌂ *Box 563, Kamuela 96743* ☎ *808/885–8550* ⊕ *www.waimeagardens.com* ⌐ *2 cottages, 1 studio* ᗽ *In-room: no a/c, kitchen, Wi-Fi* ⊟ *No credit cards* ⫙ *Breakfast.*

THE HAMAKUA COAST

A stretch of coastline between Waimea and Hilo, the Hamakua Coast is an ideal spot for those seeking peace, tranquility, and beautiful views, which is why it can be a favorite with honeymooners. Several über-romantic bed-and-breakfasts dot the coast, each with its own personality and views. As with Hilo, the beaches are an hour's drive away or more, so most visitors spend a few nights here and a few closer to the beaches on the west side. A handful of vacation homes provide an extra level of privacy for couples, groups, or families, but the nearest grocery stores are in either Hilo or Waimea.

$$ ⊞ **The Palms Cliff House Inn.** This handsome Victorian-style mansion,
B&B/INN 15 minutes north of downtown Hilo, is perched on the sea cliffs 100
feet above the crashing surf of the tropical coast. **Pros:** stunning views;
terrific breakfast; comfortable rooms with every amenity; all rooms
have private entrances from the exterior. **Cons:** no pool; no lunch or
dinner on site; remote location means you have to drive to Hilo town
for dinner. ⊠ *28-3514 Mamalahoa Hwy., Honomu* ☎ *866/963–6076,
808/963–6076* ⊕ *www.palmscliffhouse.com* ⤵ *4 rooms, 4 suites* ⚒ *In-
room: a/c, safe. In-hotel: business center* ¶◯| *Breakfast.*

$$ ⊞ **Waianuhea.** Defining Hawaiian upcountry elegance, this gorgeous
B&B/INN country inn, which is fully self-contained and runs off solar power,
Fodor's Choice sits in a forested area on the Hamakua Coast in Ahualoa. **Pros:** eco-
★ friendly hotel; hot and healthy breakfast; beautiful views. **Cons:** very
remote location; unreliable phone access. ⊠ *45-3503 Kahana Dr., Box
185, Honokaa* ☎ *888/775–2577, 808/775–1118* ⊕ *www.waianuhea.
com* ⤵ *4 rooms, 1 suite* ⚒ *In-room: no a/c. In-hotel: business center*
¶◯| *Breakfast.*

$ ⊞ **Waipio Wayside.** Nestled amid the avocado, mango, coffee, and kukui
B&B/INN trees of a historic plantation estate (circa 1932), this serene inn provides
a retreat close to the Waipio Valley. **Pros:** close to Waipio; authentic
Hawaiian feel; hammocks with views. **Cons:** remote location; no lunch
or dinner on property. ⊠ *Waipio Valley Rd., Hwy. 240, 42-4226 Honokaa Waipio Road, Honokaa* ☎ *808/775–0275, 800/833–8849* ⊕ *www.
waipiowayside.com* ⤵ *5 rooms* ⚒ *In-room: no a/c, Wi-Fi* ¶◯| *Breakfast.*

HILO

Hilo is the wetter, more lush eastern side of the Big Island, which means
if you stay here you'll be close to waterfalls and rain-forest hikes, but
not to the warm, dry, white-sand beaches of the Kohala Coast. Locals
have taken a greater interest in Hilo; signs of that interest are showing in new restaurants, restored buildings, and a handful of clean and
pleasant parks. Hilo has a few decent hotels, but none of the high-end
resorts that are the domain of the west side. So, get into the groove
at one of Hilo's fantastic bed-and-breakfasts. Most have taken over
lovely historic homes and serve breakfast comprised of ingredients from
backyard gardens. The volcano is only a 30- to 40-minute drive, as are
the sights of the Puna region. There are also a number of nice beaches,
though not in the class of the resort beaches of South Kohala.

$ ⊞ **The Bay House.** Overlooking Hilo Bay and just steps away from
B&B/INN the "Singing Bridge" into Hilo's historic downtown area, this small,
quiet bed-and-breakfast is vibrantly decorated, with Hawaiian-quilted
beds and private lanai. **Pros:** cliffside hot tub; Hilo Bay views. **Cons:**
no hot breakfast; only two people per room. ⊠ *42 Pukihae St., Hilo*
☎ *888/235–8195, 808/961–6311* ⊕ *www.bayhousehawaii.com* ⤵ *3
rooms* ⚒ *In-room: no a/c, Wi-Fi* ¶◯| *Breakfast.*

$ ⊞ **Dolphin Bay Hotel.** Units in this circa-1950s motor lodge are modest,
HOTEL but charming, clean, and inexpensive. **Pros:** great value; full kitchens in
☺ all units; extremely helpful and pleasant staff; weekly rates are a good
deal. **Cons:** no pool; no phones in the rooms. ⊠ *333 Iliahi St., Hilo*

9

☎ *808/935–1466* ⊕ *www.dolphinbayhotel.com* ⤳ *18 rooms, 12 studios, 4 1-bedroom units, 1 2-bedroom unit* ♿ *In-room: no a/c, kitchen, Wi-Fi* ¶⊙¶ *No meals.*

$ ⊞ **Hale Kai.** On a bluff above Hilo Bay, this 5,400-square-foot modern
B&B/INN home is 2 mi from downtown Hilo, and features four rooms—each with patios, deluxe bedding, and grand ocean views within earshot of the surf. **Pros:** delicious hot breakfast; panoramic views; hot tub. **Cons:** no kids under 13. ⊠ *111 Honolii Place, Hilo* ☎ *808/935–6330* ⊕ *www. halekaihawaii.com* ⤳ *3 rooms, 1 suite* ♿ *In-room: no a/c, Wi-Fi. In-hotel: pool, some age restrictions* ¶⊙¶ *Breakfast.*

$$ ⊞ **Hilo Hawaiian Hotel.** Though it does show its age and some of the
HOTEL rooms are in dire need of a refresh, this older hotel has large bay-front rooms offering spectacular views of Mauna Kea and Coconut Island on Hilo Bay. **Pros:** Hilo Bay views; private lanai in most rooms; large rooms. **Cons:** worse for wear; prices high for quality of rooms. ⊠ *71 Banyan Dr., Hilo* ☎ *808/935–9361, 800/367–5004 from mainland, 800/272–5275 interisland* ⊕ *www.castleresorts.com* ⤳ *264 rooms, 21 suites* ♿ *In-room: a/c, kitchen, Internet, Wi-Fi. In-hotel: restaurant, bar, pool, laundry facilities* ¶⊙¶ *No meals.*

$ ⊞ **Hilo Honu Inn.** A charming old Craftsman home lovingly restored by
B&B/INN a friendly and hospitable couple from North Carolina, the Hilo Honu offers quite a bit of variety. **Pros:** beautifully restored home; spectacular Hilo Bay views; delicious breakfast; free Wi-Fi. **Cons:** no toddlers in the upstairs suite. ⊠ *465 Haili St., Hilo* ☎ *808/935–4325* ⊕ *www. hilohonu.com* ⤳ *3 rooms* ♿ *In-room: a/c, Wi-Fi. In-hotel: some age restrictions* ¶⊙¶ *Breakfast.*

$ ⊞ **The Inn at Kulaniapia Falls.** Overlooking downtown Hilo and the ocean
B&B/INN beyond, the Inn at Kulaniapia sits adjacent to a 120-foot waterfall that tumbles into a 300-foot-wide natural pond. **Pros:** waterfalls on property; good value. **Cons:** isolated; dark road challenging to navigate at night. ⌂ *Box 11338, 1 Kulaniapia Dr., Hilo 96720* ☎ *808/935–8088, 888/838–6373* ⊕ *www.waterfall.net* ⤳ *4 rooms* ♿ *In-room: no a/c, kitchen, Wi-Fi. In-hotel: spa* ¶⊙¶ *Breakfast.*

$ ⊞ **Naniloa Volcanoes Resort.** The Naniloa's recently renovated guest
RESORT rooms in the Mauna Kea tower are a vast improvement over the old ones at this landmark hotel, which is a great home base for exploring the Big Island's unspoiled east side. **Pros:** some renovated rooms; great views of Hilo Bay and Mauna Kea and Mauna Loa volcanoes from some rooms. **Cons:** ongoing renovations; limited dining options. ⊠ *93 Banyan Dr., Hilo* ☎ *808/969–3333* ⊕ *www.volcanohousehotel. com/naniloa_volcanoes_resort.htm* ⤳ *313 rooms, 7 suites* ♿ *In-room: a/c, Internet. In-hotel: restaurant, golf course, pool, laundry facilities* ¶⊙¶ *No meals.*

$$ ⊞ **Shipman House Bed & Breakfast Inn.** This bed-and-breakfast is on 5½
B&B/INN verdant acres on Reed's Island; the house is furnished with antique koa and period pieces, some dating from the days when Queen Liliuokalani came to tea. **Pros:** 10-minute walk to downtown Hilo; historic home; friendly and knowledgeable local hosts. **Cons:** not a great spot for kids. ⊠ *131 Kaiulani St., Hilo* ☎ *808/934–8002, 800/627–8447* ⊕ *www.hilo-*

hawaii.com ⌨ *3 rooms, 2 cottage rooms* ☐ *In-room: no a/c, no TV, Wi-Fi* ⎮❍⎮ *Breakfast.*

PUNA

Puna is a world apart—wild jungles, volcanically heated hot springs, and not a resort for miles around. There are, however, a handful of vacation homes and bed-and-breakfasts, most of which are a great deal—Puna doesn't attract nearly as many visitors as other regions on the island. This is not a typical vacation spot: there are a few black-sand beaches (some of them clothing-optional), few dining or entertainment options, and quite a few, er, interesting locals. That said, for those who want to have a unique experience, get away from everything, witness molten lava flowing into the ocean (depending on conditions), and don't mind the sound of the chirping coqui frogs at night, this is the place to do it. The volcano and Hilo are all within driving distance.

$ ▦ **Bed & Breakfast Mountain View.** This modern home on a secluded 4-acre
B&B/INN estate has extensive floral gardens and a fishpond and is surrounded by rolling forest and farmland. **Pros:** reasonable prices; local artist hosts; beautiful landscaping. **Cons:** rooms could use some updating; location is remote. ✉ *18-3717 South Kulani Rd., Kurtistown* ☎ *808/968–6868, 888/698–9896* ⊕ *www.bbmtview.com* ⌨ *4 rooms, 2 with shared bath* ☐ *In-room: no a/c, Wi-Fi. In-hotel: some age restrictions* ⎮❍⎮ *Breakfast.*

$ ▦ **Coconut Cottage Bed & Breakfast.** Coconut Cottage has quickly become
B&B/INN a favorite among visitors for its beautiful grounds, the hosts' attention to detail, and its proximity to different island adventures. **Pros:** great breakfast; convenient to the lava-flow area, black-sand beach, and Kapoho tide pools for snorkeling. **Cons:** some may have a hard time sleeping with the coqui frogs chirping. ✉ *13-1139 Leilani Ave., Pahoa* ☎ *808/965–0973, 866/204–7444* ⊕ *www.coconutcottagehawaii.com* ⌨ *3 rooms, 1 bungalow* ☐ *In-room: no a/c, Wi-Fi. In-hotel: laundry facilities* ⎮❍⎮ *Breakfast.*

$ ▦ **Yoga Oasis.** With its exposed redwood beams, Balinese doorways,
B&B/INN and imported art, Yoga Oasis draws those who seek relaxation and rejuvenation, and perhaps a free morning yoga lesson or two. **Pros:** daily yoga; focus on relaxation; very low prices. **Cons:** remote location; shared bathrooms in the main building. ✉ *Pohoiki Rd., Box 1935, 13-677 Pohoiki Rd., Pahoa* ☎ *808/936–7710, 800/274–4446* ⊕ *www.yogaoasis.org* ⌨ *4 rooms with shared bath, 4 deluxe cabins, 1 Bali house* ☐ *In-room: no a/c, no TV, Wi-Fi* ⎮❍⎮ *No meals.*

9

HAWAII VOLCANOES NATIONAL PARK AND VICINITY

If you are going to visit Hawaii Volcanoes National Park, and we highly recommend that you do, stay the night in Volcano Village. This allows you to see the glow of Halemaumau Crater at night—if there's activity, that is—without worrying about driving an hour or more back to your condo, hotel, or bed-and-breakfast. There are plenty of places to stay

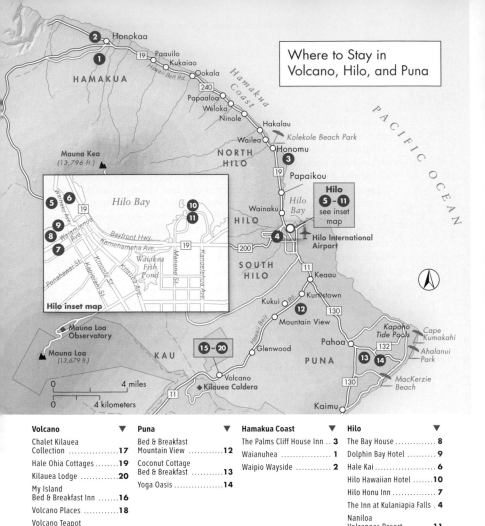

Where to Stay in Volcano, Hilo, and Puna

HAMAKUA

Honokaa

Paauilo

Kukaiao

Ookala

Papaaloa

Weloka

Ninole

Hakalau

Kolekole Beach Park

Wailea

Honomu

NORTH HILO

Papaikou

Wainaku

HILO

Hilo Bay

Hilo — see inset map

Hilo International Airport

SOUTH HILO

Keaau

Kurtistown

Kukui

Mountain View

Pahoa

PUNA

Glenwood

Kapoho Tide Pools

Cape Kumakahi

Ahalanui Park

MacKerzie Beach

Kaimu

Volcano

Kilauea Caldera

KAU

Mauna Loa Observatory

Mauna Loa (13,679 ft.)

Mauna Kea (13,796 ft.)

Hilo inset map

Hilo Bay

Wailoa River State Park

Waiakea Fish Pond

Bayfront Hwy.

Kamehameha Ave.

0   4 miles

0   4 kilometers

PACIFIC OCEAN

Hamakua Coast

Hawaii Belt Rd.

in the area, and many of them are both charming and reasonable. Volcano Village has just enough dining and shopping options to satisfy you for a day or two, and you're also close to Hilo, the Puna region, and Punaluu's black-sand beach, should you decide to make Volcano your home base for longer.

$
B&B/INN
Chalet Kilauea Collection. The Collection comprises three inns and lodges and five vacation houses in and around Volcano Village. **Pros:** free Wi-Fi at all facilities; free afternoon tea at main office; large variety of lodging types to choose from; hot tub; fireplace. **Cons:** office closes at 5 pm—late arrivals allowed but you need to formally check in the following morning. ⊠ *19-4178 Wright Rd., Volcano* ☎ *808/967–7786, 800/937–7786* ⊕ *www.volcano-hawaii.com* ⊅ *14 rooms, 3 suites, 5 houses* ⚲ *In-room: no a/c, Wi-Fi* ⦿ *No meals.*

$
RENTAL
Hale Ohia Cottages. A stately and comfortable Queen Anne–style mansion, Hale Ohia was built in the 1930s as a summer home for a wealthy Scotsman (the property is listed on the State Historic Register). **Pros:** unique architecture; central, quiet location; privacy. **Cons:** no TVs. ⊠ *11-3968 Hale Ohia Rd., off Hwy. 11, Volcano* ☎ *808/967–7786, 800/455–3803* ⊕ *www.haleohia.com* ⊅ *4 rooms, 3 cottages, 1 suite* ⚲ *In-room: no a/c, kitchen, no TV, Wi-Fi* ⦿ *Breakfast.*

$
HOTEL
Kilauea Lodge. A mile from the entrance of Hawaii Volcanoes National Park, this lodge was initially built as a YMCA camp in the 1930s. **Pros:** great restaurant; close to volcano; fireplaces. **Cons:** a little pricey for the area; no TV or phone in room. ⊠ *19-3948 Old Volcano Rd., 1 mi northeast of Volcano Store, Box 116, Volcano* ☎ *808/967 7366* ⊕ *www.kilauealodge.com* ⊅ *12 rooms, 4 cottages (off property)* ⚲ *In-room: no a/c, no TV, Wi-Fi. In-hotel: restaurant* ⦿ *Breakfast.*

$
B&B/INN
My Island Bed & Breakfast Inn. This three-story, family-operated inn is in a historic home built in 1886 by the Lyman missionary family and set on a 7-acre botanical estate. **Pros:** historic home; full breakfast. **Cons:** some shared bathrooms; not every room has a TV. ⊠ *19-3896 Old Volcano Hwy., Volcano Village* ✆ *Box 100, Volcano 96785* ☎ *808/967–7216* ⊕ *www.myislandinnhawaii.com* ⊅ *6 rooms, 1 guesthouse* ⚲ *In-room: no a/c, no TV* ⦿ *Breakfast.*

$
RENTAL
Volcano Places. A collection of lovely vacation rental cottages, these accommodations range from a simple cottage in the rain forest to the stunning cedar-paneling Nohea, with its own hot tub. **Pros:** unique architecture; accommodates families; competitively priced; total privacy. **Cons:** no nightlife nearby. ⊠ *19-3951 Laukapu Rd., Volcano* ☎ *808/967–7990, 877/967–7990* ⊕ *www.volcanoplaces.com* ⊅ *2 2-bedroom cottages, 1 1-bedroom unit, 1 studio* ⚲ *In-room: no a/c, kitchen, Wi-Fi* ⦿ *No meals.*

$$
RENTAL
Volcano Teapot Cottage. A near-perfect spot for couples seeking a romantic getaway in Volcano Village, this cute two-bedroom red-and-white cottage is completely private and lovingly decorated. **Pros:**

9

claw-foot tub; hot tub; fireplace; laundry facilities. **Cons:** single or double occupancy only. ✉ *19-4041 Kilauea Rd., Volcano Village* ✉ *Box 511, Volcano 96785* ☎ *808/967–7112* ⊕ *www.volcanoteapot.com* ⬎ *1 cottage* & *In-room: no a/c, kitchen, Wi-Fi* ❖| *Breakfast.*

KAU

Far from the Big Island's resorts, Kau is a good place for those looking to get away from it all. You won't find much in terms of amenities, but there are a few nice rental and B&B options here.

$$

B&B/INN

❖ **Kalaekilohana.** You wouldn't really expect to find a top-notch bed-and-breakfast in Kau, but just up the road from South Point, this grand yellow residence offers large, comfortable private suites with beautiful, locally harvested hardwood floors, private lanai with ocean and mountain views, and big, comfy beds decked out with high-thread-count sheets and fluffy down comforters. **Pros:** luxurious beds; beautiful decor reminiscent of Old Hawaii; delicious breakfast. **Cons:** not for children under 10; no pool. ✉ *94-2152 South Point Rd., Naalehu* ☎ *808/939–8052* ⊕ *www.kau-hawaii.com* ⬎ *4 rooms* & *In-room: no a/c, Wi-Fi. In-hotel: laundry facilities* ❖| *Breakfast.*

$

RENTAL

❖ **South Point Banyan Tree House.** Ideal for romance, this charming little tree cottage is built into a Chinese banyan tree. **Pros:** secluded and romantic, interesting architecture, hot tub with a view. **Cons:** remote location, not within walking distance to grocery store or restaurants, no pool or beach. ✉ *Hwy. 11 at Pinao St. (near South Point), Waiohinu* ☎ *715/212–9946, 808/217–2504* ⊕ *www.southpointbth.com* ⬎ *1 cottage* & *In-room: no a/c, kitchen, Wi-Fi. In-hotel: laundry facilities* ❖| *No meals.*

UNDERSTANDING
BIG ISLAND

Hawaiian Vocabulary

HAWAIIAN VOCABULARY

Although an understanding of Hawaiian is by no means required on a trip to the Aloha State, a *malihini,* or newcomer, will find plenty of opportunities to pick up a few of the local words and phrases. Traditional names and expressions are widely used in the Islands. You're likely to read or hear at least a few words each day of your stay.

With a basic understanding and some uninhibited practice, anyone can have enough command of the local tongue to ask for directions and to order from a restaurant menu. One visitor announced she would not leave until she could pronounce the name of the state fish, the *humuhumunukunukuāpua'a.*

Simplifying the learning process is the fact that the Hawaiian language contains only eight consonants—H, K, L, M, N, P, W, and the silent *'okina,* or glottal stop, written '—plus one or more of the five vowels. All syllables, and therefore all words, end in a vowel. Each vowel, with the exception of a few diphthongized double vowels such as *au* (pronounced "ow") or *ai* (pronounced "eye"), is pronounced separately. Thus *'Iolani* is four syllables (ee-oh-la-nee), not three (yo-la-nee). Although some Hawaiian words have only vowels, most also contain some consonants, but consonants are never doubled.

Pronunciation is simple. Pronounce *A* "ah" as in *father*; *E* "ay" as in *weigh*; *I* "ee" as in *marine*; *O* "oh" as in *no*; *U* "oo" as in *true.*

Consonants mirror their English equivalents, with the exception of W. When the letter begins any syllable other than the first one in a word, it is usually pronounced as a V. *'Awa,* the Polynesian drink, is pronounced "ava," *'ewa* is pronounced "eva."

Almost all long Hawaiian words are combinations of shorter words; they are not difficult to pronounce if you segment them. *Kalaniana'ole,* the highway running east from Honolulu, is easily understood as *Kalani ana 'ole.* Apply the standard pronunciation rules—the stress falls on the next-to-last syllable of most two- or three-syllable Hawaiian words—and Kalaniana'ole Highway is as easy to say as Main Street.

Now about that fish. Try *humu-humu nuku-nuku āpu a'a.*

The other unusual element in Hawaiian language is the *kahakō,* or macron, written as a short line (¯) placed over a vowel. Like the accent (´) in Spanish, the kahakō puts emphasis on a syllable that would normally not be stressed. The most familiar example is probably *Waikīkī.* With no macrons, the stress would fall on the middle syllable; with only one macron, on the last syllable, the stress would fall on the first and last syllables. Some words become plural with the addition of a macron, often on a syllable that would have been stressed anyway. No Hawaiian word becomes plural with the addition of an *S,* since that letter does not exist in the language.

The Hawaiian diacritical marks are not printed in this guide.

Pidgin

You may hear pidgin, the unofficial language of Hawai'i. It is a Creole language, with its own grammar, evolved from the mixture of English, Hawaiian, Japanese, Portuguese, and other languages spoken in 19th-century Hawai'i, and it is heard everywhere.

Glossary

What follows is a glossary of some of the most commonly used Hawaiian words. Hawaiian residents appreciate visitors who at least try to pick up the local language.

'a'ā: rough, crumbling lava, contrasting with *pāhoehoe,* which is smooth.

'ae: yes.

aikane: friend.

āina: land.

akamai: smart, clever, possessing savoir faire.

akua: god.

ala: a road, path, or trail.

ali'i: a Hawaiian chief, a member of the chiefly class.

aloha: love, affection, kindness; also a salutation meaning both greetings and farewell.

'ānuenue: rainbow.

'a'ole: no.

'apōpō: tomorrow.

'auwai: a ditch.

auwē: alas, woe is me!

'ehu: a red-haired Hawaiian.

'ewa: in the direction of 'Ewa plantation, west of Honolulu.

hala: the pandanus tree, whose leaves (*lau hala*) are used to make baskets and plaited mats.

hālau: school.

hale: a house.

hale pule: church, house of worship.

ha mea iki or **ha mea 'ole:** you're welcome.

hana: to work.

haole: ghost. Since the first foreigners were Caucasian, *haole* now means a Caucasian person.

hapa: a part, sometimes a half; often used as a short form of *hapa haole*, to mean a person who is part-Caucasian.

hau'oli: to rejoice. *Hau'oli Makahiki Hou* means Happy New Year. *Hau'oli lā hānau* means Happy Birthday.

heiau: an outdoor stone platform; an ancient Hawaiian place of worship.

holo: to run.

holoholo: to go for a walk, ride, or sail.

holokū: a long Hawaiian dress, somewhat fitted, with a yoke and a train. Influenced by European fashion, it was worn at court, and at least one local translates the word as "expensive mu'umu'u."

holomū: a post–World War II cross between a *holokū* and a mu'umu'u, less fitted than the former but less voluminous than the latter, and having no train.

honi: to kiss; a kiss. A phrase that some tourists may find useful, quoted from a popular hula, is *Honi Ka'ua Wikiwiki:* Kiss me quick!

honu: turtle.

ho'omalimali: flattery, a deceptive "line," bunk, baloney, hooey.

huhū: angry.

hui: a group, club, or assembly. A church may refer to its congregation as a *hui* and a social club may be called a *hui*.

hukilau: a seine; a communal fishing party in which everyone helps to drive the fish into a huge net, pull it in, and divide the catch.

hula: the dance of Hawai'i.

iki: little.

ipo: sweetheart.

ka: the. This is the definite article for most singular words; for plural nouns, the definite article is usually *nā*. Since there is no *S* in Hawaiian, the article may be your only clue that a noun is plural.

kahuna: a priest, doctor, or other trained person of old Hawai'i, endowed with special professional skills that often included prophecy or other supernatural powers; the plural form is kāhuna.

kai: the sea, saltwater.

kalo: the taro plant from whose root *poi* (paste) is made.

kamā'aina: literally, a child of the soil; refers to people who were born in the Islands or have lived there for a long time.

kanaka: originally a man or humanity, it is now used to denote a male Hawaiian or part-Hawaiian, but is occasionally taken as a slur when used by non-Hawaiians. *Kanaka maoli,* originally a full-blooded Hawaiian person, is used by some Native Hawaiian rights activists to embrace part-Hawaiians as well.

kāne: a man, a husband. If you see this word on a door, it's the men's room. If you see *kane* on a door, it's probably a misspelling; that is the Hawaiian name for the skin fungus tinea.

kapa: also called by its Tahitian name, *tapa,* a cloth made of beaten bark and usually dyed and stamped with a repeat design.

kapakahi: crooked, cockeyed, uneven. You've got your hat on *kapakahi*.

kapu: keep out, prohibited. This is the Hawaiian version of the more widely known Tongan word *tabu* (taboo).

kapuna: grandparent; elder.

kēia lā: today.

keiki: a child; *keikikāne* is a boy, *keikiwahine* a girl.

kona: the leeward side of the Islands, the direction (south) from which the *kona* wind and *kona* rain come.

kula: upland.

kuleana: a homestead or small plot of ground on which a family has been installed for some generations without necessarily owning it. By extension, *kuleana* is used to denote any area or department in which one has a special interest or prerogative. You'll hear it used this way: If you want to hire a surfboard, see Moki; that's his *kuleana*.

lā: sun.

lamalama: to fish with a torch.

lānai: a porch, a balcony, an outdoor living room. Almost every house in Hawai'i has one. Don't confuse this two-syllable word with the three-syllable name of the island, Lāna'i.

lani: heaven, the sky.

lau hala: the leaf of the *hala*, or pandanus tree, widely used in handicrafts.

lei: a garland of flowers.

limu: sun.

lolo: stupid.

luna: a plantation overseer or foreman.

mahalo: thank you.

makai: toward the ocean.

malihini: a newcomer to the Islands.

mana: the spiritual power that the Hawaiians believe inhabit all things and creatures.

manō: shark.

manuwahi: free, gratis.

mauka: toward the mountains.

mauna: mountain.

mele: a Hawaiian song or chant, often of epic proportions.

Mele Kalikimaka: Merry Christmas (a transliteration from the English phrase).

Menehune: a Hawaiian pixie. The *Menehune* were a legendary race of little people who accomplished prodigious work, such as building fishponds and temples in the course of a single night.

moana: the ocean.

mu'umu'u: the voluminous dress in which the missionaries enveloped Hawaiian women. Now made in bright printed cottons and silks, it is an indispensable garment. Culturally sensitive locals have embraced the Hawaiian spelling but often shorten the spoken word to "mu'u." Most English dictionaries include the spelling "muumuu."

nani: beautiful.

nui: big.

ohana: family.

'ono: delicious.

pāhoehoe: smooth, unbroken, satiny lava.

Pākē: Chinese. This *Pākē* carver makes beautiful things.

palapala: document, printed matter.

pali: a cliff, precipice.

pānini: prickly pear cactus.

paniolo: a Hawaiian cowboy, a rough transliteration of *español*, the language of the Islands' earliest cowboys.

pau: finished, done.

pilikia: trouble. The Hawaiian word is much more widely used here than its English equivalent.

puka: a hole.

pupule: crazy, like the celebrated Princess Pupule. This word has replaced its English equivalent in local usage.

pu'u: volcanic cinder cone.

waha: mouth.

wahine: a female, a woman, a wife, and a sign on the ladies' room door; the plural form is *wāhine*.

wai: freshwater, as opposed to saltwater, which is *kai*.

wailele: waterfall.

wikiwiki: to hurry, hurry up (since this is a reduplication of *wiki*, quick, neither W is pronounced as a V).

Travel Smart
Big Island

GETTING HERE AND AROUND

Unless your cousin is a travel agent, you're probably among the millions of people who make most of their travel arrangements online. But have you ever wondered about the differences between an online travel agent (a Web site through which you make reservations instead of going directly to the airline, hotel, or car-rental company), a discounter (a firm that does a high volume of business with a hotel chain or airline and accordingly gets good prices), a wholesaler (one that makes cheap reservations in bulk and then resells them to people like you), and an aggregator (one that compares all the offerings so you don't have to)? Is it truly better to book directly on an airline or hotel Web site? And when does a real live travel agent come in handy?

▌ AIR TRAVEL

Flying time to the Big Island is about 10 hours from New York, eight hours from Chicago, five hours from Los Angeles, and 15 hours from London, not including layovers. Some of the major airline carriers serving Hawaii fly direct to the Big Island, allowing you to bypass connecting flights out of Honolulu and Maui. If you're a more spontaneous traveler, island-hopping is easy; flights depart daily every 20 to 30 minutes or so.

Although the Big Island's airports are smaller and more casual than Honolulu International, during peak times they can also be quite busy. Allow extra travel time getting to all airports during morning and afternoon rush-hour traffic periods. Plan to arrive at the airport 45 to 60 minutes before departure for inter-island flights.

Plants and plant products are highly restricted by the Department of Agriculture, both on entering and leaving Hawaii. When you leave the Islands, your bags will be screened and tagged at one of the airport's agricultural inspection stations. Pineapples and coconuts with the packer's agricultural inspection stamp pass freely; papayas must be treated, inspected, and stamped. All other fruits are banned for export to the U.S. mainland. Flowers pass except for gardenia, rose leaves, jade vine, and mauna loa. Also banned are insects, snails, soil, cotton, cacti, sugarcane, and all berry plants.

You'll have to leave dogs and other pets at home. A 120-day quarantine is imposed to prevent the introduction of rabies, which is nonexistent in Hawaii. If specific pre- and post-arrival requirements are met, animals may qualify for a 30-day or five-day-or-less quarantine.

Airlines and Airports Airline and Airport Links.com ⊕ *www.airlineandairportlinks.com.*

Airline Security Issues Transportation Security Administration ⊕ *www.tsa.gov.*

Air Travel Resources in Hawaii State of Hawaii Airports Division Offices ☎ *808/836–6413* ⊕ *www.hawaii.gov/hnl.*

AIRPORTS

Honolulu International Airport (HNL) is the main gateway for most domestic and international flights into Hawaii. From Honolulu, there are interisland flights to the Big Island departing regularly from early morning until evening. From Honolulu, the travel time is about 35 minutes. From Maui, it's about 20 minutes. Some carriers now offer nonstop service directly from the mainland to the Kona International Airport at Keahole (KOA) and Hilo International Airport (ITO). Like many of Hawaii's airports, the two Big Island airports are "open-air," meaning you can enjoy those trade-wind breezes until the moment you step on the plane.

HONOLULU/OAHU AIRPORT

Hawaii's major airport is Honolulu International, on Oahu, 20 minutes (9 mi) west of Waikiki. To travel to the Big Island from

Honolulu, you will depart from either the interisland terminal or the commuter-airline terminal (also called the "old interisland terminal" by locals), located in two separate structures adjacent to the main overseas terminal building. A free shuttle bus, the Wiki Wiki Shuttle, operates between terminals.

Information Honolulu International Airport (HNL) ☎ *808/836-6413* ⊕ *www. honoluluairport.com.*

BIG ISLAND AIRPORTS
Those flying to the Big Island of Hawaii regularly land at one of two fields. Kona International Airport at Keahole, on the west side, serves Kailua-Kona, Keauhou, and the Kohala Coast and points south. There are Visitor Information Program (VIP) booths located at all baggage-claim areas to assist travelers. Additionally, the airport is home to newsstands and lei stands, Maxwell's Landing restaurant, and a small gift shop.

Hilo International Airport is more appropriate for those planning visits to the east side of the island. Here, you'll find VIP booths across from the Centerplate Coffee Shop near the departure lobby and in the arrival areas at each end of the terminal. In addition to the coffee shop, services include a Bank of Hawaii automatic teller machine, a gift shop, and newsstands and lei stands. Waimea-Kohala Airport, called Kamuela Airport by residents, is used primarily for private flights between islands.

Information Hilo International Airport (ITO) ☎ *808/961-9300* ⊕ *www.hawaii.gov/ito.* **Kona International Airport at Keahole (KOA)** ☎ *808/329-3423* ⊕ *www.hawaii.gov/koa.* **Waimea-Kohala Airport (MUE)** ☎ *808/887-8126* ⊕ *www.hawaii.gov/mue.*

GROUND TRANSPORTATION
Check with your hotel to see if it runs an airport shuttle. If you're not renting a car, you can choose from among 17 taxi companies serving the Hilo Airport. The approximate taxi rate is $3 for the initial fare, plus 30¢ every 1/8 mi, with surcharges for waiting time (30¢ per minute)

and baggage ($1 per bag). Cab fares to locations around the island are estimated as follows: Banyan Drive hotels $11, Hilo town $12, Hilo Pier $13, Volcano $75, Keaau $22, Pahoa $50, Honokaa $105, Kamuela/Waimea $148, Waikoloa $188, and Kailua town $240.

At the Kona International Airport, taxis are available. SpeediShuttle also offers transportation between the airport and hotels, resorts, and condominium complexes from Waimea to Keauhou.

Contacts SpeediShuttle ☎ *877/242-5777* ⊕ *www.speedishuttle.com.*

FLIGHTS
Serving Kona are Air Canada, Alaska Air, American, Delta, go! Mokulele, Hawaiian, Island Air, United, U.S. Airways, and Westjet. Hawaiian, United, and Go! Mokulele all fly into Hilo. Airlines schedule flights seasonally, meaning the number of daily flights varies according to demand.

Airline Contacts Air Canada ☎ *888/247-2262* ⊕ *www.aircanada.com.* **Alaska Airlines** ☎ *800/252-7522* ⊕ *www.alaskaair.com.* **American Airlines** ☎ *800/433-7300* ⊕ *www. aa.com.* **Delta Airlines** ☎ *800/221-1212 for U.S. reservations* ⊕ *www.delta.com.* **United Airlines** ☎ *800/864-8331 for U.S. reservations, 800/538-2929 for international reservations* ⊕ *www.united.com.* **US Airways** ☎ *800/428-4322* ⊕ *www.usairways.com.* **Westjet** ☎ *888/937-8538* ⊕ *www.westjet.com.*

INTERISLAND FLIGHTS
Should you wish to visit neighboring islands, go! Mokulele, Hawaiian, and Island Air offer regular service. Prices for interisland flights have increased quite a bit in recent years, while flight schedule availability has been reduced. Planning ahead is your best bet.

Interisland Carriers Go! Mokulele Airlines ☎ *888/435-9462* ⊕ *www.iflygo.com.* **Hawaiian Airlines** ☎ *800/367-5320* ⊕ *www.hawaiianair. com.* **Island Air** ☎ *800/388-1105* ⊕ *www. islandair.com.* **PW Express** (☎ *888/866-5022* ⊕ *www.flypwx.com*).

CHARTER FLIGHTS

Iolani Air Taxi, based on the Big Island, offers on-demand service between islands. If you're interested in getting off the beaten track, Iolani can fly you to remote airstrips.

Charter Companies Iolani Air Taxi
☎ 808/329–0018, 800/538–7590 ⊕ www. iolaniair.com.

▌ BUS TRAVEL

Travelers can take advantage of the Hawaii County Mass Transit Agency's Hele-On Bus, which travels several routes throughout the island. Mostly serving local commuters, the Hele-On Bus costs $1 per person. You can wait at a scheduled stop or stand along a route and simply flag down the bus. A one-way journey between Hilo and Kona will take about four hours. There's regular service in and around downtown Hilo, Kailua-Kona, Waimea, North and South Kohala, Honokaa, and Pahoa.

Visitors staying in Hilo can take advantage of the Transit Agency's Shared Ride Taxi program, which provides door-to-door transportation in the area. A one-way fare is $2, and a book of 15 coupons can be purchased for $30. Visitors to Kona can also take advantage of free shuttles operated by local shopping centers.

Information Hele-On Bus ☎ 808/961–8744 ⊕ www.heleonbus.org.

▌ CAR TRAVEL

Technically, the Big Island of Hawaii is the only island you can completely circle by car, and driving is the best way to enjoy the sightseeing opportunities afforded by the miles of scenic roadway.

In addition to using compass directions, Hawaii residents often refer to places as being either *mauka* (toward the mountains) or *makai* (toward the ocean). Hawaii has a strict seat-belt law that applies to both drivers and passengers. The fine for not wearing a seat belt is $92.

Jaywalking is also very common, so pay careful attention to the roads, especially while driving in rural areas.

Many police officers drive their own cars while on duty, strapping the warning lights to the roof. Because of the color of the lights, locals call them "blue lights."

GASOLINE

You can count on having to pay more at the pump for gasoline on the Big Island than almost anywhere on the U.S. mainland. Prices tend to be cheaper in Hilo.

PARKING

Parking can be a challenge in downtown Kailua Village. If you're willing to walk several blocks, you might be able to find free parking on some of the residential streets branching off Alii Drive. A few municipal lots near Alii Drive offer convenient parking on an honor system. (You'll be ticketed if you don't pay.) In Hilo, you'll find plenty of free parking. As always, use common sense: don't leave valuables in a rental car, and lock up.

ROAD CONDITIONS

It's difficult to get lost along the main roads of the Big Island. Although their names may challenge the visitor's tongue, most roads are well marked. Free publications containing good-quality road maps can be found at most convenience stores.

Roads on the Big Island are generally well maintained and can be easily negotiated. Most of the roads are two-lane highways with limited shoulders—and yes, even in paradise, there is traffic, especially during the morning and afternoon rush hours. Gas stations in rural areas can be few and far between, and it's not unusual for them to close early. If you notice that your tank is getting low, don't take any chances. In Hawaii, turning right on a red light is legal, except where noted. Use caution during heavy downpours, especially if you see signs warning of flash floods and falling rocks.

Car Rental Resources

Automobile Associations

American Automobile Association	☎ 315/797–5000	⊕ www.aaa.com
National Automobile Club	☎ 650/294–7000	⊕ www.thenac.com; CA residents only

Local Agencies

AA Aloha Cars-R-Us	☎ 800/655–7989	⊕ www.hawaiicarrental.com
Harper Car and Truck Rental (Big Island)	☎ 800/852–9993	⊕ www.harpershawaii.com
Hawaiian Discount Car Rentals	☎ 800/882–9007	⊕ www.hawaiidrive-o.com
Kona Harley-Davidson	☎ 866/326–9887	⊕ www.hawaiiharleyrental.com
Happy Campers Hawaii	☎ 888/550–3918	⊕ www.happycampershawaii.com

Major Agencies

Alamo	☎ 800/479–0000	⊕ www.alamo.com
Avis	☎ 800/831–2847	⊕ www.avis.com
Budget	☎ 800/221–8822	⊕ www.budget.com
Dollar	☎ 877-492–9379	⊕ www.dollar.com
Enterprise	☎ 808-334–1810	⊕ www.enterprise.com
Hertz	☎ 800/654–3131	⊕ www.hertz.com
National Car Rental	☎ 800/227–7368	⊕ www.nationalcar.com
Thrifty	☎ 800/847–4389	⊕ www.thrifty.com

RENTALS

Should you plan to do any sightseeing on the Big Island, it is best to rent a car due to the size of the island. With more than 260 mi of coastline—and attractions as varied as Hawaii Volcanoes National Park, Akaka Falls State Park, Puuhonua o Honaunau National Historic Park, and Puukohola Heiau National Historic Site—ideally you should split up your stay between the east and west coasts of the island. Even if all you want to do is relax at your resort, you may want to hop in the car to check out one of the island's popular restaurants.

While on the Big Island, you can rent anything from an econobox to a sports car to a motor home. Rates are usually better if you reserve though a rental agency's Web site. It's wise to make reservations far in advance and make sure that a confirmed reservation guarantees you a car, especially if visiting during peak seasons or for major conventions or sporting events. It's not uncommon to find several car categories sold out during major events on the island, like the Merrie Monarch Festival in Hilo in April or the Ironman Triathlon World Championship in Kailua-Kona in October. ■TIP➜ If you're planning on driving to the 13,796-foot summit of Mauna Kea for stargazing, you'll need a four-wheel-drive vehicle. Harper Car and Truck Rental, with offices in Hilo and Kona, is a good source for 4x4 vehicles.

For some, renting an RV or motor home might be an appealing way to see the island. Harper's has motor homes available and Hilo-based Happy Campers Hawaii rents out classic Volkswagon Westfalia camping vans. And if exploring the island on two wheels is more your speed, Kona Harley-Davidson rents motorcycles.

Rates begin at about $25 to $35 a day for an economy car with air-conditioning, automatic transmission, and unlimited mileage. This does not include the airport concession fee, general excise tax, rental vehicle surcharge, or vehicle license fee. When you reserve a car, ask about cancellation penalties and drop-off charges should you plan to pick up the car in one location and return it to another. Many rental companies in Hawaii offer coupons for discounts at various attractions that could save you money later on in your trip.

In Hawaii, you must be 21 years of age to rent a car and you must have a valid driver's license and a major credit card. Those under 25 will pay a daily surcharge of $15 to $25. Request car seats and extras such as GPS when you book. Hawaii's Child Restraint Law requires that all children three years and younger be in an approved child safety seat in the backseat of a vehicle. Children ages four to seven must be seated in a rear booster seat or child restraint such as a lap and shoulder belt. Car seats and boosters range from $5 to $8 per day.

In Hawaii, a valid mainland driver's license is valid for rental for up to 90 days.

Because the road circling the Big Island is so narrow, be sure to allow plenty of time to return your vehicle so that you can make your flight. Traffic can be heavy during morning and afternoon rush hours, especially in the Kona area. Roadworks projects are ongoing and often unscheduled. Give yourself about 3½ hours before departure time to return your vehicle.

CAR-RENTAL INSURANCE

Everyone who rents a car wonders whether the insurance that the rental companies offer is worth the expense. No one—including us—has a simple answer. It all depends on how much regular insurance you have, how comfortable you are with risk and whether or not money is an issue.

If you own a car and carry comprehensive car insurance for both collision and liability, your personal auto insurance will probably cover a rental, but call your auto insurance company to confirm. If you don't have auto insurance, then you will probably need to buy the collision- or loss-damage waiver (CDW or LDW) from the rental company. Some credit cards offer CDW coverage, but it's usually supplemental to your own insurance and rarely covers SUVs, minivans, luxury models, and the like. If your coverage is secondary, you may still be liable for loss-of-use costs from the car-rental company (again, read the fine print). But no credit-card insurance is valid unless you use that card for *all* transactions, from reserving to paying the final bill.

■**TIP→** Diners Club offers primary CDW coverage on all rentals reserved and paid for with the card. This means that Diners Club's company—not your own car insurance—pays in case of an accident. It doesn't mean that your car-insurance company won't raise your rates once it discovers you had an accident.

You may also be offered supplemental liability coverage; the car-rental company is required to carry a minimal level of liability coverage insuring all renters, but it's rarely enough to cover claims in a really serious accident if you're at fault. Your own auto-insurance policy will protect you if you own a car; if you don't, you have to decide whether you are willing to take the risk.

U.S. rental companies sell CDWs and LDWs for about $15 to $25 a day; supplemental liability is usually more than $10 a day. The car-rental company may offer you all sorts of other policies, but they're rarely worth the cost. Personal accident insurance, which is basic hospitalization coverage, is an especially egregious rip-off if you already have health insurance.

■ TIP→ You can decline the insurance from the rental company and purchase it through a third-party provider such as Travel Guard (⊕ www.travelguard.com)—$9 per day for $35,000 of coverage. That's sometimes just under half the price of the CDW offered by some car-rental companies.

ESSENTIALS

■ COMMUNICATIONS

INTERNET

If you've brought your laptop with you to the Big Island, you should have no problem checking email or connecting to the Internet. Most of the major hotels and resorts offer high-speed access in rooms or lobbies. You should check with your hotel in advance to confirm that access is wireless; if not, ask whether in-room cables are provided. In some cases, there will be an hourly or daily charge posted to your room. If you're staying at a small inn or bed-and-breakfast without Internet access, ask the proprietor for the nearest café or shopping center with wireless access.

Contacts Cybercafes. Cybercafes lists over 4,000 Internet cafés worldwide. ⊕ *www. cybercafes.com.*

■ HEALTH

Hawaii is known as the Health State. The life expectancy here is 79 years, the longest in the nation. Balmy weather makes it easy to remain active year-round, and the low-stress aloha attitude certainly contributes to general well-being. When visiting the Islands, however, there are a few health issues to keep in mind.

The Hawaii State Department of Health recommends that you drink 16 ounces of water per hour to avoid dehydration when hiking or spending time in the sun. Use sunblock, wear UV-reflective sunglasses, and protect your head with a visor or hat for shade. If you're not acclimated to warm, humid weather you should allow plenty of time for rest stops and refreshments. When visiting freshwater streams, be aware of the tropical disease leptospirosis, which is spread by animal urine and carried into streams and mud. Symptoms include fever, headache, nausea, and red eyes. If left untreated it can cause liver

WORD OF MOUTH

Did the resort look as good in real life as it did in the photos? Did you sleep like a baby, or were the walls paper-thin? Did you get your money's worth? Rate hotels and write your own reviews in Travel Ratings or start a discussion about your favorite places in the Forums on ⊕ *www. fodors.com.* Your comments might even appear in our books. Yes, you, too, can be a correspondent!

and kidney damage, respiratory failure, internal bleeding, and even death. To avoid this, don't swim or wade in freshwater streams or ponds if you have open sores and don't drink from any freshwater streams or ponds.

On the Big Island, you may experience the effects of "vog," an airborne stew of gases released from volcanic vents at Kilauea. Depending on volcanic activity, you may notice a strong sulfur smell and hazy horizons. These gases can wreak havoc with respiratory and other health conditions, especially asthma or emphysema. If susceptible, stay indoors and get emergency assistance if needed.

The Islands have their share of bugs and insects that enjoy the tropical climate as much as visitors do. Most are harmless but annoying. When planning to spend time outdoors in hiking areas, wear long-sleeve clothing and pants and use mosquito repellent containing DEET. In very damp or rocky places, you may encounter the dreaded local centipede. Blue or brown in color, the centipedes can be as long as eight inches. If surprised they might sting you, and the result is similar to that of a bee and wasp. When camping, shake out your sleeping bag before climbing in, and check your shoes in the morning, as the centipedes like cozy places. If planning on hiking or traveling in remote areas, always carry a first-aid kit and appropriate medications for sting reactions.

■ HOURS OF OPERATION

Even people in paradise have to work. Generally local business hours are weekdays 8–5. Banks are usually open Monday–Thursday 8:30–3 and until 6 on Friday. Some banks have Saturday-morning hours.

Only a handful of service stations are open around the clock. Many operate from around 7 am until 9 pm. U.S. post offices are open weekdays 8:30 am–4:30 pm and Saturday 8:30–noon.

Most museums generally open their doors between 9 am and 10 am and stay open until 5 pm Tuesday–Saturday. Many museums operate with afternoon hours only on Sunday and close on Monday. Visitor-attraction hours vary throughout the state, but most sights are open daily with the exception of major holidays such as Christmas.

Stores in resort areas sometimes open as early as 8 am, with shopping-center opening hours varying from 9:30 to 10 am on weekdays and Saturday, a bit later on Sunday. Bigger malls stay open until 9 pm weekdays and Saturday and close at 5 pm on Sunday. Boutiques in resort areas may stay open as late as 11 pm.

■ MONEY

Automatic teller machines for easy access to cash are everywhere on the Islands. ATMs can be found in shopping centers, small convenience and grocery stores, inside hotels and resorts, as well as outside most bank branches. For a directory of locations, call ☎ 800/424–7787 for the MasterCard/Cirrus/Maestro network or ☎ 800/843–7587 for the Visa/Plus network.

CREDIT CARDS

It's a good idea to inform your credit-card company before you travel, especially if you're going abroad and don't travel internationally very often. Otherwise, the credit-card company might put a hold on your card owing to unusual activity—not a good thing halfway through your trip. Record all your credit-card numbers—as well as the phone numbers to call if your cards are lost or stolen—in a safe place, so you're prepared should something go wrong. Both MasterCard and Visa have general numbers you can call (collect if you're abroad) if your card is lost, but you're better off calling the number of your issuing bank, since MasterCard and Visa usually just transfer you to your bank. Your bank's number is usually printed on your card.

Reporting Lost Cards American Express ☎ 800/528–4800 in the U.S., 336/393–1111 collect from abroad ⊕ www.americanexpress. com. **Diners Club** ☎ 800/234–6377 in the U.S., 303/799–1504 collect from abroad ⊕ www.dinersclub.com. **Discover** ☎ 800/347–2683 in the U.S., 801/902–3100 collect from abroad ⊕ www.discovercard.com. **MasterCard** ☎ 800/622–7747 in the U.S., 636/722–7111 collect from abroad ⊕ www.mastercard.com. **Visa** ☎ 800/847–2911 in the U.S., 410/581–9994 collect from abroad ⊕ www.visa.com.

TRAVELER'S CHECKS

Some consider this the currency of the caveman, and it's true that fewer establishments accept traveler's checks these days. Nevertheless, they're a cheap and secure way to carry extra money, particularly on trips to urban areas. Both Citibank (under the Visa brand) and American Express issue traveler's checks in the United States, but Amex is better known and more widely accepted; you can also avoid hefty surcharges by cashing Amex checks at Amex offices. Whatever you do, keep track of all the serial numbers in case the checks are lost or stolen.

Contacts American Express ☎ 800/528-4800 in the U.S., 801/945–9450 outside of the U.S. ⊕ www.americanexpress.com.

LOCAL DO'S AND TABOOS

GREETINGS

Hawaii is a very friendly place and this is reflected in the day-to-day encounters with friends, family, and even business associates. Women will often hug and kiss one another on the cheek and men will shake hands and sometimes combine that with a friendly hug. Children often refer to elders as "auntie" or "uncle," even if they aren't related, which reflects the strong sense of family.

When you disembark from long flight, perhaps a bit groggy and stiff, nothing quite compares with a Hawaiian lei greeting. This charming custom ranks as one of the fastest ways to make the transition from the worries of home to the joys of your vacation.

If you've booked a vacation with a wholesaler or tour company, a lei greeting might be included in your package, so check before you leave. If not, it's easy to arrange a lei greeting for yourself or for your companions before you arrive. Contact Kamaaina Leis, Flowers & Greeters if you're arriving into Kona International Airport. A plumeria or dendrobium orchid lei are considered standard and cost about $22 per person. Hilo International Airport does not allow companies to provide lei greeting services, but there are lei vendors at the airport should you wish to purchase lei upon arrival.

Information Kamaaina Leis, Flowers & Greeters ☎ *800/367–5183, 808/836–3246* ⊕ *www.alohaleigreetings.com.*

LANGUAGE

Hawaii was admitted to the Union in 1959, so residents can be sensitive when visitors refer to their own hometowns as "back in the States." When in Hawaii, refer to the contiguous 48 states as "the mainland" and not as the United States. When you do, you won't appear to be such a *malahini* (newcomer).

English is the primary language on the Islands. Making the effort to learn some Hawaiian words can be rewarding, however. Despite the length of many Hawaiian words, the Hawaiian alphabet is actually one of the world's shortest, with only 12 letters: the five vowels, *a, e, i, o, u,* and seven consonants, *h, k, l, m, n, p, w.* Hawaiian words you're most likely to encounter during your visit to the Islands are *aloha, mahalo* (thank you), *keiki* (child), *haole* (Caucasian or foreigner), *mauka* (toward the mountains), *makai* (toward the ocean), and *pau* (finished, all done).

Hawaiian history includes waves of immigrants, each bringing their own languages. To communicate with each other, they developed a sort of slang known as "pidgin." If you listen closely, you'll know what is being said by the inflections and by the extensive use of body language. For example, when you know what you want to say but don't know how to say it, just say "you know, da kine." For an informative and sometimes hilarious view of things Hawaiian, check out Jerry Hopkins's series of books titled *Pidgin to the Max* and *Fax to the Max,* available at most local bookstores in the Hawaiiana sections.

▌ PACKING

Hawaii is casual: sandals, bathing suits, and comfortable, informal clothing are the norm. In summer synthetic slacks and shirts, although easy to care for, can be uncomfortably warm.

One of the most important things to tuck into your suitcase is sunscreen. Hats and sunglasses offer important sun protection, too. Both are easy to find in island shops, but if you already have a favorite packable hat or sun visor, bring it with you. All major hotels in Hawaii provide beach towels.

As for clothing in the Hawaiian Islands, there's a saying that when a man wears a suit during the day, he's either going for a loan or he's a lawyer trying a case. Only a few upscale restaurants require a jacket for dinner. The *aloha* shirt is accepted dress in Hawaii for business and most social occasions. Shorts are acceptable daytime attire, along with a T-shirt or polo shirt. There's no need to buy expensive sandals on the mainland— here you can get flip-flops (called "slippers" by locals) for under $5. Golfers should remember that many courses have dress codes requiring a collared shirt; call courses you're interested in for details. If you're not prepared, you can pick up appropriate clothing at resort pro shops. If you're visiting in winter, bring a sweater or light- to medium-weight jacket. A polar fleece pullover is ideal, and makes a great impromptu pillow.

If your vacation plans include Hilo, you'll want to pack a folding umbrella and a light poncho. And if you'll be exploring Hawaii Volcanoes National Park, make sure you pack appropriately as weather ranges from hot and dry along the shore to chilly, foggy, and rainy at the summit. Sturdy boots are recommended if you'll be hiking or camping in the park.

▌ SAFETY

Hawaii is generally a safe tourist destination, but it's still wise to follow the same commonsense safety precautions you would normally follow in your own hometown. Hotel and visitor-center staff can provide information should you decide to head out on your own to more remote areas. Rental cars are magnets for break-ins, so don't leave any valuables in the car, not even in a locked trunk. Avoid poorly lighted areas, beach parks, and isolated areas after dark as a precaution. When hiking, stay on marked trails, no matter how alluring the temptation might be to stray. Weather conditions can cause landscapes to become muddy, slippery, and tenuous, so staying on marked trails will lessen the possibility of a fall or getting lost.

Ocean safety is of the utmost importance when visiting an island destination. Don't swim alone, and follow the international signage posted at beaches that alerts swimmers to strong currents, man-of-wars or box jellyfish, sharp coral, high surf, sharks, and dangerous shore breaks. At coastal lookouts along cliff tops, heed the signs indicating that waves can climb over the ledges. Check with lifeguards at each beach for current conditions, and if the red flags are up, indicating swimming and surfing are not allowed, don't go in. Waters that look calm on the surface can harbor strong currents and undertows, and not a few people who were "just wading" have been dragged out to sea.

Women traveling alone are generally safe on the Islands, but always follow the same safety precautions you would use in any major destination. When booking hotels, request rooms closest to the elevator, and always keep your hotel-room door and balcony doors locked. Stay away from isolated areas after dark; camping and hiking solo are not advised. If you stay out late visiting nightclubs and bars, use caution when exiting night spots and returning to your car or lodging.

▌ TAXES

Businesses in Hawaii charge a 4.2% general excise tax on all purchases, including food and services. A hotel room tax of 7.25%, combined with the excise tax, equals an 11.45% rate added to your hotel bill. A $3-per-day road tax is also assessed on each rental vehicle.

▌ TIME

Hawaii is on Hawaiian Standard Time, five hours behind New York, two hours behind Los Angeles, and 10 hours behind London.

When the U.S. mainland is on daylight saving time, Hawaii is not, so add an extra hour of time difference between the Islands and U.S. mainland destinations.

▌ TIPPING

Hawaii is a major vacation destination and many of the people who work at the hotels and resorts rely on tips to supplement their wages, so tipping is common. Tip cabdrivers 15% of the fare. Standard tips at restaurants and spas run from 15% to 20% of the bill, depending on the quality of service; bartenders expect about $1 per drink. Bellhops at hotels usually receive $1 per bag, more if you have bulky items like bicycles or surfboards. Tip the hotel maid $1 per night, paid daily. Tip doormen $1 to $5 for assistance with taxis, bags, or golf clubs; tips for concierges vary depending on the service.

▌ TOURS

GENERAL-INTEREST TOURS

Globus has three Hawaii itineraries that include the Big Island, one of which is an escorted cruise on Norwegian Cruise Lines' *Pride of America* that includes one day each in Kona and Hilo. Tauck Travel and Trafalgar offer several land-based Hawaii itineraries that include two to three nights on the Big Island, depending on the tour. Both companies offer similar itineraries. In all cases, visits to Hawaii Volcanoes National Park are included.

EscortedHawaiiTours.com, owned and operated by Atlas Cruises & Tours, sells more than a dozen Hawaii trips ranging from 7 to 12 nights operated by various guided-tour companies including Globus, Tauck, and Trafalgar.

Recommended Companies Atlas Cruises & Tours ☎ *800/942–3301* ⊕ *www.escortedhawaiitours.com.* **Globus** ☎ *866/755–8581* ⊕ *www.globusjourneys.com.* **Tauck Travel** ☎ *800/788–7885* ⊕ *www.tauck. com.* **Trafalgar** ☎ *866/544–4434* ⊕ *www. trafalgar.com.*

SPECIAL-INTEREST TOURS

ADVENTURE STUDY

A tour of Kilauea Volcano—the most active volcano on earth— is even better with an actual geologist. With tours tailored to small groups, Volcano Discovery offers detailed information about such geologic features as lava tubes, vents, and fumaroles. Big Island Volcano Tours offers an Evening Eco Tour inside the park that includes stops at the Kilauea Iki overlook, Black Sands Beach, Jagger Museum, and the Kalapana viewing area.

Contacts Big Island Volcano Discovery Tours ☎ *808/690–9054* ⊕ *www. bigislandvolcanotours.com.* **Volcano Discovery** ☎ *808/640–4165* ⊕ *hawaii. volcanodiscovery.com.*

ART

Whether you want to learn about Hawaiian arts, history, and culture; astronomy, ecology, or botany; or the geology of the Hawaiian volcanoes, Volcano Art Center can design a program for your group that utilizes the talents of local artists, scientists, performers, historians, park rangers, storytellers, and guides. The staff arranges transportation, accommodations, meals, classes, and lectures.

Contact Volcano Art Center ☎ *866/967– 7565* ⊕ *www.volcanoartcenter.org.*

BIKING

If you're a bicycling enthusiast, you've got exciting options on the Big Island. Bicycle Adventures has a seven-day Hawaii tour that costs about $3,180 per person and includes biking, hiking, snorkeling, sailing, and whale-watching. A six-day budget tour is priced at about $2,410 per person. Both include accommodations, meals, and park admissions.

WomanTours has a seven-night bike tour that circumnavigates the entire island. Included in the $2,790 per person price are accommodations, some meals, and guides.

■TIP→ Most airlines accommodate bikes as luggage, provided they're dismantled and boxed.

Contacts Bicycle Adventures ☎ 800/443–6060 ⊕ www.bicycleadventures.com. WomanTours ☎ 800/247–1444 ⊕ www.womantours.com.

BIRD-WATCHING

More than 150 species of birds live in the Hawaiian Islands. Field Guides has a three-island, 11-day guided bird-watching trip that focuses on endemic land birds and specialty seabirds. While on the Big Island, birders will try to spot forest birds including the Hawaiian hawk, Hawaiian thrush, Hawaiian goose, and the Hawaii creeper. Participants might also get a glimpse of the rare *palila*, the only finchlike Hawaiian honeycreeper that remains on the main islands. The trip costs $4,475 per person and includes accommodations, meals, ground transportation, interisland flights, and guided excursions.

Victor Emanuel Nature Tours has multiday trips that include the Big Island. The guide for both tours is Bob Sundstrom, who has been leading birding tours in Hawaii and other destinations since 1989. Birders will see such indigenous birds as the *amakihi, apapane, elepaio*, and the comical scarlet *iiwi*, as well as endemic birds such as the *omao, palila*, and *akepa* honeycreepers.

Contacts Field Guides ☎ 800/728–4953 ⊕ www.fieldguides.com. Victor Emanuel

Nature Tours ☎ 800/328–8368 ⊕ www.ventbird.com.

CULTURE

Road Scholar, a nonprofit organization that has been leading all-inclusive learning adventures for more than 20 years, offers several cultural and educational tours of Hawaii. A 14-night tour of the Big Island, presented by experts on local culture, includes lectures, excursions, and performances. Coordinated by Lyman House and Mission House, the tour includes excursions to Hawaii Volcanoes National Park, visits to Hilo, and walks around the quaint seaside village of Kailua-Kona. Prices start at $3,210.

Contacts Road Scholar ☎ 800/454–5766 ⊕ www.roadscholar.org.

CULINARY

Epitourean's five-day Hawaiian Culinary Safari features cooking classes using locally grown produce. This package includes ocean-view accommodations in a renovated historic ranch house perched along the scenic Kohala coast. Packages start at $1,695.

Contacts Epitourean ☎ 800/390–3292 ⊕ www.epitourean.com. Exploritas ☎ 800/454–5768 ⊕ www.exploritas.org.

ECO TOURS

Locally owned and operated Hawaii Forest & Trail, in business since 1993, seeks to educate, inspire, and entertain visitors. The company showcases the island's amazing diversity with adventures to waterfalls, rain forests, and nature preserves. With access to thousands of acres of private land, the company can offer offthe-beaten-path adventures. Trips might include tours of coffee plantations, sunset views of volcanic eruptions, or explorations of the dazzling night sky. Prices vary depending on activities chosen and size of group.

Hawaiian Walkways, run by longtime hiker Hugh Montgomery, offers ecofriendly tours of the Waipio Valley, Kilauea Volcano, and other destinations.

Personalized tours can be arranged for small groups.

Contacts **Hawaii Forest & Trail** ☎ *800/464–1993* ⊕ *www.hawaii-forest.com.* **Hawaiian Walkways** ☎ *800/457–7759* ⊕ *www.hawaiianwalkways.com.*

HIKING

Offered by The World Outdoors, which has been leading adventure tours since 1988, the Hawaii Three Island Hiker is a eight-day tour of the Big Island, Kauai, and Maui. Included in the per-person price of $3,898 are accommodations, meals, interisland airfare, and professional guides. You also get a T-shirt and water bottle. You'll spend two nights on the Big Island exploring Hawaii Volcanoes National Park.

Timberline Adventures has an eight-day tour combining Kauai and the Big Island. It includes visits to Hawaii Volcanoes National Park and the Kona Coast. The package costs about $3,095 per person, and includes accommodations, meals, ground transportation, and activities.

Contacts **The World Outdoors** ☎ *800/488–8483* ⊕ *www.theworldoutdoors.com.* **Timberline Adventures** ☎ *800/417–2453* ⊕ *www.timbertours.com.*

▌VISITOR INFORMATION

Before you go, contact the Big Island Visitors Bureau to request a free official vacation planner with information on accommodations, transportation, sports and activities, dining, arts and entertainment, and culture. Take a virtual visit to the Big Island on the Web, which can be helpful in planning your vacation. The site also has a calendar section that allows you to see what local events coincide with your visit.

The Hawaii Island Chamber of Commerce has links to dozens of museums, attractions, bed-and-breakfasts, and parks on its Web site. The Kona-Kohala Chamber of Commerce lists local activities. The Volcano Art Center offers a host of activities at Kilauea, including classes and workshops, music, dance, and theater performances, art shows, and volcano runs, which you may want to participate in while on the island.

Contacts **Big Island Visitors Bureau** ☎ *808/961–5797, 800/648–2441* ⊕ *www.bigisland.org.* **Hawaii Island Chamber of Commerce** ☎ *808/935–7178* ⊕ *www.hicc.biz.* **Kona-Kohala Chamber of Commerce** ☎ *808/329–1758* ⊕ *www.kona-kohala.com.* **Volcano Art Center** ☎ *866/967–7565, 808/967–7565* ⊕ *www.volcanoartcenter.org.*

INDEX

PHOTO CREDITS

1, Douglas Peebles/eStock Photo. 3, Polynesian Cultural Center. Chapter 1: Experience the Big Island: 6-7, Pacific Stock/SuperStock. 8 and 9 (all), Big Island Visitors Bureau. 11 (left), Photodisc.11 (right), WaterFrame/Alamy. 14 (top left), Photo Resource Hawaii/Alamy. 14 (bottom left), Corn-forth Images/Alamy. 14 (top center), Photo Resource Hawaii/Alamy. 14 (bottom center), Waterframe/Alamy. 14 (right), Douglas Peebles Photography/Alamy. 15 (left), Big Island Visitors Bureau. 15 (top center), Andre Seale/age fotostock. 15 (bottom center), Hemis/Alamy. 15 (top right), Photo Resource Hawaii/Alamy. 15 (bottom right), Stephen Frink Collection/Alamy. 17 (left), SuperStock/age fotostock. 17 (right), Photo Resource Hawaii/Alamy. 19, Katja Govorushchenko/iStockphoto. 21, iStockphoto. 23, Jay Spooner/iStockphoto. 24, Hilton Hawaii. 25 (left), Photo Resource Hawaii/Alamy. 25 (right), Stephanie Horrocks/iStockphoto. 27, iStockphoto. 29, Photo Resource Hawaii/Alamy. 31 (left), Douglas Peebles/age fotostock. 31 (right), Castle Resorts & Hotels. 35 (both), Hilton Hawaii. 36, Bryan Lowry/Alamy. Chapter 2: Exploring the Big Island: 37, Douglas Peebles/eStock Photo. 38, George Burba/Shutterstock. 39, Big Island Visitors Bureau. 49, Big Island Visitors Bureau. 51-52, Pacific Stock/SuperStock. 55, Greg Vaughn/Alamy. 56, Pacific Stock/SuperStock. 61, Pacific Stock/SuperStock. 62, Photo Resource Hawaii/Alamy. 69, Russ Bishop/Alamy. 70, Cornforth Images/Alamy. 78, SuperStock/age fotostock. 84, Big Island Visitors Bureau. 85, Russ Bishop/age fotostock. 87, Photo Resource Hawaii/Alamy. 88, Cornforth Images/Alamy. 89 (top), Pacific Stock/SuperStock. 89 (bottom), Linda Robshaw/Alamy. 90, Interfoto Pressebildagentur/Alamy. Chapter 3: Beaches: 95, Preferred Hotels & Resorts Worldwide. 96, Kushch Dmitry/Shutterstock. 99, Luis Castanedox/agefotostock. 103, Pacific Stock/SuperStock. 106, Cornforth Images/Alamy. 108, Douglas Peebles/eStock Photo. Chapter 4: Water Activities & Tours: 111, WaterFrame/Alamy. 112, Hawaii Tourism Authority (HTA) / Tor Johnson.113, Russ Bishop/Alamy. 115, Blaine Harrington III/Alamy. 125, Andre Seale/Alamy. 127, Ron Dahlquist/HVCB. 128, SuperStock/age fotostock. 130 (top), SPrada/iStockphoto. 130 (bottom), Gert Vrey/iStockphoto.131, sweetlifephotos/iStockphoto. 134, David Fleetham/Alamy. 135, Stephen Frink Collection/Alamy. Chapter 5: Golf, Hiking & Outdoor Activities: 137, HTJ. 138, Kushch Dmitry/Shutterstock.139, Douglas Peebles/eStock Photo. 145, Pacific Stock/SuperStock. 149, Luca Tettoni/viestiphoto.com. 150, Kaua'I Visitors Bureau. 151(bottom), Jack Jeffrey. 152, Pacific Stock/SuperStock. 155, Photo Resource Hawaii/Alamy. Chapter 6: Shops & Spas: 157, Hilton Hawaii. 158, Fairmont Hotels & Resorts, 165, Sri Maiava Rusden/HVCB. 167 (top), Linda Ching/HVCB. 167 (bottom), Sri Maiava Rusden/HVCB. 168, Michael Soo/Alamy. 169 (top), leisofhawaii.com. 169 (2nd from top), kellyalexanderphotography.com. 169 (3rd, 4th, and 5th from top), leisofhawaii.com. 169 (bottom), kellyalexanderphotography.com. 177 (top), Kevin Syms/Fairmont Hotels & Resorts. 177 (bottom left), Chad Kirkpatrick I Witness to Beauty ® I PHOTOGRAPHY and DESIGN. 177 (bottom right), Mauna Lani Spa. Chapter 7: Entertainment & Nightlife: 179, Hilton Hawaii. 180, Hawaii Tourism Authority (HTA) / Tor Johnson. 184, Hawaii Visitors & Convention Bureau. 185, Thinkstock LLC. 187, Hawaii Visitors & Convention Bureau. Chapter 8: Where to Eat: 191, Four Seasons Hotels & Resorts, 192, Don Riddle Images/Four Seasons Hotels & Resorts. 205, Kevin Syms/Fairmont Hotels & Resorts. 206, Kevin Syms/Fairmont Hotels & Resorts. 213, Polynesian Cultural Center. 214 (top), Douglas Peebles Photography. 214 (top center), Douglas Peebles Photography/Alamy. 214 (center), Dana Edmunds/Polynesian Cultural Center. 214 (bottom center), Douglas Peebles Photography/Alamy. 214 (bottom), Purcell Team/Alamy. 215 (top, top center, and bottom center), HTJ/HVCB. 215 (bottom), Oahu Visitors Bureau. Chapter 9: Where to Stay: 225, Waianuhea. 226, DANA EDMUNDS/Fairmont Hotels & Resorts. 237 (top), Four Seasons Hualalai/Rothenborg, Kyle. 237 (bottom), Otter Rock Films, Inc. 240 (top), Fairmont Hotels & Resorts. 240 (bottom), TOMOHITO YAMANISHI/Mauna Kea Beach Hotel. 243 (top), Preferred Hotel Group. 243 (bottom left), Puakea Ranch. 243 (bottom right), Waianuhea.